Fragmentation vs the Constitutionalisation of International Law

The current system of international law is experiencing profound transformations. Indeed, the simultaneous processes of globalization combined with the disintegration of international systems of governance and law-making pose complex challenges for legal scholarship. The doctrinal response to these challenges has been theorized within two seemingly contradictory discourses in international law: fragmentation and constitutionalisation.

This book takes an innovative approach to international law, viewing the processes of the fragmentation and constitutionalisation as being profoundly interconnected and reflective of each other. It brings together a select group of contributors, including both established and emerging scholars and practitioners, in order to explore the ways in which the problems of fragmentation and constitutionalisation are viscerally linked one to the other and thus mutually conditioning and stimulating. The book considers the theory and practice of international law looking at the two phenomena in relation to the various fields of international law such as international criminal law, cultural heritage law and international environmental law.

Andrzej Jakubowski is Assistant Professor at the Institute of Law Studies of the Polish Academy of Sciences. He has authored a monograph *State Succession in Cultural Property* (OUP 2015) and edited a volume *Cultural Rights as Collective Rights – An International Law Perspective* (Brill 2016).

Karolina Wierczyńska is Assistant Professor at the Institute of Law Studies of the Polish Academy of Sciences where she serves as a managing editor of the *Polish Yearbook of International Law*. Her current research relates to the admissibility issues before the ICC.

Routledge Research in International Law

Available:

International Law and the Third World
Reshaping Justice
Edited by Richard Falk, Balakrishnan Rajagopal and Jacqueline Stevens

International Legal Theory
Essays and Engagements, 1966–2006
Nicholas Onuf

The Problem of Enforcement in International Law
Countermeasures, the Non-Injured State and the Idea of International Community
Elena Katselli Proukaki

International Economic Actors and Human Rights
Adam McBeth

The Law of Consular Access
A Documentary Guide
John Quigley, William J. Aceves and S. Adele Shank

State Accountability under International Law
Holding States Accountable for a Breach of Jus Cogens Norms
Lisa Yarwood

International Organizations and the Idea of Autonomy
Institutional Independence in the International Legal Order
Edited by Richard Collins and Nigel D. White

Self-Determination in the Post-9/11 Era
Elizabeth Chadwick

Participants in the International Legal System
Multiple Perspectives on Non-State Actors in International Law
Edited by Jean d'Aspremont

Sovereignty and Jurisdiction in the Airspace and Outer Space
Legal Criteria for Spatial Delimitation
Gbenga Oduntan

International Law in a Multipolar World
Edited by Matthew Happold

The Law on the Use of Force
A Feminist Analysis
Gina Heathcote

The ICJ and the Evolution of International Law
The Enduring Impact of the Corfu Channel Case
Edited by Karine Bannelier, Théodore Christakis and Sarah Heathcote

UNHCR and International Refugee Law
From Treaties to Innovation
Corinne Lewis

Asian Approaches to International Law and the Legacy of Colonialism
The Law of the Sea, Territorial Disputes and International Dispute Settlement
Edited by Jin-Hyun Paik, Seok-Woo Lee, Kevin Y. L. Tan

The Right to Self-Determination Under International Law
"Selfistans," Secession, and the Rule of the Great Powers
Milena Sterio

Reforming the UN Security Council Membership
The Illusion of Representativeness
Sabine Hassler

Threats of Force
International Law and Strategy
Francis Grimal

The Changing Role of Nationality in International Law
Edited by Alessandra Annoni and Serena Forlati

Criminal Responsibility for the Crime of Aggression
Patrycja Grzebyk

Regional Maintenance of Peace and Security under International Law
The Distorted Mirrors
Dace Winther

International Law-making
Essays in Honour of Jan Klabbers
Edited by Rain Liivoja and Jarna Petman

Resolving Claims to Self-Determination
Is There a Role for the International Court of Justice?
Andrew Coleman

The Rise of Tamil Separatism in Sri Lanka
From Communalism to Secession
Gnanapala Welhengama and Nirmala Pillay

The United Nations and Collective Security
Gary Wilson

Justice for Victims before the International Criminal Court
Luke Moffett

Public-Private Partnerships and Responsibility under International Law
A Global Health Perspective
Lisa Clarke

Cultural Diversity in International Law
The Effectiveness of the UNESCO Convention on the Protection and Promotion of the Diversity of Cultural Expressions
Edited by Lilian Richieri Hanania

Incitement in International Law
Wibke K. Timmermann

The Cuban Embargo under International Law
El Bloqueo
Nigel D. White

Resisting United Nations Security Council Resolutions
Sufyan Droubi

The Changing Nature of Customary International Law
Methods of Interpreting the Concept of Custom in International Criminal Tribunals
Noora Arajärvi

The International Criminal Court in Search of its Purpose and Identity
Edited by Triestino Mariniello

Power and Law in International Society
International Relations as the Sociology of International Law
Mark Klamberg

The International Criminal Court and Global Social Control in Late Modernity
International Criminal Justice in Late Modernity
Nerida Chazal

International Law and Boundary Disputes in Africa
Gbenga Oduntan

Means of Transportation and Registration of Nationality
Transportation Registered by International Organizations
Vincent P. Cogliati-Bantz

Reciprocity in International Law
Its Impact and Function
Shahrad Nasrolahi Fard

The Responsibility to Protect in International Law
An Emerging Paradigm Shift
Susan Breau

Seeking Justice in International Law
The Significance and Implications of the UN Declaration on the Rights of Indigenous Peoples
Mauro Barelli

Legal Accountability and Britain's Wars 2000–2015
Peter Rowe

Forthcoming titles in this series include:

Technology and the Law on the Use of Force
New Security Challenges in the Twenty First Century
Jackson Maogoto

International Law and the Rights of those Displaced by Armed Conflict
Elena Katselli Proukaki

International Criminal Law and Sexual Violence against Women
The Interpretation of Gender in the Contemporary International Criminal Trial
Daniela Nadj

Fighting and Victimhood in International Criminal Law
Joanna Nicholson

Fragmentation vs the Constitutionalisation of International Law

A Practical Inquiry

Edited by

Andrzej Jakubowski and Karolina Wierczyńska

Routledge
Taylor & Francis Group
LONDON AND NEW YORK

First published 2016
by Routledge
605 Third Avenue, New York, NY 10017
4 Park Square, Milton Park, Abingdon, Oxon OX14 4RN

First issued in paperback 2017

Routledge is an imprint of the Taylor & Francis Group, an informa business

British Library Cataloguing in Publication Data
A catalogue record for this book is available from the British Library

Library of Congress Cataloguing in Publication Data
Names: Jakubowski, Andrzej, 1980– editor. | Wierczyńska, Karolina, editor.
Title: Fragmentation vs the constitutionalisation of international law : a practical inquiry / edited by Andrzej Jakubowski and Karolina Wierczyńska.
Description: Abingdon, Oxon; New York, NY : Routledge, 2016.
Identifiers: LCCN 2015050922 | ISBN 9781138119727 (hbk) | ISBN 9781315652177 (ebk)
Subjects: LCSH: International law. | Constitutional law–Philosophy.
Classification: LCC KZ3410.F73 2016 | DDC 341.01–dc23
LC record available at http://lccn.loc.gov/2015050922

ISBN 13: 978-0-8153-5529-8 (pbk)
ISBN 13: 978-1-138-11972-7 (hbk)

Typeset in Galliard
by Out of House Publishing

Contents

Notes on contributors xii
Foreword xvi
Acknowledgments xviii
Select abbreviations xix
Table of legislation xxi

Introduction 1
ANDRZEJ JAKUBOWSKI AND KAROLINA WIERCZYŃSKA

PART I
International constitutionalisation as a claim 13

1 Constitutionalisation: a new philosophy of international law? 15
JERZY ZAJADŁO AND TOMASZ WIDŁAK

2 From the internationalisation of national constitutions to the "constitutionalisation" of international law: the role of human rights 32
VASSILIS P. TZEVELEKOS AND LUCAS LIXINSKI

3 International constitutionalism, language in legal discourse, and the functions of international law scholarship 53
ROMAN KWIECIEŃ

4 The creeping constitutionalisation and fragmentation of international law: from 'constitutional' to 'consistent' interpretation 69
MAURIZIO ARCARI

PART II
Fragmentation of international law as a challenge to its constitutionalisation 87

5 The paradoxes of fragmentation: does regional constitutionalisation constitute a fragmentation threat to the international legal order? 89
FRANÇOIS FINCK

6 International constitutionalisation of protection of privacy on the internet: the *Google* case example 106
KRYSTYNA KOWALIK-BAŃCZYK

7 The "revival" of sovereignty via the complementarity regime and the "doctrinal" idea of responsibility to protect; what about constitutionalisation? 118
MARIA VARAKI

8 Fragmentation of the law of targeting: a comfortable excuse or a dangerous trap? 132
PATRYCJA GRZEBYK

9 The Rome Statute and the debate surrounding the constitutionalisation, fragmentation and pluralisation of international criminal law 146
KAROLINA WIERCZYŃSKA

PART III
Constitutionalisation through fragmentation 161

10 Justifying 'fragmentation' and constitutional reforms of international law in terms of justice, human rights and 'cosmopolitan constitutionalism' 163
ERNST-ULRICH PETERSMANN

11 A constitutionalised legal order: exploring the role of the World Heritage Convention (1972) 183
ANDRZEJ JAKUBOWSKI

12 Constitutionalisation through fragmented adjudication? 203
MÓNIKA AMBRUS

13 From fragmentation to coherence: a constitutionalist take on the trade and public health debates 222
CHIEN-HUEI WU

14 Access to environmental justice for NGOs: interplay between the Aarhus Convention, the EU Lisbon Treaty and the European Convention on Human Rights 244
MARJOLEIN SCHAAP · RUBIO IMBERS

15 The reconciliatory approach: how multilateral environmental agreements can harmonise international legal obligations 265
BRITTA SJÖSTEDT

Index 288

Notes on contributors

Mónika Ambrus is a Senior Researcher at the Institute of Legal Sciences of the Hungarian Academy of Sciences, Budapest. Before that she served as an Assistant Professor at the University of Groningen and the Erasmus University Rotterdam, The Netherlands. Mónika is also the Managing Editor of the *Netherlands Yearbook of International Law*, and has recently co-edited (with R.A. Wessel) its 2015 volume entitled 'Between Pragmatism and Predictability: Temporariness in International Law'. Her current research projects include: risk across international law, the standard of proof in the practice of the European Court of Human Rights, access to water services from a human rights perspective, and the comparative law method across various international courts and tribunals.

Maurizio Arcari is Professor of International Law at the School of Law of the University of Milano-Bicocca, Milan (Italy). He has authored and co-authored several books and studies on collective security, global peace and international responsibility. He also serves as editor-in-chief of the e-journal *QIL-Questions of International Law*, and as co-director of the book series *La ricerca del diritto nella Comunità internazionale* [Research in the Law of the International Community] (Editoriale Scientifica, Naples).

François Finck is a Senior Academic Assistant (Law) at the College of Europe, Natolin (Warsaw, Poland). He graduated from the Law Faculty of the University of Strasbourg, where his PhD was awarded the Prize for the best doctoral dissertation in Public Law in 2011. His main areas of research focus on EU law and public international law.

Patrycja Grzebyk is an Assistant Professor at the Institute of International Relations of the University of Warsaw. She is a graduate of the departments of international relations and law at the University of Warsaw. She has published in the area of international criminal law, international humanitarian law and international human rights law. She has authored the monograph *Criminal Responsibility for the Crime of Aggression* (Routledge 2013) and numerous other publications.

Andrzej Jakubowski is an Assistant Professor at the Institute of Law Studies of the Polish Academy of Sciences, in Warsaw (Poland), where he currently chairs an international collaborative research project 'HEURIGHT – The Right to Cultural Heritage – Its Protection and Enforcement through Cooperation in the European Union'. He has authored *inter alia* a monograph *State Succession in Cultural Property* (OUP 2015) and edited a volume *Cultural Rights as Collective Rights – An International Law Perspective* (Brill 2016).

Krystyna Kowalik-Bańczyk is Associate Professor at the Institute of Law Studies of the Polish Academy of Sciences. She specializes in general EU Law, EU Competition Law and EU Internet Law. She holds an LLM in European Law from College of Europe (Bruges) and a DEA from the University of Social Sciences of Toulouse. In September 2016 she will assume the position of judge at the General Court of the European Union.

Roman Kwiecień serves as Full Professor of Law at Maria Curie-Skłodowska University in Lublin, Faculty of Law and Administration. He teaches international law and public EU law. He is also a member of the Legal Advisory Committee to the Polish Minister of Foreign Affairs and an alternate member in the Court of Conciliation and Arbitration within the Organization for Security and Co-operation in Europe (OSCE).

Lucas Lixinski is a Senior Lecturer at the Faculty of Law, UNSW Australia. He holds a PhD in Law from the European University Institute. He has been a Postgraduate Fellow at the University of Texas School of Law, and a visiting researcher at New York University School of Law (2009) and Columbia Law School (2007). He worked as a judicial clerk for the Inter-American Court of Human Rights in San José, Costa Rica. His teaching and research interests focus on international law, particularly international human rights law, international cultural heritage law and international law and development.

Ernst-Ulrich Petersmann is Emeritus Professor of International and European law and former head of the Law Department of the European University Institute in Florence, Italy. During 35 years, he combined a career as legal practitioner in German, European, UN and GATT/WTO institutions with an academic career at numerous universities in Germany, Switzerland, Italy, the USA and Asian countries. He has published some 30 books and 300 book contributions, articles and book reviews.

Marjolein Schaap - Rubio Imbers is a Doctoral Candidate and Lecturer in international law at the department of International and European Union Law, Erasmus School of Law, Erasmus University, Rotterdam. She holds a LL.M. in international and European Public Law (2009) and a LL.B. in Dutch Law (2008). She has been a visiting scholar at the Max Planck institute for Comparative Public Law and International Law (2013 and 2014). Her research project focuses on the accountability of international institutions, more particularly on the inclusion (access to information, participation and review) of affected individuals in decision-making procedures by international institutions.

Britta Sjöstedt is a Doctoral Candidate and Lecturer at the Faculty of Law, Lund University and at the Raoul Wallenberg Institute, Sweden. She also worked at the UN International Law Commission and at the Swedish Administrative Court in Stockholm. Her research project concerns how international humanitarian law could be strengthened to adequately protect the environment during armed conflict. In particular she assesses how multilateral environmental agreements can apply and reconcile with international humanitarian law, being *lex specialis* in times of armed conflict. She has recently performed field work in the Democratic Republic of the Congo.

Vassilis P. Tzevelekos is a Senior Lecturer in Law at the University of Liverpool, School of Law and Social Justice. He holds a PhD in Law from the European University Institute. He has been a visiting scholar at Columbia Law School (2008) and a research scholar at Michigan Law School (2009–2010). He is a qualified lawyer with the Athens Bar in Greece, specialising in international human rights protection and practicing before both national and international human rights courts. His teaching and research interests focus on general international law and human rights protection.

Maria Varaki is an Assistant Professor in International Law at Kadir Has University, Faculty of Law, in Istanbul. Before joining Kadir Has University, she was a post-doctoral researcher at the Law Faculty of Hebrew University in Jerusalem and a visiting fellow at the i Courts Centre of the University of Copenhagen. She holds a PhD in International Criminal Law from the Irish Centre for Human Rights in Galway, Ireland and two LLM degrees in International and Comparative Law, one from Tulane University, School of Law and one from New York University, School of Law. Her current research interests focus on legal theory concerning the principle of legitimacy, international responsibility with regard to refugee law and international courts and tribunals.

Tomasz Widłak is an Assistant Professor to the Chair of Theory and Philosophy of Law and State at the Faculty of Law and Administration, University of Gdańsk, Poland. He graduated from the University of Gdańsk and the University of Antwerp, Belgium (*maxima cum laude*). He has authored and co-authored publications in theory and philosophy of law, human rights, international law, medical law – major monographs include *International Community* (2012) and *From International Society to International Community: The Constitutional Evolution of International Law* (in English, 2015). He also co-edited the volume *Humanitarian Interventions* (2010).

Karolina Wierczyńska is an Assistant Professor at the Institute of Law Studies of the Polish Academy of Sciences, in Warsaw (Poland). Her current research relates to the problem of admissibility issues before the ICC, and the scope of individual responsibility. Karolina has recently co-authored a book *Deference in International Courts and Tribunals Standard of Review and Margin of Appreciation* (edited by L. Gruszczynski and W. Werner; OUP 2014). She also serves as a managing editor of the *Polish Yearbook of International Law*.

Chien-Huei Wu is an Associate Research Professor at the Institute of European and American Studies, Academia Sinica in Taipei, Taiwan. He holds a PhD in Law from the European University Institute. He also worked for the Ministry of Justice in Taiwan as a district attorney. His research interests cover EU external relations law and international economic law. He follows closely EU – China and EU – ASEAN relations and pays particular attention to Asian regionalism and WTO – IMF linkage. He is the author of *WTO and the Greater China: Economic Integration and Dispute Resolution* (Nijhoff 2012).

Jerzy Zajadło serves as Full Professor of Law at the University of Gdańsk, where he holds a Chair of Theory and Philosophy of Law and State. He is a member of the Polish Academy of Arts and Sciences. He has authored and co-authored numerous publications in the general area of law, in particular theory and philosophy of law, human rights and international law – major monographs and edited volumes include: *Radbruch's Formula* (2001), *Responsibility for the Wall Trials of the Snipers at the Berlin Wall* (2003), *Dilemmas of Humanitarian Intervention* (2005), *Fascinating Paths of the Philosophy of Law* (2008), *Humanitarian Interventions* (2010) and *Philosophy of Law in Questions and Answers* (2013).

Foreword

Processes commonly associated with "global governance" or "globalization" affect the structures of public international law. In the heyday of the nation state, public international law was predominantly conceived of as the law located "in-between" states, where international legal arrangements were to fulfil a very specific function: enabling the translation of political disputes into legal claims – and thus the peaceful resolution of conflicts. This conceptualization of international law as a specific form of political self-constraint provides an inaccurate picture of today's legal arrangements in several respects. International law faces important structural changes: from the advent of novel forms of warfare, the resurrection of targeted killings, and the managerial structures of governance across fields to the degradation of the global environment or the challenges posed by global economic crises. These challenges escape the constitutive confines of the state system and require new solutions.

For some, the legal system is in need of a new constitution and a new hierarchy of norms. Proponents of this thesis point to new supranational rules, human rights, transnational judicial cooperation, general principles of law and procedural guarantees. Since the 1990s, the use of constitutional language has gained increasing popularity in international legal parlance. The vocabulary of constitutionalism has been used in different contexts, from in-depth critiques of existing international law to analyses of international tribunals, the revitalization of international organizations, the self-understanding of European organizations or the development of core values in international law.

Others, however, witness a fragmentation of international law, arguing that the functional differentiation of international law challenges its unity and hierarchy. In this context, scholars have often pointed out the rise of managerialism and expert rule and the blurring line between public and private authority. While constitutionalisation builds on the uniforming aspects of globalization, fragmentation follows from the differentiation of functional systems, while managerialism challenges the formality of law as such.

Existing scholarship has long treated the processes of constitutionalisation and fragmentation as separate phenomena or as opposite lenses through which to study the development of international law. Only recently has academic literature started to explore the possible interlinkages between the constitutionalisation, fragmentation and politicization of international law. This was also the main focus of the COST Action IS1003 "*International Law between Constitutionalisation and Fragmentation. The Role of Law in the Post-national Constellation*" – a vehicle that allowed for scientific collaboration between researchers from various European universities. In particular, the Action concentrated its investigative endeavours on the problems posed by the existing interplay between fragmentation, constitutionalisation and the politicization of international law, seeing these elements as different dimensions of a more systemic change taking place in the international legal order.

The current volume builds on this stream of literature and represents an important part of the research efforts that were undertaken within the COST Action IS1003. It offers a more contextualized perspective on the constitutionalisation and fragmentation discourse. At the same time, it highlights the close interconnectedness of the processes of constitutionalisation and fragmentation in international law. We are confident that the papers included in this volume will allow readers to look at certain developments in international law from fresh (and sometimes surprising) perspectives, contributing to the current academic discussion on the changing structure of international law.

Last but not least, we also would like to acknowledge the financial support provided by the Polish National Science Centre (NSC) within its Harmonia programme, which facilitated the participation of Polish researchers in the activities of the COST Action. In particular, the NSC co-financed the organization of the conference entitled "*Constitutionalisation and Fragmentation of International Law Revisited*", held in November 2013 in Warsaw. This meeting became a basis for subsequent collaboration between its participants and eventually led to the publication of the present volume.

Prof. Wouter Werner
VU University Amsterdam
Prof. Łukasz Gruszczyński
Institute of Law Studies
Polish Academy of Sciences

Acknowledgments

This book is a fruit of cooperation between the participants of the conference "*Constitutionalisation and Fragmentation of International Law Revisited*", held in November 2013 in Warsaw. The event constituted one of the activities within a broad research agenda of the COST Action IS1003 "*International Law between Constitutionalisation and Fragmentation. The Role of Law in the Post-national Constellation*" and was co-financed by the Polish National Science Centre (NSC; grant no. UMO-2011/01/M/HS5/03846). We are very thankful to Wouter Werner, Chair of the COST Action, and Łukasz Gruszczyński, Head of the NSC research team at the Institute of Law Studies of the Polish Academy of Sciences, for their unfailing encouragement and insightful comments offered during the entire journey which has led to the completion of this book. We would also like to acknowledge the institutional support rendered by Władysław Czapliński, Director of the Institute. We wish to express our gratitude to Tamás Hoffmann, Tomer Broude and Nikolas Rajkovic for their most precious comments on the initial stage of the research on this book. We would also like to thank the reviewers of this book for their most precious feedback. We are immensely grateful for the contributions made by the individual authors, Mónika Ambrus, Maurizio Arcari, François Finck, Patrycja Grzebyk, Krystyna Kowalik-Bańczyk, Roman Kwiecień, Lucas Lixinski, Ernst-Ulrich Petersmann, Marjolein Schaap – Rubio Imbers, Britta Sjöstedt, Vassilis Tzevelekos, Maria Varaki, Tomasz Widłak, Chien-Huei Wu and Jerzy Zajadło. Each has committed to the richness and broadness of the analysis offered in this collection. Special thanks go to Olivia Manley, Linda Ridley-Paulus and the staff at Routledge for making the production of this book a pleasant process.

Last but not least, we would like to thank Ania, Ewa, Grzegorz, Irenka and Staś for their support and patience.

Andrzej Jakubowski and Karolina Wierczyńska
Warsaw

Select abbreviations

AJIL	*American Journal of International Law*
BYIL	*British Yearbook of International Law*
CAH	Crimes against Humanity
CFI	Court of First Instance of the European Union
CJEU	Court of Justice of the European Union
CUP	Cambridge University Press
ECHR	European Convention on Human Rights
ECJ	European Court of Justice
ECtHR	European Court of Human Rights
EEA	European Economic Area
EFTA	European Free Trade Area
EJIL	*European Journal of International Law*
EJLS	*European Journal of Legal Studies*
EU	European Union
EUCFR	Charter of Fundamental Rights of the EU
FAO	Food and Agriculture Organization
GAL	Global Administrative Law
GATT 1994	General Agreement on Tariffs and Trade 1994
GYIL	*German Yearbook of International Law*
HILJ	*Harvard International Law Journal*
HRL	*Human Rights Law*
ICC	International Criminal Court
ICCPR	International Covenant on Civil and Political Rights
ICESCR	International Covenant on Economic, Social and Cultural Rights
ICJ	International Court of Justice
ICJ Reports	*International Court of Justice Reports of Judgments, Advisory Opinions and Orders*
ICL	International Criminal Law
ICLQ	*International and Comparative Law Quarterly*
ICSID	International Centre for the Settlement of Investment Disputes

ICTR	International Criminal Tribunal for Rwanda
ICTY	International Criminal Tribunal for the Former Yugoslavia
IEL	International Economic Law
IHL	International Humanitarian Law
IJCP	*International Journal of Cultural Property*
IJHR	*International Journal of Human Rights*
ILC	International Law Commission
ILM	*International Legal Materials*
ILO	International Labour Organization
JICJ	*Journal of International Criminal Justice*
LJIL	*Leiden Journal of International Law*
MTN	Multilateral trade negotiations
NAFTA	North American Free Trade Agreement
Nijhoff	Martinus Nijhoff Publishers
NJIL	*Nordic Journal of International Law*
OHCHR	Office of the High Commissioner for Human Rights
OIE WORLD	Organization of Animal Health
OTP	Office of the Prosecutor (ICC)
OUP	Oxford University Press
PGs	Public goods
PYIL	*Polish Yearbook of International Law*
R2P	Responsibility to Protect (doctrine)
RGDIP	*Revue Générale de Droit International Public*
RS	Rome Statute of the International Criminal Court
SCSL	Special Court for Sierra Leone
TEU	Treaty on the European Union
TFEU	Treaty on the Functioning of the European Union
TRIPS	Agreement on Trade-Related Aspects of Intellectual Property Rights
TTIP	Transatlantic Trade and Investment Partnership
UN	United Nations
UN Charter	Charter of the United Nations
UNSC	United Nations Security Council
UNESCO	The United Nations Educational, Scientific and Cultural Organization
UNGA	United Nations General Assembly
UNMIK	United Nations Interim Administration Mission in Kosovo
UNTS	*United Nations Treaty Series*
VCLT	Vienna Convention on the Law of Treaties
WHA	World Health Assembly
WHO	World Health Organization
WHO FCTC	WHO Framework Convention on Tobacco Control
WTO	World Trade Organization
ZaöRV	*Zeitschrift für ausländisches öffentliches Recht und Völkerrecht*

Table of legislation

Agreement between the European Union and the United States of America on the Processing and Transfer of Financial Messaging Data from the European Union to the United States for the Purposes of the Terrorist Finance Tracking Program, Brussels, 28 June 2010 ... 109

Agreement between the United States of America and the European Union on the Use and Transfer of Passenger Name Records to the United States Department of Homeland Security, Brussels, 14 Dec. 2011 ... 109

Agreement Establishing the World Trade Organization, Marrakesh, 15 Apr. 1994 ... 223

Agreement on the Application of Sanitary and Phytosanitary Measures, Marrakesh, 15 Apr. 1994 ... 212, 222

Agreement on Trade-Related Aspects of Intellectual Property Rights, Marrakesh, 15 Apr. 1994 ... 222

American Convention on Human Rights (Pact of San José), San José, 22 Nov. 1969 ... 136–37

Charter of the United Nations, San Francisco, 26 June 1945 ... 7, 27, 56, 62, 71–7, 80, 85, 97–8, 105, 124–25, 144–45, 148–51, 166–67, 171, 174, 179, 267, 278, 280, 283, 285

Constitution of the World Health Organization, New York, 22 July 1946 ... 226

Convention (I) for the Amelioration of the Condition of the Wounded and Sick in Armed Forces in the Field, Geneva, 12 Aug. 1949 ... 135, 136, 138, 143, 192, 226

Convention (II) for the Amelioration of the Condition of Wounded, Sick and Shipwrecked Members of Armed Forces at Sea, Geneva, 12 Aug. 1949 ... 135, 136, 138, 143, 192, 226

Convention (III) relative to the Treatment of Prisoners of War, Geneva, 12 Aug. 1949 .... 135, 136, 138, 143, 192, 226

Convention (IV) relative to the Protection of Civilian Persons in Time of War, Geneva, 12 Aug. 1949 .... 135, 136, 138, 143, 192, 226

Convention Concerning the Protection of World Natural and Cultural Heritage, Paris, 16 Nov. 1972 .... 10, 183, 184, 186, 188, 188–90, 194, 196–202, 265–67, 272–76, 278, 280–87

Convention for the Protection of Cultural Property in the Event of Armed Conflict with Regulations for the Execution of the Convention 1954, The Hague, 14 May 1954 .... 185, 191, 278, 280

Convention for the Protection of Human Rights and Fundamental Freedoms, Rome, 4 Nov. 1950 .... 11, 47, 76–8, 82–5, 96–101, 110, 114, 116, 134–35, 137, 164, 166, 169, 173, 180, 182, 208–9, 211, 215–17, 244–45, 257–63

Convention for the Protection of Individuals with regard to Automatic Processing of Personal Data No 108, Strasbourg, 28 Jan. 1981 110

Convention for the Protection of the Marine Environment of the North-East Atlantic, Paris, 22 Sep. 1992 274

Convention for the Protection of the Ozone Layer, Vienna, 22 Mar. 1985 .... 265, 271

Convention for the Safeguarding of the Intangible Cultural Heritage, Paris, 17 Oct. 2003 186

Convention of International Trade in Endangered Species of Wild Fauna and Flora, Washington, 3 Mar. 1973 .... 265, 269, 271, 276

Convention on Access to Information, Public Participation in Decision-Making and Access to Justice in Environmental Matters, Aarhus, 25 June 1998 245–46

Convention on Biological Diversity, Rio de Janeiro, 5 June 1992 .... 230, 265, 272

Convention on Long-Range Transboundary Air Pollution, Geneva, 13 Nov. 1979 274

Convention on Stolen and Illegally Exported Cultural Objects, Rome, 24 June 1995 185

Convention on the Conservation of European Wildlife and Natural Habitats, Bern, 19 Sep. 1979 276

Convention on the Means of Prohibiting and Preventing the Illicit Import, Export and Transfer of Ownership of Cultural Property, Paris, 14 Nov. 1970 185

Convention on the Prevention and Punishment of Genocide, New York, 9 Dec. 1948 .... 149, 217–19, 221

Convention on the Protection and Promotion of the Diversity of Cultural Expressions, Paris, 20 Oct. 2005 186–87

Convention on the Protection of the Marine Environment of the Baltic Sea Area, Helsinki, 9 Apr. 1992 274

Convention on the Protection of the Underwater Cultural Heritage, Paris, 2 Nov. 2001 186

Council Decision 2005/370/EC on the Conclusion, on behalf of the European Community, of the Convention on Access to Information, Public Participation in Decision-Making and Access to Justice in Environmental Matters, 17 Feb. 2005 247

Council Directive 2000/78/EC Establishing a General Framework for Equal Treatment in Employment and Occupation, 27 Nov. 2000 208

Council Directive 2000/43/EC Implementing the Principle of Equal Treatment between Persons Irrespective of Racial or Ethnic Origin, 29 June 2000 208

Council Directive 75/117/EEC on the Approximation of the Laws of the Member States Relating to the Application of the Principle of Equal Pay for Women and Men, 10 Feb. 1975 208

Council Directive 97/80/EC on the Burden of Proof in Cases of Sex Discrimination, 15 Dec. 1997 208

Council Directive 76/207/EEC on the Implementation of the Principle of Equal Treatment for Women and Men with respect to Access to Employment, Vocational Training and Promotion, and Working Conditions, 9 Feb. 1976 208

Decision on the Implementation of the WHO Framework Convention on Tobacco Control, Punta del Este, 19 Nov. 2010 .... 223, 235

Directive 2003/4/EC of the European Parliament and of the Council on Public Access to Environmental Information and Repealing Council Directive 90/313/EEC, 28 Jan. 2003 248

Directive 95/46/EC of the European Parliament and of the Council on the Protection of Individuals with regard to the Processing of Personal Data and on the Free Movement of Such Data, 24 Oct. 1995 .... 107, 110–11, 113, 115

Directive 2003/35/EC of the European Parliament and of the Council Providing for Public Participation in respect of the Drawing Up of Certain Plans and Programmes Relating to the Environment and

Amending with regard to Public Participation and Access to Justice Council Directives 85/337/EEC and 96/61/EC, 26 May 2003 248

Final Act Embodying the Results of the Uruguay Round of Multilateral Trade Negotiations, Marrakesh, 15 Apr. 1994 222

Framework Convention on Climate Change, New York, 9 May 1992.... 265

General Agreement on Tariffs and Trade 1994, Marrakesh, 15 Apr. 1994 .... 164, 224, 230, 235, 237–38, 240

International Covenant on Civil and Political Rights, New York, 19 Dec. 1966 .... 100, 106, 108, 134–37, 143

International Covenant on Economic, Social and Cultural Rights, New York, 16 Dec. 1966 .... 143, 215, 237

North American Free Trade Agreement, Washington, Ottawa, Mexico City, 8, 11, 14 and 17 Dec. 1992 .... 170, 179, 195–96

Protocol No 12 to the European Convention on Human Rights and Fundamental Freedoms on the Prohibition of Discrimination, Rome, 4 Nov. 2000 208

Protocol Additional to the Geneva Conventions of 12 August 1949, and Relating to the Protection of Victims of International Armed Conflicts (Protocol I), Geneva, 8 June 1977 .... 136, 138, 143, 192

Protocol Additional to the Geneva Conventions of 12 August 1949, and Relating to the Protection of Victims of Non-International Armed Conflicts (Protocol II), Geneva, 8 June 1977 .... 136, 138, 143

Protocol to the Convention for the Protection of Cultural Property in the Event of Armed Conflict 1954, The Hague, 14 May 1954 .... 186, 278

Regulation EC No. 1367/2006 of the European Parliament and of the Council on the Application of the Provisions of the Aarhus Convention on Access to Information, Public Participation in Decision-Making and Access to Justice in Environmental Matters to Community Institutions and Bodies, 6 Sep. 2006 248

Second Protocol to the Hague Convention of 1954 for the Protection of Cultural Property in the Event of Armed Conflict, The Hague, 26 Mar. 1999 .... 191–92, 278

Statute of the International Criminal Court, Rome, 17 July 1998 .... 9, 121, 139, 148, 193, 217

Statute of the International Criminal Tribunal for the Prosecution of Persons Responsible for Genocide and Other Serious Violations of International Humanitarian Law Committed in the Territory of Rwanda and Rwandan Citizens Responsible for Genocide and Other Such Violations Committed in the Territory of Neighbouring States, between 1 January 1994 and 31 December 1994, 8 Nov. 1994 .... 154–55, 158, 217–19

Statute of the International Tribunal for the Prosecution of Persons Responsible for Serious Violations of International Humanitarian Law Committed in the Territory of the Former Yugoslavia since 1991, 25 May 1993 .... 154–55, 158, 217–19

Treaty of Lisbon Amending the Treaty on European Union and the Treaty Establishing the European Community, Lisbon, 13 Dec. 2007 .... 174, 244, 245, 250, 254

Treaty on European Union, Maastricht, 7 Feb. 1992 .... 105, 178, 256

Treaty on the Functioning of the European Union (formerly Treaty establishing the European Economic Community), Rome, 25 Mar. 1957 .... 208, 248, 250–53, 255–57

United Nations Security Council Resolution 1493, 28 July 2003.. 280, 283

United Nations Security Council Resolution 1565, 1 Oct. 2004 283

United Nations Security Council Resolution 1592, 30 Mar. 2005 283

United Nations Security Council Resolution 1625, 14 Sep. 2005.......... 284

United Nations Security Council Resolution 1674, 28 April 2006......... 126

United Nations Security Council Resolution 1756, 15 May 2007 283

United Nations Security Council Resolution 1856, 22 Dec. 2008 283

United Nations Security Council Resolution 1906, 23 Dec. 2009 283

United Nations Security Council Resolution 1925, 28 May 2010 283

United Nations Security Council Resolution 1991, 22 June 2011 283

United Nations Security Council Resolution 2150, 16 April 2014......... 126

Vienna Convention on the Law of Treaties, Vienna, 23 May 1969 .... 20, 42, 77, 79, 85, 90, 139, 145, 163, 165, 167, 174, 177–78, 181, 229–31, 233–36, 241, 243, 254–55, 257, 268, 270, 276

WHO Framework Convention on Tobacco Control, Geneva, 21 May 2003... 223, 226, 231–37

WHO International Health Regulation, Geneva, 23 May 2005 225

Introduction

Andrzej Jakubowski and Karolina Wierczyńska

The current system of international law is experiencing profound structural and dogmatic transformations. Indeed, the simultaneous processes of globalization combined with the disintegration of international systems of governance and law-making pose complex challenges for legal scholarship. The doctrinal response to these challenges has been framed within two influential theories in international law: fragmentation and constitutionalisation. These describe and analyze the trends affecting the international legal order, which are often considered to be opposite or separate tendencies. Fragmentation basically refers to the profound systemic rupture in the structure of international law, reflected in the lack of well-developed and established hierarchies or other techniques to deal with normative conflicts and tensions between general international law norms and its specialized regimes, as well as between those regimes *inter se*. In turn, the constitutionalisation thesis suggests that international law has reached a certain degree of autonomy and objectivity *vis-à-vis* state sovereignty. As such, international law is seen as recognizing and enforcing the common interest of humanity, thus transcending the particular interests of individual states. Hence it is argued that today's international law possesses certain common constitutional features comparable to those characterizing national constitutional systems.

If nothing else, the concepts of fragmentation and constitutionalisation are at least two competing models of reasoning. As such, they constitute a valuable exercise in normative theory and contribute to understanding the ongoing changes in the structure of international law and international society.[1] However, should they be seen as inherently contradictory doctrines, or are they rather profoundly interconnected, merely evidencing and interpreting various dimensions of such systemic changes? In fact, both fragmentation and constitutionalisation are arguably founded on the concept of unity in public international law,[2] although they offer differing conceptualizations of

1 A Peters, 'Constitutional Fragments: On the Interaction of Constitutionalization and Fragmentation in International Law' (2015) 2 *Working Paper* (Centre for Global Constitutionalism, University of St Andrews).

2 M Prost, *The Concept of Unity in Public International Law* (Hart 2012); R Deplano, 'Fragmentation and Constitutionalisation of International Law: A Theoretical Inquiry' (2013) 6 *EJLS* 67, 69.

the remedies needed to counteract or alleviate a rupture of the international legal order.

The arguments on fragmentation, which begin from 'a predetermined position on unity,'[3] refer to the concepts of politicization, pluralization and regionalization of international law. Accordingly, fragmentation has generally posited that the expansion of international law into new areas has created problems of harmony between its different branches, institutions and norm-systems.[4] Such threats to the coherence of the international legal order have usually been framed in terms of a deconstruction of the hierarchy of norms and the difficulty, due to the plurality of different regulatory contexts, in maintaining shared principles and interpretations across international law.[5] Fragmentation is also seen as an effect of globalization, leading to a profound compartmentalization and functional specialization in international law. Moreover, fragmentation is usually perceived not only as a challenge to the coherence and unity of international law, but also as a contributing factor to its erosion.[6] Yet at the same time there is no universally accepted legal definition of fragmentation and the debate itself often appears to be a search for a solution or compromise 'on how the tension between unity and diversity is and should be managed'.[7] Therefore, the prevailing doctrinal approach essentially focuses on remedies to the fragmentation process within international law's various layers (normative, territorial, functional and structural), aimed at enabling a greater integration both at the level of international law-making as well as with respect to legal authorities.[8] The suggested remedies are usually pragmatic in nature, often advocating 'the politics of tolerance and pluralism' rather than 'universalist voices' based on dogmatic 'consistency' stemming from 'humanitarianism, human rights, trade or the environment'.[9] In essence, they are designed to mitigate the

3 See Prost (n 2) 15.

4 Study Group of the International Law Commission, 'Fragmentation of International Law: Difficulties Arising from the Diversification and Expansion of International Law', Report Finalized by M Koskenniemi, UN Doc. A/CN.4/L.682.

5 MA Young (ed), *Regime Interaction in International Law Facing Fragmentation* (CUP 2012); N Krisch, *Beyond Constitutionalism. The Pluralist Structure of Postnational Law* (OUP 2010).

6 S Singh, 'The Potential of International Law: Fragmentation and Ethics' (2011) 24 *LJIL* 23, 24–25.

7 AC Martineau, 'The Rhetoric of Fragmentation: Fear and Faith in International Law' (2009) 22 *LJIL* 1, 27.

8 G Hafner, 'Pros and Cons Ensuing from Fragmentation of International Law' (2004) 25 *Michigan Journal of International Law* 849; A Fisher-Lescano, G Teubner, 'Regime Collisions: The Vain Search for Legal Unity in the Fragmentation of Global Law' (2004) 25 *Michigan Journal of International Law* 999; T Broude, 'Fragmentation(s) of International Law: On Normative Integration as Authority Allocation' in T Broude, Y Shany (eds), *The Shifting Allocation of Authority in International Law* (Hart 2008) 99–122; T Komori, 'Integrating the Fragmented International Public Order: A Theoretical Perspective' in E Rieter, H de Waele (eds), *Evolving Principles of International Law: Studies in Honour of Karel C. Wellens* (Nijhoff 2012) 103–135.

9 M Koskenniemi, P Leino, 'Fragmentation of International Law?: Postmodern Anxieties' (2002) 15 *LJIL* 553, 578–579.

fragmentation of international law, rather than to eliminate it and (re)build its unity and coherence. Importantly, certain trends towards the mitigation or 'de-fragmentation' of international law have been observed in the practice of international tribunals and that of national courts adjudicating claims based on international law.[10] It has been noted that 'both international and national courts have recognized that they do not operate in isolation from the larger international legal system, and have found various ways to counteract the process of fragmentation that may result from their jurisdictional limitations'.[11]

At the same time, the theoretical efforts to describe and explain societal changes affecting the unity of international law have been framed with more consistency within the concept of international or global constitutionalisation, seeing the phenomenon of globalization as a unifying factor in the international legal order rather than as a source of its fragmentation. Yet the vocabulary of parallel constitutional discourses has been applied to a great variety of contexts and dimensions of international law, and thus it too is characterized more by methodological and conceptual diversity[12] than homogeneity or unity.

In the first place, the theory of constitutionalisation implicates a 'de-constitutionalisation' at the domestic level.[13] In other words, national constitutional systems no longer regulate the entirety of governance and the exercise of governmental power, i.e. no longer retain total sovereignty. Thus alternative systems for providing basic constitutional guaranties have evolved, including those of powerful international organizations.[14] This perspective is related to another context, wherein voices can be heard proposing analogies between domestic hierarchical constitutional systems and those laying beyond the state at the international level.[15] These embrace various claims,

10 K Fauchald, A Nollkaemper (eds), *The Practice of International and National Courts and the (De-)Fragmentation of International Law* (Hart 2014), intro.
11 Ibid.
12 See Chapter 3 in this book.
13 A Peters, 'Compensatory Constitutionalism, The Function and Potential of Fundamental International Norms and Structures' (2006) 19 *LJIL* 579, 580.
14 J Klabbers, A Peters, G Ulfstein (eds), *The Constitutionalization of International Law* (OUP 2009).
15 WM Reisman, 'The Constitutional Crisis in the United Nations' (1993) 87 *AJIL* 83; T Franck, *Recourse to Force, State Action Against Threats and Armed Attacks* (CUP 2002); N Blokker, S Muller, *Towards more Effective Supervision by International Organizations* (Nijhoff 1994); JE Alvarez, 'Judging the Security Council' (1996) 90 *AJIL* 1; C Walter, 'Constitutionalizing (Inter)national Governance. Possibilities for and Limits to the Development of an International Constitutional Law' (2001) 44 *GYIL* 170; J Klabbers, *An Introduction to International Institutional Law* (CUP 2002); N Walker, 'Postnational Constitutionalism and the Problem of Translation' in JH Weiler & M Wind (eds), *European Constitutionalism Beyond the State* (CUP 2003) 27–54; E De Wet, A Nollkaemper (eds), *Review of the Security Council by Member States* (Intersentia 2003); D Cass, *Constitutionalisation of WTO: Legitimacy, Democracy, and Community in the International Trading System* (OUP 2005); N Tsagourias, 'Introduction – Constitutionalism: A Theoretical Roadmap', in N.

from compensatory constitutionalism to institutional constitutionalisation of the international legal order and system of justice (with reference to international adjudication).

The next context refers to normative constitutionalisation, which touches upon the foundations of the international legal order and the development of core values in international law. This has been discussed in relation to the consolidation of the catalogue of international *jus cogens* norms and the proliferation of obligations *erga omnes* – giving a normative power to the values and interests commonly shared by the international community as a whole.[16] In this regard, the claims to constitutionalisation are mostly founded on the value and objective of promotion and protection of human dignity, traversing various layers and regimes within the body of international law. This aspect is sometimes referred to as the humanization of international law.[17] Such new developments within the body of public international law raise questions about the generation of global normativity beyond the nation state. In light of the growing number of 'constitutional' international legal norms, in part arising from world order treaties and the constitutional nature of universal organizations (in particular the United Nations and the legislative activity of the Security Council), one may legitimately speak of corresponding limitations on state sovereignty.

Last but not least, the constitutionalisation thesis has been addressed in relation to social constitutionalism, which uses the concept of 'community' at both the domestic and global governance levels to identify the holders of constituent and constituted power within a constitutional legal order.[18] In other words, constitutionalisation is seen through the lens of governance and the protection of various social relations emerging at the international level, beyond the realm of state sovereignty, with particular focus on the international community.[19]

The above-mentioned approaches to international constitutionalisation recognize that the effective protection and enforcement of universally

Tsagourias (ed.), *Transnational Constitutionalism. International and European Perspectives* (CUP 2007) 1–14; EU Petersmann, 'Time for a United Nations "Global Compact" for Integrating Human Rights into the Law of World Wide Organisations: Lessons from European Integration' (2002) 13 *EJIL* 621; EU Petersmann, 'Human Rights, Constitutionalism and the World Trade Organization: Challenges for the World Trade Organization Jurisprudence and Civil Society' (2006) 19 *LJIL* 633; M Cremona, et al. (eds), *Reflections on the Constitutionalisation of International Economic Law* (Nijhoff 2014).

16 A Cassese, *International Law* (OUP 2005); E De Wet, J Vidmar (eds), *Hierarchy in International Law: The Place of Human Rights* (OUP 2012).

17 AA Cançado Trindade, *International Law for Humankind: Towards a New Jus Gentium* (2nd edn., Nijhoff 2013) 393 ff.

18 CEJ Schwöbel, *Global Constitutionalism in International Legal Perspective* (Nijhoff 2011); A O'Donoghue, *Constitutionalism in Global Constitutionalisation* (CUP 2014).

19 RSJ Macdonald, DM Johnston (eds), *Towards World Constitutionalism. Issues in the Legal Ordering of the International Community* (Nijhoff 2005).

recognized constitutional values may create inevitable tensions and conflicts within the decentralized system of international decision-making, on the one hand, and within the normative hierarchy of the international legal order on the other. The constitutional approach postulates that these tensions and conflicts can be alleviated by a more profound reform of the international legal order than by the pragmatic solutions propagated by the fragmentation scholarship. Such reformist theses, largely grounded on moral considerations, perceive a constitutional order, with its hierarchically supreme constitutional principles, as a remedy to the deficits engrained in the very essence of international law,[20] that is, its decentralization and diversity and state-oriented paradigm. Thus, the constitutionalisation may be seen not only as an ongoing process within the international legal order, but also as a solution to counteract or alleviate its rupture.

The core idea of this volume is to offer a 'practical inquiry' into the fragmentation-constitutionalisation debate. It aims to contextualize these theoretical positions, which often may seem merely abstract or purely dogmatic, at the substantive level. Indeed, the diverse contributions presented in the volume do not develop or adhere to any of these singular positions on the constitutionalisation and fragmentation of international law, nor do they treat them as fully autonomous theories of international law. Rather, they recognize them as scholarly narratives, used in different ways and contexts and to different extents in order to describe and explain the complexity of the current developments in the international legal order. Moreover, fragmentation and constitutionalisation are seen as interconnected, or even dependent on one another.[21] In fact, some of the authors of this book seem to share the arguments voiced by Jeffrey L. Dunoff and Joel P. Trachtman[22] and present fragmentation as an inherent element of, or even a basis for, constitutionalisation within the practice of international law. Viewed through such a prism, the nature of the interplay between fragmentation and constitutionalisation is analyzed both with regard to international legal scholarship and within distinct areas of the practice of international law. In fact, this practical aspect of the analysis facilitates understanding of the mechanisms mitigating or counteracting the fragmentation of international law and drives all the contributions to this volume, offering insights in relation to various factual and legal contexts.

The volume is divided in three parts, addressing the use of constitutionalisation and fragmentation theories in specific contexts and by determinant actors. The four contributions in Part I – *International constitutionalisation*

20 T Kleinlein, *Konstitutionalisierung im Völkerrecht / Constitutionalization in International Law: Konstruktion und Elemente einer idealistischen Völkerrechtslehre* (Springer 2012) 703.

21 Cf Peters, 'Constitutional Fragments' (n 1).

22 JL Dunoff, JP Trachtman, 'A Functional Approach to International constitutionalization' in JL Dunoff, JP Trachtman (eds), *Ruling the World? Constitutionalism, International Law, and Global Governance* (CUP 2009) 3–35.

as a claim, deal with the foundations of the constitutionalisation thesis in international law scholarship and legal philosophy. They proceed from a more general perspective on constitutional discourses and explore the reasons and purposes of constitutional claims, critically assessing their relevance to the general understanding of various axiological, normative and societal changes in the international legal order. Jerzy Zajadło and Tomasz Widłak, in *Constitutionalisation: a new philosophy of international law?*, perceive constitutionalisation is an intellectual movement fostered by academics rather than lawmakers. They argue that it has indeed both an interpretative (descriptive) as well as constitutive (creational) potential. Since the concept of constitutionalisation is extremely value-laden, it may result in constructing reality by building 'a particular intellectual framework upon the fabric of international law.' Yet the effects of constitutionalisation may also have a profound impact on the very essence of international law as a normative category, but only if such a process is accompanied by the evolution of international society towards a 'true' (more coherent) international community. In the next chapter, *From the internationalisation of national constitutions to the 'constitutionalisation' of international law: the role of human rights*, Vassilis Tzevelekos and Lucas Lixinski also link constitutionalisation with the formation of a more homogenous international community 'as to its core values and their collective protection.' They argue that by instituting a number of changes of systemic proportions in the international legal order, the internationalization of national constitutions has led to the 'constitutionalisation' of international law, highlighting the fact that international law has always contained some general 'constitutional' features that are particular to its systemic physiognomy. Tzevelekos and Lixinski focus on human rights and explain how this special branch of international law expands beyond the so-called 'humanization of the international law narrative' and acts as an important ingredient in a number of other narratives, such as the constitutionalisation of international law and others comparable to it, like legal pluralism and fragmentation. With respect to the systemic changes that the internationalization of human rights has brought to the order of public international law, the examples given are those of collective enforcement at the decentralized level for the protection of common interests/values and the idea of the responsibility of states to act in a protective manner, linked with the principle of due diligence, as well as the so-called 'positive effect' that human rights develop. They conclude that the 'constitutional' changes brought into international law by human rights have prepared that order to effectively accommodate further areas of national (constitutional) law aimed at safeguarding values that societies see as vital.

The other two chapters in Part I provide more critical, polemic responses to the constitutional theories in international law. Roman Kwiecień, in *International constitutionalism, language in legal discourse, and the functions of international law scholarship*, focuses on the weaknesses in the constitutionalist approach which justify scepticism about the constitutionalisation of international law, whether considered as a legal process within international society or as a research agenda. He points out three main sources giving rise to scepticism with respect to the constitutional argument: i) such theses can fail to explain the contemporary world in its moral and political diversity, since they are based on a 'homogeneity of values and political aims'; ii) due to its inherent limitations constitutionalisation may not necessarily contribute to the stronger protection of human rights envisaged by international constitutionalists; and iii) international law does not seem to have reached the level of universality, unity and coherence to allow for its constitutionalisation. Against the background of these observations, Kwiecień argues that rather than its constitutionalisation, contemporary international law requires structural and systemic changes in order to enhance its effectiveness. In this regard, he opts for a systemic approach to international law since the desired aim of the constitutionalist doctrine (the constitutionalisation of international law) is not possible without certain systemic features (coherence, unity, universality). In turn, Maurizio Arcari, in his chapter entitled *The creeping constitutionalisation and fragmentation of international law: from 'constitutional' to 'consistent' interpretation*, considers the different interpretive methods used to deal with the phenomena of the constitutionalisation and fragmentation of international law. He explains that while the technique of 'constitutional' interpretation has traditionally been developed and applied with reference to the UN Charter,[23] the expansion of other constitutionally-oriented regimes, at both universal and regional levels, has increased the threat to the coherence of the international legal order. In this respect he examines the principle of systemic integration as a legal panacea for the coordination of the different normative layers of international law. Insofar as systemic integration aims at minimizing normative conflicts and is predicated on the presumption of compatibility between the different rules at stake, it can be posited that the principle of 'consistent interpretation' represents one of its fundamental conceptual underpinnings. However, consistent interpretation as a legal technique has been traditionally reserved for a constitutional legal environment, and thus its application at the international level is likely to produce unintended 'constitutionally-oriented' legal effects. Arcari observes that the various interpretive methods considered operate, through the dynamic of reciprocal interferences, in a 'creeping' fashion to promote, rather paradoxically, both the constitutionalisation and fragmentation of international law. As such, they are symptomatic of legal pluralism and of the complexities that characterize modern international law.

Part II – *Fragmentation of international law as a challenge to its constitutionalisation*, contains contributions exploring the claims for international

23 Charter of the United Nations, signed on 26 June 1945, entered into force on 24 October 1945 (1 UNTS XVI), amended in 1963 (557 UNTS 143), in 1965 (638 UNTS 308), and in 1971 (892 UNTS 119).

constitutionalisation tested against particular challenges which arise as a result of the alleged fragmentation within selected areas of international law and its practice. These contributions encompass interpretations of the challenges and threats to the unity and coherence of international law and offer some tentative responses on how they can be overcome. In fact each chapter in this part of the book analyzes whether the constitutional theory may aid in overcoming the collisions between distinct regimes and prevent further erosions within the system of international law. In *The paradoxes of fragmentation – does regional constitutionalisation constitute a fragmentation threat to the international legal order?* François Finck focuses on the question of 'regional constitutionalisation', specifically the international regimes founded on a geographical basis, in opposition to international legal regimes governing certain areas of international law. By using examples concerning the relations between the European Union (EU) and the European Convention on Human Rights and the decisions of United Nations' organs, he tries to demonstrate that while in fact regional constitutionalisation only realizes some core constitutional functions at a regional level, at the same time it challenges the global governance system. Finck argues that this challenge in turn forces the global governance level to adopt at least some 'constitutional' elements, albeit in a rudimentary manner. European law is also the point of reference for Krystyna Kowalik-Bańczyk who, in her chapter entitled *International constitutionalisation of protection of privacy on the internet – the* Google *case example*, deals with individuals' right to privacy as perceived by the EU legislation and the jurisprudence of the Court of Justice of the European Union (CJEU). The judgment of the latter in the *Google Spain* case[24] is taken as an example of European influence on the way privacy is protected worldwide, thus highlighting the possible unification of its definition and methods of protection. She argues that the *Google* case may also be echoed in the US approach to privacy issues, perhaps leading to the working out of a common US/EU denominator, at least for the issue of the right to be forgotten, which she assesses as a first step towards an international constitutionalisation of Internet users' rights.

The remaining three chapters in Part II take into account international criminal law and international humanitarian law. They discuss certain similarities and common trends characterizing these branches of international law, which can be framed within the vocabulary of both fragmentation and constitutionalisation. The authors aim to demonstrate and reconcile paradoxes that might stem out from the adoption of such perspectives, against the background of more general questions relating to international law and politics, international justice, and the general interest of humanity. Maria Varaki, in *The 'revival' of sovereignty via the complementarity regime and the 'doctrinal'*

24 Case C-131/12, *Google Spain SL, Google Inc v Agencia Espanola de Proteccion de Datos, Mario Costeja González* [2014].

idea of responsibility to protect?, deals with the notion of sovereignty. In fact, this 'S' word is a starting point for her analysis of the complementarity regime of the Rome Statute[25] (Article 17) and the so-called 'doctrine of responsibility to protect', which focuses on the concept of state sovereignty as a source of primary responsibility and action in the field of accountability and prevention of gross violations of human rights and humanitarian law. By examining the two cases of Syria and Libya, Varaki underlines a certain transformation of the notion of state sovereignty, where state consent remains paramount, with the state playing a contradictory but eminent role in the terrain of global governance when issues of human rights and international crimes are at stake. In the next chapter, titled *Fragmentation of the law of targeting – a comfortable excuse or dangerous trap?*, Patrycja Grzebyk deals with the law of targeting and offers a critical analysis of the fragmented nature of international humanitarian law. By referring to the various regimes of international law (humanitarian law, international criminal law and human rights) that set the rules on targeting, she assesses both the positive and negative consequences of such a functional fragmentation on the practice of those engaged in hostilities, as well as on the judicial assessment of responsibility of states and criminal responsibility of individual perpetrators. In such a context, Grzebyk ponders what remedies might be used, including the arguments on constitutionalisation, to alleviate or overcome the defects in the fragmented law on targeting. Karolina Wierczyńska, in *The Rome Statute and the debate surrounding the constitutionalization, fragmentation and pluralisation of international criminal law*, demonstrates how the simultaneous use of different doctrinal narratives might, in fact, be useful in describing and explaining the complex reality of international criminal justice. She argues that certain features of the International Criminal Court (ICC)'s legal regime might be interpreted through a 'constitutional' prism, whereas other of its characteristics could be definitely viewed through the lenses of fragmentation and/or diversification of international law, especially when referring to the decentralization of International Criminal Law (ICL). In addition, she points out that the 'pluralist' perspective can also provide valuable insights, as the Rome Statute can, on the one hand, be seen as linking criminal justice with, for example, human rights values, while on the other its complementary character demands deference towards national systems of justice and some leniency in the context of national procedures. Thus, the differing narratives of 'constitutionalisation' and 'fragmentation' do not result in opposite conceptualizations of the ICC, but conversely offer interconnected and complementary insights on the ICC's legal position and its functioning within the international legal order. Her observations constitute an excellent link to the next part of the book.

25 Statute of the International Criminal Court (Rome Statute), adopted on 17 July 1998, entered into force on 1 July 2002, UN Doc. A/CONF.183/9 (2187 UNTS 90).

Part III, *Constitutionalisation through fragmentation*, critically discusses current developments in various areas of international law which are deeply affected by the process of fragmentation. In such a context, the contributions explore whether the analyzed practices might not also be perceived as leading to a greater coherence and/or constitutionalisation of international law. In this vein, they attempt to conceive of fragmentation as a part of or vehicle for the constitutionalisation of international law, identifying the roles of various actors and mechanisms involved in the processes of de-fragmentation and the constitutionalisation of international law. Ernst-Ulrich Petersmann, in *Justifying 'fragmentation' and constitutional reforms of international law in terms of justice, human rights and 'cosmopolitan constitutionalism'*, endeavours to demonstrate that the 'fragmentation' of international law among states through democratic and judicial control of multilevel governance of international public goods (PGs) is often a necessary strategy for reforming the power-oriented UN and WTO legal regimes for the benefit of citizens. He further argues that justice and human rights require integration of the competing private and public, national and international approaches to international economic law on the basis of a 'cosmopolitan constitutionalism' aimed at protecting the rights of citizens as 'constituent powers' *vis-à-vis* abuses of limited governance powers over the collective supply of PGs. Power-oriented 'management approaches' must be 'constitutionalised' through functionally limited 'multilevel constitutionalism', empowering citizens through cosmopolitan rights and judicial remedies to hold governments accountable for their failures to protect transnational 'aggregate PGs'. This reference to common goods is also reflected in Andrzej Jakubowski's chapter entitled *A constitutionalised legal order – exploring the role of the World Heritage Convention (1972)*. He deals with international cultural heritage law, sometimes perceived as a specific branch of international law, internally fragmented into functionally diversified sectors (e.g. intangible cultural heritage, world heritage, import and export restrictions on cultural property) and greatly affected by the exclusive interest of states and unequal power/knowledge relations between experts' and human communities' interests. Against this general background, he explains that the international legal protection of cultural heritage is currently being re-conceptualized and is becoming treated as an international common good, perceived as an essential element for the full realization of all human rights, including cultural rights. Taking the example of the 1972 World Heritage Convention, Jakubowski seeks to identify which elements of its legal regime are the most plausible candidates to obtain the status of 'universal' or 'constitutional' principles of the international legal order. This analysis aims to demonstrate whether and how different 'fragmented' practices of international law may contribute to the consolidation of universal regime for the protection of cultural heritage globally. In turn, Mónika Ambrus, in *Constitutionalisation through fragmented adjudication?*, deals with the 'structural fragmentation' of international law caused by its proliferation, that is, the situation when (quasi) judicial bodies working within the same field of law use different approaches to address a similar concept/problem. She argues that the impact of such proliferation on the substantive fragmentation of international law still lacks a consistent and systematic analysis which relies on a comparative assessment of different aspects of judicial decision-making. In order to gain insights into the actual effects of proliferation (i.e. fragmented adjudication) on the substantive fragmentation of international law, Ambrus explores the extent of divergence/convergence in judicial practices in relation to procedural norms, on the one hand, and substantive norms on the other, in terms of both structural and sectoral fragmentation.

The final three contributions to Part III consider the interrelationship between various seemingly fragmented branches or 'sectors' of international law and analyze how they are, or should be, reconciled and approached in order to achieve a more coherent system for the protection of certain universal 'constitutional' values. Chien-Huei Wu, in *From fragmentation to coherence: a constitutionalist take on the trade and public health debates*, locates trade and public health in the context of fragmentation and argues for a constitutional construction of the relationship between the WTO and WHO. Accordingly, he explores different areas where trade and public health cross paths, such as food safety, communicable diseases, non-communicable diseases and access to medicine. Wu proposes four concrete approaches to resolve the problems arising from such fragmentation: interpretative, legislative, human rights, and the global principle of subsidiarity. He argues that these four approaches should then be linked by a constitutionalist approach toward international law, thus calling for a more consistent global constitutional order. In the next chapter, *Access to environmental justice for NGOs: interplay between the Aarhus Convention, the EU Lisbon Treaty, and the European Convention on Human Rights*, Marjolein Schaap - Rubio Imbers explores the interplay of the three treaty regimes binding all EU Member States and takes as a point of departure the (procedural) right of access to environmental justice for NGOs as guaranteed by the Aarhus Convention. She examines how this right is shaped in Europe, considering the complex relationship between the three conventions, with each having its own oversight mechanism and with no clear hierarchy established. By recounting the recent case law of the CJEU and the European Court of Human Rights, she attempts to answer the question whether this interaction between the treaty regimes and overlapping mandates may lead to a constitutionalisation of the right of access to environmental justice for NGOs, or at a minimum lead to further development of the right at stake. Britta Sjöstedt's contribution, entitled *The reconciliatory approach: how multilateral environmental agreements can harmonize international legal obligations*, concludes the discussion offered in this volume with an analysis of global responses to trans-boundary environmental problems. Indeed these pose a specific challenge to the international legal system, as they often demand instruments providing for collective and far-reaching measures on a global scale. Such measures may collide with other areas of international law, including trade law, human rights law and international humanitarian law, which may give rise to conflicting behaviours. Arguably, the particular structure of environmental treaties, also referred to as multilateral environmental agreements (MEAs), allows their treaty institutions to adopt a 'reconciliatory approach'. The article describes how normative and institutional interactions take place under MEAs for the purpose of avoiding conflicts and tensions with other international legal obligations, while at the same time furthering the common concern to mitigate global environmental problems by going beyond the traditional mechanisms of treaty interpretation. By recounting the practice of protecting natural world heritage sites in the war-torn Democratic Republic of the Congo (DRC), Sjöstedt argues that the 'reconciliatory approach' may contribute to overcoming the fragmentation of international law.

The analyses presented in this volume are by no means exhaustive. Still, by demonstrating how the parallel debates of fragmentation and constitutionalisation materialize in various substantive legal contexts, they contribute to an understanding of the international legal discourse and the interactions between different spheres and actors. In fact the topics selected and included in this volume refer to highly significant areas of international law, on which general conclusions can be drawn about the practice of international law with respect to the fragmentation and constitutionalisation debates. Moreover, the variety of areas of international law analyzed in the book offer new contextual dimensions to the discussion, such as environmental or cultural issues, illustrating various aspects of the operationalisation of the fragmentation-constitutonalisation debate in the practice of international law.

Part I

International constitutionalisation as a claim

1 Constitutionalisation

A new philosophy of international law?

Jerzy Zajadło and Tomasz Widłak

1 Introduction: is constitutionalisation in need of revision?

At the beginning of our analysis of the problem of the constitutionalisation of international law, we would like to make three reservations. The first two of these to the original title for the research project proposed to us by the editors of this volume ('Constitutionalisation and Fragmentation of International Law Revisited'), which preceded its publication. This formulation raised substantial doubts, but at the same time it has given us food for thought as the starting point for this reflection.

First of all, a hidden normative claim had been included that the right time had come to *revisit*, or consider afresh, the notions of both the constitutionalisation and the fragmentation of international law. While distancing ourselves from the part of this thesis pertaining to fragmentation, which may indeed have recently undergone a revision, or at least a transformation, we wish to direct our attention to the somewhat more perplexing concept of the constitutionalisation of international law. We simply believe that there is as yet nothing to be 'revisited' as far as global constitutionalism is concerned. This contribution will sustain the view that the discussion on the constitutionalisation of international law has not yet matured to a point that allows definite conclusions amounting to any sort of possible revision of its central theses.[1] Instead, the debate on constitutionalisation may just have placed itself in the very starting blocks before taking a definite leap towards a more robust development as a meaningful doctrinal tool or perhaps even a new philosophy of international law. It is indeed an intellectual movement driven by academics rather than lawmakers, and it has both interpretative (descriptive) as well as constitutive (creational) potential. Let us quote the following opinion of Anne Peters: 'The constitutionalisation process of international

1 There are, however, also different opinions. For example T Kleinlein concludes that: 'The debate on constitutionalisation seems to have reached certain conclusions that may no longer be seriously challenged', T Kleinlein, 'On Holism, Pluralism, and Democracy: Approaches to Constitutionalism beyond the State' (2011) 21 *EJIL* 1083.

law is mainly driven by academics and to some extent by international courts, not by governments and treaty-makers'.[2] Also, she points out:

> Global constitutionalism is an intellectual movement which both reads (or reconstructs) some features of the status quo of international relations as 'constitutional' and 'constitutionalist' (positive analysis), and also seeks to provide arguments for their further development in a specific direction (normative analysis).[3]

Secondly, we interpret the conjunction 'and' in the above-mentioned formulation as pointing towards certain normative theses that we support: namely that the two processes of constitutionalisation and fragmentation are parallel and to a substantial degree autonomous in relation to each other.[4] These are not necessarily two opposite ends of the same process (if they were, the formulation would read, for example, 'from fragmentation to constitutionalisation'[5]). Likewise, international law itself is not and does not have to be torn between the two; the question is not about 'international law between constitutionalisation and fragmentation'. Therefore, we interpret the use of the word 'versus' in the title of this volume ('Fragmentation vs the Constitutionalisation of International Law: A Practical Inquiry') not as suggesting any antagonism between the two but rather as a reference to them being dynamically interconnected with a substantial degree of autonomy towards each other. This allows us to focus our inquiry on constitutionalisation but without denying in any way the link between the two notions.

The last reservation (by no means the least, however) is that our comments are not made from the point of view of scholars of international law, or to put it differently, from *the inside* of the discipline, but rather from the perspective of legal philosophers, or from *the outside* of the doctrine of international law. Our methodological point of departure can be described as that of the philosophy of international law, which we believe is at present one of the most dynamic and transformative areas of law and philosophy. For that reason, it is not only international lawyers who are interested in the robust processes represented by the constitutionalisation of international law; as will become evident in this chapter, legal, social and political philosophers are also interested. To mention just one example at this point (but a very significant

2 A Peters, 'Are we Moving towards Constitutionalization of the World Community?' in A Cassese (ed), *Realizing Utopia. The Future of International Law* (OUP 2012) 118 and 119.

3 Ibid., 119.

4 See in that regard recent research on the relation between fragmentation and constitutionalisation as relatively autonomous concepts: R Deplano, 'Fragmentation and Constitutionalisation of International Law: A Theoretical Inquiry' (2013) 6 *EJLS* 67.

5 See e.g. HG Cohen, 'The Global Impact and Implementation of Human Rights Norms: From Fragmentation to Constitutionalization' (2012) 25 *McGeorge Global Business & Development Law Journal* 381.

example) that demonstrates the centrality of the problems of international law in the modern philosophy of law: one of the most influential contemporary American legal philosophers, the late Professor Ronald Dworkin, recently devoted his last paper (published *post mortem*) entirely to the key problem of the grounds of international law.[6] Clearly, one *prima facie* observation is undeniable: *something* is happening with and within international law, and moreover that something should be written with a capital 'S'. The statement seems to be widely accepted in the doctrine of public international law, since the dramatic changes of the last two or three decades in the functioning and merits of international law are quite evident. However, we believe that this may not be just a substantial change in the content of international law but rather a qualitative shift in paradigms. In that regard, constitutionalisation can serve not only as an exemplification or expression of this change, but also as a point of departure in constructing an entirely new philosophy of international law.

2 Constitutionalisation, constitution and sovereignty in international law

For a long time philosophy has been committed to a certain provocative question – do the language and concepts we use only reflect a state of affairs, or can they also construct reality?[7] Notwithstanding the answer given, there is no doubt that the question has a particular significance in relation to the language used in the public sphere, which also includes the study of law. In reference to the topic of this paper, one may of course ask about the possibilities, meanings and effects of the application of the term 'constitutionalisation' in the area of international law. Nagging doubts about the use of language, which keep tormenting philosophers, appear to be particularly relevant at this point – the phenomenon of 'global' and 'postnational' constitutionalism lies exactly at the intersection of 'the law and the language',[8] and is connected with the 'problem of translation'.[9] Moreover, the historical development of international law and its scholarly study shows some specific features. For example, Stephen Beaulac draws attention to this process by referring to the immense transformative power that the word 'sovereignty' has had over the centuries. In his opinion, it is the concept of centralised power first created

6 R Dworkin, 'A New Philosophy for International Law' (2013) 41 *Philosophy & Public Affairs* 1; Professor Dworkin died on 14 February 2013. The title of his article served as an inspiration for the authors in their work on this chapter.

7 R Sarkowicz and J Stelmach, *Teoria Prawa* [Theory of Law] (Wydawnictwo Uniwersytetu Jagiellońskiego 1998) 39. The authors point in that regard, on the one hand, to L Wittgenstein, and on the other to BL Whorf, E Sapir and W von Humboldt.

8 M-S Kuo, 'Between Law and Language: When Constitutionalism Goes Plural in a Globalising World' (2010) 73(5) *Modern Law Review* 858.

9 N Walker, 'Postnational Constitutionalism and the Problem of Translation' in JHH Weiler and M Wind (eds), *European Constitutionalism Beyond the State* (CUP 2003).

by Jean Bodin (in the sixteenth century) and then extrapolated by Emerich de Vattel (in the eighteenth century) to the external ground of international relations that has shaped the paradigm of *ius inter gentes*.[10] Of course, this is not to say that the historical role of this specific kind of linguistic determinism should be exaggerated, but it is difficult not to agree – at least to some extent – with the opinion that it was a revolution in ideas that led to a revolution in terms of sovereignty, which in turn shaped the state system that defines the world politics of the present day.[11] Contrary to appearances, this has a very close connection with the problem of the modern constitutionalisation of international law, because in philosophy, politics and international relations theory so far it has been precisely the principle of sovereignty that has been recognised as the constitutional foundation of the international community.

From this point of view, the contemporary doctrinal phenomenon under discussion here is actually an attempt to shift this paradigm. The main objective of contemporary proponents of the constitutionalisation of international law is a broad acknowledgment of the statement that it is not sovereignty, or, being more precise, not primarily sovereignty, that should form the basis of the 'constitution of the international community'.[12] Paraphrasing a famous saying by Cicero, 'where there is a society, there is the state, and there is the law' (*ubi societas, ibi civitas, ibi ius*); one may say that if the international community is no longer merely a mechanical collection of sovereign entities, but has evolved into a structurally complex community based on generally accepted axiology, then sooner or later a constitutional basis for its existence and functioning must be built (*ubi societas, ibi communitas, ibi constitutio*).[13]

If we recall the controversy associated with the process of the constitutionalisation of European Union law,[14] then it is easy to imagine the difficulties piling up before lawyers who are trying to convey this concept in relation to the even broader and far more precarious area of international law. Some lawyers may even have the impression that it is, *prima facie*, oxymoronic to think about a combination of the instruments of constitutional law on the one hand and international law on the other. This is even more likely to be true because

10 S Beaulac, *The Power of Language in the Making of International Law: The Word Sovereignty in Bodin and Vattel and the Myth of Westphalia* (Nijhoff 2004) 102, 128.

11 D Philpott, *Revolutions in Sovereignty. How Ideas Shaped Modern International Relations* (Princeton University Press 2001) 8.

12 Ibid., 10–27; see also C Reus-Smit, 'International Law' in J Baylis and S Smith (eds), *The Globalization of World Politics: An Introduction to International Relations* (6th edn, OUP 2014) 274.

13 J Zajadło, 'Społeczność międzynarodowa czy wspólnota międzynarodowa? [International Society or International Community?]' (2005) 9 *Państwo i Prawo* 34; T Widłak, *From International Society to International Community: The Constitutional Evolution of International Law* (University of Gdańsk Press 2015).

14 See e.g. the articles of D Grimm, J Habermas, JHH Kompens and U Di Fabio published under the title 'Czy Europa potrzebuje konstytucji? [Does Europe Need a Constitution?]' (2005) 1 *Nowa Europa. Przegląd Natoliński* 17.

the word 'constitutionalisation' has a relatively well defined and commonly accepted meaning in the field of municipal law, where it is connected with an idea of the transmission of the constitution (as the supreme legal act) and its values onto the entire system and legal order. However, in the context of international law a completely different sense of this word is relevant – the development of international law towards a constitutional system.[15] On the other hand, in recent years one can witness the gradual expansion of the relationships between constitutional law and international law; Brun-Otto Bryde very aptly referred to this process as 'the internationalisation of constitutional law' and the 'constitutionalisation of international law'.[16] Anne Peters points to a slightly different aspect of this relationship. According to her, the processes of globalisation have caused the de-constitutionalisation of national legal systems, and, therefore, a reverse process at the international level can act to compensate for this loophole.[17]

3 Connotations of constitutionalisation in international law

When the word 'constitution' appeared from time to time in international law, especially in the titles of treaties setting up and defining the structure and functioning of international organisations, no attention was paid to it.[18] In particular, there were no attempts to construct a philosophy of an international legal constitutionalism *sui generis* on this basis. However, as far as the process of constitutionalisation is concerned, the case is about something different altogether in terms of quality. As long as the terminology of constitutions was involved only to the point of naming international agreements, it was difficult to couple it with the concept of constitutionalism as a manifestation of a certain ideology or normative political theory. Nevertheless, the situation has changed radically because the statutes of international organisations have developed clearly constitutional elements, as was the case with the transformation of the GATT into the WTO.[19] There is no doubt that the issue of constitutionalisation is, on the one hand, one of the most controversial questions and, on the other hand, a widely and fervently debated issue in the

15 M Knauff, 'Konstitutionalisierung im inner- und überstaatlichen Recht – Konvergenz oder Divergenz? [Constitutionalisation in National and Supranational Law – Convergence or Divergence?]' (2008) 68 *ZaöRV* 489.

16 B-O Bryde, 'Konstitutionalisierung des Völkerrechts und Internationalisierung des Verfassungsrechts [Constitutionalisation of International Law and Internationalisation of Constitutional Law]' (2003) 42 *Der Staat* 61; see also Knauff (n 15) 482ff.

17 A Peters, 'Compensatory Constitutionalism: The Function and Potential of Fundamental International Norms and Structures' (2006) 19 *LJIL* 579.

18 E.g. the International Labour Organization (ILO), World Health Organization (WHO), United Nations Education Science and Culture Organization (UNESCO).

19 For more on this topic see e.g. DZ Cass, *The Constitutionalization of the World Trade Organization. Legitimacy, Democracy, and Community in the International Trading System* (OUP 2005).

contemporary study of international law.[20] In the initial phase, the problem was raised mainly in German scholarship, but it has now grown to be a subject of wider interest.[21] However, even the declared proponents of this concept are well aware of its controversy, and some of them even end the titles of their works on the subject with a question mark.[22] For example, Anne Peters juxtaposes a number of arguments for and against the constitutionalisation of international law that are present in the literature: the former refer to 'protection against uncontrolled deformalisation of international law', 'compensation for the process of deconstitutionalisation [of municipal law – authors] caused by globalisation and global governance' as well as the 'critical potential of the concept'; whereas the latter include accusations (which these authors are trying to fend off) such as a 'lack of constitutional mythology [or a revolutionary pedigree – authors]', 'excessive expectations', 'unrealism', 'the [apparent – authors] end of politics', 'anti-revolutionism', 'constitutional imperialism', 'Eurocentrism' and 'anti-democratic juristocracy'.[23]

Indeed, it is very difficult to analyse and give an unequivocal evaluation of the phenomenon of the constitutionalisation of international law. There are a number of reasons for this. First, the treatment of the problem depends on whether we consider the constitutionalisation of international law

20 See Chapter 12 in this book.

21 Among the newest literature see, in particular, RStJ Macdonald and DG Johnston (eds), *Towards World Constitutionalism* (Nijhoff 2005); N Tsagourias (ed), *Transitional Constitutionalism. International and European Perspective* (CUP 2007); B Fassbender, *The United Nations Charter as the Constitution of the International Community* (Nijhoff 2009); J Klabbers, A Peters and G Ulfstein, *The Constitutionalization of International Law* (OUP 2009); JL Dunoff and JP Trachtman (eds), *Ruling the World? Constitutionalism, International Law, and Global Governance* (CUP 2009); P Dobner and M Loughlin (eds), *The Twilight of Constitutionalism?* (OUP 2010); N Krisch, *Beyond Constitutionalism. The Pluralist Structure of Postnational Law* (OUP 2010); F Pfeil, *Globale Verrechtlichung: Global Governance und die Konstitutionalisierung des internationalen Rechts* [Global Juridification: Global Governance and the Constitutionalisation of International Law] (Nomos 2011); T Kleinlein, *Konstitutionalisierung im Völkerrecht: Konstruktion und Elemente einer idealistischen Völkerrechtslehre* [Constitutionalisation of International Law: Design and Elements of An Idealistic International Legal Doctrine] (Springer 2011); CEJ Schwöbel, *Global Constitutionalism in International Legal Perspective* (Brill 2011); JL Cohen, *Globalization and Sovereignty: Rethinking Legality, Legitimacy, and Constitutionalism* (CUP 2012).

22 This way of formulating titles in the form of a question is common not only among the critics (e.g. U Haltern, 'Internationales Verfassungsrecht? Anmerkungen zu einer kopernikanischen Wende' [International Constitutional Law? Notes on a Copernican Revolution] (2003) 128(4) *Archiv des öffentlichen Rechts* 511), but also among authors having a more sympathetic attitude towards the constitutionalisation of international law (e.g. S Kadelbach and T Kleinlein, 'International Law – A Constitution of Mankind?' (2007) 50 *GYIL* 303 and O Diggelmann and T Altwicker, 'Is There Something Like a Constitution of International Law? A Critical Analysis of the Debate on World Constitutionalism' 2008 68(3) *ZaöRV* 623).

23 A Peters, 'Reconstruction Constitutionnaliste du Droit International: Arguments pour et contre' [Constitutionalist Reconstruction of International Law: Pros and Cons] in E Jouannet and others (eds), *Select Proceedings of the European Society of International Law*, vol 1 (OUP 2008).

as the actual process that takes place in the normative dimension or, alternatively, only as a certain *de lege ferenda* projection constructed by some scholars.[24] Some alternative explanations propose a middle way between these two positions; for example, they view the constitutionalisation of international law as a hermeneutical device. This means that the process may be seen as an attempt to assume a constitutional pre-understanding (*Vorverständnis*) when interpreting international law, or as an attempt to bestow a certain cognitive constitutional framework on international law without actually changing the law *de lege lata*.[25] Recently, it has also been pointed out that constitutionalism goes well with constructivist theories of international relations that help to define it as a mindset shared between subjects that works as a powerful tool for arguments in the legal discourse on legitimacy deficits at the level of exercising authority beyond the state.[26] Secondly, the issue is clearly of an interdisciplinary nature, because it is discussed not only by scholars of international law but also by constitutionalists, as well as by political philosophers, legal philosophers, sociologists and theorists of international relations. Thirdly, in this debate, alongside the term 'constitutionalisation' one will also find related terms such as 'constitution' and 'constitutionalism'; as a result we have to deal with a specific transfer to the field of public international law of the methodological instruments that have been developed for an entirely different branch of the law.[27] Fourthly and finally, the term has not been created, and does not operate, in a vacuum. On the one hand, contrary to all appearances, the constitutionalisation of international law has a fairly long history (most notably one should mention Alfred Verdross and his students,[28] as well as the New Haven school[29]). On the other hand, the constitutionalisation of international law is today primarily a result of other processes or of reactions to them; these processes include fragmentation, globalisation,[30] hierarchy (verticalisation)[31]

24 See Chapter 2 in this book.

25 For more on that issue, see T. Widłak, 'Konstytucjonalizacja prawa międzynarodowego jako narzędzie hermeneutyczne' [Constitutionalisation of International Law as a Hermeneutical Device], in A Samonek (ed), *Teoria prawa między nowoczesnością a ponowoczesnością* [Theory of Law Between Modernity and Postmodernity] (Wydawnictwo Uniwersytetu Jagiellońskiego 2012); Klabbers, Peters and Ulfstein (n 21) 348.

26 T Kleinlein, 'Between Myths and Norms: Constructivist Constitutionalism and the Potential of Constitutional Principles in International Law' (2012) 81 *NJIL* 79.

27 A Peters and K Armingeon, 'Introduction – Global Constitutionalism from an Interdisciplinary Perspective' (2009) 16(2) *Indiana J Global Legal Studies* 385; see also M Loughlin, 'What is Constitutionalization?' in Dobner and Loughlin (n 21).

28 For more on the role of Alfred Verdross, see T Kleinlein, 'Alfred Verdross as a Founding Father of International Constitutionalism?' (2012) 4(2) *Goettingen Journal of International Law* 385.

29 Fassbender (n 21) 28–41.

30 See e.g. DJ Bederman, *Globalization and International Law* (Palgrave Macmillan 2008).

31 See E de Wet and J Vidmar (eds), *Hierarchy in International Law. The Place of Human Rights* (OUP 2012); D Shelton, 'Normative Hierarchy in International Law' (2006) 100 *AJIL* 291.

and the privatisation[32] of international law. One of the leading protagonists of the idea of constitutionalisation, Jan Klabbers, rightly notes that constitutionalisation, fragmentation and verticalisation are the 'holy trinity of international legal debate in the early 21st century'.[33]

4 Constitutionalisation and the transformation of international law

The constitutionalisation of international law is part of a broader phenomenon that can be summarised in the following questions: does the contemporary paradigm of international law undergo axiological and normative transformations and, if so, why, and in what ways? If one gives a positive answer to the first of these questions, there are, *prima facie*, three positions that can be taken towards the issue:

1) Even if any changes, such as in relation to the concept of state sovereignty being the fundamental category of international law, are observable, these should not affect the substance of international law as a normative category, and especially should not lead to any transformation of its consensual nature or any changes in other aspects of the phenomenon of the law (its creation, application, interpretation, validity or compliance). From this point of view we are just dealing with a normal evolutionary development of international law, which is of the same nature as a development in any other branch of the law such as administrative, civil, criminal, constitutional law, etc. As a result, many hard-line international legal scholars[34] as well as some political philosophers[35] warn us against fiddling with the essence of international law by means of constitutionalisation, because this apparently violates the 'critical mass' of international law;
2) The scale of the process is so far-reaching that it affects the very essence of international law as a normative category. The result is that we should, on the one hand, develop a new philosophy of international law,[36] and, on the other hand, verify the current position of the philosophy of law *in genere* towards the very essence of international law *in specie*, because in both aspects the current state of affairs does not reflect the scale of the progressive qualitative changes (for example, the fact that the ultimate goal of the exercise of national sovereignty should be the good of

32 See e.g. O Dörr, 'Privatisierung des Völkerrechts' [Privatisation of International Law] (2005) 60(19) *Juristen Zeitung* 905.
33 J Klabbers, 'Setting the Scene' in Klabbers, Peters and Ulfstein (n 21) 1.
34 JL Goldsmith and EA Posner, *The Limits of International Law* (OUP 2005).
35 C Delsol, *Unjust Justice. Against the Tyranny of International Law* (ISI Books 2008).
36 S Besson and J Tasioulas (eds), *The Philosophy of International Law* (OUP 2010); see also J Zajadło, 'Filozofia prawa międzynarodowego? [Philosophy of International Law?]' (2007) 2 *Państwo i Prawo* 16.

all humanity). This view is represented both by some international legal scholars (especially representatives of German science such as Hermann Mosler, Jochen Frowein, Bruno Simma, and Christian Tomuschat[37]), as well as some political philosophers;[38]

3) The scale of these phenomena is so far-reaching that we should not be limited to a change in the philosophy of international law and in the relation of the philosophy of law to international law. According to some authors, we are dealing, on the one hand, with a paradigmatic crisis in international law,[39] and, on the other, with such a new and substantially different entity in terms of normative categories that we should perhaps talk about the creation of a completely new law, a law that is sometimes referred to as global law or, in a slightly different perspective, the law of humanity. Although this should not replace the classical international law, it can be complementary to it and create a sort of 'superstructure' for it. The qualitative change lies primarily in the fact that it is not the sovereign states that are placed at the centre of this new system, but rather human beings and the international community as a whole. In this case, too, one can point to lawyers[40] as well as philosophers[41] as the proponents of the approach.

The problem of the constitutionalisation of international law is discussed primarily in the context of the second of the positions mentioned above. The supporters of this view argue that it is a specific process that cannot be assessed only from the perspective of terminology simply borrowed from the dogmatic constructs of constitutional law. As a result, in the case of global constitutionalism such concepts as 'constitution' and 'constitutionalism' take a slightly different or completely different meaning.[42] This is admitted even by the authors, who refer directly not only to the 'constitutionalisation of international law', but simply to 'international constitutional law'. For example, Brado Fassbender believes that the United Nations Charter can indeed be perceived as a kind of 'constitution of the international community'; however, at the same time he defines this as an autonomous phenomenon and warns against the simplified search for analogies with the 'constitution' for the purposes of national law.[43] The heart of the matter

37 Fassbender (n 21) 41–51.

38 A Buchanan, *Justice, Legitimacy, and Self-Determination. Moral Foundations of International Law* (OUP 2004).

39 R Domingo, 'The Crisis of International Law' (2009) 42(5) *Vanderbilt Journal of Transnational Law* 1543.

40 R Domingo, *The New Global Law* (CUP 2010); R Teitel, *Humanity's Law* (OUP 2011).

41 P Singer, *One World. The Ethics of Globalization* (Yale University Press 2002).

42 See A Surowiecka, 'Konstytucja – aspekty historyczne, definicyjne i współczesne kierunki rozwoju [Constitution – Historical, Definitional Aspects and Contemporary Trends]' (2012) 21(2) *Perspectiva. Legnickie Studia Teologiczno-Historyczne* 163–164.

43 Fassbender (n 21) 170.

is not so much the 'constitution in a formal sense' but rather a series of events that are evidence of certain constitutional processes taking place in the international community. These processes include, among others, the progressive legalisation of international relations,[44] the development of an international judiciary, the humanisation and/or moralisation of international law, an increasing number of *jus cogens* (or peremptory) norms, an increasing number of international obligations *erga omnes*, the hierarchisation of international law, the supranational role of the Security Council, international agreements (sometimes called world order treaties) that have the character of mini-constitutions, etc.[45] These elements taken individually are insufficient to allow one to speak persuasively about the constitutionalisation of international law – for example, legalisation, understood as an extension of the volume of the legal regulation of international relations, is only a quantitative change and nothing more. However, the same legalisation when combined with the other processes and phenomena mentioned above creates not only a new quantity, but indeed also a new quality.

The constitutionalisation of international law so conceived is by no means homogeneous and does not constitute a static phenomenon, but rather is diverse and dynamic and takes place in very different aspects of international law, from its creation, application and interpretation, to the system of its institutions, the issue of legal subjectivity, and the structure of the international community, its system of values, and its organisational and procedural rules. In this sense, constitutionalisation is the process of implementing a normative political theory (constitutionalism), which will perhaps result in the creation of a normative structure (a constitution). The essence of this phenomenon is, however, very differently conceived. As already mentioned above, some authors believe it to be the common denominator of the actual processes that are taking place in the contemporary international community; for others, it is the basis for building new hermeneutical rules of interpretation of international law; and for yet others it creates a horizon for the *de lege ferenda* perspective of the international order. With such diverse approaches, it is difficult to predict what the fate of this concept will be. It seems, however, that we are dealing with a process that it will be challenging to stop, because it is accompanied by the above-mentioned evolution of international society towards a true international community. In other words, using the terminology of the English school of international relations, just as once there was a move from a realistic (coexistence) to a pluralistic (co-operation) model in international society, so we are witnessing the rise of a solidarist (cosmopolitan) model,[46] for the problem of the constitutionalisation of international law is closely associated with cosmopolitism, especially in contemporary political

44 See e.g. JL Goldstein and others (eds), *Legalization and World Politics* (MIT Press 2001).

45 T Widłak, 'From International Society to International Community' (n 13); Diggelmann and Altwicker (n 22) 625–628.

46 AJ Bellamy, 'Introduction: International Society and the English School' in AJ Bellamy (ed), *International Society and its Critics* (OUP 2005); J Zajadło, 'Koncepcja odpowiedzialności za ochronę – nowa filozofia prawa międzynarodowego? [The Concept of Responsibility

philosophy.[47] In passing, it should be noted, however, that there has also been criticism of these assumptions for forcing the predominance of a particular orthodox liberal-democratic vision of constitutionalism with an almost religious zeal that in fact threatens fundamental values such as constitutional pluralism as well as the neutrality of constitutional ideas.[48]

5 Fuller vs. Hart: constitutionalisation as the systematisation of international law

The change in the philosophical and legal understanding of the nature of international law certainly encourages the discussion of the constitutionalisation of international law. For many years, the paradigm in force was the one proposed by Herbert LA Hart – according to him, international law is indeed law, but law only in terms of a set of primary rules.[49] It does not constitute a fully-fledged system of law because it lacks secondary rules. In recent years, however, in the philosophy of law there has been a shift away from this paradigm in the direction of the proposals of Hart's main opponent – Lon L Fuller.[50] Fuller himself wrote relatively little about international law, but he also never questioned its juridical character. On the contrary, he was even fascinated by some elements of it, such as the horizontal process of its creation, the mutual and consensual nature of its legal commitments, its interactive nature and diversity, and the informality of its sources.[51] However, he also had some doubts, mainly concerning the ineffectiveness of the system of international justice – that is, to some extent, the rules of adjudication in Hart's terminology. In the final instance, however, while recognising the incompleteness of international law as a system, Fuller saw the possibility of applying the principle of the rule of law to the international legal system.[52] A recourse to Fuller's concept means that international law is indeed created in the horizontal plane rather than the vertical one, but this

to Protect – a New Philosophy of International Law?]' in J Kranz (ed), *Świat współczesny wobec użycia siły zbrojnej* [The Contemporary World and the Use of Armed Force] (Instytut Wydawniczy Euro Prawo 2009).

47 The typical example of this may be given by J Habermas, who infers the constitutionalisation of international law from I Kant's cosmopolitism – see J Habermas, 'Hat die Konstitutionalisierung des Völkrrechts noch eine Chance?' in J Habermas (ed) *Die gespaltene Westen* (Suhrkamp 2004).

48 CEJ Schwöbel, 'The Holy Trinity of International Legal Debate' (2011) 24 *LJIL* 1035.

49 HLA Hart, *The Concept of Law* (2nd edn, OUP 1994).

50 LL Fuller, *The Morality of Law* (2nd edn, Yale University Press 1969).

51 J Brunnée and SJ Toope, *Legitimacy and Legality in International Law. An Interactional Account* (CUP 2010) 33–52.

52 The only text in which Fuller made comments about international law is *The Forms and Limits of Adjudication*; this was published in 1959 and in its original form was a lecture given at a meeting of the American Society of International Law under the title *Adjudication and the Rule of Law*. Its final version was published only after Fuller's death in 1978 in 92 *Harvard Law Review* 353). The details of this interesting case, together with the private correspondence between Fuller and President Richard Nixon is given by K Knop in 'The Hart-Fuller Debate's Silence on Human Rights' in P Cane (ed), *The Hart-Fuller Debate in the Twenty-First Century* (Hart 2010).

does not necessarily imply that it cannot be considered in terms of a system. On the contrary, it can be subjected to the same criteria for evaluating the so-called internal morality of law as are applied in the process of the assessment of municipal law.[53] From this point of view, there is only one step needed to systematise, and therefore international law is constitutionalised in the process of resolving the conflict between its legality and its legitimacy.[54]

Indeed, all three concepts discussed here – constitution, constitutionalism and constitutionalisation – are, to varying degrees, connected with the concept of the system, and separately from it they are essentially meaningless.[55] Therefore, even if international law does not yet constitute a system, the ultimate goal of constitutionalisation as the process of the implementation of the principles of constitutionalism is an attempt to confer such a feature upon it. Therefore, first of all one must determine exactly what these principles are. In this context, Jeffrey L Dunoff and Joel P Trachtman have formulated the following catalogue: the creation of the institutions of authority and their horizontal and vertical allocation, the supremacy of constitutional norms, a qualified mode of change, the guarantee of the fundamental rights of the individual, the control of the constitutionality of the law, and accountability and democracy.[56] Indeed, clearly this is all about the basic foundational rules of constitutionalism as formulated on the grounds of national law. The best proof of these tendencies is the fact that in 2012 Cambridge University Press started to issue a new scientific journal with a very characteristic title: 'Global Constitutionalism – Human Rights, Democracy and the Rule of Law'.[57] The transfer of these principles – human rights, democracy and the rule of law – to the grounds of international law and the understanding of the process of constitutionalisation requires, however, some findings about terminology as well as some systemic and functional assumptions to be made in advance.

First of all, the authors who refer to this concept define the nature and the scale of the necessary appropriation of the constitutional terminology in very different ways. Otto Diggelmann and Thomas Altwicker indicate the existence of three basic strategies for the 'legitimization of the constitutional language in international relations': the semantic strategy, the correspondence strategy and the ethical and pragmatic strategy.[58] The semantic strategy is simply a direct borrowing of the constitutional terminology, with an adjustment *mutatis mutandis* to the specifics of international law. It requires, however, the assumption that there is an international community that

53 J Klabbers, 'Constitutionalism and the Making of International Law. Fuller's Procedural Natural Law' (2008) 5 *No Foundations – Journal of Extreme Legal Positivism* 84.
54 Brunnée and Toope (n 51).
55 Diggelmann and Altwicker (n 22) 629.
56 JL Dunoff and JP Trachtman, 'A Functional Approach to International Constitutionalization' in Dunoff and Trachtman (n 21) 19–21.
57 Cambridge Journals <http://journals.cambridge.org/action/displayIssue?jid=GCN&tab=currentissue>, accessed: 6.08.2015
58 Diggelmann and Altwicker (n 22) 632–640.

ought to be based on constitutional principles corresponding to the law's structural and axiological needs. This version – in its various mutations – is referred to by such authors as Bado Fassbender, Bruno Simma, Christian Thomuschat, and Ronald St J Macdonald. The correspondence strategy is based on a search of the international sphere for constitutional functions, features and content. Unlike the semantic strategy, it does not require any transformations of the classical constitutional language to be made, but instead it applies this language directly to the above-mentioned features, elements and content. The use of different variants of this strategy is attributed to authors such as Brun-Otto Bryde, Daniel Thürer, Erika de Wet, Anne Peters, and Pierre-Marie Dupuy. The last strategy is to extend the legal discourse to arguments of ethical rationality (the state on its own identifies itself with the international constitutional order – this is favoured by, for example, Jürgen Habermas) or pragmatic rationality (it is practical reason that points to the need for a global constitution – a proponent of this view is Angelika Emmerich-Fritsche).

Secondly, the particular strategy for dealing with constitutional terminology does not by itself determine the nature of the phenomenon under analysis. Therefore, Christine EJ Schwöbel has recently described four different models of global constitutionalism: social, institutional, normative and analogous.[59] The first of these, represented in the works of Günther Teubner and Andreas Fischer-Lescano, generally separates the issue from the realm of the state and moves it entirely to the level of global civil society.[60] The second model, represented in the work of Brado Fassbender, is primarily a search for the central seat of power at the global level that is legitimised through institutionalisation – the major point of focus here is the United Nations and the constitutional nature of the UN Charter. The third of the above-mentioned models, normative constitutionalism, underlines the exceptional role, the binding force and the position within the hierarchy of international legal norms of the *jus cogens* (peremptory) norms of international law as the fundamental and, therefore, constitutional standards (this type of global constitutionalism is represented in the works of Erika de Wet, Angelika Emmerich-Fritsche and Michael Byers[61]). Last but not least, analogous constitutionalism, represented in the works of Mattias Kumm and Robert

59 Schwöbel, *Global Constitutionalism in International Legal Perspective* (n 21); CEJ Schwöbel, 'Organic Global Constitutionalism' (2010) 23 *LJIL* 529.

60 G Teubner, 'Societal Constitutionalism: Alternatives to State-Centered Constitutional Theory?' in C Joerges, I-J Sand and G Teubner (eds), *Constitutionalism and Transnational Governance* (OUP 2004); A Fischer-Lescano, *Globalverfassung* (Velbrück Wissenschaft 2005).

61 E de Wet, 'The Emergence of International and Regional Value Systems as a Manifestation of the Emerging International Constitutional Order' (2006) 19 *LJIL* 611; E de Wet, 'The International Constitutional Order' (2006) 55(1) *ICLQ* 51; A Emmerich-Fritsche, *Vom Völkerrecht zum Weltrecht* [From International Law to World Law] (Duncker & Humblot 2007); M Byers, 'Conceptualising the Relationship between Jus Cogens and Erga Omnes Rules' (1997) 66 *NJIL* 211.

Uerpmann,[62] is primarily focused on demonstrating the similarities between intra-national and international constitutionalism.

Thirdly, depending on the strategy for the transplantation of terminology and the global constitutionalism model chosen, various functions and/or objectives of the constitutionalisation of international law can be highlighted. The literature on this subject indicates, *inter alia*, such objectives as: the allocation of the centre of power and the delimitation of its competence, the legal regulation of the functioning of the international community and the search for legitimacy in international law.[63]

Fourthly, manifestations of the constitutionalisation of international law as they are variously understood may take place at different levels. They may in fact relate to international law as a whole or to its general principles, but they may also refer to some of its regimes or parts (such as human rights, international trade law, criminal law, law of the sea, etc.), or they may only have a regional (e.g. European) dimension.[64]

6 Towards a philosophy of the constitutionalisation of international law?

Constitutionalisation is a term 'equally attractive as mysterious'.[65] International constitutionalism, in turn, has for some time now been admitted as a subject of analysis by lawyers, philosophers, political scientists, sociologists and theorists of international relations, but at the same time it remains an 'unsolved riddle'.[66] Returning to the question posed at the outset of this chapter, the attempt to answer can be summarised in the following way: the concept of the constitutionalisation of international law both reflects and at the same time shapes reality. In this context, the latter role seems to be particularly interesting, as it seems to confirm the immense power of words and/or ideas in the field of international law that is mentioned above. We have already indicated the importance of the concept of sovereignty in the history of international relations. At this point, one can take into account yet another, more recent, example – the concept of the Responsibility to Protect (R2P).[67] What only yesterday seemed like an elusive daydream of a group of intellectuals has today become an official doctrine of the United Nations, and tomorrow will possibly mature into a binding norm of law. The constitutionalisation of international law may, perhaps, follow the same path. What today seems to be an exaggerated theoretical generalisation of

62 M Kumm, 'The Legitimacy of International Law: A Constitutionalist Framework of Analysis' (2004) 15(5) *EJIL* 907; R Uerpmann, 'Internationales Verfassungsrecht' (2001) 56 *Juristen-Zeitung* 565.

63 Schwöbel, *Global Constitutionalism in International Legal Perspective* (n 21).

64 Knauff (n 15) 456, 475.

65 Ibid.

66 I de la Rasilla del Moral, 'The Unsolved Riddle of International Constitutionalism' (2010) 12 *International Community Law Review* 81.

67 For more on that issue, see G Evans, *The Responsibility to Protect. Ending Mass Atrocity Crimes Once and for All* (The Brookings Institution Press 2008); also see Zajadło, 'Koncepcja odpowiedzialności za ochronę' (n 46).

certain objective phenomena is tomorrow likely to become a binding normative paradigm, because, in the words of Anne Peters who is paraphrasing Immanuel Kant, 'there is nothing more practical than a good theory'.[68] In this respect, international law indeed demonstrates a certain particularity – 'it is what international lawyers make of it'.[69]

Obviously, it was not the purpose of this chapter to conduct a comprehensive analysis and evaluation of the concept of constitutionalisation as a new philosophical proposal for international law. Because of editorial limitations, we were forced to leave out a number of issues and phenomena that are being discussed in the global debate on the subject, such as the so-called problems of constitutional multi-levels, or constitutional pluralism related to fragmentation as the other side of the 'constitutional coin'. We have also abstained from undertaking any sort of final assessment of this phenomenon from the point of view of the methodology of law. It is, however, difficult not to agree with Jörg Kammerhofer in his argument that the use of, for example, Kelsen's pure theory of law in the problem of the constitutionalisation of international law raises certain methodological problems, since it forces one to acknowledge the debate as being of a more political than legal character.[70] This does not change the fact that the voice of a more geographically diverse doctrine of international law has somehow been missing from this discussion – particularly because the observations above are made by a theorist and philosopher of the law, not a scholar of international law. However, the issue raises a plethora of theoretical as well as practical problems that must be of interest to both theorists and dogmatists all over the globe. One of the examples of this kind of problem is the question of the collision of laws.[71] Constitutionalisation and fragmentation, in this context, are not just about the continuing dispute between monists and dualists with regard to the relationship between domestic law and international law. On the contrary, they are also about the problem of competition between and within supranational normative systems. It is not by accident that one of the most important monographs on the constitutionalisation of international law begins with an analysis of the high-profile judgments in the *Yusuf and Al Barakaat* and *Kadi* cases, because they are 'a microcosm of some of the most fundamental disputes in modern international law'.[72]

68 A Peters, 'There is Nothing more Practical than a Good Theory. An Overview of Contemporary Approaches to International Law' (2001) 44 *GYIL* 37.

69 M Koskenniemi, *From Apology to Utopia. The Structure of International Legal Argument* (CUP 2005) 615.

70 J Kammerhofer, 'Constitutionalism and the Myth of Practical Reason: Kelsenian Responses to Methodological Problems' (2010) 23(4) *LJIL* 723.

71 A Peters, 'Rechtsordnungen und Konstitutionalisierung: Zur Neubestimmung der Verhältnisse' [Jurisdictions and Constitutionalisation: Redefining the Relationships] (2010) 65 *Zeitschrift für öffentliches Recht* 3.

72 Klabbers, 'Setting the Scene' (n 21); the cases are T-306/01 *Yusuf and Al Barakaat v Council and Commission* [2005] ECR II-3533 and T-315-01 *Kadi v Council and Commission* [2005] ECR II-3649.

7 Conclusion: constitutionalisation as the new philosophy for international law

The aim of this chapter was to introduce the reader to the philosophical map of the discussion on constitutionalisation and the potentially transformative power of constitutionalisation for the structure and essence of international law. As expected from the introduction to this contribution, the phenomenon of the constitutionalisation of international law is far from being a definite doctrine or even a compact theory. It lacks one clear formulation or dominating current that could at this point be 'revisited' or restated. Nevertheless, its descriptive and creative potential is notable, and it may play a role in setting the course for the transformation of international law in the twenty-first century.

We believe that the notion of 'constitutionalisation' is first and foremost that of a transformative process. Its effect, however, may not necessarily be an explicit change in the wording of international law as it stands – in fact, this is rather unlikely. The notion of constitutionalisation is extremely value-laden and, given the use of an appropriate strategy for transplanting the constitutional terminology at hand, it may well end up constructing reality by building a particular intellectual framework upon the fabric of international law. For instance, the constitutional interpretation of international law explicitly introduces and sanctions the normative hierarchy in the doctrine on the sources of international law, and for the first time aims to treat the *jus cogens* doctrine seriously. Moreover, it is capable of embracing what have been called 'community interests'[73] or 'public interest norms',[74] which are often included in the neglected *erga omnes* rules. Last but not least, in this understanding constitutionalisation facilitates the international project by appealing to the systemic nature of international law and thereby remedying the potential defects of fragmentation. Therefore, we believe that, of the three general approaches to the issue of constitutionalisation, the middle position is the most pragmatic and desirable. It acknowledges the transformative momentum that international law arguably has today, and sees constitutionalisation as a reformative but not a revolutionary solution.

***

Timothy Dunne, writing about new ways to conceptualise international society, told a story from Albert Einstein's life: '"Professor Einstein, do you realize that this is the same exam paper that you set last year?", asked the examination officer. "Ah", began the reply, "the questions are the same, it's the answers that have changed"'.[75] This anecdote could be used in an equally

73 See U Fastenrath and others (eds), *From Bilateralism to Community Interest. Essays in Honour of Judge Bruno Simma* (OUP 2011).

74 Peters, 'Compensatory Constitutionalism' (n 17) 601.

75 T Dunne, 'New Thinking on International Society' (2001) 3 *British Journal of Politics and International Relations* 223.

apt way to illustrate the development of the idea of the constitutionalisation of international law from the time of Alfred Verdross until now. Indeed, the questions are the same, but the answers have radically changed. One of the questions concerns the ultimate purpose of the constitutionalisation of international law. Paraphrasing Jose Alvarez,[76] we could say that for an optimist it is 'the virtue of the Law's Empire', but for a pessimist it is 'the peril of the Empire's Law'.

76 JE Alvarez, 'Contemporary International Law: An "Empire of Law" or the "Law of Empire"' (2009) 24(5) *American University International Law Review* 811.

2 From the internationalisation of national constitutions to the "constitutionalisation" of international law

The role of human rights*

Vassilis P. Tzevelekos and Lucas Lixinski

1 The link between international law's humanisation and constitutionalisation, and the chapter's scope

The theory of the *humanisation* of international law might be seen as contiguous or even complementary to the theory – or theories – on the *constitutionalisation* of international law.[1] This is one of the claims that the first author of this chapter has made in his introduction to a relatively recent paper he wrote for a special issue of a journal edited by the second author. As it is well known, the humanisation theory argues that human rights have had, and continue to have, major impact on numerous areas of international law, which, owing to that influence, is now perceived as an increasingly humanised legal system.[2] While there is no single conceptual denotation of constitutionalisation, the second author of this chapter has summarised it as an intellectual "project, which argues that the international legal order beyond the state exists and has a backbone, a foundational set of norms".[3] Human rights could be seen as part of that foundational set of norms, and a common *locus* that bridges the two named, separate, but interlinked narratives of international law and the international legal order. "Other than the object of the humanization of international law, human rights are one of the 'ingredients' of [its] constitutionalization".[4]

* We are particularly thankful to Dr David Kosar for the many conversations with respect to Part 3 of this chapter. All errors remain our own. The chapter is part of a broader study published at the *Leiden Journal of International Law*.

1 VP Tzevelekos, 'Revisiting the Humanisation of International Law: Limits and Potential – Obligations *Erga Omnes*, Hierarchy of Rules and the Principle of Due Diligence as the Basis for Further Humanisation' (2013) 6 *Erasmus Law Review* 63.

2 Ibid., 62, where a list with scholar works on the humanisation of international law is given. For a collection of essays on the topic, see MT Kamminga and M Scheinin (eds), *The Impact of Human Rights Law on General International Law* (OUP 2009).

3 L Lixinski, 'Narratives of the International Legal Order and Why They Matter' (2013) 6 *Erasmus Law Review* 2.

4 Tzevelekos (n 1) 63.

This chapter focuses on that common ingredient -i.e. human rights- of the two named theories. It seeks to highlight how the transplantation of (mainly civil and political) human rights from *national* constitutions to *international* law has generated major systemic changes in the latter's order that could be described by proponents of the constitutionalisation theory as constitutional in nature. The core assumption of this chapter is that of its title: the *internationalisation* of national constitutions leads to the "*constitutionalisation*" of international law. Two preliminary explanations are due at this point.

First, there is a reason why the term "constitutionalisation" is between quotation marks in the previous paragraph as well as in the chapter's title. In essence, we are somewhat critically "agnostic" about the constitutionalisation narrative. The reasons for our scepticism are briefly discussed in Part 2 of the chapter, but for now we would like to preface our position to the reader by saying that international law, like all legal orders, has always contained certain systemic characteristics that underpin its order,[5] and which are exclusive to it and stem from the nature of the society that developed it for its own needs and use. International law is a state-centric, decentralised, quasi-anarchic legal system. Such is the *être* of its constitutive society. Its core principles, sovereignty and equality, reflect the basic feature of its main "actors", i.e. states exercising the ultimate power and authority on a certain territory and over certain people, and the fact that sovereign states live in a society that recognises no superior authority than their very own sovereignty, leading thereby to the horizontality of the relationship between equals. The absence of centralisation produces inter-subjective relations (*ergo*, the deficiency -in principle- of objectiveness[6]), based on reciprocity and self-help. These are the key features of the Westphalian model,[7] which, of course, modern international law (also because of human rights, as this chapter will argue) has gradually mitigated and tempered. However, these very characteristics, as well as others such as the absence of the Hartial rule of recognition,[8] which for reasons of brevity cannot be mentioned here, remain central to international law, forming the basis that founds its system. Thus, in a sense they are "constitutional".

If by constitutionalisation we mean the existence of certain structural features of the legal order, then international law has always had a "constitution". This constitution is informal in its nature and delineates the structure (but also the confines) of its legal order. Yet, the term constitutionalisation

5 J Combacau, 'Le Droit International: Bric-à-Brac ou Système?' (1986) 31 *Archives de philosophie du droit* 85.

6 Ibid., 95–101.

7 On the impact of Westphalia on international law, see AS Hershey, 'History of International Law Since the Peace of Westphalia' (1912) 6 *AJIL* 30–69. For a critical perspective, see Stéphane Beaulac, 'The Westphalian Model in Defining International Law: Challenging the Myth' (2004) 9 *Australian Journal of Legal History* 181.

8 HLA Hart, *The Concept of Law* (3rd edn, OUP 2012) 214. Although, according to Hart, custom could be seen as a rule of recognition (256, postscript).

refers to something emerging;[9] rather than pointing to the aforementioned well known, and very old "constitutional" attributes of international law, it aspires to trace the signs of a dynamic transformative process marked by the emergence of a renewed constitutional "edifice". However, to effectively debate the forces and nature of any transformation observed in the international legal system, we ought not to lose sight or underrate the foundational "constitutional" features of the international system. For the metaphor to be valid, *in lieu* of "constitutionalisation", the word should be that of a "constitutional reform" – and such a reform cannot be but equally informal, as the "constitution" of international law is, and has always been. Human rights are part of that "reform" and associated with changes affecting the general systemic features of international law.

Second, thus far, scholarship has largely referred to constitutionalisation in the context of explaining why and how international law is developing what authors see as elements of a constitution. Next to that basic strand, one could add scholarly work studying how international law (and especially human rights) affects national constitutions.[10] We would like to add to that literature by framing some of its core contributions within debates on the constitutionalisation of international law, but also by adding a third strand of debate concerning the impact national constitutions and their human rights provisions (prevailingly regarding first generation rights) have or have had on the systemic premises and basic features of international law.

Thus, in this chapter, we take a step back in the debate(s) on the constitutionalisation of international law by identifying the origins of that transformative (and circular,[11] in essence) process. Our core contention is that the internationalisation of human rights law – to the extent that it is reflected in

9 A Peters, 'Are We Moving Towards Constitutionalization of the World Community' in A Cassese (ed), *Realizing Utopia: The Future of International Law* (OUP 2012) 118–135, especially 119.

10 See, for instance, J Waldron, 'Foreign Law and the Modern *Ius Gentium*' (2005) 19 *Harvard Law Review* 129; SH Cleveland, 'Our International Constitution' (2006) 31 *Yale Journal of International Law* 1; J Lobel, 'Fundamental Norms, International Law, and the Extra-Territorial Constitution' (2011) 36 *Yale Journal of International Law* 307, especially 333ff. In that category, one could also add the burgeoning literature on judicial dialogue and legal pluralism. To give just a few examples: BF Kerr, 'The Conversation between Strasbourg and National Courts: Dialogue or Dictation?' (2009) 44 *Irish Jurist* 1; G Martinico and O Pollicino, *The Interaction Between Europe's Legal Systems: Judicial Dialogue and the Creation of Supranational Laws* (Edward Elgar 2012); and in the context of legal pluralism, MP Maduro, 'Courts and Pluralism: Essay on a Theory of Judicial Adjudication in the Context of Legal and Constitutional Pluralism' in JL Dunoff and JP Trachtman (eds), *Ruling the World? Constitutionalism, International Law and Global Governance* (CUP 2009).

11 In the sense that the internationalisation of national constitutions allowed human rights to develop their effects and be developed at the international level, which now have an impact on domestic law and national constitutions. Seen from that perspective, the chapter explores the link between modernity's state-centered constitutionalism, and the current era of post-national constitutionalism.

positive international law and not simply a moral aspiration[12] – has led to the development of certain significant features that were initially either anaemic, or even entirely absent from "classic" international law. These new features that the order of international law has acquired through the internationalisation of human rights – and this is what makes them in a sense constitutional – amount now to structural elements of the international system that apply well beyond human rights as a specialised field of international law. Had they been exclusive to human rights, they would only be characteristics of self-contained-ness, and not essential, organisational, underlying constituents of the system of international law as such.

This is besides what makes the theory of the humanisation of international law contiguous to that of constitutionalisation. The shift in the protection of human rights from the national to the international level made it necessary for certain new systemic features to be developed in the order of international law. That is, for international law to effectively accommodate human rights protection, it had to change. These changes can be seen as a sign of a type of humanisation that – unlike other special questions[13] or subject-matters on which human rights were understood as having an impact – affects the systemic premises of the international order. For those who endorse the constitutionalisation metaphor, these are "constitutional" features. This is what justifies the chapter's title, and main argument, namely, that the internationalisation of national constitutions has led to the "constitutionalisation" of international law.

As mentioned above, Part 2 of this chapter critically evaluates the main tenet of the theory of constitutionalisation and its principal assertion that international law develops a constitution. Part 3 discusses the links between human rights and the constitutionalisation of international law. Although human rights are not exclusive to that particular account of the international legal order (i.e. the constitutionalisation), they are central to it, and they fit easily within the constitutional narrative, and in many ways advance it. Part 4 discusses the internationalisation of human rights and how that regime of international law has contributed to the change of the international order, in that its system had to develop certain systemic tools to allow human rights to develop their full *effet utile*, and facilitate effectiveness through collective enforcement. In that respect, the chapter identifies two main changes: i. collective enforcement at the decentralised level for the protection of common interests and/or values; and ii. responsibility of states to protect (linked with the principle of due diligence and the so-called positive effect that human rights develop). It goes without saying that the "privileged" place human rights occupy as a branch of international law within its system and the idea of their *specialty* (which,

12 A Pellet, '"Human Rightism" and International Law' (2000) 10 *Italian Yearbook of International Law* 3, especially 5.

13 Such as the law on reservations to treaties, which is a question that has been thoroughly discussed over the last two decades. See, for instance, I Boerefijn, 'Impact on the Law on Treaty Reservations' in MT Kamminga and M Scheinin (eds), *The Impact of Human Rights Law on General International Law* (OUP 2009).

besides, is linked to the two named systemic changes) cannot be dissociated from the values found in their very existential core or, to use a more technical term, the material sources that nourish them. Part 5 concludes.

2 Critiquing the constitutionalisation of international law

Is international law developing a constitution? This is the principal question at the heart of the scholarly debate on the constitutionalisation of international law. There are two main critical comments that can be made in that respect.

Before that, a competence "disclaimer" is due. Constitutionalisation is more of a constitutional law question, and less of an international law one. Therefore, the debate on the constitutionalisation of international law needs to be firmly situated within the context of domestic constitutionalism.[14] This is a precondition for a systematic analysis of what in essence remains (from a methodological point of view) an interesting hypothesis or research question. For, this is what the constitutionalisation of international law is, beyond a mindset:[15] a research question that seems to be of little consequence in practice. We all know that raising a hypothesis or asking a question is the basis for building a thesis. Yet, what we, international law lawyers, are missing is the tools that will enable us to actually try and answer that question, and validate or reject the hypothesis. What is a constitution? What is constitutionalism? Is there a constituent power[16] in the decentralised structure of international law – other maybe than all states together (the idea of the international community) and nobody in particular? Can there be a constitution without a constituent power or demos? How is a constitution found in such a system? And what, after all, allows using the language of constitutional law for the international society, which is by no means akin to a polity? What would the function of a constitution be in the context of the international order and its society? Is there an added value in the use of the constitutional lens? In practical terms, what would/will it change if international law had/has a constitution? Would that make it more legitimate[17] or effective?

Moving then to the first critical comment, to duly frame the question on the constitutionalisation of international law, we need to build a common understanding of what a constitution and constitutionalism are. The absence of such a consensus might explain why the language used lacks unity as to

14 On constitutionalism, and its pertinence beyond the state, see N Walker, 'Taking Constitutionalism Beyond the State' (2008) 56 *Political Studies* 519, and especially 525ff.

15 M Koskenniemi, 'Constitutionalism as Mindset: Reflections on Kantian Themes about International Law and Globalization' (2007) 8 *Theoretical Inquiries in Law* 9, especially 18ff.

16 For a collection of essays, M Loughlin and N Walker (eds), *The Paradox of Constitutionalism: Constituent Power and Constitutional Form* (OUP 2007). See especially B Fassbender, '"We the Peoples of the United Nations": Constituent Power and Constitutional Form in International Law' at 269.

17 M Kumm, 'The Legitimacy of International Law: A Constitutionalist Framework of Analysis' (2004) 15 *EJIL* 907; see also Chapters 1, 3 and 10 in this book.

whether that constitutionalism is international[18] or transnational,[19] global[20] or pluralistic.[21] It might also explain why De Wet,[22] for instance, emphasises normative hierarchy (which is a point with which, under certain conditions, we agree, although we would not necessarily call it constitutionalisation) as a consequence of human rights, whereas Fassbender[23] situates the constitutionalisation of international law in the framework and organisational structure of international organisations,[24] especially of the UN, the Charter of which is seen an a exhibition of constitutionalism. It might further explain why Dunoff and Trachtman[25] approach the question from a purposive, functionalist perspective that focuses on the function of the constitutional rules – leaving much to be complemented by practice, that would prove that, indeed, there is a commitment in the international community to lift those rules to the constitutional level. Be they thought-provoking and pointing to elements of international law of gravity, these approaches fail to establish common ground as to what are the essential constitutional elements of international law; in some instances, they mix positive law with normative aspirations[26] (that is, the *lex lata* with the *lex ferenda*), but also, and most importantly, they miss the fundamental question of what makes these elements constitutional in nature – beyond what could be described as (an admittedly inflated) analogy or metaphor.[27]

18 B Fassbender, 'The United Nations Charter as Constitution of the International Community' (1998) 36 *Columbia Journal of Transnational Law* 529.

19 N Tsagourias (ed), *Transnational Constitutionalism: International and European Perspectives* (CUP 2007).

20 A Peters, 'The Merits of Global Constitutionalism' (2009) 16 *Indiana Journal of Global Legal Studies* 397.

21 JL Cohen, 'A Global State of Emergency or the Further Constituionalization of International Law: A Pluralist Approach' (2008) 15 *Constellations* 456; J Klabbers, 'Setting the Scene' in J Klabbers, A Peters and G Ulfstein (eds), *The Constitutionalization of International Law* (OUP 2009) 25ff; N Krisch, *Beyond Constitutionalism: The Pluralist Structure of Postnational Law* (OUP 2010).

22 Among other publications, see E De Wet, 'The International Constitutional Order' (2006) 55 *ICLQ* 51, especially 57ff, and by the same author, 'The Emergence of International and Regional Value Systems as a Manifestation of the Emerging International Constitutional Order' (2006) 19 *LJIL* 611.

23 Among other publications by B Fassbender, *The United Nations Charter as Constitution of the International Community* (Nijhoff 2009).

24 See also JO McGinnis and ML Movsesian, 'The World Trade Constitution' (2000) 114 *Harvard Law Review* 511.

25 JL Dunoff and JP Trachtman, 'A Functional Approach to International Constitutionalization' in JL Dunoff and JP Trachtman (eds), *Ruling the World? Constitutionalism, International Law and Global Governance* (CUP 2009).

26 J Kammerhofer, 'Constitutionalism and the Myth of Practical Reason: Kelsenian Responses to Methodological Problems' (2010) 23 *LJIL* 723. See also, JG Van Mullingen, 'Global Constitutionalism and the Objective Purport of the International Legal Order' (2011) 24 *LJIL* 277.

27 No scholar has argued (to the best of our knowledge) that this is a full analogy or that a constitution similar to the national ones exists at the global level.

The second objection has to do with disagreements regarding the impact and effect of those elements in terms of positive international law. An example is the idea of the verticalisation of international law, through the establishment of normative hierarchies (linked to human rights), defended by many authors and (as already mentioned) explicitly perceived as an attribute of constitutionalism by De Wet,[28] as opposed to the non-hierarchical, pluralistic vision of the international legal system defended, for instance, by Kirsch.[29] This disagreement is more than two different accounts of constitutionalisation or a simple divergence in the way the two scholars perceive positive international law. Moreover, what these two opposing interpretations reveal goes beyond a merely different understanding of the ambit of human rights (i.e. pluralist v. universalist). Indeed, we may wonder if behind such a discrepancy over what is allegedly the same phenomenon, i.e. the constitutionalisation of international law, certain (ideological) preferences are hidden, translated in selection bias regarding what are the constitutional elements of international law, but also how these ought to be conceived and interpreted.[30] But it may also be that there is no truly empirically observable constitutionalisation process, and that concept owes its very existence to scholar creativity, that is, to our "collective imaginary" that has constructed a notion using the language of constitutional law that needs now to be given legal content at the international level.[31] Of course, the absence of a clear-cut distinction between positive law and normative aspirations[32] (a problem which is inherent to the -lacking centralisation- international law) adds complexity by giving scholars wider discretion as to what they can exclude or include in their own narrative of constitutionalisation.

Thus, one cannot but agree with Kennedy, who perceives constitutionalisation as yet another "project" next to other ones (one may think for instance of global administrative law, third world approaches, the process school, or even "New World Order" and the global norms it identifies[33] – aspiring to provide "new thinking about how the global order coheres").[34] We wonder however if in the case of constitutionalisation, rather than a common "tale",

28 Especially with regard to normative hierarchy in international law, see the 'Introduction' and the 'Conclusions' in E De Wet and J Vidmar (eds), *Hierarchy in International Law: The Place of Human Rights* (OUP 2012)

29 N Krisch, *Beyond Constitutionalism: The Pluralist Structure of Postnational Law* (OUP 2010).

30 On "[g]lobal [c]onstitutionalism as a [h]ermeneutic [d]evice", see A Petters, 'Conclusions' in J Klabbers, A Peters and G Ulfstein (eds), *The Constitutionalization of International Law* (OUP 2009).

31 See MS Kuo, who argues that global constitutionalism "sits at the crossroads of law and language", 'Between Law and Language: When Constitutionalism Goes Plural in a Globalising World' (2010) 73 *Modern Law Review* 872, 878ff.

32 J Klabbers, 'International Legal Positivism and Constitutionalism' in J Kammerhofer and J D'Aspremont, *International Legal Positivism in a Post-Modern World* (CUP 2014) 268ff.

33 AM Saughter, *A New World Order* (Princeton University Press 2004) 244ff.

34 D Kennedy, 'The Mystery of Global Governance' in L Dunoff and JP Trachtman (eds), *Ruling the World? Constitutionalism, International Law and Global Governance* (CUP 2009).

there are disparate perceptions of it. It seems that international law is undergoing several constitutionalisation processes at once, with the term acting as an all-encompassing "umbrella" with multiple meanings, and perceptions allowing it to host wide-ranging narratives. The common theme is that international law is changing with regards to its foundational rules, with globalisation turning sovereignty thinner and these changes making its system more constitutionalised – whatever this may mean to each one of us.

3 Linking human rights to grand narratives of the international legal order

Having finished with this brief, critical account of the constitutionalisation narrative(s), and declared our lack of competence as international law lawyers to confirm or reject it/them and, consequently, our critical "agnosticism" vis-à-vis it/them, we now move to the next step in our analysis, which aims at demonstrating that human rights are part of said narrative(s). The field of human rights is always in the background of several grand narratives of international law, but hardly ever at the foreground. We bring international human rights law to the foreground and take on claims about the role human rights play in particular in three grand "projects" of the international legal order, namely fragmentation,[35] international legal pluralism[36] and, of course, constitutionalisation.[37] Admittedly, human rights are assigned a role and occupy a privileged place within other narratives of international law as well. However, space contraints require that our brief discussion be limited to only those narratives that are comparable with and can be directly juxtaposed to constitutionalisation. Our focus is the latter in an effort to highlight its links with human rights. Particularly, we wish to advance the claim that human rights law is an integral part to a constitutionalised reading of the international legal order, and in many respects serves to advance it.

35 See, for instance, L Lixinski, 'Choice of Forum in International Human Rights Adjudication and the Unity / Fragmentation Debate: Is Plurality the Way Ahead?' 18 (2008) *Italian Yearbook of International Law* 183; M Koskenniemi, 'International Law and Hegemony: A Reconfiguration' (2004) 17 *Cambridge Review of International Affairs* 197; or D Kennedy, *The Dark Sides of Virtue: Reassessing International Humanitarianism* (Princeton University Press 2004).

36 See, for instance, M Delmas-Marty, *Ordering Pluralism: A Conceptual Framework for Understanding the Transnational Legal World* (Hart 2008); N Krisch (n 21); or the symposium on 'Global Public Goods and the Plurality of Legal Orders' in (2012) 21(3) *EJIL*; J Klabbers and T Piiparinen (eds), *Normative Pluralism and International Law* (CUP 2013).

37 See, for instance, J Klabbers, A Peters and G Ulfstein (eds), *The Constitutionalization of International Law* (OUP 2009); LR Helfer, 'Constitutional Analogies in the International Legal System' (2003) 37 *Loyola of Los Angeles Law Review* 193; A von Bogdandy, 'Constitutionalism in International Law: Comments on a Proposal from Germany' (2006) 47 *HILJ* 223; A Peters, 'The Merits of Global Constitutionalism' (2009) 16 *Indiana Journal of Global Legal Studies*; JL Dunoff and JP Trachtman (eds), *Ruling the World? Constitutionalism, International Law and Global Governance* (CUP 2009); or N Walker, 'Taking Constitutionalism Beyond the State' (2008) *Political Studies* 519.

The named three projects are comparable in that fragmentation and pluralism work as two sides of the same coin (fragmentation seen from "above" is pluralism seen from "below"),[38] and both can work as a counter-narrative to constitutionalisation (challenging its centralising nature). But then pluralism can also be seen as constitutionalising, at least as far as judicialised international law is concerned, in the sense that it contributes to more cross-fertilisation and cooperation between courts and their converging towards a central normative focal point.[39]

Scholars working on the grand narratives of international law seem to assume that human rights played a somewhat marginal role in projects of the international legal order, or, even when some more central role was given to human rights, it was never fully fleshed out. To articulate this, it is necessary to first try to place human rights discourse in current narratives of the international legal order, and address what seems to be one of the biggest factors behind what can be described as a certain reluctance towards human rights in many of these projects, namely, the claim of human rights' role in the hegemonic tendencies of international law, at least inasmuch as it advances an Euro-centric perspective on the values behind human rights law and law-making. Scholars aligned with the constitutionalisation project[40] tend to look at human rights as indeed a very central part of their normative aspirations, particularly by looking at the reception and entrenchment of human rights in domestic legal orders and at the ways through which judicial and other institutions assert and protect human rights.[41] In this sense, human rights law operates both as the cultural context (or the "entrenched" law necessary to the constitutionalist project) and as the background against which the entire project is built. Human rights is one of the ingredients of the constitutionalisation narrative.[42] The constitutionalist project also usually assumes some sort of charter of rights is a part of their project (even

38 Lixinski (n 3).

39 See Krisch (n 21).

40 Note that there are at least three streams within the constitutionalisation project. The first examines constitutionalisation of the United Nations (see, for instance, R Macdonald, 'The Charter of United Nations in Constitutional Perspective' (1999) 20 *Australian Year Book of International Law* 205; RSJ Macdonald and DM Johnston (eds), *Towards World Constitutionalism: Issues in the Legal Ordering of the World Community* (Nijhoff 2005); B Fassbender, *The United Nations Charter as Constitution of the International Community* (Martinoff Nijhoff 2009); or J Crawford, *The Charter of the United Nations as a Constitution* in H Fox (ed), *The Changing Constitution of the United Nations* (British Institute of International and Comparative Law 1997)). The second focuses on the "constitutionalisation" of the World Trade Organization (see, for instance, DZ Cass, *The Constitutionalisation of the World Trade Organisation* (OUP 2005); or EU Petersmann, 'Constitutionalism and International Organizations' (1996) 17 *Northwestern Journal of International Law and Business* 398). The third argues that the entire international law is undergoing constitutionalisation (see literature cited (n 22)).

41 One such example is Geir Ulfstein's contributions to J Klabbers, A Peters and G Ulfstein (eds), *The Constitutionalization of International Law* (OUP 2009).

42 Tzevelekos (n 1) 63.

if scholars aligned with this project often fail to explore the content of any such charter)[43] and suggests that international human rights law has the potential to become the *Grundnorm* of the international legal order.[44] The reliance of this project on institutions is somewhat limited, as proposed by Mattias Kumm, whose idea of "cosmopolitan constitutionalism" is less dependent on institutionalism, while still relying on human rights as a fundamental normative aspiration of a constitutionalised international legal order.[45]

The fragmentation project, at least to the extent it is perceived as a counter-narrative to the constitutionalisation project, is very critical of institutionalisation, particularly with respect to human rights. For some, the "inchoate institutional character" of international law is one of the greatest obstacles to a unified international legal order.[46] In a way, fragmentation tends to stick to a deceptively descriptive account of international law as a means to avoid committing to any sort of normative project. The problem is that this position in itself is normative.[47] Fragmentation, by being this empty shell, easily becomes prey to the status quo, only under new guise, through mechanisms like "strategic fragmentation", but also others.[48]

Fragmentation, by being non-committal on the surface, tends to skirt accusations of participating in what Martti Koskenniemi, referring to international human rights law, calls a hegemonic strategy of international law.[49] According to him, international human rights law is an essential part of the hegemonic strategy to the extent human rights is an ideology and political project.[50] The solution to the hegemonic strategy of international law seems to be, according to Koskenniemi, a return to formalism.[51] This call to formalism finds followers

43 For instance, JL Dunoff and JP Trachtman, 'A Functional Approach to International Constitutionalization' in JL Dunoff and JP Trachtman (eds), *Ruling the World? Constitutionalism, International Law and Global Governance* (CUP 2009).

44 See, for instance, L Lixinski, 'The Quest for a Founding Norm: Constitutionalization of International Law Revisited – A Review of Nicholas Tsagourias, ed, Transnational Constitutionalism: International and European Models' (2008) 9 *German Law Journal* 2263.

45 M Kumm, 'The Cosmopolitan Turn in Constitutionalism: On the Relationship between Constitutionalism in and beyond the State' in JL Dunoff and JP Trachtman (eds), *Ruling the World? Constitutionalism, International Law and Global Governance* (CUP 2009).

46 A Carty, 'The Yearning for Unity and the Eternal Return of the Tower of Babel' (2007) 1 *EJLS* 1.

47 See generally N Rajkovic, 'On Fragments and Geometry: The International Legal Order as Metaphor and How It Matters' (2013) 6 *Erasmus Law Review* 6.

48 E Benvenisti and GW Downs, 'The Empire's New Clothes: Political Economy and the Fragmentation of International Law' (2007) 60 *Stanford Law Review* 595.

49 M Koskenniemi, 'Human Rights Mainstreaming as a Strategy for Institutional Power' (2010) 1 *Humanity* 47.

50 M Koskenniemi, 'International Law and Hegemony: A Reconfiguration' (2004) 17 *Cambridge Review of International Affairs* 197, reprinted in M Koskenniemi, *The Politics of International Law* (Hart 2011).

51 M Koskenniemi, 'What is International Law For?' in MD Evans (ed), *International Law* (OUP 2003), reprinted in M Koskenniemi, *The Politics of International Law* (Hart 2011).

also among scholars in the constitutionalisation project, particularly Anne Peters.[52] This return to formalism seems to be the principal claim of the fragmentation narrative, particularly with respect to international human rights law. Of course, the main problem with it is that formalism does not avoid political commitments. It simply reinforces the status quo.

There are two ways to look at the relationship between international human rights law and the fragmentation of international law. From an internal perspective, the question is how different human rights bodies relate to one another, and how their different instruments are interpreted, especially in light of very similar (or identical) factual situations.[53] From an external perspective, the key question is how international human rights law relates to other bodies of international law.[54] The former perspective (or a version of it) is the most relevant for our current purposes (because we are trying to understand how human rights law operates endemically, even if on a domestic/international interplay), but a few words might be needed with respect to the latter.

Regional human rights courts have used "foreign" (that is, non-human rights) instruments extensively in expanding the scope and reach of rights protected under their constitutive instruments.[55] The reason why foreign instruments have only been applied "indirectly" is because the Inter-American and European human rights courts have only the competence to declare violations of the American and European Conventions, respectively. Thus, because of their constitutive constraints, they are forced to "translate" all legal issues before them into human rights issues. This translation effort has two main effects: on the one hand, it promotes some sort of unity, by bringing all of international law under the human rights umbrella, which means to say that international legal norms are considered in light of their impact upon human lives (which is, arguably, the reason why law exists in the first place – to have an impact upon human lives). This unity further enhances the legitimacy of international human rights law. On the other hand, by bringing everything under the human rights umbrella, human rights courts create an informal or de facto hierarchy of international legal rules, putting human rights norms at the top of the pyramid. International human rights law affects the "systemic premises" of other areas of international law through this interaction,[56] with

52 J Klabbers, A Peters and G Ulfstein (eds), *The Constitutionalization of International Law* (OUP 2009) 350–351.

53 See Lixinski, 'Choice of Forum' (n 35).

54 See Lixinski, 'Treaty Interpretation by the Inter-American Court of Human Rights: Expansionism at the Service of the Unity of International Law' (2010) 21 *EJIL* 585.

55 See, for instance, VP Tzevelekos, 'The Use of Article 31(3)(c) of the VCLT in the Case-law of the ECtHR: an Effective Anti-Fragmentation Tool or a Selective Loophole for the Reinforcement of the Teleology of Human Rights? Between Evolution and Systemic Integration' (2010) 31 *Michigan Journal of International Law* 621.

56 Tzevelekos (n 1) 63.

one consequence being a possibility for hierarchisation. This consequence is, again, mandated by the constitutional constraints of these courts, and their popularity makes this hierarchisation seem all the more pervasive, and it easily becomes part of the hegemonic project Koskenniemi is so critical of.

Finally, international legal pluralism lies somewhere in between the constitutionalisation and fragmentation narratives (while challenging both) and echoes the constitutional pluralism debate in the European Union.[57] It "provides a normative vision of restructuring *plural* orders into *pluralist* ones – that is, re-envisaging them from fragmented, closed, sovereign legal orders into an open, interacting, interlinked, interdependent, multi-level structure of legal ordering".[58] However, it does not have the unification agenda and accepts a fragmented plurality of legal orders out of which none necessarily prevails.

The main perceived power of international legal pluralism is precisely to offer a counterpoint to the constitutionalist narrative, and a response to the dangers of constitutionalism, and also fragmentation: it is something of a positive spin on fragmentation focusing on the potential of a diverging legal order, as opposed to its apparent chaos. While fragmentation undermines international law, pluralism strengthens it,[59] even if what looks like fragmentation seen from above can easily look like pluralism seen from below.

International legal pluralism generally lacks an overarching hierarchical structure, favoring the openness of different legal systems. Unlike constitutionalism's search for *Grundnorm(s)*, pluralism accepts the notion that there is no such common point of reference.[60] Pluralism can be either systemic or institutional, with the latter dealing with institutional viewpoints, whereas the former addresses more substantive issues across plural fora.[61] In a way, it is a mirror image of institutional and systemic fragmentation.

57 On the latter, see, for instance, M Avbelj and J Komárek (eds), *Constitutional Pluralism in the European Union and Beyond* (Hart 2012). Cfr M Delmas-Marty, *Ordering Pluralism: A Conceptual Framework for Understanding the Transnational Legal World* (Hart 2008) 110 (noting that Europe 'holds no monopoly' as a 'laboratory' for the ordering of a global legal pluralism). See also at 125–129 (noting the development of the human rights regime in Europe and its impact on the EU trade regime, constituting a 'school of democracies'). For a critique of legal pluralism in the European Union in the context of human rights and the accession of the European Union to the ECHR, see L Lixinski, 'Taming the Fragmentation Monster through Human Rights? International Constitutionalism, 'Pluralism Lite' and the Common Territory of the two European Legal Orders' in V Kosta, N Skoutaris and VP Tzevelekos (eds), *The EU Accession to the ECHR* (Hart 2014) 219–233.

58 G Shaffer, 'International Law and Global Public Goods in a Legal Pluralist World' (2012) 23(3) *EJIL* 669, 671.

59 WW Burke-White, 'International Legal Pluralism' (2003) 25 *Michigan Journal of International Law* 963.

60 See, for instance, N Krisch, *Beyond Constitutionalism: The Pluralist Structure of Postnational Law* (OUP 2010) 5–6.

61 Burke-White (n 59) 964.

The pluralist narrative seems to be the most apt to enable international human rights law and values to form an integral part of a project about the international legal order, alongside Mattias Kumm's "cosmopolitan constitutionalism".[62] But human rights courts seem to be more focused on the constitutional narrative, because that narrative privileges adjudicators, at least to the extent it mirrors domestic constitutional systems, which are anchored on judicial systems for their functioning. Additionally, how does the promise of pluralism (or cosmopolitan constitutionalism) react in light of the phenomenon of fragmentation of international law, which puts in evidence the difficulty of consistent interpretations of international legal norms across different fora? The (quasi-)adjudicatory practice of human rights can contribute or become a hurdle to narratives of the international legal order.

The specificity of human rights law, which is (to give an example) connected to the way it is interpreted (*evolutive* or *pro homine* interpretation, as opposed to ordinary meaning),[63] challenges the capacity of international human rights law being fully a part of general international law, seen as it chooses to play by its own rules. This idiosyncrasy is created by, and reinforces, the expertisation and specialty of international human rights law,[64] which is an important element in the fragmentation of all areas of international law. At the same time, though, the endemic practice of human rights institutions, and particularly of human rights courts, is to see themselves as playing a part in a constitutionalist project of international law, especially as they can often be perceived as engaging directly with domestic courts (even if they will reject the notion of being a "court of fourth instance").[65]

4 The specialty of human rights: the impact of the internationalisation of national constitutions on the system of international law

Having argued that human rights are interlinked with the constitutionalisation of international law, the chapter now turns to its main assertion, namely that the internationalisation of human rights protection has helped the international legal order to develop certain systemic, "constitutional" features that mitigate the rigidity of the Westphalian structure.

62 M Kumm, 'The Cosmopolitan Turn in Constitutionalism: On the Relationship between Constitutionalism in and beyond the State' in JL Dunoff and JP Trachtman (eds), *Ruling the World? Constitutionalism, International Law and Global Governance* (CUP 2009) 258–324.

63 See, for instance, J Tobin, 'Seeking to Persuade: A Constructive Approach to Human Rights Treaty Interpretation' (2010) 23 *Harvard Human Rights Journal* 1.

64 See, for instance, Kennedy (n 35).

65 *Centro Europa 7 S.r.l. and Di Stefano v Italy* App no 38433/09 (ECtHR, 7 June 2012) para. 197. See also *Nejdet Şahin and Perihan Şahin v Turkey* App no 13279/05 (ECtHR, 20 October 2011) para. 88; *García Ruiz v Spain* App no 30544/96 (ECtHR, 21 January 1999) para. 28; *Kemmache v France (No 3)* (1994) Series A no 296-C para. 44; and, at the Inter-American Court, see IACtHR, *Cabreara García and Montiel Flores v Mexico*, Judgment of 26 November 2010 paras 16–22.

In its general lines, the legal history of human rights in the West and its landmarks, the *Magna Carta*, the English Bill of Rights and the American and French revolutions in the era of Enlightenment, are well known. Gradually, human rights attained the form and strength of constitutional rights aiming to limit public power, but also to invite public authorities to develop policies to guarantee and enhance the well-being of the persons under their jurisdiction. That these bills of rights were included in the "basic" (to borrow the German term) law of a polity reflects their importance for the society and the idea that they are part and parcel of its constitutive/constitutional legal act and the social contract underlying it. Thus, apart from organising power, the polity and the functioning of its institutions, national constitutions were also employed as a means to subject the acts and omissions of the polity's organs (governmental, but also beyond the executive) to the societal values that shape its public order, impose limits and preclude conducts that cannot be tolerated within it. This is a rough sketch of the national constitutional model in the West, we concede, but it should suffice for our present purposes.

WWII, its atrocities – and especially Shoah – came to prove in a tragic way the dramatic inadequacy of that model. Before the era of internationalisation, flagrant human right breaches principally constituted a matter of municipal law, falling within a sort of (what nowadays seems to be an) overstated *domaine réservé*. Protecting human rights at the national level alone had proven to be ineffective – especially where democratic roots were weak – allowing states to hide behind the veil of sovereignty and the prohibition of the interference with domestic affairs. Yet, to paraphrase G. Clemenceau, human rights are too important a matter to be left to national constitutions.

Human rights need to be effective. Their internationalisation[66] came just to address that very social necessity. However, that process required more than simply "copying-and-pasting" the rights one could commonly find in national constitutions. An area of law *originally and in principle* related to the relationship of the individual/citizen with public power had to be transplanted within a system *originally and in principle* regulating inter-state relationships. Thus, for constitutional human rights to be converted into international human rights, they had to be not only posited by the means of the sources of international law (such as treaties or custom), but also adapted to its systemic features. Their teleology and overall function have both remained unchanged. But, they now produce their effect within an entirely different context, society and legal framework. Consequently, the mindset changes too. This time, the scheme is rather *oblique*. States "promise" one another that they shall safeguard the rights of the human person. Thereby, they recognise the right of other states to lawfully react to violations

66 For a concise account, see D Shelton, *An Introduction to the History of International Human Rights Law* (2007) George Washington University Legal Studies Research Paper 326 <http://papers.ssrn.com/sol3/papers.cfm?abstract_id=1010489##> accessed 15 April 2015.

occurring within their national legal sphere. Hence, sovereignty becomes thinner, more transparent and states acquire a *droit de regard*, that is, the right to monitor human rights performance inside other states. The human being is still the primary beneficiary of the obligations at issue, but these are owed by the state to other states *and* also to the human being itself. The latter aspect is closely linked to the self-executing nature of human rights treaties,[67] allowing them to be invoked by the individual before domestic courts, as well as to the fact that certain instruments provide for control and establish international institutions – such as the UN Human Rights Committee, or the Inter-American Commission and Court – endowed with the competence to receive individual petitions for human right breaches.

However, the admittance of the human being as a recipient of rights directly at the international level could not leave the legal system unaffected. The study gives the example of two main changes in the systemic premises of international law, which partially owe to human rights as well. The first stems from the *erga omnes* (*partes*) quality of human rights rules, whereas the second is linked to the principle of due diligence. The point made here is that the influence of human rights on the system of international law goes well beyond the obvious fact that the individual came to be added to the list with the subjects of international law,[68] expanding thereby its span, and also bringing to an end the exclusiveness of states, which however remain the primary subjects of the system.[69] The changes discussed below are of systemic, i.e. in a sense "constitutional" proportions.

4.1 Collective enforcement at the decentralised level for the protection of common interests and values

The main such influence of human rights is that their protection bestowed international law with rules that reflect values and aim to safeguard interests that are not exclusive to each state individually, but to all of them *collectively*. This has rendered necessary that they are also protected collectively. Definitely, this is not the only area of international law with this characteristic. The same applies in the

67 On self-executing treaties, their doctrinal underpinnings and reception within the US see CM Vázquez, 'The Four Doctrines of Self-Executing Treaties' (1995) 89 *AJIL* 694.

68 Among several others, T Franck, 'Individuals and Groups of Individuals as Subjects of International Law' in R Hofmann and N Geissler (eds), *Non-State Actors as New Subjects of International Law: International Law: From the Traditional State Order Towards the Law of the Global Community* (Duncker & Humblot 1999). See also J Spiropoulos, ('L'individu et le droit international' (1929) 30 *Recueil des Cours de l'Académie de Droit International* 228) who was one of the first to discuss the question, linking the legal personality of the human being with *jus gentium*. *Contra*, of course, D Anzilotti, *Cours De Droit International*, re-edition (LGDJ 1999) 122–3.

69 This is why Verhoeven describes the human being as a "passive" international person that owes its personality to the state. J Verhoeven, *Droit International Public* (Larcier 2000) 295ff. On the attributes of that personality and their evolution, see K Parlett, *The Individual in the International Legal System: Continuity and Change in International Law* (CUP 2011).

case of environmental protection, for instance, or in the protection of cultural heritage.[70] However, this is not a trivial development. Human rights prepared the soil for the emergence of what could be seen as an international public order for the protection of common interests/values – and this also explains why human rights are associated with the constitutionalisation of international law.

For international law to effectively accommodate human rights, it was inevitable that its system would change too. This involved developing certain features and tools that were not necessary to it when its operation was confined to merely reciprocal obligations destined to safeguard under the logic of self-help individual state interests – that is, in the framework of the *jus inter gentes*, marked by the idea of absolute state sovereignty. As already explained, the ambit of the change brought by human rights in that respect is a rather controversial issue among scholars – and we tend to think that the humanisation theory is indeed inflated.[71] Yet, it is incontestable that human rights are entwined with the concepts of *jus cogens* and obligations *erga omnes*.[72]

Erga omnes (which, besides, encompass *jus cogens* in the sense that all peremptory norms have an *erga omnes* (*partes*) effect) were first confirmed as part of international law by the ICJ in its famous *obiter dictum* in *Barcelona Traction*.[73] That class of rules has found its place in the ILC norms on state responsibility, which recognise the ability of non-(directly) injured states to invoke the responsibility of the state breaking an obligation it owes *erga omnes*.[74] Practically speaking, any state may invoke the responsibility and react (possibly by countermeasures as well[75]) to the wrongful contact of a state breaking an obligation it owes *erga omnes*. This has found numerous applications in international law,[76] one of which is the idea of inter-state applications for human rights breaches before international *fora*, such as the ECtHR.[77] As far as the reason why obligations *erga omnes*, such as human rights, are owed towards all (as the term literally suggests), this is so because they refer to issues

70 For a collection of studies in these areas, see F Lenzerini and AF Vrdoljak (eds), *International Law for Common Goods – Normative Perspectives on Human Rights, Culture and Nature* (Hart 2014).

71 Tzevelekos (n 1) 64–66.

72 Among others, E De Wet, 'Jus Cogens and Obligations Erga Omnes' in D Shelton (ed), *The Oxford Handbook of International Human Rights Law* (OUP 2013) 541; M Byers, 'Conceptualising the Relationship between Jus Cogens and Erga Omnes Rules' (1997) 66 *NJIL* 211.

73 *Case Concerning the Barcelona Traction, Light and Power Company, Limited (Belgium v Spain)* (Second Phase) [1970] ICJ Rep 3, para. 34.

74 ILC Articles on the Responsibility of States (A/56/83), Article 48(1), especially (b).

75 On countermeasures by non-injured states, see generally, EK Proukaki, *The Problem of Enforcement in International Law: Countermeasures, the Non-Injured State and the Idea of International Community* (Routledge 2010). See also A Bird, 'Third State Responsibility for Human Rights Violations' (2011) 21 *EJIL* 896.

76 See, for instance, P Okowa, 'Issues of Admissibility and the Law on International Responsibility' in M Evans (ed), *International Law* (4th edn, OUP 2014) 494ff.

77 European Convention on Human Rights (ECHR), Article 33.

that concern everyone in the society, i.e. they reflect shared interests/values. If an obligation is owed towards all other states, in the case of general international law, or all other states-parties, in the case of a treaty law, then it flows naturally that all those states be allowed to react to wrongfulness.

Seen from a strictly legal viewpoint, human rights are special because they are owed *erga omnes*. Yet, the reason why they are owed *erga omnes* is because they are materially special, that is, because they reflect common values and collective interests that are considered to be important[78] and, therefore, worthy enough to benefit from collective enforcement. When a given right of the individual is recognised[79] as a human right, it is automatically acknowledged as having a special *erga omnes* normative effect. This allows maximising its effectiveness and fostering its enforcement, which, given the absence in principle of centralised authorities in international law, will continue to operate at the decentralised level, albeit (ideally) in more a communitarian,[80] or collective, manner. Thus, the entrance of an area of law like human rights in international law has generated changes within its system by rendering necessary the development of new mechanisms, such as obligations *erga omnes*, that enable the collective enforcement and protection of "legitimate community interests".[81] In the absence of a centralised public authority similar to the one that exists within states, the decentralised system of international law invites (but does not oblige) each and every state in the world to partake in the collective enforcement of the values shaping the international public order.

However, outside the framework of international organisations (which may have the power to sanction human rights breaches within an institutional, hence partially centralised, structure), collective enforcement of *erga omnes* rules continues to operate under the same decentralised logic that underpins the

78 Importance may translate to occasional normative priority in favour of *erga omnes* (*partes*) rules. This could be seen as a form of normative primacy. See Tzevelekos (n 1) at 70–72. For a different reasoning in favour of the normative primacy of *erga omnes* rules see U Linderfalk, 'International Legal Hierarchy Revisited – The Status of Obligations *Erga Omnes*' (2011) 80 *NJIL* 1, 5ff, and the authors to which Linderfalk refers. See also B Simma, 'Universality of International Law from the Perspective of a Practitioner' (2009) 20 *EJIL* 265, 272ff. *Contra*, United Nations International Law Commission, 'Fragmentation of International Law: Difficulties Arising from the Diversification and Expansion of International Law – Report of the Study Group of the International Law Commission' (2006) UN Doc A/CN.4/L.682, para. 408. See also J Vidmar, 'Norm Conflicts and Hierarchy in International Law: Towards a Vertical International Legal System' in E De Wet and J Vidmar (eds), *Hierarchy in International Law. The Place of Human Rights* (OUP 2012) 23–25.

79 See, for instance, *Avena and Other Mexican Nationals (Mexico v United States of America)* [2004] ICJ Rep 12, para. 124. See also the critique by Alston against Petersmann's understanding of trade as a human right. P Alston, 'Resisting the Merger and Acquisition of Human Rights by Trade Law: A Reply to Petersmann' (2002) 13 *EJIL* 815.

80 Tzevelekos (n 1) 68.

81 UNHRC 'General Comment No. 31, The Nature of the General Legal Obligation Imposed on States Parties to the Covenant' (26 May 2004) UN Doc CCPR/C/21/Rev.1/Add.13, para. 2.

international legal system. It is not reciprocity *stricto sensu* that applies.[82] Rather, it is a renewed, broader concept of mutuality that enlarges the circle of concerned/affected states, and allows them as non-directly injured parties to react to wrongfulness, that is to partake in the collective enforcement of common values, through lawful means of action.[83] The broader framework and its logic (i.e. the decentralised structure of the system) remain in essence unchanged. Yet, within that framework, reasonable adjustments are made so that the community of states is allowed to collectively enforce the rules that are special to it.

4.2 Due diligence and the responsibility of states to protect

Moving to the second area discussed in this chapter where the internationalisation of human rights may be associated with signs of systemic change in positive international law, this corresponds to the positive effect of human rights,[84] and more generally to the idea of their protection[85] (as opposed to the strands of respect and fulfilment), that are linked to the well-known principle of due diligence.[86] Undeniably, this is an old principle of international law that applies in many areas that go well beyond human rights. Discussing in full detail due diligence and its ramifications (especially with regard to state fault and the law of international responsibility)[87] exceeds the scope of the chapter. Suffice it here to highlight the links with human rights, and their constitutional protection at the national level.

National constitutional provisions on human rights were originally conceived as merely vertical, with a view to restrict the exercise of public power and shield the individual-subject of the State-Leviathan (with a capital "s"), from its arbitrariness. This corresponds to the so-called negative dimension

82 If State A breaks the rights of its citizens, State B cannot react by breaking the rights of its own citizens, as this would be both unlawful and meaningless.

83 See ILC Norms on State Responsibility (A/56/83), Articles 48 and 54. This is linked to what Simma has described as the passage from bilateralism to protection of community interests. B Simma, 'From Bilateralism to Community Interests' (1994) 250 *Recueil des Cours de l'Académie de Droit International de La Haye* 217. On reciprocity and human rights, see A Paulus, 'Whether Universal Values can Prevail over Bilateralism and Reciprocity' in A Cassese (ed), *Realizing Utopia: The Future of International Law* (OUP 2011) 91ff.

84 Among several others, D Spielmann, 'Obligations Positives et Effet Horizontal des Dispositions de la Convention' in F Sudre (ed), *L'Interprétation de la Convention Européenne des Droits de l'Homme* (Bryulant 1998) 133–74.

85 A Eide, 'Economic, Social and Cultural Rights as Human Rights' in A Eide, C Krause and A Rosas (eds), *Economic, Social and Cultural Rights* (Springer 2001) 9. See also O De Schutter, *International Human Rights Law: Cases, Materials, Commentary* (CUP 2010) 242ff.

86 RP Mazzeschi, 'The Due Diligence Rule and the Nature of the International Responsibility of States' (1992) 35 *GYIL* 9. Timo Koivurova, 'Due Diligence' in *Max Planck Encyclopedia of Public International Law* (OUP 2013).

87 See VP Tzevelekos, 'Reconstructing the Effective Control Criterion in Extraterritorial Human Rights Breaches: Direct Attribution of Wrongfulness, Due Diligence, and Concurrent Responsibility' (2015) 36 *Michigan Journal of International Law* 152 and the references contained there.

of (traditionally, civil and political) human rights, prohibiting state organs from directly causing wrongful results. The evolution of human rights protection at the national level has led to the expansion of their scope by adding a positive axis, next to the negative one. The positive dimension of human rights reflects the idea of a state that, far from abstaining or being neutral, has a legal obligation to be pro-active in the protection of rights (through prevention, punishment etc.) by employing means available to it.[88] This applies beyond the horizontal effect of human rights, but it is that dimension that was mainly developed at the national level, through the theory of *Drittwirkung* that requires the state to protect people under its jurisdiction from the wrongful conduct not only of its own organs (directly caused by the state, hence directly attributable to it),[89] but of other individuals as well (even if indirectly). The horizontal effect of human rights was adopted by international human rights *fora*, that placed it in the broader framework of protection, which in international law is linked to the principle of due diligence. Thus, that old principle of international law found ample application within the regime of international human rights law, which has promoted the due diligence and put it again emphatically on the map of international law, (plausibly) contributing to its use in other areas of law.[90]

Last but not least, the broader impact due diligence (in the context of human rights) may have on international law is evidenced in the (still immature in terms of positive international law) doctrine of Responsibility to Protect (R2P),[91] inviting states first – and, in case of failure, the international community – to protect people under their jurisdiction from heinous crimes such as genocide or ethnic cleansing.[92] One could argue that the rationale behind R2P is identical to that of protection under due diligence.[93] Thus, to the extent that

88 This implies that positive obligations are obligations of conduct or means. On that class of obligations see A Tunk, 'La Distinction des Obligations de Résultat et des Obligations de Diligence' (1945) *La Semaine Juridique (Juris-Classeur Periodique)* 449. See also, *United States Diplomatic and Consular Staff in Tehran (USA v Iran)* [1980] ICJ Rep 3, para. 68 and *Application of the Convention on the Prevention and Punishment of the Crime of Genocide (Bosnia and Herzegovina v Serbia and Montenegro)* [2007] ICJ Rep 43, para. 430.

89 As opposed to "indirect responsibility". See J Salmon (ed), *Dictionnaire de Droit International Public* (Bruylant 2001) 996. See also the critical comments by JA Hessbruegge, 'The Historical Development of the Doctrines of Attribution and Due Diligence in International Law' (2004) 36 *NYU Journal of International Law and Politics* 265, 268–69.

90 *Pulp Mills on River Uruguay (Argentina v Uruguay)* [2010] ICJ Rep 14, para. 101.

91 The literature on R2P is vast. Among several others, see S Zifcak, 'The Responsibility to Protect' in MD Evans (ed) *International Law* (4th edn, OUP 2014) 509–533. See also UNGA '2005 World Summit Outcome Document' (24 October 2015) A/RES/60/1, paras 138 and 139.

92 UNGA 'Implementing the Responsibility to Protect: Report of the Secretary-General' (12 January 2009) UN Doc A/63/677. The United Nations Secretary General's 2009 report established the renowned three-pillar structure of R2P.

93 Indeed, to the extent that R2P might amount to a positive international law duty, this will be of means/due diligence. For a discussion of the links between R2P and due diligence, see RA Barnes and VP Tzevelekos, 'Beyond Responsibility to Protect: Ceci n'est pas une Pipe'

these two concepts coincide (i.e. lawful measures adopted by a state in light of its obligation to demonstrate diligence that serve the purposes of R2P) the latter doctrine may be seen as acquiring a compulsory, hard law dimension as well. Yet, the most important similarity between the two concepts for our purposes is that, now, sovereignty is not only seen as a right, but also as responsibility[94] to protect through pro-active, diligent conduct. This is yet another sign of erosion, or transformation of sovereignty,[95] which is one of the systemic, foundational, that is, "constitutional" cornerstones of international law.

5 Conclusion

Be it inflated, the humanisation narrative offers a useful lens to comprehend the impact human rights have on the systemic premises of international law. Because of their material "specialty", their transfer from the national to the international order could not leave the system of international law unaffected. Hence, international law has developed within the confines of its decentralised structure special "tools" and features enabling it to accommodate human rights, which, likewise, had to adapt to the idiosyncrasy of a structure that has been modelled in different terms and under a different logic than the vertical and centralised one that characterises the domestic level. The constitutionalised version of international human rights law seems to be favoured by the practice of international human rights institutions, and thereby aligns with a narrative of human rights as standing in the dialogue between the domestic and the international.

These emerging features, such as the reconceptualisation of sovereignty as a prerogative that comes with obligations and responsibilities, and the entitlement of states to be actively engaged in the protection of what they deem important, are linked to and indeed descending from the concepts of obligations *erga omnes*, and due diligence. It might be that due diligence[96] – as well as possibly *jus cogens*[97] – predate the internationalisation era of human rights,

in RA Barnes and VP Tzevelekos (eds), *Beyond Responsibility to Protect: Generating Change in International Law* (Intersentia 2016)11–19.

94 Among others, see L Axworthy, 'RtoP and the Evolution of State Sovereignty' in J Genser and I Cotler (eds), *The Responsibility to Protect: The Promise of Stopping Mass Atrocities in our Time* (OUP 2012) and A Orford, *International Authority and Responsibility to Protect* (CUP 2011) and the sources to which that author refers. See also HG Dederer, '"Responsibility to Protect" and "Functional Sovereignty"' in P Hilpold (ed), *The Responsibility to Protect (R2P): A New Paradigm of International Law* (Brill Nijhoff 2011).

95 See N Tsagourias, 'R2P: An Inquiry into its Transformative Potential' in RA Barnes and VP Tzevelekos (eds), *Beyond Responsibility to Protect: Generating Change in International Law* (Intersentia 2016) 435.

96 See, for instance, *Corfu Channel Case (UK v Albania)* (Merits) [1949] ICJ Rep 4, para. 22 (recognising that every state has an "obligation not to allow knowingly its territory to be used for acts contrary to the rights of other States").

97 A Verdross, 'Forbidden Treaties in International Law. Comments on Professor Garner's Report on "The Law of Treaties"' (1937) 31 *AJIL* 571.

but it is through that regime of international law that they acquired solid flesh and bones. Besides, that they are not exclusive to human rights, that is, that they extend in a number of other areas and regimes of international law, makes them "systemic" elements of modern international law. If this is a form of constitutionalisation (which is not up to us to tell) then international law has, indeed, restructured its constitutional features, and that restructuring owes a lot to the internationalisation of national constitutional provisions on human rights. Our anticipation is that this is an ongoing process that has more to bring. Its potential for further evolution may be evidenced in the emergence, for instance, of obligations for individuals (with soft law on corporations[98] being the most notorious example in that respect), or the development of individual criminal responsibility.

Yet, there is another, broader, potential as well. The recalibration of the system of international law that this chapter attempted to portray in its general lines means that, apart from readjusting its physiognomy by developing certain features that made possible the accommodation of human rights, international law is now equipped with what is necessary for it to lodge, under similar terms, other (less established or developed within international law) areas of law as well – as long as these present similarities to human rights, mainly in that they aim at safeguarding collective interests/values. In other words, the "constitutional" change brought in international law by human rights has prepared that order to effectively accommodate further areas of national (constitutional) law aiming to safeguard values that societies rank as important. In a nutshell, while remaining decentralised and sovereignty-based[99] the international legal system is now prepared to host public order rules. The framework has been updated. What remains is to give it substance. The more the public order dimension will flourish and become tangible, the more the reconceptualisation of sovereignty and the decline of the old, Westphalian model will be discernible, and the international society of states will be transformed into a more homogeneous as to its core values and their collective protection "community".[100]

98 For instance, UN ECOSOC, Sub-Commission on the Promotion and Protection of Human Rights, Economic, Social and Cultural Rights, 'Norms on the Responsibilities of Transnational Corporations and Other Business Enterprises with Regard to Human Rights' (26 August 2003) UN Doc E/CN.4/Sub.2/2003/12/Rev.2.

99 L Condorelli and A Cassese, 'Is Leviathan Still Holding Sway over International Dealings' and JE Alvarez, 'State Sovereignty is Not Withering Away: A Few Lessons for the Future' in A Cassese (ed), *Realizing Utopia: The Future of International Law* (OUP 2012) 14 and 26 respectively.

100 On the origins and meanings of the term in international law, see R Kolb, 'Quelques Réflexions sur la "Communauté Internationale"' (2002) 10 *African Yearbook of International Law* 431.

3 International constitutionalism, language in legal discourse, and the functions of international law scholarship

Roman Kwiecień

1 Introduction

It is almost a truism to say that one of the most prominent, visible and, at the same time, controversial issues in the framework of a broad and meaningful intellectual debate on legal transformations within international society, is that of constitutionalisation of the international legal order. Indeed, the doctrine of international constitutionalism is so comprehensive that the constitutionalist theory of international law is even seen by some scholars as a 'sub-discipline of public international law'.[1] At the same time, looking at the ongoing debate on constitutionalisation of international law one can be struck by the lack of common language within the debate. The consequences of that for international legal scholarship and for international law itself are far-reaching because the lack of common language makes impossible speaking about a common legal reality. This factor can call into question usefulness of international constitutionalism vocabulary for better understanding of legal changes within contemporary international society. The mentioned problem is directly connected with another one, namely, a role of legal scholarship which more and more often leaves its traditional cognitive function and sometimes gets close to a role of 'political activists'. It is a debate concerning constitutionalisation of international law that clearly shows this phenomenon.

This chapter rather does not support the constitutionalist theory of international law and an idea of constitutionalisation of international law. Quite a contrary, it seeks to point out some weaknesses of the constitutionalist approach which can justify scepticism about constitutionalisation of international law conceived both as a legal process within international society and as a research agenda. There are three main sources of my scepticism about constitutionalisation of international law and the doctrine of international

1 In this way B Fassbender, 'The Meaning of International Constitutional Law' in N Tsagourias (ed), *Transnational Constitutionalism: International and European Perspectives* (CUP 2007) 307–308.

constitutionalism. The first source concerns an accuracy of the concepts 'constitution' and 'constitutionalisation' to international law. As known, they are grounded in national constitutional tradition. In other words, the first reason of scepticism concerns an accuracy of constitutionalist vocabulary beyond the state, which touches an issue of the role of language in legal discourse. The second source of my scepticism is connected with a supposed novelty of the doctrine of international constitutionalism. The third one boils down to the following question: does international law need constitutional straitjacket to be explained and developed? The contribution starts from presenting an outline of the doctrine of international constitutionalism. Next it addresses issues concerning the role of language and society of scholars in constitutionalist discourse as well as the mentioned sources of scepticism to international constitutionalism.

2 An outline of the doctrine of international constitutionalism

The doctrine of international constitutionalism is too rich a trend in legal scholarship to be considered a uniform approach to international law.[2] The idea of international constitutionalism itself is not a new one. The political and legal changes following World War I resulted in new expectations as regards the role and function of international law. They were guided by the hope of instilling the rule of law in international relations. The establishment of a few new international organizations and institutions, including the League of Nations, and the Permanent Court of International Justice, justified the recognition of the post-war situation as a real 'constitutional moment' for international society, ie a specific historical situation which offered favorable conditions for introducing significant changes in the political, legal, and organizational structure of international society.[3] Not accidentally, it was then that the doctrine of international constitutionalism was formed. The views that were typical of the doctrine were the ones presented by Georges

2 Jean d'Aspremont makes the same point. J d'Aspremont, *Formalism and the Sources of International Law. A Theory of the Ascertainment of Legal Rules* (OUP 2011) 77. Cf also N Tsagourias, 'Introduction' in N Tsagourias (ed) (n 1) 8.

3 Such opinion was presented in the interwar period (eg MO Hudson, *Progress in International Organization* (Rothman 1932) 6, 23, 42, 45) and is still expressed in today's doctrine. See C Walter, 'Progress in International Organization: A Constitutionalist Reading' in RA Miller and RM Bratspies (eds), *Progress in International Law* (Nijhoff 2008) 133, 136; CEJ Schwöbel, *Global Constitutionalism in International Legal Perspective* (Nijhoff 2011) 81; R Kwiecień, 'The Permanent Court of International Justice and the Constitutional Dimension of International Law: from Expectations to Reality' in M Fitzmaurice and C Tams (eds), *Legacies of the Permanent Court of International Justice* (Nijhoff 2013) 361. On the concept 'constitutional moment' see B Ackerman, 'Constitutional Politics/Constitutional Law' (1989) 99 *Yale Law Journal* 453, 489; AM Slaughter and W Burke-White, 'An International Constitutional Moment' (2002) 43 *HILJ* 1.

Scelle, Borys Mirkine-Guetzévitch, as well the representatives of the Vienna school of law: Hans Kelsen and Alfred Verdross.

All these scholars were representatives of the so-called monistic doctrine. As is well known, this doctrine was not uniform in explaining the bases of the relationship between international law and domestic legal orders. The mentioned scholars also represented differing views regarding the understanding and the role of constitution in international law, or even the meanings given to the term 'international constitutional law'. To Kelsen, constitution, whose function was served by hypothetical *Grundnorm*, was a logical and, in this sense, necessary consequence of thinking about the system of law. Without it – according to Kelsen – the basis of the binding force of law and legal obligations cannot be justified.[4] Verdross represented a different approach. What he recognized as the constitutional underpinnings of international law were meta-principles that indicate the sources of international law, its subjects, and determine the division and exercise of authority between States.[5] Yet another approach on the position of constitution in international law was given by Georges Scelle. The core of his construction was a then unique thesis on the reference of all legal norms, irrespective of their sources, to individuals as the primary legal subjects (theory of *dédoublement fonctionnel*). What Scelle understood as 'international constitutional law' (*droit constitutionnel international*) were customary rules that served three functions in international relations: legislative, administrative and judicial. International constitutional law determines the scopes of operations of such branches of international law as administrative law, contract law or criminal law. According to Scelle, constitutional rules do not have to be clearly defined norms. They may seem, thus, as *incertaine et irregulière*. Nevertheless, they are of fundamental significance to international society, as without them, it would lack the normative core. To international society, constitutional law is its *droit constructif*.[6] The author who greatly contributed to the spread of

4 H Kelsen, *Reine Rechtslehre. Einleitung in die Rechtswissenschaftliche Problematik* (Deuticke 1934) 115–119, 147–154.

5 A Verdross, *Die Verfassung der Völkerrechtsgemeinschaft* (Springer 1926) v. Surprisingly enough, Christine Schwöbel states that Verdross's interwar vision of global constitutionalism 'can almost be regarded as utopian'. Schwöbel (n 3) 8. Verdross's vision was not utopian. It was just an attempt to point out systemic basis and features of international law. More controversial seems to be Verdross's the post-war view recognizing the Charter of the United Nations as a constitution of international society. See A Verdross, *Völkerrecht* (5. Aufl., Springer 1964) 135–136; A Verdross and B Simma, *Universelles Völkerrecht. Theorie und Praxis* (3. Aufl., Duncker & Humblot 1984) vii-viii, 72, 221.

6 See G Scelle, *Le Pacte des Nations et sa Liaison avec le Traité de Paix* (Recueil Sirey 1919) 101–107; G Scelle, 'Essai de Systematique de Droit International (Plan d'un Cours de Droit International Public)' (1923) 30 *RGDIP* 116, 124–141; G Scelle, *Précis de Droit des Gens. Principes et Systématique*, vol 2 *Droit Constitutionnel International* (Recueil Sirey 1934) 7–11. It is worth mentioning in passing an apt criticism of Scelle's views which shows that his theory postulating to be based on social facts would, indeed, deny them. Scelle would, for instance, recognize the politically-motivated actions of States as the execution of constitutional functions by States. Cf T Opsahl, 'An "International Constitutional Law"?' (1961) 10 *ICLQ* 760,

the term 'international constitutional law' (*droit constitutionnel international*) in the twenty-year interwar period was a then well-known scholar examining the relationship between international law and States' constitutional law, Borys Mirkine-Guetzévitch. He would, however, give it a different meaning than Verdross, or even Scelle. Mirkine-Guetzévitch viewed international constitutional law as a new branch of public law that was formed as a result of the contents of domestic constitutions being saturated with the international legal issues. The result of the opening of domestic constitutions to international relations was the formation of 'the unity of public law' (*l'unité du droit public*).[7] International constitutional law was, thus, not so much part of international law, as a manifestation of close, monistic relations between international law and domestic legal orders. As can be seen, the doctrine of international constitutionalism from the very beginning was characterized by methodological and conceptual diversity not unity. What is more, a certain conceptual confusion was characteristic of it, because the mentioned authors were inclined to call different, even disproportional, legal phenomena a single concept of constitution. Today, one can notice such a practice still clearer.

After World War II new constitutional expectations have been especially embedded in the UN Charter.[8] There are two mutually opposing phenomena in contemporary international society that support the constitutional vocabulary. On the one hand, we must notice the expansion of international law beyond the inter-State sphere, establishing a hierarchy of norms, a value-oriented approach, departure from horizontal structure of law and from law-making solely based on the consent of States, as well as the existence of institutions and procedures for the enforcement of community interests at the international level. On the other hand, however, deformalisation of international legal regulations, their fragmentation, and hegemonic aspirations are often believed to be perils for the unity of international law. In such a configuration, international constitutionalism is an intellectual 'mindset', that is a program of moral and political regeneration.[9]

766; M Koskenniemi, *The Gentle Civilizer of Nations. The Rise and Fall of International Law 1870–1960* (CUP 2002) 333–338.

7 B Mirkine-Guetzévitch, 'Droit International et Droit Constitutionnel' (1931) 38 *Recueil des Cours de l'Académie de Droit International* 307, 319–324; B Mirkine-Guetzévitch, *Droit Constitutionnel International* (Recueil Sirey 1933) 7–8.

8 See eg P-M Dupuy, 'The Constitutional Dimension of the Charter of the United Nations Revisited' (1997) 1 *Max Planck Yearbook of United Nations Law* 1; B Fassbender, 'The United Nations Charter as Constitution of the International Community' (1998) 36 *Columbia Journal of Transnational Law* 529; T Franck, 'Is the UN Charter a Constitution?' in JA Frowein (ed), *Verhandeln für den Frieden – Negotiating for Peace: Liber Amicorum Tono Eitel* (Springer 2003) 95, 96–99; R Chemain and A Pellet (eds), *La Charte des Nations Unies. Constitution Mondiale?* (Pedone 2006); B Fassbender, 'Rediscovering a Forgotten Constitution: Notes on the Place of the UN Charter in the International Legal Order' in JL Dunoff and JP Trachtman (eds), *Ruling the World? Constitutionalism, International Law, and Global Governance* (CUP 2009) 133; MW Doyle, 'The UN Charter – A Global Constitution?' in Dunoff and Trachtman (eds) (this n) 113.

9 M Koskenniemi, 'Constitutionalism as Mindset: Reflections on Kantian Themes about International Law and Globalization' (2007) 8 *Theoretical Inquiries in Law* 9, 18. Martti

Some scholars strongly enhance the modern *l'esprit d'internationalité* which is commitment to the general, the global – as opposed to the particular, the local. Such an approach is also labelled as 'cosmopolitanism' and today is visible as enthusiasm about global governance[10] which is cognate with constitutionalism. Global constitutionalism as an academic approach is treated as a hermeneutic device for better understanding of legal processes within international society.[11] The constitutionalist reading of international law is often seen as a progressive and reformist agenda that is able to humanize the dominant State-centric understanding of international law and promote a new normative pattern of internationalism, substantive unity, and legal control of politics. The enthusiasm about global governance leads, among other things, to the idea of 'multilevel global constitutionalism' based on value-oriented approach, that is to say, on the significance of human rights and their protection. Within this perspective, global constitutionalism is functionally limited, but necessary complement to national constitutionalism because only those two levels of global governance taken together can give an effective protection for human rights and democratic self-determination in a globally integrating world. Multilevel global constitutionalism is here presented as functional unity for the protection and promotion of freedom and human rights in multilevel governance at 'home and abroad'.[12] From a global constitutionalist perspective, the relevant society is humankind in its totality, and the core issue of constitutionalism is the relationship between governmental power and human liberty. As such, the idea of multilevel global constitutionalism continues, at least to some extent, Immanuel Kant's idea of *jus cosmopoliticum (Cosmopolitan Right, Weltbürgerrecht)*.[13]

Koskenniemi argues that thinking of constitutionalism as a mindset instead of as architecture 'implies a kind of Copernican turn in legal theory' (at 31). Mathias Kumm also speaks of Copernican turn in legal thinking which is based on 'cosmopolitan constitutionalism'. It establishes, according to Kumm, an integrative basic conceptual framework for a general theory of public law that integrates national and international law. See M Kumm, 'The Cosmopolitan Turn in Constitutionalism: On the Relationship between Constitutionalism in and Beyond the State' in Dunoff and Trachtman (eds) (n 8) 263–264.

10 D Kennedy, 'My Talk at the ASIL: What is New Thinking in International Law' (2000) 94 *ASIL Proceedings* 107.

11 A Peters, 'The Merits of Global Constitutionalism' (2009) 16 *Indiana Journal of Global Legal Studies* 397, 405–406; A Peters, 'Are We Moving Towards Constitutionalization of the World Community?' in A Cassese (ed), *Realizing Utopia. The Future of International Law* (OUP 2012) 119–123. Cf also AL Paulus, 'The International Legal System as a Constitution' in Dunoff and Trachtman (eds) (n 8) 72.

12 E-U Petersmann, 'State Sovereignty, Popular Sovereignty and Individual Sovereignty: From Constitutional Nationalism to Multilevel Constitutionalism in International Economic Law' in W Shan, P Simons and D Singh (eds), *Redefining Sovereignty in International Economic Law* (Hart 2008) 27, 37–56; E-U Petersmann, 'Multilevel Trade Governance in the WTO Requires Multilevel Constitutionalism' in C Joerges and E-U Petersman (eds), *Constitutionalism, Multilevel Trade Governance and International Economic Law* (Hart 2011) 5. See also E de Wet, 'The International Constitutional Order' (2006) 55 *ICLQ* 51–53, 56–63, 75–76.

13 M Gregor (tr), I Kant, *The Methaphysics of Morals* (Cambridge Texts in the History of Philosophy, CUP 1996) 121–122. Cf also J Habermas, 'Hat die Konstitutionalisierung

3 International constitutionalism and the role of language and 'cohesive élite' of scholars

Judging from contemporary debate on legal transformations within international society international law scholars have different aims of their activity. Part of them – call them 'minimalists' – search out their role as commentators of binding legal rules and principles, whereas 'maximalists' display greater aspirations and treat their scholarship activity as a progressive agenda which seeks to shape a legal reality. Such an approach is characteristic not only of today's international law scholarship, because from the very beginning international law scholars have played a twofold role. Philip Allott once wrote about the possibility for the writer to be a thinker and a politician at the same time. In writing about the law, Allott argues, the problem is still more acute because it seems to be inherent in the nature of legal systems that writing about the law may itself constitute law. Owing to Article 38(1)(d) of the Statute of the ICJ writing about international law has an especially significant function.[14] It is the doctrine of international constitutionalism or constitutionalism beyond the State which especially treats scholarship as a reformist agenda. At any rate, following through the debate on international constitutionalism it is hard to resist the impression that the doctrine supporting international constitutionalism and scholars criticising it address to different audiences. Philip Allott calls the audience to which the writers themselves belong as 'cohesive élite', that is to say, an 'élite sharing certain moral, political and social values, and values relating to the conduct of academic discourse'.[15] It follows that a given scientist community must have a common substratum of values broad enough to protect its coherence and permit to act. Such a scientist community exists both within the constitutionalist theory of international law and within the doctrine questioning it due to cultivating wishful thinking.

One should have in mind that the idea of constitutionalisation of international law is developed and supported by academia not by international law makers. Nonetheless, academic activity is not axiologically and politically neutral. International law scholars do not choose between law and politics, but – as Martti Koskenniemi put it[16] – between one politics of law, and another. International law scholars are *nolens volens* political actors because their value judgments normally carry political implications, though they are not, unlike States and intergovernmental organizations, law makers.[17] Their

des Völkerrechts noch eine Chance?' in J Habermas, *Der Gespaltene Westen* (Surkhamp 2004) 113.

14 P Allott, 'Language, Method and the Nature of International Law' (1971) 45 *BYIL* 118.

15 Ibid., 95.

16 M Koskenniemi, 'International Law in Europe: Between Tradition and Renewal' (2005) 16 *EJIL* 113, 123.

17 A Peters, 'Realizing Utopia as a Scholarly Endeavour' (2013) 24 *EJIL* 533, 541; see also Chapter 1 in this book.

main authority is a cognitive one. Yet they sometimes in fact act – some scholars even say that they should act – as law reformers. Such scholars mainly understand their task as 'realizing utopia'[18] in order to improve the role of law within international society. It is worth emphasizing that all supporters of the idea of constitutionalisation of international law shared the faith in the idea of constitution as a manifestation of the rule of law in international relations. They believe that referring to the idea of constitution in international law signifies rejecting the choice between realism (supremacy of power over law) and hegemonic liberalism. The constitutional approach to international law offers, among other things, a promise of spreading the rule of law over international relations, and thus refusing the political claims and usurpations of States. In this perspective, constitution is supposed to establish a strong legitimization of the international legal order.[19] It is what makes the idea of international constitutionalism so appealing and interesting. But at the same time the following question arises: does the constitutional vocabulary have epistemic (cognitive) meaning or just an emphatic one? Maybe this vocabulary is artificial and even meaningless?[20] At any rate, the approach labeled above as 'realizing utopia' transforms scholars into 'political activists' who are led by the temptation to engage with factors beyond law.[21] Constitutionalist reading of international law is seen – as mentioned above – as a progressive and reformist agenda that is able to humanize the dominant State-centric understanding of international law and promote a new normative pattern of internationalism, substantive unity, and legal control of politics especially by scholars 'realizing utopia'. As a consequence, the language of the doctrine which *only* seeks to explain binding international rules and principles differs from the language of the scholarship which wants to change them. The former is, using Immanuel Kant's vocabulary, a 'theoretical reason language', whereas the latter a 'practical reason language'. In other words, the former concerns *Sein*, the latter *Sollen*. Reformist enthusiasm of scholars 'realizing utopia' leads them sometimes to confuse *Sollen* and *Sein*, which consequently can change established meanings of legal concepts. Scholars as political activists often articulate their fears about efficiency and

18 Peters (n 17) 537–540; A Cassese, 'Introduction' in Cassese (ed) (n 11) xxi.

19 See M Kumm, 'The Legitimacy of International Law: A Constitutionalist Framework of Analysis' (2004) 15 *EJIL* 907; J Klabbers, A Peters and G Ulfstein, *The Constitutionalization of International Law* (OUP 2011) 37–44; Paulus (n 11) 87; Schwöbel (n 3) 103–104, 143–145.

20 In this way many years ago eg Opsahl (n 6) 782–784. Altwicker and Diggelmann rightly underline that the global constitutionalism is an approach which typically works with the assumption that the struggle for the 'right terminology' is also a struggle for the 'right reality'. T Altwicker and O Diggelmann, 'How is Progress Constructed in International Legal Scholarship?' (2014) 25 *EJIL* 442–443.

21 Critically on scholars as 'political activists' see J Kammerhofer, 'Ortodox Generalists and Political Activists in International Legal Scholarship' in M Happold (ed), *International Law in a Multipolar World* (Routledge 2010) 13. But see contra GI Hernández, 'The Activist Academic in International Legal Scholarship' (2013) 2 *ESIL Reflections* 11.

legitimacy of international law. That is why, they try to introduce into legal language new, progressive concepts or new meanings of existing concepts as a remedy for unsatisfactory status quo. That is exactly in the language of scholars-reformers one can notice a phenomenon of reification, that is to say, regarding conceptual entities as real things. Reification has been characteristic of social scientists for a long time. It is especially visible in the 'utopian aspirations', that is, where aspirations are strongly motivated by political and moral aims.[22] At the same time, scholars as political reformers seek to prove a difference between law and politics in order to justify the complete normative legitimacy of international law.[23] That is precisely typical of the constitutionalist theory of international law which language possesses many borrowings from political and moral discourse language. In this meaning international law is not a self-contained normative system. When international legal language borrows from moral and political discourse, the legal terminology inheres some of this normativity. That is why the normative significance of the conceptual terms used in legal discourse turn not on the normativity of law as such, but rather on the normativity associated with the moral or political concepts drawn upon. It follows that using concepts as intermediate links in legal inferences may work to provoke reactions that international law itself cannot provoke. This is what Ulf Linderfalk calls 'the normative functionality of conceptual terms in international law'.[24]

Language of the constitutionalist theory often expresses personal preferences in *Sollen* of international law and disappointment in its *Sein*. On account of that one can notice a practice of changing meanings of established legal concepts. It is true that language is a 'living structure'. Yet in scholars – political activists, the emotive function of language takes precedence over its explanatory function. Consequently, it leads not only to the mentioned above reification and 'multiplying entities beyond necessity', but also to depreciation of binding legal rules and principles. Such a practice constitutes in itself a serious source of scepticism towards the constitutionalist approach to international law.

4 The sources of scepticism to constitutionalisation of international law and the constitutionalist theory of international law

There arises a question as to what extent the theory of international constitutionalism attempts to explain a new normative quality in the law of international society, and to what extent it is only a hermeneutic, that

22 J Boyle, 'Ideals and Things: International Legal Scholarship and the Prison-house of Language' (1985) 26 *HILJ* 327, 349–351.
23 Ibid., 331.
24 U Linderfalk, 'The Functionality of Conceptual Terms in International Law and International Legal Discourse' (2013/2014) 6 *EJLS* 27, 37.

is, exactly constitutional, interpretation of international law. In the latter case, it would provide not so much a description and explanation of legal reality, as an expression of the belief in the causative force of the idea of constitution, and its ability to influence the practice of international law. Many scholars-reformers simply believe in the transformative power of such ideas like 'international constitution', 'constitutionalisation beyond the State', 'global constitutionalism', 'multilevel constitutionalism'. In other words, they give the priority of 'practical reason' over 'theoretical reason'. Such an approach is frequently seen in the contemporary debate on the constitutionalisation of international law.[25]

I could agree with Philip Allott that it is ideas or ideals not theories that really matter in law.[26] But science of law also needs good theories to explain convincingly. Thus, one can pose a question whether the constitutionalist theory of international law does so?

An extent of expectations placing in promises given by the constitutionalist theory depends on a meaning of the concept of constitution. Meanwhile, this concept is not unambiguous. There are two essential meanings of the concept of constitution. It may be defined in the descriptive ('weak' meaning of constitution also known as 'thin' constitution) or normative ('strong' meaning of constitution known as 'thick' constitution) senses.[27] In the former sense, constitution consists of the long-term rules of a higher rank and of general and abstract nature. It is an act of universal scope which regulates the execution of the political authority within a given society, and should be binding

25 See eg C Walter, 'Constitutionalising (Inter)national Governance – Possibilities for and Limits to the Development of an International Constitutional Law' (2001) 44 *GYIL* 192ff; P Allott, *The Health of Nations. Society and Law beyond the State* (CUP 2002) 342–379; A von Bogdandy, 'Constitutionalism in International Law: Comment on a Proposal from Germany' (2006) 47 *HILJ* 223ff; W Werner, 'The Never-ending Closure: Constitutionalism and International Law' in Tsagourias (ed) (n 1) 329–330; J Klabbers, 'Constitutionalism and the Making of International Law. Fuller's Procedural Natural Law' (2008) 5 No Foundation. *Journal of Extreme Legal Positivism* 84ff <http://www.helsinki.fi/nofo/NoFo5Klabbers.html> accessed 31 July 2015; S Besson, 'Whose Constitution(s)? International Law, Constitutionalism, and Democracy' in Dunoff and Trachtman (eds) (n 8) 381; T Giegerich, 'The *Is* and the *Ought* of International Constitutionalism: How Far We Come on Habermas's Road to a "Well-Considered Constitutionalisation of International Law"?' (2009) 10 *German Law Journal* 31ff; Paulus (n 11) 69; Klabbers, Peters and Ulfstein (n 19) 37–44, 153–157; Schwöbel (n 3) 133–165; Peters, 'Are We Moving' (n 11) 118; Petersmann, 'Multilevel' (n 12) 5; M Rosenfeld, 'Is Global Constitutionalism Meaningful or Desirable?' (2014) 25 *EJIL* 177, 196–199.

26 'Law, like life and love, does not need theory to work effectively (…) but like life and love, law needs good ideas to make it better'. P Allott, 'Reviews of Books' (2009) 80 *British Yearbook of International Law* 409.

27 Cf Dupuy (n 8) 1, 3; T Cottier and M Hertig, 'The Prospects of 21st Century Constitutionalism' (2003) 7 *Max Planck Yearbook of UN Law* 261ff; J Crawford, 'Multilateral Rights and Obligations in International Law' (2006) 319 *Recueil des Cours de l'Académie de Droit International* 325, 372–383; Walter, 'Progress' (n 3) 138–142; Giegerich (n 25) 42–46.

on all the society members without discrimination.[28] In this sense, however, constitution does not guarantee complete subordination of the authority's activities to the rule of law. This requirement is met by the constitution in the 'strong' meaning, which is a manifestation of the Enlightenment ideal of the rule of law over the arbitrary rule of man. It embodies a modern trust in the ability of humankind to rationally govern itself, in the power of reason in the design of political institutions, and in the strength of those institutions in realizing a common good.[29] Understood in this way, constitution plays an important integrating role in the society.[30]

While referring to such a constitutional ideal, one needs to reject the possibility of recognizing as a constitution of international society, at least in the 'strong' sense, the acts and/or principles that do not cement the identity of this society; the acts and/or principles that do not concern the authority and do not determine the boundaries to any exercise of public authority for the sake of individual rights, and do not determine the institutional and procedural framework of settling disputes within the society. The only acts and/or principles that may aspire to the rank of constitution are the ones that provide stable bases of the legal system, thus being the main point of reference in the relations between the subjects of the legal order. Such acts and/or principles *ipso facto* legitimize the legal order. However, there still remains an open question whether the legitimization by means of constitution is the only, and necessary in this sense, form of legitimization of the legal order, the international legal order in particular.

A constitution as a form of the legitimacy of the legal order, only exists within a true community, that is to say, such a community where relations are based on stable principles, around which the identity of a community is formed. Such a constitution in the community is what unites it and is a counterweight to the atomization of social ties.[31] Thus, a question arises whether there is a homogeneity of values, interests and norms in international society which transforms this society into a true community? Looking at the controversies concerning a constitutional position of the UN Charter in the strong meaning of the term, deficiencies in enforcement of international *jus cogens*, the absence of judicial control over political organs of most intergovernmental organizations, including the UN, weak democratic legitimacy of international legal process and difficulties arising from ineffectiveness of many

28 Petersmann, 'Multilevel' (n 12) 15 speaks in this context of 'formal' elements of constitutionalism.

29 N Krisch, *Beyond Constitutionalism. The Pluralist Structure of Postnational Law* (OUP 2010) 67. See also Petersmann, 'Multilevel' (n 12) 15–18; see also Chapters 10 and 11 in this book.

30 See D Grimm, 'Integration durch Verfassung' Vortrag an der Humboldt-Universität zu Berlin am 12. Juli 2004 (FCE 6/04) <http://whi-berlin.de/documents/grimm.pdf> accessed 31 July 2015.

31 Cf Allott, *The Health* (n 25) 344 who writes: 'Constitutionalism is a *theory*, that is to say, a mental ordering of the reality within which a particular society constitutes itself. It is an explanatory and justificatory theory of a society's self-constituting'.

international norms in national legal orders, the answer cannot be affirmative. International society simply suffers from the lack of a strong uniting factor which does not allow speak about the constitutionalised international legal order. The main constitutive characteristic of international law is still sovereign equality of States, and international legal obligations of States basically follow from their consent. The restrictive interpretation of the limitations of the freedom of States' actions that stems from it, supports rather well the protection of States' individual interests, than so-called 'community interests'. In today's international law this still remains to be true. Although one may speak about 'community interests' that are clearly being formed, their enforcement and protection are largely conditioned by the protection of the individual interests of States.[32] The latter of them often remain outside the judicial control, which emphasizes the inadequacy of a constitutional schema towards international law. The international legal order has few of the constitutional features comparable to those found in national law. In this sense international law seems to be beyond constitutionalisation and the vision of international constitutionalism itself seems to be rather wishful thinking than an agenda explaining convincingly today's international law.

And yet, this state of affairs has another, more optimistic, side to it. Namely, it shows the autonomous character of international law and its normative independence from national law. It is hard to identify them with each other in the context of their normative systemic underpinnings. An independent approach to international law allows to see it as a legal order that is not so much primitive owing to the lack of a 'formal' constitution, as simply different from national law. And perhaps this autonomy of international law is a greater value than the striving for its constitutional interpretation that makes this law rather artificially similar to the national constitutional ideal. Moreover, one should have in mind that the idea of constitutionalisation can be unsuitable for the explanation of contemporary world which is characterized by moral and political pluralism.[33] Meanwhile, the idea of constitution supposes a homogeneity of values and political aims.

32 Cf A Paulus, 'International Adjudication' in S Besson and J Tasioulas (eds), *The Philosophy of International Law* (OUP 2010) 207, 210–212; S Villalpando, 'The Legal Dimension of the International Community: How Community Interests Are Protected in International Law' (2010) 21 *EJIL* 387; R. Kwiecień, *Interesy indywidualne państw a interesy wspólnotowe w prawie społeczności międzynarodowej (Individual Interests of States and Community Interests in the Law of International Society)* (Wydawnictwo UMCS 2015) 102–118. Cf also O Spiermann, 'Twentieth Century Internationalism in Law' (2007) 18 *EJIL* 785, 812–814 and especially a direct contribution to constitutional debate by J Dunoff and J Trachtman, 'The Lotus Eaters' in Klabbers, Peters and Ulfstein (n 19) 369–373. See, however, contra Peters, 'The Merits' (n 11) 398–399; Kumm, 'The Cosmopolitan' (n 9) 260–263; F Fabbrini, 'The Constitutionalization of International Law: A Comparative Federal Perspective' (2013/2014) 6 *EJLS* 7, 15–19. Peters and Kumm criticize so-called 'sovereignist thinking' which is, according to them, tantamount to a statist paradigm of thought, which conceives of constitutionalism exclusively through the vocabulary of sovereignty.

33 For that reason the idea of constitutionalisation has been rejected by Nico Krisch in his vision of postnational law. Krisch argues that the idea of settling the central questions of postnational

This doubt inclines to address another source of skepticism about international constitutionalism which concerns a cognitive novelty of the constitutionalist theory of international law.

As mentioned above, many scholars support constitutionalisation of international law because of ensuring stronger protection of human dignity and rights of individuals. As such, it is parallel to a trend called 'humanization of international law'. It seems to me that 'Ockham's razor' ('entities must not be multiplied beyond necessity') should be an important methodological pattern also in legal scholarship. The point is that there has been a well-established human-centric trend based on so-called Grotian tradition of international law in international legal scholarship that has supported conceiving international law as universal law of humanity (eg Lauterpacht) or as common law of mankind (eg Jenks). I do not think that the doctrine of global constitutionalism contributes something new to this trend. Both the Grotian tradition and the doctrine of global constitutionalism are based on a monistic vision of legal reality within which the primary responsibility of internal and international institutions for the protection of human rights is underlined. There is no need to invoke to the constitutional vocabulary in order to strengthen the protection of human rights.

There is another doubt concerning novelty of the doctrine of international constitutionalism. It concerns interaction between different levels of legal regulation which is so important for today's doctrine of global governance. The idea of multilevel regulations is not also a new one. This idea has been, for instance, developed from the 1950s by New Haven School. A global order is presented within the conception of 'world legal order' as

global society in constitutionalist form may not only seem unachievable but also undesirable due to the respect for diversity of contemporary world. Krisch (n 29) 27–68. Likewise M Loughlin, 'Constitutional Pluralism: An Oxymoron?' (2014) 3 *Global Constitutionalism. Human Rights, Democracy, Rule of Law* 9. See, however, Koskenniemi, 'Constitutionalism' (n 9) 36, who states that 'constitutional politics is resistant, indeed opposed, to managerialism.[…] In a fundamentally unfree and unequal world, constitutionalism, as Kant might have put it, carries the ideal of a free and self-determining humanity'. According to Koskenniemi, constitutionalism is opposed to 'empire', that is, the emergence of patterns of constraint to advance the objectives of a single dominant actor, either through the law or irrespective of it. See Koskenniemi, 'Constitutionalism' (n 9) 13. In another paper of 2007 Koskenniemi seems to argue against international constitutionalism owing to a threat to international law from 'empire'. 'The debate on an international constitution – Koskenniemi speaks – will not resemble domestic constitution-making. This is so not only because the international realm lacks a *pouvoir constituent* but because if such presented itself, it would be empire, and the constitution it would enact would not be one of an international but an imperial realm'. M Koskenniemi, 'The Fate of Public International Law: Between Technique and Politics' (2007) 70 *MLR* 1, 19. See, however, contra AS Sweet, 'Constitutionalism, Legal Pluralism, and International Regimes' (2009) 16 *Indiana Journal of Global Legal Studies* 621, 631–639; P Zumbansen, 'Comparative, Global and Transnational Constitutionalism: The Emergence of a Transnational Legal-pluralist Order' (2012) 1 *Global Constitutionalism. Human Rights, Democracy, Rule of Law* 16; Fabbrini (n 32) 20–22. Cf also D Kennedy, 'The Mystery of Global Governance' in Dunoff and Trachtman (eds) (n 8) 42; Schwöbel (n 3) 87–132; Peters, 'Are We Moving' (n 11) 126–128.

a conglomeration of different legal orders (nationals, transnationals, and intergovernmental) acting on different levels of regulation. A constitution conceived as a process holds – according to McDougall and Lasswell – those normative levels together. Actually, international constitution is here seen as a constitutionalisation, that is a flexible process coming up international actors' expectations.[34] The contemporary doctrine of multilevel international constitutionalism does not add new normative justification to old well-diagnosed processes. That questions a need of using the constitutional vocabulary due to Ockham's razor. Thus, the doctrine of international constitutionalism does not contribute – unlike eg Geir Ulfstein argues[35] – the 'value added' to scholarship except for some *de lege ferenda* demands concerning the limitations to exercise of public power by States for the sake of individual rights. In this sense, it is as a reformist agenda aimed at 'realizing utopia'.

The third source of my skepticism about constitutionalisation of international law boils down to a most important issue, namely: does international law need constitutional straitjacket to be explained and developed? In my opinion, instead of constitutionalisation it is coherence, universalism, and unity of international law that should be striving for and protecting. If international law scholars want international law to be improved they should underline its universalism and its systemic character. The very nature of those features can cope with fragmentation of legal regulations and proliferation of judicial bodies. The first sentence that opens the *Conclusions of the Study Group of ILC on the Fragmentation of International Law* states as follows: 'International law is a legal system'. And next:

> Its rules and principles (i.e. its norms) act in relation to and should be interpreted against the background of other rules and principles. As a legal system, international law is not a random collection of such norms. There are meaningful relationships between them.[36]

It is true that the constitutionalist theory of international law points out key phenomena in contemporary international society. But scholars do not need to be 'cool'[37] and adopt a new vocabulary in order to explain those phenomena. What scholarship can, needs and ought to do is enhancing unity

34 See eg MS McDougal, HD Lasswell, 'The Identification and Appraisal of Diverse Systems of Public Order' in MS McDougal and others, *Studies in World Public Order* (Yale University Press 1960) 3; M Reisman, 'The Constitutional Crisis in the United Nations' (1993) 87 *AJIL* 94–96. See also N Onuf, 'The Constitution of International Society' (1994) 5 *EJIL* 1, 7–8; Allott, *The Health* (n 25) 342–344, 351–354.

35 G Ulfstein in Klabbers, Peters and Ulfstein (n 19) 387–388.

36 ILC, 'Conclusions of the Work of the Study Group on the Fragmentation of International Law: Difficulties arising from the Diversification and Expansion of International Law' UN Doc A/Res/61/34, para. 1(1).

37 In this ironical way Bruno Simma labels a part of German scholarship developing the idea of international constitutionalism. See B Simma, 'Universality of International Law from the Perspective of a Practitioner' (2009) 20 *EJIL* 268, 297.

and systemic features of the international legal order. It seems better – as rightly argues Bruno Simma – presenting the development of international law just as a process of its progressive universalization.[38] Universalism and unity of international law are really a good enough cure for its fragmentation.

If, as some scholars argue,[39] a coherence and unity of international law concern systemic (formal) features of this law and the debate on constitutional character of international law applies to the substantive principles a question arises whether those two aspects can do without each other. The doctrine of international constitutionalism is aimed at substantive unity and hierarchy of international legal principles, including peremptory norms. It, however, seems doubtful whether the substantive unity can be reached without formal and institutional coherence. The substantive unity is not possible without coherence of substantive norms which are given a constitutional importance because the relationships between them are not clear. Substantive norms and principles themselves simply do not clarify the conditions of their own application. That is why, *The Conclusions of the Study Group of ILC on the Fragmentation of International Law* attaches such a great significance to coherence, especially to the principle of systemic integration. What scholars have to face up to is a constant adjudication between substantive norms and rule-systems, deciding on institutional powers of international bodies, and formulating legal principles. The truth is that dealing with those problems can lead to the conclusion that, as Koskenniemi argues,[40] a practice does exist of 'constitutionalizing' international relations even in the absence of a formal constitution. But it is only a 'mindset',[41] that is to say, a research approach which is, in fact, tantamount to the systemic approach to international law.

A significant relationship between universality and unity of international legal regulations was underlined above. This significance in the age of fragmentation cannot be underestimated because *erga omnes* effects of alleged constitutional norms cannot simply appear without their universality. So called 'partial' or 'segment' constitutions which are formed within self-contained regimes are unable to counter the effects of the fragmentation phenomenon. Quite a contrary, they threaten the unity of international law. It follows that it is universalism and coherence of international law, not its constitutionalisation, that really matter. It means, that alleged constitutional underpinnings of the law of international society are conditioned by universality and coherence of international legal regulations. Thus, the process of constitutionalisation of international law cannot exist without universality, unity and coherence of its principles and other rules. Thus, the foregoing sceptical remarks may be finished by posing the following question: is today's international law

38 Simma (n 37) 297.
39 See eg Paulus, 'The International Legal System' (n 11) 86–87.
40 Koskenniemi, 'Constitutionalism' (n 9) 21.
41 That is why Koskenniemi states that the report of the Study Group of ILC on Fragmentation illustrates 'the constitutional mindset at work'. Koskenniemi, 'Constituionalism' (n 9) 21.

universal, united and coherent enough to be subjected to a process of its constitutionalising?

5 Conclusions

Reflection on the significance of legal language arrives at the conclusion that perception, cognition and understanding of reality is conditioned by ideas of a given language. And in this sense understanding of ideas creates examined reality. Looking at the world from the perspective of the language is, in fact, a metaphysical perspective. The famous thesis by Ludwik Wittgenstein is worth reminding: 'That the world is *my* world, shows itself in the fact that the limits of the language (*the* language which I understand) mean the limits of *my* world'.[42]

Many scientific disputes derive from using by scholars different languages, especially from giving too flexible meanings to existing concepts. Lack of common vocabulary makes difficult, and sometimes even prevents, a real discourse, because of a lack of common reference point. Scholars using different languages simply speak about different worlds. The debate on constitutionalisation of international law illustrates it very clearly. There are within this debate two opposing 'cohesive élites', that is to say, two élites sharing different moral, political and social values, and different aims relating to the conduct of academic discourse. Scholars belonging to the doctrine of international constitutionalism are legal reformers who seek to change the international legal order, whereas critics of international constitutionalism are mainly concentrated on explanation of binding rules and principles. The former speak 'practical reason' language which puts emphasis on *Sollen* of the international legal order. However the latter 'cohesive élite' uses 'theoretical reason' language which main attention pays to *Sein*. That is why those two 'cohesive élites' explore different legal realities. Moreover, a phenomenon of reification often characterises legal reformers aiming at 'realizing utopia', which consists in regarding conceptual entities as real things. Such a practice is rejected by critics of international constitutionalism owing to its wishful thinking approach.

Critical examination of binding international legal rules and principles is useful, even necessary, for effectiveness of international law. However, *de lege ferenda* remarks should follow thorough explanation of status quo. In other words, 'theoretical reason' should precede 'practical reason'. Taking this directive into account, the following conclusion can be drawn: contemporary international law needs structural and systemic changes in order to enhance its effectiveness, but it does not demand reforms calling for the doctrine

42 L Wittgenstein, *Tractatus Logico-Philosophicus* (Kegan Paul 1922) 87, para. 5.62. In German: 'Dass die Welt meine Welt ist, das zeigt sich darin, dass die Grenzen der Sprache (der Sprache, die allein ich verstehe) die Grenzen meiner Welt Bedeuten' (ibid.).

of international constitutionalism. It is enhancement of structural coherence, substantive unity, and universality that are necessary for effectiveness of international law. It follows that it is rather systemic than constitutionalist approach to international law that has a greater research value, because desirable by the constitutionalist doctrine constitutionalisation of international law without the mentioned above systemic features (coherence, unity, universality) is simply not possible.

4 The creeping constitutionalisation and fragmentation of international law

From 'constitutional' to 'consistent' interpretation

Maurizio Arcari

1 Introduction

A sketch of contemporary legal writings on international law conveys the impression that constitutionalisation and fragmentation stand together as terms representing an odd but inseparable couple. In the words of a prominent author, it may be said that '[i]f anyone were to propose a pairing of phrases to characterize current developments in international law, the smart money would surely be on constitutionalization and fragmentation.'[1] Far from being astonishing, this is actually something which is not really new. Assuming that pluralism and normative dispersion have always been present in modern international law,[2] and that they are nothing but an expression of 'her infinite variety',[3] 'constitutionalism' – together with its operational variation, 'constitutionalisation' – stand out among the possible responses to ensure the systemic coherence of the international legal order.[4] Indeed, it can be noted that constitutionalisation, rather paradoxically, contains within itself the seeds of the very problem it purports to solve, namely 'fragmentation'. In fact, constitutionalism as a theoretical approach and process has been applied and developed in international law on a fragmented basis, in the context of the institutional settings of diverse international organizations and/or of

1 *See* J Klabbers, 'Constitutionalism Lite' (2004) 1 *International Organizations Law Review* 31. For other examples of the parallel treatment of the problems of constitutionalisation and fragmentation, *see* J Klabbers, A Peters, G Ulfstein, *The Constitutionalization of International Law* (OUP 2009) 11–19; A Paulus, 'The International Legal System as a Constitution' in JL Dunoff, JP Trachtman (eds), *Ruling the World? Constitutionalism, International Law and Global Governance* (CUP 2009) 69–109.

2 *See* B Conforti, 'Unité et Fragmentation du Droit International: "Glissez, mortels, n'appuyez pas!"' (2007) 111 *RGDIP* 5.

3 RR Baxter, 'International Law in "Her Infinite Variety"' (1980) 29 *ICLQ* 549.

4 Klabbers, *Constitutionalism Lite* (n 1) 31: 'On the one hand, many international lawyers raise worries about fragmentation of international law (...). On the other hand, and partly in response, international law is also heavily engaged in a countermove: many international lawyers propose that treaty regimes be constitutionalized.'

specific treaty regimes, such as those protecting basic human rights or the natural environment. Inasmuch as the trend towards constitutional pluralism in international law is likely to promote the consolidation of multiple autonomous and competing regimes,[5] the final result of constitutionalisation will inescapably be a dispersed international legal landscape.

Considering the very extensive legal literature on the subject, the present contribution does not intend to dwell on the substantive features of the phenomena of constitutionalisation and fragmentation in international law. Rather, it purports to explore the dynamics of their reciprocal interaction by considering some of the interpretive methods which can be used by international law practitioners to deal with the above phenomena. Leaving aside for the moment the question whether the interpretive principles included in Article 31 of the 1969 Vienna Convention on the Law of Treaties (VCLT) can be deemed to have a constitutional character or any constitutional implications,[6] it is a matter of record that both constitutionalisation and fragmentation have been, and indeed still are, constantly addressed by judges and scholars through the lens of interpretative techniques.

On the one hand, the early attempts at 'constitutionalising' the international legal order have been carried out through a functional and purpose-oriented reading of some constituent treaties of universal international organizations, such as the Covenant of the League of Nations and the United Nations Charter, that were supposed to incorporate the basic values of the international community.[7] Therefore, it can comfortably be said that, at least initially, the process of the constitutionalisation of international law developed in a rather 'creeping' fashion, through the prism of a 'constitutional' interpretation that was nothing but an adaptation of the traditional principles of teleological interpretation and effectiveness enshrined in Article 31.1 of the VCLT.

On the other hand, the response to the (allegedly) contemporary problem of the fragmentation of international law, exacerbated by the juxtaposition of partial and competing constitutional regimes, has also been elaborated through recourse to interpretive techniques. To this effect, one may recall the emphasis contemporary legal discourse has put on the principle of 'systemic integration', drawn from Article 31.3(c) of the VCLT, which is presented as the legal panacea which would ensure, through mutual coordination rather than antagonism, the coexistence of the different layers of international law.[8]

5 The phenomenon labeled as 'constitutional pluralism' lies at the origin of the so-called 'auto-constitutional regimes' in international law; see A Fischer-Lescano, G Teubner, 'Regime-collisions: The Vain Search for Legal Unity in the Fragmentation of Global Law' (2003–2004) 25 *Michigan Journal of International Law* 999, 1014–1017.

6 This question is interestingly addressed in Klabbers, Peters, Ulfstein (n 1) 24–25.

7 See below section 2 and the authorities quoted in (n 9). For an early attempt concerning the Covenant of the League of Nations, see H Lauterpacht, 'The Covenant as the Higher Law' (1936) 17 *BYIL* 54.

8 See below section 3 and the authorities quoted in (n 28) and (n 42).

In fact, while systemic interpretation is based on a presumption of consistency between the different norms and regimes of international law, it is often applied in a constitutional environment, i.e., in the context of 'constitutional' regimes, which assume that competing provisions are to be construed in the light of the higher norms, principles and values appertaining to a specific regime. In this perspective, systemic interpretation can be turned into a principle of 'consistent interpretation', i.e., one which upholds a constitutional and hierarchically-oriented – rather than conciliatory – outcome of the conflict between the norms and values at stake.

The points above will be developed following a three-step approach. First, some instances of constitutional interpretation will be illustrated with reference to the UN Charter. Second, the difficulties arising from the proliferation of constitutional regimes in international law will be illustrated and the basic features of the principle of systemic interpretation – intended as a tool for reframing this proliferation and solving the consequent fragmentation – will be considered. Third, some egregious examples in which the principle of systemic interpretation has become transformed into a principle of consistent interpretation, with the effect of promoting a constitutional and value-oriented outcome of legal disputes, will be explored.

2 Instances of 'constitutional' interpretation in international law, as applied to the UN charter

There is no room here for assessing the legal merits and foundations of legal theories that look at the Charter of the United Nations as the proper constitution for the international community (not to mention humankind).[9] Suffice it to say that if one accepts that the basic aim of constitutionalisation is to subject all types of public power (whatever the medium of their exercise) to the structures, processes, principles and values encapsulated in a basic document called a 'constitution',[10] then there is enough in the UN Charter

9 The legal literature on the subject is impressive. Just to list some of the most recent contributions, see B Sloan, 'The United Nations Charter as a Constitution' (1989) 1 *Pace Yearbook of International Law* 61; PM Dupuy, 'The Constitutional Dimension of the Charter of the United Nations Revisited' (1997) 1 *Max Planck Yearbook of United Nations Law* 1; J Crawford, 'The Charter of the United Nations as a Constitution' in H Fox (ed), *The Changing Constitution of the United Nations* (The British Institute of International and Comparative Law 1997) 3–16; S Szurek, *La Charte des Nations Unies, Constitution Mondiale*, in JP Cot, A Pellet, M Forteau (eds), *La Charte des Nations Unies* vol. 1 (3rd ed. Economica 2005) 29–68; R Chemain, A Pellet (eds), *La Charte des Nations Unies, Constitution Mondiale?* (Pédone 2006); B Fassbender, *The United Nations Charter as the Constitution of the International Community* (Njjhoff 2009). An excellent synthesis of the main doctrinal opinions can be found in K Zemanek, 'Can International Law Be "Constitutionalized"?' in M Kohen, R Kolb, DL Tehindrazanarivelo (eds), *Perspectives of International Law in the 21st Century. Liber Amicorum Professor Christian Dominicé* (Nijhoff 2012) 27–33.

10 See M Loughlin, 'What is Constitutionalization?' in Petra Dobner, Martin Laughlin (eds), *The Twilight of Constitutionalism?* (OUP 2010) 49.

to encourage a constitutionally-oriented construction. Just to mention some elements: the Charter stands out as an instrument of universal reach and vocation, which captures in its Purposes and Principles some of the basic values of the international community;[11] sets forth a framework of organs and institutions endowed with the powers to pursue such values;[12] and – as a final but very relevant factor – also presumes a hierarchical ordering of the sources of international law by proclaiming its priority over conflicting external (treaty) obligations.[13] Considering all these evidentiary elements, it should come as no surprise that the parallelism between domestic constitutions (especially the US Constitution) and the UN Charter is frequently evoked by scholars, together with the suitability of adopting a constitutionally-oriented approach for the interpretation of the latter instrument.[14] Indeed, the early instances of constitutional interpretation in international law have been construed with reference to the UN Charter and date back to several landmark cases. However, given the fact that the Charter is a treaty – albeit one 'having certain special characteristics'[15] – with respect to which one can hardly escape the application of the classic principles of treaty interpretation, the constitutional discourse was initially developed by judges in a rather transversal way.

While not worded in openly constitutional terms, the functional interpretation of UN powers proposed by the International Court of Justice (ICJ) in its 1949 and 1954 advisory opinions concerning, respectively the *Reparation for Injuries Suffered in the Service of the United Nations*,[16] and the *Effects of Awards of Compensation Made by the United Nations Administrative Tribunal*,[17] was based on the prominent consideration of the object and purpose of the UN Charter and on privileging the method of teleological interpretation of treaties. In its hermeneutical construction, the World Court paid special attention to the purposes and principles of the UN Charter, thereby espousing the approach usually reserved for the interpretation of domestic constitutions. If it is true that 'when interpreting a constitution one has to keep its principles constantly in mind, because it is in their light that the

11 See Arts 1 and 2 of the Charter.

12 See, especially, with reference to the competences and powers of the Security Council, Arts 24–25 and 39–42 of the Charter.

13 See Art. 103 of the Charter.

14 On the analogies between the UN Charter and the US Constitution, see in particular Sloan, (n 9), passim and especially pp. 87 ff. for the constitutional interpretation of both instruments. However, for a critical consideration of such analogies, see G Arangio-Ruiz, 'The Federal Analogy and UN Charter Interpretation: A Crucial Issue' (1997) 1 *EJIL* 1.

15 As perspicuously pointed out by the ICJ in the case concerning *Certain Expenses of the United Nations (Article 17, Paragraph 2, of the Charter)* (Advisory Opinion 20 July 1962) [1962] ICJ Rep, p. 157.

16 *Reparation for Injuries Suffered in the Service of the United Nations* (Advisory Opinion 11 April 1949) [1949] ICJ Rep, p. 174.

17 *Effects of Awards of Compensation Made by the United Nations Administrative Tribunal* (Advisory Opinion 13 July 1954) [1954] ICJ Rep, p. 47.

provisions have to be construed',[18] this was exactly the course followed by the ICJ in the *Effects of Awards of Compensation* case, when it underscored that it 'would hardly be consistent with the expressed aim of the Charter to promote freedom and justice for individuals' to leave the staff of the Organization without any judicial protection or remedy.[19] This constitutional reasoning was pushed another step forward in the 1962 advisory opinion on *Certain Expenses of the United Nations*, where the World Court ascribed 'a primary place' among the purposes of the UN to the maintenance of international peace and justice, thereby suggesting that these purposes, as well as the provisions functional to their attainment, can be ordered hierarchically, according to a constitutional perspective.[20]

More than thirty years later, the World Court reconsidered its earlier constitutional reading of the UN Charter by re-situating it against the broader context of the 'system' of UN specialized agencies. In 1996 the ICJ rejected the World Health Organization's (WHO) request for an advisory opinion concerning the legality of the use of nuclear weapons in time of armed conflict, arguing that this question fell outside the scope of the activities of the requesting agency. This conclusion was grounded on the assumption that the competences and powers of the WHO must be interpreted taking into account 'not only the general principle of speciality, but also the logic of the overall system contemplated by the Charter.' Following this perspective, the Court held that the responsibilities of the WHO should necessarily be confined to the sphere of public health and cannot encroach on 'other parts of the United Nations system', in particular on the question of legality of the use of force and of disarmament, lying within the competence of the principal organs of the United Nations.[21] If, as it has been suggested by an author, this reasoning reveals an attempt on the part of the ICJ to infuse a constitutional design into the governance of world affairs,[22] one cannot avoid noting the central place assigned to the Charter of the United Nations in this context.

Apart from these early – or at least relatively less recent – examples drawn from the case law of the World Court, the constitutionalist approach towards the interpretation of the constituent instrument of the UN has had its vitality confirmed in more recent case law. Such an approach has been particularly enhanced with the reactivation of the Security Council's (SC) powers following the end of the cold war. Among a number of prominent examples, the 2003 decision of the Trial Chamber of the International Criminal Tribunal for the Former Yugoslavia (ICTFY) in the *Prosecutor v Milutinovic et al.* case should be recalled. In this decision the principle of

18 See Zemanek (n 9) 29.

19 ICJ, *Effects of Awards for Compensation* (n 17) 57.

20 ICJ, *Certain Expenses of the United Nations* (n 15) 168.

21 *Legality of the Use by a State of Nuclear Weapons in Armed Conflict* (Advisory Opinion 8 July 1996) [1996] ICJ Rep, p. 80.

22 J Klabbers, 'Global Governance before the ICJ: Re-reading the WHA Opinion' (2009) 13 *Max Planck Yearbook of United Nations Law* 1 27–28.

effectiveness of the UN system of collective security was evoked to assert the universal reach of SC decisions adopted under Chapter VII and their applicability to non-member States. In elaborating this conclusion, the ICTFY expressly mentioned 'the constitutional character of the Charter', and 'the critical importance to the international community of the goal of the maintenance of international peace and security', as being among the crucial factors that could render the SC resolution establishing the Tribunal applicable to any country that was a part of the former Yugoslavia, irrespective of its actual membership in the UN.[23]

Indeed, the most far-reaching expression of the constitutional interpretation of the UN Charter and of the powers of UN organs (and especially the SC) under the Charter has been developed with reference to Article 103 of the Charter. It is well known that one of the essential features of the constitutional character of a legal text lies in its hierarchical primacy over other (external) normative sources. In the case of the UN Charter, this feature is granted by Article 103, which however confines the priority effect to the hypothesis of a conflict between the obligations arising under the Charter and other treaty obligations assumed by Member States. This principle of primacy is also deemed to apply to SC resolutions adopted under Chapter VII.[24] It is therefore not surprising that Article 103 has been extensively invoked and applied by courts evaluating the impact of SC targeted sanctions on individuals in order to assert the primacy of SC decisions over conflicting human rights treaty obligations of UN Member States.[25] What is striking, however, are the current attempts to enlarge, by way of interpretation, the scope of Article 103 of the Charter. On one side it has been suggested that the *primauté* granted by Article 103 of the Charter cannot be limited to conflicting treaty obligations of UN Member States, but must be extended to any obligations arising under customary international law, because otherwise the primacy effect assigned to SC decisions would be easily circumvented.[26] On the other side it has been

23 ICTY, *Prosecutor v Milan Milutinovic, Dragoljub Ojdanic, Nikola Sainovic*, No IT-99-37-PT, Decision on Motion Challenging Jurisdiction of 6 May 2003, available at http://www.icty.org, paras 45–63 and especially para. 62.

24 Case Concerning *Questions of Interpretation and Application of the 1971 Montreal Convention arising from the Aerial Incident at Lockerbie (Libyan Arab Jamahiriya v UK; Libyan Arab Jamahiriya v US)* (Request for the Indication of Provisional Measures, Orders 14 April 1002) [1992] ICJ Rep, pp. 3 and 114 respectively.

25 See especially, the judgment rendered by Tribunal of First Instance of the European Communities in the first phase of the *Kadi* affair: case T-315/01, *Yassin Abdullah Kadi v Council of the European Union and Commission of the European Communities*, Judgment 21 September 2005 [2005] ECR II-3706. For an application in domestic case law, see *Tribunal Fédéral Suisse, A. c.* Département Fédéral de l'Economie (2A.783/2006), Judgment 23 January 2008, available at http://www.bger.ch. On this question, see generally P De Sena, MC Vitucci, 'The European Courts and the Security Council: Between Dédoublement Fonctionnel and Balancing of Values' (2009) 20 *EJIL* 193.

26 See N Krisch, 'Introduction to Chapter VII: The General Framework' in B Simma, DE Khan, G Nolte, A Paulus (eds), *The Charter of the United Nations. A Commentary* (3rd

submitted that, in order to ensure the effectiveness of UN action in the field of maintenance of international peace and security, the 'authorizations' to use all necessary means granted by the SC to Member States must also be considered to be on the same footing as Chapter VII binding 'decisions' for the purposes of application of Article 103 of the UN Charter.[27]

A common feature of the trends outlined above is that the maintenance of international peace and security is constantly considered, according to a constitutional-type perspective, as the primary goal of the international community organized under the UN Charter, and this is the crucial factor legitimizing interpretations aimed at enhancing the effectiveness of the action of UN organs in that field. As such, the above-mentioned instances can be ranked among the most significant and far-reaching emanations of the principle of constitutional interpretation in modern international law.

3 Conflicting constitutional regimes in international law and interpretative tools for avoiding fragmentation: from 'constitutional' to 'systemic' interpretation

As already mentioned, one of the most challenging issues of modern international law is the fragmentation arising from the proliferation of autonomous international regimes, whose different norms may come into conflict and jeopardize the global coherence of the international legal order.[28] For the present purposes, it must be kept in mind that the risks of fragmentation can also stem from the coexistence of different constitutional regimes and constitutional sub-systems of international law. In fact, apart from the prominent case of the UN Charter, the possibility also exists that a constitutional discourse can be pursued within particular treaty regimes

edn, OUP 2012) 1262; R Kolb, *Interprétation et Création du Droit International* (Bruylant 2006) 580. The argument that the priority rule of Art. 103 of the Charter applies to both conventional and customary obligations of UN Member States was also advanced by the EU Council and Commission in the first phase of the *Kadi* case: ECJ, *Yassin Abdullah Kadi v Council of the European Union* (n 25) para. 156.

27 For an application in domestic case law, see *R (on application of Al-Jedda) v Secretary of State for Defence*, Opinions of the Lords of Appeal for Judgment 12 December 2007, [2007] UKHL 58, reprinted in (2008) 47 *ILM* 607, paras 30–34 (Lord Bingham of Cornhill), para. 117 (Lord Rodger of Earlsferry) and paras 131–135 (Lord Carswell). For a review of the underlying legal arguments, see R Kolb, 'Does Article 103 of the Charter of the United Nations Apply only to Decisions or also to Authorizations Adopted by the Security Council?' (2004) 64 *ZaöRV* 21.

28 Besides the authors cited above, notes 1 to 5, on the problem of fragmentation of international law also see: M Koskenniemi, P Leino, 'Fragmentation of International Law? Postmodern Anxieties' (2002) 15 *Leiden Journal of International Law* 553; J Pauwelyn, 'Bridging Fragmentation and Unity: International Law as a Universe of Inter-connected Islands' (2003–2004) 25 *Michigan Journal of International Law* 903; T Treves, 'Fragmentation of International Law: The Judicial Perspective' (2007) 23 *Comunicazioni e Studi* 822; MA Young (ed), *Regime Interaction in International Law. Facing Fragmentation* (CUP 2012).

presenting, in a more or less advanced form, typical characteristics of a constitutional order. Examples in international law of partial regimes which are construed and interpreted according to a constitutional perspective range from the World Trade Organization (WTO) – at the universal level – to the European Union (EU) or the European Convention on Human Rights (ECHR) system on a regional scale. While in the context of international trade and economic law the constitutional discourse has mainly been pursued in a theoretical and doctrinal perspective,[29] the case law of regional judicial organs contains a large number of decisions premised on a constitutional interpretation of the basic instruments of their particular regime. This is the case, for example, for the EU Court of Justice (ECJ), which since 1986 has spoken of the Treaty establishing the (then) European Community in terms of 'a basic constitutional charter'.[30] Albeit more occasionally, the European Court of Human Rights (ECtHR) has also referred in its case law to the ECHR as a 'constitutional instrument of European public order', usually to exclude reservations made by a State party that would diminish the effectiveness of the Convention[31] or to affirm the existence of jurisdiction under Article 1 of the Convention, including outside the territory covered by the Council of Europe Member States.[32]

Recent case law has demonstrated, however, that in some extreme situations, norms reflecting or incorporating the basic values of different constitutional regimes may come into conflict. In those instances, the picture is further complicated by the fact that – with the sole and possible exception of the UN Charter – none of the different 'constitutional rules' at stake can usually claim any inherent superior ranking, as they are in principle endowed with equivalent normative force.

A case in point are the intricate legal issues, and the related judicial sagas, stemming from the targeted sanctions ordered by the UNSC against persons included in the blacklist of suspected terrorists. Both the content of the targeted measures and the procedure for compiling the list of targeted persons are deemed to infringe on some basic individual rights, such as the right to property, the right to freedom of movement and (especially) the right to a fair process, all of which are protected under both the EU Charter

29 Among others see DZ Cass, *The Constitutionalization of the World Trade Organization* (OUP 2005); JP Trachtman, 'The Constitutions of the WTO' (2006) 17 *EJIL* 623.

30 Case 294/83 *Parti écologiste 'Les Verts' v European Parliament*, Judgment 23 April 1986, [1986] ECR I-1365, para. 23. It is impossible to review here the vast legal literature existing on the subject of the EU's constitutional dimension. The reader can usefully refer to the synthesis of the debate, carried out from an international law perspective, contained in J d'Aspremont, F Dopagne, 'Two Constitutionalisms in Europe: Pursuing an Articulation of the European and International Legal Orders' (2008) 68 *ZaöRV* 939.

31 *Loizidou v Turkey (Preliminary Objections)* (15318/89), ECtHR Judgment 23 March 1995, paras 75 ff.

32 *Al-Skeini and Others v the United Kingdom* (55721/07), Grand Chamber, ECtHR Judgment 7 July 2011, paras 141–142 and ff.

of Fundamental Rights and the ECHR.[33] The developments of the *Kadi* case before the judicial organs of the EU show how unfortunate the attempt to resolve the legal issues involved by following a strict constitutional perspective can be. The initial effort, in 2005, by the (then) Tribunal of First Instance to assign a hierarchical priority to the imperatives of peace maintenance enshrined in the UN Charter over the conflicting human rights,[34] was dramatically reversed in 2008 by the Court of Justice. This Court embraced a rigid 'dualistic' approach for resolution of the case, premised on the blunt separation of the two concurring constitutional legal orders at stake, and claimed the need to ensure the full review of the lawfulness of all EU acts in the light of fundamental rights, even when such acts were designed to give effect to SC resolutions adopted under Chapter VII of the UN Charter.[35] This approach led to the annulment of EU regulations implementing UN sanctions, and was substantially confirmed in the judicial decisions concerning the second round of the *Kadi* dispute.[36] Insofar as such an approach can be deemed to promote the fragmentation rather than the coherence of the international legal order, the search for more moderate solutions seems inescapable. In this vein, a more nuanced path appears to have been explored by the ECtHR in the 2011 and 2012 judgments in the *Al-Jedda* and *Nada* cases, both involving similar questions arising from the conflict between the SC resolutions and the protection of fundamental human rights.[37] As will be further examined below, in these cases the ECtHR attempted to strike a balance between the different values at stake by suggesting that a feasible way out of the legal conundrum may consist in taking into account human rights requirements during the implementation of SC decisions by individual States.[38]

The reasoning developed by the ECtHR in the above-mentioned cases reflects a modern approach to the problem of competing regimes in international law, premised on the notion of 'systemic' interpretation. This approach is inspired by Article 31.3(c) of the VCLT, according to which, in interpreting a treaty, account must be taken of 'any relevant rules of international law applicable in the relations between the parties.' This assumes that international legal norms and obligations included in a certain

33 On this question, see generally A Ciampi, 'Security Council Targeted Sanctions and Human Rights' in B Fassbender, *Securing Human Rights? Achievements and Challenges of UN Security Council* (OUP 2011) 98–140, as well as the authorities quoted (n 25).

34 See (n 25).

35 Case C-402/05/P *Yassin Abdullah Kadi, Al Barakaat International Foundation v Council of the European Union and Commission of the European Communities*, Judgment 3 September 2008 [2008] ECR I-06351, especially para. 326.

36 Case C-584/10/P, *Commission and Others v Yassin Abdullah Kadi*, Judgment 18 July 2013.

37 See respectively, *Al-Jedda v the United Kingdom* (27021/08) Grand Chamber, ECtHR Judgment 7 July 2011 [hereinafter Al-Jedda Judgment] and *Nada v Switzerland* (10593/08) Grand Chamber, ECtHR Judgment 12 September 2012 [hereinafter Nada judgment].

38 See section 4.2 below.

international regime or sub-system must not be read in 'clinical isolation'[39] or in a 'legal vacuum',[40] but are to be integrated into the overall framework of international norms, both of conventional and customary origin, that may be relevant and applicable in each case.[41] This corresponds to the notion of 'systemic integration' propounded by the UN International Law Commission (ILC) study group on fragmentation as the appropriate legal tool for avoiding the fragmentation of the international legal system and guaranteeing its overall consistency.[42]

One of the basic tenets of the principle of systemic integration is that the harmonization of different legal regimes and norms of international law can be attained by minimizing the possibility of their conflict through interpretive techniques. As explained by the ILC study group on fragmentation, 'rules appear to be compatible or in conflict as a result of interpretation', and in an international legal system made up of rules dispersed across different sub-systems but sharing a common 'normative environment', an effort must be made to harmonize apparently conflicting rules so as to render them compatible.[43] In other words, it must be presumed that norms belonging to different legal subsystems of international law are mutually consistent and that they can be applied simultaneously, so that normative conflicts will be exceptional and in principle limited to the most extreme cases. In sum, '[i]n international law, there is a strong presumption against normative conflicts.'[44]

As will be more closely examined below, this stance was unambiguously endorsed by the ECtHR in the *Nada* case as a premise for assessing the compatibility with the ECHR of the restrictive measures adopted by Switzerland on the basis of SC resolutions:

> Where a number of apparently contradictory instruments are simultaneously applicable, international case-law and academic opinion endeavour to construe them in such a way as to coordinate their effects and avoid any opposition between them. Two diverging commitments must

39 WTO, Report of the Appellate Body, *United States – Standards for Reformulated and Conventional Gasoline* (WT/DS2/AB/R), 29 April 1996, reprinted in (1996) 35 *ILM* 605, p. 621: 'the General Agreement [GATT] is not to be read in clinical isolation from public international law.'

40 See Nada Judgment, para. 169 ('The Court reiterates that the Convention cannot be interpreted in a vacuum but must be interpreted in harmony with the general principles of international law').

41 See generally C McLachlan, 'The Principle of Systemic Integration and Article 31(3)(c) of the Vienna Convention' (2005) 54 *ICLQ* 279.

42 Study Group of the International Law Commission, 'Fragmentation of International Law: Difficulties Arising from the Diversifi cation and Expansion of International Law', Report Finalized by M Koskenniemi, UN Doc. A/CN.4/L.682.

43 Ibid., paras 411–412 and 423.

44 Ibid., para. 37.

therefore be harmonized as far as possible so that they produce effects that are fully in accordance with existing law.[45]

However, the question can be asked how far this presumption of consistency between international norms and regimes can be pushed when normative conflicts involve rules belonging to a 'constitutional' regime or, as a most extreme hypothesis, when a clash between different 'constitutional' regimes is at stake. A closer look at the pertinent case law reveals that the answer to this question is far from unequivocal.

4 From 'systemic' to 'consistent' interpretation

Based on the premise that normative conflicts in international law must be avoided or conciliated through interpretation, one can infer that the so-called 'principle of consistent interpretation' is an essential part of systemic integration and conclude that its role will be critical in promoting the effective harmonization of the international legal order. Indeed, one must not forget the origin and the theoretical underpinnings of the principle of consistent interpretation. Consistent interpretation is an interpretive technique well known in domestic legal systems, where it is extensively used to avoid or resolve conflicts between constitutional principles and subordinate normative sources. Moreover, consistent interpretation also serves, in the context of the international/domestic law dialectic, as a means for enhancing the application of international law within domestic legal orders, insofar as it presupposes that domestic law will be applied and interpreted in conformity with the international legal obligations of the State.[46] In both cases, the interpretive technique called 'consistent interpretation' is premised on the assumption that – to avoid normative conflicts at the domestic level, or to avoid breaches of the obligations of States at the international level – the interpretation of one of the rules at stake must be deferential to other rules of the system endowed with a superior normative ranking or force. In other words, the mechanism of consistent interpretation has been conceived to work in a legal environment

45 See Nada Judgement, para. 170, whereby the principle of systemic integration as well as the ILC study group report on fragmentation are both explicitly evoked. For a comprehensive overview and analysis of the application by the ECtHR of the principle of systemic integration, see VP Tzevelekos, 'The Use of Article 31(3)(c) of the VCLT in the Case Law of the ECtHR: An Effective Anti-fragmentation Tool or a Selective Loophole for the Reinforcement of Human Rights Teleology?' (2010) 31 *Michigan Journal of International Law* 621.

46 For more on this principle and its application in domestic law for dealing with the relationship between domestic and international or EU law, see especially G Betlem, A Nollkaemper, 'Giving Effect to Public International Law and European Community Law before Domestic Courts. A Comparative Analysis of the Practice of Consistent Interpretation' (2003) 14 *EJIL* 569; A Nollkaemper, *National Courts and the International Rule of Law* (OUP 2011) 139–165.

where rules are co-ordinated according to some kind of normative hierarchy, with the consequence that the 'presumption of conformity' lying behind the concept is often intended to work in a unidirectional mode, rather than on a bilateral and reciprocal basis.

While it is not unusual that consistent interpretation is employed by judges operating in the context of specific regimes of international law to resolve questions relating to their coordination with 'external' sources (such as in dialectic between EU/WTO rules or EU/international law rules),[47] one may ask whether the same principle can deploy its intended 'conciliatory' effects when normative conflicts involve the higher rules or values belonging to constitutionally-oriented international regimes. The two case-studies below may illustrate some of the unpredictable implications of the principle of consistent interpretation as applied at international law level.

4.1 The relationship between the UN Charter and the secondary norms on international responsibility

The first illustration can be drawn from the relationship between the primary obligations existing under the UN Charter, especially SC decisions adopted under Chapter VII, and the secondary obligations arising in the field of international responsibility from the commission of internationally wrongful acts.[48] As is widely known, such secondary obligations have been codified by the ILC in two sets of Draft Articles, devoted respectively to the Responsibility of States and to the Responsibility of International Organizations.[49] Both sets of ILC Draft Articles contain the same (rather ambiguous) final clause, devoted to the relationship with the UN Charter, which provides that 'these articles are without prejudice to the Charter of the United Nations.'[50] The scope of this 'non-prejudice clause' is tentatively clarified in the ILC commentaries to the two draft articles, both stressing the key role that Article 103 of the UN Charter is called on to play in this regard, especially in cases where decisions of political organs of the UN may have a bearing on questions involving the responsibility of States or of International Organizations. On this point, the commentary to Article 59 of the State Responsibility Draft

47 See generally G Gattinara, 'Consistent Interpretation of WTO Rulings in the EU Legal Order?' in E Cannizzaro, P Palchetti, RA Wessel (eds), *International Law as Law of the European Union* (Nijhoff 2012) 269–287; F Casolari,' Giving Indirect Effect to International Law within EU Legal Order: The Doctrine of Consistent Interpretation', ibid., 395–415.

48 On this question, see generally V Gowlland-Debbas, 'Responsibility and the United Nations Charter' in B Simma *et al.* (n 26) 117–138.

49 See General Assembly Resolutions 56/83 of 12 December 2001 and 66/100 of 9 December 2011, endorsing respectively the ILC Draft Articles on the Responsibility of States for internationally wrongful acts [hereinafter SR Draft Articles] and the ILC Draft Articles on the Responsibility of International Organizations [hereinafter IOR Draft Articles].

50 See, respectively, Art. 59 of the SR Draft Articles and Art. 67 of IOR Draft Articles.

directly recalls the situation that materialized in the well-known *Lockerbie* case,[51] while the commentary to Article 67 of the International Organizations Draft specifies that the non-prejudice clause applies not only to obligations directly provided for in the UN Charter, but especially to 'those flowing from binding decisions of the Security Council, which according to the International Court of Justice similarly prevail over other obligations under international law on the basis of Article 103 of the United Nations Charter.'[52] One may wonder if this insistence on the prevailing effect of Artcle 103 of the UN Charter is appropriate in the context of two sets of draft articles that are deemed to reflect, in whole or in part, the general and customary principles of the law of international responsibility. As already mentioned, Artcle 103 is intended to settle the conflicts between Charter obligations and other treaty obligations of UN Member States, and in principle it will be of little or no avail in the hypothetical case of a clash between the Charter obligations and the secondary principles of responsibility embodied in the ILC Draft Articles. This conclusion appears to be even stronger when issues concerning the responsibility of International Organizations are involved, insofar as International Organizations are not members of the UN, or parties to the UN Charter, and therefore cannot be bound by the priority rule set forth in Artcle 103 of the Charter.[53]

The real implications of the references to Artcle 103 of UN Charter in the ILC commentaries are eventually disclosed in the very final phrase of the commentary to Artcle 59 of the State Responsibility Draft, which unambiguously refers to the principle of 'consistent interpretation', by stating that '[t]he articles are in all respects to be interpreted *in conformity with* the Charter.'[54] In fact, to assert that a principle of 'consistent interpretation' with the UN Charter must be observed in the application of the rules governing international responsibility amounts to a *petitio principii*, which can hardly be sustained except on the assumption of the higher ranking accorded to the former instrument.

The example at hand seems to reveal the real implications of the principle of consistent interpretation as applied in a 'constitutional' environment, i.e., one whose basic principles, rules and values are accompanied by a presumption of a higher hierarchical ranking: in the event of conflict between the 'constitutional' principles and other, 'external' rules, the latter rules are to

51 See para. 1 of the commentary to Art. 59 of SR Draft Articles, reproduced in [2001] II(2) *Yearbook of the International Law Commission* 143.

52 See para. 1 of the commentary to Art. 67 of IOR Draft Articles, in *Report of the International Law Commission, Sixty-third Session*, UN doc. A/66/10 (2011), p. 173.

53 For more details on this, *see* M Arcari, 'Parallel Words, Parallel Clauses: Remarks on the Relationship Between the Two Sets of ILC Articles on International Responsibility and the UN Charter' in M Ragazzi (ed), *Responsibility of International Organizations. Essays in Memory of Sir Ian Brownlie* (Nijhoff 2013) 101–102.

54 See para. 2 of the commentary to Art. 59 of SR Draft Articles, (n 51) (emphasis added).

be interpreted so as to 'bow to' or 'defer to' the former, and the presumption of consistency is ultimately meant to work in a uni-directional way. Ultimately, this means that the constitutional principles and rules of the system are deemed to prevail by way of a result-oriented interpretation of any other rules external to the regime that may be applicable in a given case. It is of significance that the ILC, perhaps aware of these unwanted implications, has refrained from inserting into the commentary to Artcle 67 the Draft on the Responsibility of International Organizations a statement similar to that appearing in Artcle 59 of the Draft on State Responsibility to the effect that the Commission's articles had to be interpreted in conformity with the UN Charter. Instead of this, the final phrase of the commentary to Artcle 67 includes a more prudent proviso, warning that 'the present article is not intended to exclude the applicability of the principles and rules set forth in the preceding articles to the international responsibility of the United Nations'.[55]

4.2 The relationship between the UN Charter and the European Convention on Human Rights

Other insights into the principle of consistent interpretation can be drawn from consideration of the case law of the ECtHR relating to the impact of SC decisions on human rights, namely the *Al-Jedda* and *Nada* cases already referred to.[56]

Al-Jedda concerned the detention of a joint Iraqi/British national – supposedly in breach of Artcle 5 of the ECHR – by British forces operating in Iraq under the authority of SC resolution 1546 (2004). Mr. Al-Jedda's complaints were considered and rejected by British Courts, especially by the House of Lords,[57] on the basis that SC resolution 1546 (2004), by authorizing UN Member States to take all the necessary measures to contribute to the maintenance of security and stability in Iraq, created an obligation on the part of the United Kingdom to subject the applicant to security internment, and that, under Artcle 103 of the UN Charter, this obligation prevailed over the conflicting right to personal liberty provided for in Artcle 5 of the ECHR. In its judgment of 2011, the ECtHR reversed this conclusion by interpreting the scope of the authorization delivered by the SC in resolution 1546 (2004) in a very different manner. In fact, the ECtHR deliberately called into question the applicability of Artcle 103 of the UN Charter, preliminarily asking itself whether an opposition existed in the case at hand between the SC-authorized measures and the United Kingdom's human rights obligations under the ECHR.[58] In the relevant paragraph, the Court

55 See para. 3 of the commentary to Art. 67 of IOR Draft Articles (n 52), 172.

56 See references in n 37.

57 See references in n 27.

58 *Al-Jedda* Judgment, para. 101: 'Before it can consider whether Article 103 had any application in the present case, the Court must determine whether there was a conflict between

recalled both the purposes of the maintenance of international peace and of the promotion of human rights and fundamental freedoms, as enshrined in Artcle 1.1 and 3, of the UN Charter, and underscored that, under Artcle 24 of the same instrument, the SC, in discharging its responsibilities, shall act in accordance with the above purposes and principles. In this way, the Court apparently suggested that the mentioned purposes must be considered on an equal footing in the assessment of the legality of SC actions. Against this background, the ECtHR argued that 'there must be a presumption that the Security Council does not intend to impose any obligation on Member States to breach fundamental principles of human rights', and added that in the event of any ambiguity in the terms of a SC resolution, 'the Court must [...] choose the interpretation which is most in harmony with the requirements of the Convention and which avoids any conflict of obligations.'[59] Eventually, the Court concluded that, absent 'clear and explicit language' by which the SC intended to oblige States to take particular measures conflicting with human rights law, no opposition existed in the case at hand between United Kingdom's obligations under the UN Charter and under Article 5 of the ECHR, and held the State to have breached the latter provision.[60]

This is an outstanding example of application of the principle of consistent interpretation, whose immediate effect is to avoid the conflict between concurring obligations and to promote their coordinated application. As perspicuously noted by an author, in the case at hand the ECtHR created a very strong interpretative presumption in favour of the human rights obligations contained in the ECHR, which can be rebutted only by a clear and unequivocal decision by the SC to the effect that specific human rights guarantees must be discarded in a particular instance. However, as the same author points out, it would have been hardly conceivable for the ECtHR to accept that the SC can displace the ECHR, which is 'the constitutional instrument of European public order' and of which the Court is the ultimate guardian.[61]

The Court had the occasion to clarify its point in the subsequent *Nada* case. The question at stake in this case was the compatibility with the ECHR of restrictive measures adopted by Switzerland following the inclusion of the applicant in the blacklist of persons associated with Al-Qaida, and his subjection to SC targeted sanctions. In its 2012 judgment, the ECtHR correctly found that the situation at hand was different from that existing in the *Al-Jedda* case, insofar as SC resolution 1390 (2002) used 'clear and explicit language' requiring States to adopt measures capable of breaching

the United Kingdom's obligations under United Nations Security Council Resolution 1546 and its obligations under Article 5 § 1 of the Convention. In other words, the key question is whether Resolution 1546 placed the United Kingdom under an obligation to hold the applicant in internment'.

59 Al-Jedda Judgment, para. 102.

60 Ibid., paras 103–110.

61 See M Milanovic, *Al-Skeini and Al-Jedda in Strasbourg* (2012) 23 *EJIL* 121, 137–138.

human rights. As a consequence, the presumption of compatibility between SC decisions and human rights obligations that operated in *Al-Jedda* was rebutted in the present case.[62] Notwithstanding such an unequivocal finding, the ECtHR, in the remainder of its reasoning, underscored the fact that the UN Charter 'does not impose a particular model for the implementation of the resolutions adopted by the Security Council' but 'leaves to UN member States a free choice among the various possible models for transposition of those resolutions into their domestic legal order.' In reliance on the alleged latitude that Switzerland enjoyed in implementing the SC resolutions of the SC, the Court eventually found that the Swiss government had not taken all possible measures to adapt the sanctions regime to the applicant's individual situation and therefore breached its obligations under Arts 8 and 13 of the ECHR.[63]

It is hard to avoid the impression that the *Nada* decision amounts to an over-stretching of the technique of consistent interpretation, built on a distortion of the text of the relevant SC resolutions, the effect of which was to consolidate an almost non-rebuttable presumption that the SC did not intend to deviate from human rights standards.[64] In fact, taken together the *Al-Jedda* and *Nada* judgments confirm that the principle of consistent interpretation, when applied in a given 'constitutional environment', can be strained so as to create a presumption of priority in favour of the rules reflecting the fundamental values of the system, with the ultimate consequence of promoting a 'constitutional oriented' outcome of normative conflicts.[65]

62 See Nada Judgment, para. 172: '[I]n the present case (…), contrary to the situation in *Al-Jedda*, where the wording of the resolution at issue did not specifically mention internment without trial, Resolution 1390 (2002) expressly required States to prevent the individuals on the United Nations list from entering or transiting through their territory. As a result, the above-mentioned presumption is rebutted in the present case, having regard to the clear and explicit language, imposing an obligation to take measures capable of breaching human rights, that was used in that resolution.'

63 Ibid., paras 175–180 and 195–198.

64 See E De Wet, 'From Kadi to Nada: Judicial Techniques Favouring Human Rights over United Nations Security Council Sanctions' (2013) 12 *Chinese Journal of International Law* 787, 806.

65 The constitutionally-oriented approach followed by the ECtHR in *Al-Jedda* and *Nada* is indirectly confirmed by the outcome of the most recent case concerning SC targeted sanctions, *Al-Dulimi and Montana Management Inc v Switzerland* (5809/08), ECtHR Judgment 26 November 2013, available at http://www.echr.coe.int. In this case, any discretion of UN member States in the implementation of SC measures was *a priori* excluded by the very explicit language of SC resolution 1483 (2003), which demanded seizure of the funds of persons associated with the former regime of Saddam Hussein in Iraq. After having recognized that there was no room for a presumption of consistency between SC decisions and human rights obligations at stake, the Court held that the system of listing in place at the UN does not provide concerned individuals with a level of protection equivalent to that required by Art. 6 of the ECHR, and concluded that Switzerland, by implementing SC targeted sanctions, violated the right to fair process of the applicants (ibid., paras 113–121 and 134–135).

5 Conclusions

The above review reveals that the processes of constitutionalisation and fragmentation in international law are dealt with through recourse to specific interpretive techniques, borrowed and adapted from the general principles of treaty interpretation enshrined in Artcle 31 of the VCLT. While 'constitutional interpretation', 'systemic integration' and 'consistent interpretation' all appear ultimately intended to promote the coherence of the international legal order and the systemic construction of its rules, each interpretive technique pursues the said goals according to different theoretical perspectives, which bring with them different advantages and shortcomings.

On the one hand, the attempt to order hierarchically the entire international legal order under a superior instrument can be pursued only at the price of stretching certain key provisions, such as the priority rule enshrined in Artcle 103 of the UN Charter, beyond their scope as provided in the text. In any case, this hierarchical assumption cannot be sustained in the most extreme cases, which involve conflicts between the universal system of the UN Charter and other partial or regional subsystems also endowed with a constitutional vocation, such as the EU or the ECHR. As the *Kadi* saga seems to demonstrate, in such cases the adoption of a rigid constitutional stance can hardly avoid creating an opposition among the different subsystems involved, with the resulting systemic fragmentation.

On the other hand, attempts to conciliate normative conflicts and to avoid fragmentation of international law through the principle of 'systemic integration' and its corollary, 'consistent interpretation', cannot be pushed too far. The pertinent case law suggests that recourse to consistent interpretation at the international level may encompass implications at variance with the intended purposes of systemic integration. While the ordering of international rules according a hierarchical scale and creating a constitutionally-oriented outcome for normative struggles are goals that lie beyond the scope of systemic integration, it cannot be excluded that such unintended effects may materialize when the principle of consistent interpretation is applied to conflicts involving constitutional regimes or constitutional values. If one considers the different outcomes that recourse to consistent interpretation may generate in diverse constitutionally-oriented subsystems of international law, the question can well be posited whether this interpretive principle is apt to promote the overall coherence of the global legal order, or whether it is rather likely to perpetuate fragmentation by fuelling inter-systemic conflicts.

It is submitted here that 'constitutional', 'systemic' and 'consistent' interpretive methods are neither opposed nor complementary. Rather, they appear to be intricately entangled, insofar as their ultimate effect is that of fuelling, in a 'creeping' and often unintended fashion, both the constitutionalisation and fragmentation of the international legal order. However paradoxical this conclusion may appear, it remains true that constitutionalisation and fragmentation still represent two inseparable poles around which the legal pluralism of the international legal order gravitates. In this respect, it can easily be maintained that the inconsistencies and paradoxes accompanying the interpretive techniques used to govern the phenomena of constitutionalisation and fragmentation accurately epitomize the complexities of modern international law.

Part II

Fragmentation of international law as a challenge to its constitutionalisation

5 The paradoxes of fragmentation

Does regional constitutionalisation constitute a fragmentation threat to the international legal order?

François Finck

1 Introduction

This contribution explores the themes of constitutionalisation and fragmentation from the perspective of the relationship and mutual influence of both phenomena. It argues that the growing assertiveness of regional legal systems, a trend usually described as a symptom or a cause of fragmentation of international law may also be seen as a contribution to its progressive constitutionalisation. In other words, the purpose of this chapter is to overcome the dichotomy constitutionalisation/fragmentation by analysing phenomena which are often seen as contributing to fragmentation as, on the contrary, an instrument of spreading constitutionalist language and practice in international law. The focus of this chapter is on what I call 'regional constitutionalisation' – i.e. international regimes founded on a geographical base, in opposition to international legal regimes governing certain areas of international law – and its relations with constitutional tendencies in international law. I will use the example of the relations of the European Union and the European Convention on Human Rights to decisions of United Nations organs.

Concerns about the fragmentation of international law related in the first place to the development of international legal regimes along functional lines (international trade law, international criminal law) which could undermine the unity and coherence of international law[1], both on the normative and the institutional levels through the 'proliferation' of international tribunals and institutions.

This alarm about fragmentation of the international legal order has been famously played down as 'postmodern anxieties' of 'classical' international lawyers faced with the risk of 'pathological' conflicts between normative

1 These concerns caused the ILC to mandate a report on 'Fragmentation of international law: difficulties arising from the diversification and expansion of international law'. See Report of the Study Group, doc. A/CN.4/L.682.

systems.[2] The report of the ILC Working Group[3] also concluded that the exponential increase of international legal instruments can be dealt with thanks to the resources of general international law, in particular interpretation rules codified in the Vienna Convention on the Law of Treaties.[4]

However, similar anxieties reappeared with the evolution of the case-law of European Courts – the European Court of Justice and the European Court of Human Rights – in relation to the application of resolutions of the UN Security Council.[5] Fragmentation does not develop only along strictly functional lines, but can be based on divergences on a functional-geographical level: the challenges come from a regional human rights court or what can be described as a 'constitutional' court[6], albeit belonging to a regional international organisation.

At the same time as they were described as threats to the coherence and authority of international law, these developments – from the expansion of international regulation and judicialisation to new areas, such as international trade law[7], to the increase in the number of international organisations or the development of *jus cogens* and *erga omnes* obligations – have been widely discussed and analysed as signs of its constitutionalisation.[8]

The constitutionalisation of international law is often defined as a process of development of constitutional elements in the international legal order[9],

2 M Koskenniemi, P Leino, 'Fragmentation of International Law? Postmodern Anxieties' (2002) 15 *LJIL* 553, 559–560.

3 Report of the Study Group of the ILC (n 1).

4 Ibid., 248ff. The report also rightly pointed out that because of its decentralised structure, 'normative conflict is endemic to international law' and is not a new feature. Ibid., 246, para. 486. See also T Broude, 'Keep Calm and Carry On: Martti Koskenniemi and the Fragmentation of International Law' 2013 Fall Issue *Temple International & Comparative Law Journal* 279.

5 Ex: G de Burca, 'The European Court of Justice and the International Legal Order After Kadi' (2010) 51 *Harvard International Law Journal* 1; Joined Cases C-584/10 P, C-593/10 P and C-595/10 P *European Commission, Council of the European Union, United Kingdom of Great Britain and Northern Ireland v Yassin Abdullah Kadi* [2013] ECR-I 176 Opinion of AG Bot.

6 Both the ECJ and the ECtHR have been described as constitutional courts. See below, section 2.

7 See the important work of E-U Petersmann, A Peters and others, 'The Constitutionalisation of International Trade Law' in T Cottier, P Delimatsis (eds), *The Prospects of International Trade Regulation: From Fragmentation to Coherence* (CUP 2011); J P Trachtman 'Constitutional Economics of the World Trade Organization' in J L Dunoff, J P Trachtman (eds), *Ruling the World? Constitutionalism, International Law and Global Governance* (CUP 2009).

8 Ex: A Orakhelashvili, 'Peremptory Norms as an Aspect of Constitutionalisation in the International Legal System' in S Muller, M Frishman (eds), *The Dynamics of Constitutionalism in the Age of Globalisation* (Hague Academic Press 2010); A Peters, 'Are We Moving Towards Constitutionalization of the World Community' in A Cassese (ed), *Realizing Utopia, The Future of International Law* (OUP 2012).

9 A Peters, 'Compensatory Constitutionalism: The Function and Potential of Fundamental International Norms and Structures' (2006) 19 *LJIL* 579, 582; A Wiener and others, 'Global Constitutionalism: Human Rights, Democracy and the Rule of Law' (2012) 1 *Global Constitutionalism* 1, 5.

even though some definitions contain more substantial elements referring to a theory of constitutionalism.[10] The analysis of this process thus requires a reflection about the meaning of constitutionalism on supra- and international levels.[11]

Constitutionalism has been historically closely linked to the organisation of the political community in the State, based on a hierarchy of norms and as the expression of the common political will of the 'constitutional demos', the '*pouvoir constituant*'.[12] The 'problem of translation'[13] of constitutional language to the supranational and international levels[14], associated with the lack of unique and unequivocal definition of these terms, has provoked scepticism about the possibility or meaningfulness of using constitutional language in a non-State context.[15]

However, an approach centred on the substantive values and the functions of constitutionalism make it possible to extend constitutional analysis to sites located beyond the State.[16] The substantive principles and the functions of constitutionalism are manifold. Besides its fundamental function of organisation of the polity based on the expression of the will of the *demos* and definition of collective identity, constitutionalism organises and establishes limits to political power. Moreover, the rule of law and the judicial protection of individual rights are among 'the most basic principles of domestic

10 For example A O'Donoghue, *Constitutionalism in Global Constitutionalisation* (CUP 2014) 15 refers to constitutional functions of regulation and limitation of power.

11 'Constitutionalism' can be distinguished from 'constitutionalisation' from an analytical point of view: the latter is used to describe what is perceived as the reality of current developments of the international legal realm, whereas the former contains a normative project aiming to influence the evolution of international law towards more integration and hierarchy. For a distinction between a 'normative' and a 'functionalist' school, see A Wiener and others (n 9) 6ff. W Werner, 'The Never-ending Closure: Constitutionalism and International Law' in N Tsagourias (ed), *Transnational Constitutionalism – International and European Perspectives* (CUP 2007) 330: the language of constitutionalism is used 'with the aim of furthering a normative agenda of internationalism, integration and legal control of politics'.

12 J H H Weiler, 'In Defence of the Status Quo: Europe's Constitutional Sonderweg' in J H H Weiler, M Wind, *European Constitutionalism Beyond the State* (CUP 2003); N Walker, 'The Idea of Constitutional Pluralism' (2002) 65 *Modern Law Review* 317, 341

13 See N Walker, 'Postnational Constitutionalism and the Problem of Translation' in Weiler, Wind (n 12) 27.

14 In this regard, as European integration, as the most advanced form of international organisation, has been the subject of ample theoretical debates on constitutionalism and constitutionalisation on a supranational level, I will also draw on the debates linked to constitutionalisation in the EU context.

15 N Walker, 'The Problem of Translation' (n 13); Mattias Kumm illustrates the 'skeptic's challenge' in M Kumm, 'The Cosmopolitan Turn in Constitutionalism: On the Relationship between Constitutionalism in and beyond the State' in J L Dunoff, J P Trachtman (eds) (n 7).

16 N Walker, 'The Problem of Translation' (n 13). See also Walker, 'The Idea' (n 12); M Kumm, 'The Cosmopolitan Turn' (n 15).

constitutional orders'.[17] Limitation of power through law is one of the core functions of constitutionalism.[18] Whereas the functions related to the identity and the collective will of a polity are still overwhelmingly realised in the State context, human rights protection and power check are also being exercised in supra- or international *fora*. Constitutional language can thus be used in a non-State context as long as constitutional functions are identified in a supranational or international system.[19]

These developments at various levels of governance among competing claims to final legal authority have led to doctrinal debates about their mutual relationship and the character of international constitutionalisation/ constitutionalism.

Some authors focus on the functions of constitutionalisation, distinguishing between 'enabling, constraining, and supplemental constitutionalization'[20], or on its role as a compensatory mechanism for 'de-constitutionalisation' on domestic level.[21] Moreover, the development of constitutional claims beyond the State has given rise to theories aiming to solve the conundrum of the relations between various sources of constitutional authority. Multilevel constitutionalism and constitutional pluralism were developed to provide new analytical tools about the European Union, its 'constitutional' law and its relations with State constitutions. While the first term is limited to the debate about the EU[22], the second informed wider controversies about the relationships of national, supranational and international levels.

Constitutional pluralism acknowledges the existence of multiple sources of constitutional authority coexisting in a heterarchical relationship (as opposed to the hierarchy traditionally associated to constitutions) and posits that no claim to constitutional authority can be considered as supreme. Legal systems

17 A L Paulus, 'The International Legal System as a Constitution' in Dunoff, Trachtman (eds) (n 7) 92, 97.

18 D Halberstam, 'Systems Pluralism and Institutional Pluralism in Constitutional Law: National, Supranational and Global Governance' in M Avbelj, J Komarek (eds), *Constitutional Pluralism in the European Union and Beyond* (Hart 2012) 88, on the historical origins of 'the idea of constitutionalism as a legal limitation on power'; A Peters (n 8) 118, 129; A Wiener and others (n 9) 1.

19 See N Walker, 'The Idea…' (n 12) 334, on the necessity for a constitutionalist approach both to 'take the state seriously as a significant host to constitutional discourse' and to 'be open to the discovery of meaningful constitutional discourse and processes in non-state sites'. W Werner (n 11) 349, writes that 'the constitutional reading of international law (…) aims at the realization of some core values borrowed from modern, domestic constitutionalism', such as 'the limitation of political power through legal rules and institutions.'

20 Ibid.

21 A Peters (n 9).

22 F C Mayer, M Wendel, 'Multilevel Constitutionalism and Constitutional Pluralism' in Avbelj and Komarek (eds) (n 18). These authors show the history of the term and define it as 'two distinct (…) constitutional levels which are complementary rather in a hierarchical relationship', a 'composite Constitution', a 'complementary structure of national and European constitutions', with primacy of application of EU law, but no hierarchy.

are in a relation characterised by a 'combination of independence and mutual embedded openness'[23] to competing constitutional claims, based on the core values of constitutionalism.[24]

This contribution draws on reflections on the relationship between legal orders, but focuses on an analysis of recent developments with the aim to clarify the relation between fragmentation and constitutionalisation in practice. Constitutionalism on the supranational level is not necessarily about identifying a formal constitution, but criteria and indices[25] and constitutional functions[26] realised beyond the State.

For this reason this paper does not claim to provide a definition of constitutionalism which would be absolute and general. Instead, it will focus on this specific but central function of constitutionalism: the check of public power through law for the purpose of the protection of fundamental rights, in particular through the mechanism of judicial review by an independent jurisdiction, and contribute to the study of its development beyond the State.

The notion of constitutionalisation will thus be used as a process of spreading of constitutionalist norms and language between regional and universal levels, with a focus on one of the main functions of constitutionalism, the protection of individual rights against public power thanks to the rule of law.

The first section provides an overview of the main constitutional sites that will be addressed (2.). The paper will then turn to an analysis of the evolution of European jurisprudential assessment of UN activity, evolving from deference (3.) to challenge (4.). The consequences of this shift are assessed in the next section (5.), before concluding arguments on the relations of regional and global constitutional tendencies (6.).

2 Regional constitutional systems and the international legal order

Some proponents of a constitutionalist analysis of international law have defined the United Nations Charter as a 'world constitution'[27] on the basis of the priority of Article 103 of the Charter over Member States' obligations stemming from any other international agreement. Moreover, under Article 25, decisions of the Security Council are binding upon Member States. This argument is reinforced by the Organisation's objective legal personality, its near-universal membership and unique place in the international legal

23 Halberstam (n 18) 95.
24 Ibid., 94; Walker (n 12) 337ff; Kumm (n 15).
25 Walker, 'The Idea…' (n 12) 340.
26 Dunoff, Trachtman (n 7) 9.
27 B Fassbender, 'Rediscovering a Forgotten Constitution: Notes on the Place of the UN Charter in the International Legal Order' in Dunoff, Trachtmann (n 7); B Fassbender, 'The United Nations Charter as Constitution of the International Community' (1998) 36 *Columbia Journal of Transnational Law* 529. On a skeptical note, see Peters (n 9) 599; Paulus (n 17) 78–80.

system, as well as its proclamation of fundamental principles of coexistence of States.

However, even though the Charter undoubtedly fulfils some constitutional functions of the international community, it cannot be defined as a constitution, but rather a part of a 'constitutional compound' or system.[28] Some flaws of the UN system, especially the lack of limits to the power of the Security Council, which is in contradiction to the core values of constitutionalism, cast some doubt on its character as a Constitution.[29]

The more limited and coherent membership of regional organisations allowed for the realisation of core constitutional functions on the supranational level.

The ECtHR has clearly developed a constitutional character.[30] Its case-law has departed from classical treaty interpretation to progressively develop the rights contained in the Convention, behaving thus more like a constitutional court than a purely international jurisdiction. The Court has dismissed reservations by States parties while deciding they are still bound by the Convention[31] and consistently held that the Convention is a 'constitutional instrument of the European public order'.[32]

The ECJ has very early on defined the new organisation as an autonomous legal order[33] and consistently asserted that the Community is based on the rule of law and treated the Treaties as its constitutional charter.[34] These claims have been widely accepted in literature.[35] These developments of constitutional functions were achieved thanks to the influence of constitutional courts. The German FCC's refusal to recognise the supremacy of EC law for want of protection of fundamental rights equivalent to the protection guaranteed by the Fundamental Law[36] led the ECJ to develop its case-law on this matter and recognise that these are part of the general principles of EC law.[37] This solution, consistently reiterated and expanded[38], was the condition

28 E de Wet, 'The International Constitutional Order' (2006) 55 *ICLQ* 51; Peters (n 9) 599.
29 J Arato, 'Constitutionality and Constitutionalism beyond the State: Two Perspectives on the Material Constitution of the United Nations' (2012) 10 *International Journal of Constitutional Law* 627, 657.
30 A Stone Sweet, 'On the Constitutionalisation of the Convention: The European Court of Human Rights as a Constitutional Court' (2009) 80 *Revue Trimestrielle des Droits de l'Homme* 923.
31 *Belilos v Switzerland* (1986) Series A no 132.
32 *Loizidou v Turkey (preliminary objections)*, Series A no 310, paras 75 and 93. Also recently in judgments: *Al-Skeini and Others v the United Kingdom* ECHR (GC) 2011 para. 141; *Sargsyan v Azerbaijan* (App no 40167/06) ECtHR 16 June 2015, para. 147.
33 Case 26/62 *Van Gend en Loos v Administratie der Belastingen* [1963] ECR 00003.
34 Case 294/83 *Parti écologiste "Les Verts" v European Parliament* [1986] ECR 01339 at para. 23.
35 Ex: A Rosas, L Armati *EU Constitutional Law : An Introduction* (2nd rev. edn, Hart 2012); A von Bogdandy, J Bast, *Principles of European Constitutional Law* (2nd rev. edn, Hart 2010).
36 Case '*Solange I*' (1974) BVerfGE 37, 271.
37 Case 11/70 *Internationale Handelsgesellschaft* [1970] ECR 1125.
38 Case 36/75 *Roland Rutili v Ministre de l'intérieur* [1975] ECR 01219.

of the acceptation of primacy by national constitutional jurisdictions.[39] This high level of protection was also recognised by the ECtHR as 'equivalent protection'.[40]

These competing claims of supremacy on the global and the regional level almost inevitably gave rise to divergences and contradictions. Fragmentation is inherent to the very process of constitutionalisation in various sites.

The check on Security Council's decisions is at the heart of the question of the relationship of regional and global governance systems. The individual sanctions regime adopted under resolution 1267 (1999) and subsequent resolutions, allowing a committee subordinated to the SC to pronounce various administrative measures against persons and entities suspected of links with Al-Qaida and the Taliban, has been criticised for its lack of independent overview.

3 State acts in UN-authorised operations before the ECtHR: from deference to control

The case-law of the Strasbourg Court first focused on issues of attribution and jurisdiction (3.1) before developing a reasoning based on harmonious interpretation of international obligations (3.2).

3.1 The issue of attribution and jurisdiction

In its decision on the admissibility in the *Behrami and Saramati*[41] case, the ECtHR avoided examining the application on the merits by declaring that the actions of the defendant States' contingents in Kosovo were not attributable to them but to the United Nations.

At issue were acts carried out by contingents acting in an international framework in Kosovo, however under various conditions. The Court concluded that the acts of the body responsible for de-mining, UNMIK, a subsidiary organ of the United Nations, are attributable to the United Nations[42], and thus falling outside the jurisdiction of States parties to the Convention. However, the Court also concluded to the attribution to the UN of acts committed by national contingents of the Kosovo Force (KFOR) on the grounds of the Security Council's 'ultimate authority and control', even though the KFOR was a NATO-led operation authorised by the UNSC under 'unified command and control'.[43] Under international law, when an organ of a State is placed at the disposal of an international organisation,

39 Case '*Solange II*' (1986) BVErfGE 73, 339.

40 *Bosphorus Hava Yollari Turizm ve Ticaret Anonim Şirketi v Ireland* ECHR (GC) 2005-VI.

41 *Behrami and Behrami v France and Saramati v France, Germany and Norway* (App no 71412/01 and 78166/01) ECtHR 2 May 2007 (hereinafter *Behrami and Saramati*).

42 Ibid., para. 143.

43 Ibid., para. 140.

the criterion of attribution of an internationally wrongful act committed by this organ is *effective* control over the conduct.[44] The Court departed from the international law on responsibility of international organisations to avoid concluding to the applicability of the Convention to military operations conducted abroad by Member States in application of a UNSC resolution.[45]

The States delegated competences in the area of maintenance of international peace and security to the UN. According to the Court's earlier case-law[46], this should not allow them escaping responsibility for failures to guarantee the rights enshrined in the Convention.

The Court's stance on attribution of conduct in the context of UN-authorised operations changed in subsequent cases. In *Al-Jedda*[47] and *Al-Skeini*[48], the applications concerned acts of UK forces in Iraq under resolution 1511 allowing the deployment of a multinational force under unified command.[49] The British government relied on the *Behrami* case-law to argue that these acts were attributable to the United Nations and not to the United Kingdom.

However, the Court departed from its prior rulings and contended that mere authorization by the UNSC does not lead to the attribution of the acts committed by the authorised forces.[50] This evolution from the *Behrami and Saramati* solution is in line with the law of international responsibility. The authorisation granted by an international organisation to a State does not make the acts of States organs attributable to the organisation.[51]

In this case the respect for international law, and the correct application of its rules, goes hand in hand with the aim of enhancing the control of Member States' abidance by the European Convention on Human Rights. The accountability of international military operations in the framework of UN-authorised operations is enhanced. The applicability of the ECHR and the jurisdiction of the Court could be seen as a limitation to the Security Council's freedom of action. However, the States retain effective control over their troops, and thus the troops' actions remain State actions. Its consequence is a division of legal regime applicable to troops, depending on whether or not their home States are parties to the Convention. However,

44 Art. 7 of the Draft Articles on the responsibility of international organisations (2011), *Yearbook of the International Law Commission* vol. II, Part Two.
45 For earlier critical comments of this case, see M Milanovic, T Papic, 'As Bad as it Gets: the European Court of Human Rights' Behrami and Saramati decision and General International Law' (2009) 57 *ICLQ* 267; L-A Sicilianos 'Entre Multilatéralisme et Unilatéralisme: l'Autorisation par le Conseil de Sécurité de Recourir à la Force' (2008) 339 *Recueil des Cours de l'Académie de Droit International* 376.
46 *Bosphorus* (n 40).
47 *Al-Jedda v United Kingdom* (App no 27021/08) 2011 ECHR (GC).
48 *Al-Skeini and Others v United Kingdom* (App no 55721/07) 2011 ECHR (GC).
49 On these cases, see M Milanovic, '*Al-Skeini* and *Al-Jedda* in Strasbourg' (2012) 23 *EJIL* 121.
50 *Al-Jedda*,(n 47) para. 80.
51 See Sicilianos (n 45).

it can spur States parties to draft a more protective framework for the whole operation, as well as create accountability mechanisms to avoid cases being brought before Courts.

A tendency to avoid review of UNSC resolutions can also be seen in the EU. In its first *Kadi*[52] judgment, the Court of First Instance of the EU (now the General Court) decided that it lacked jurisdiction to review EU acts implementing UN resolutions, with the exception of the breach of a *jus cogens* rule.

The Court of First Instance based its reasoning on the superiority of the Charter over all contrary rules of international law enshrined in Article 103 of the UN Charter. However, the decisive argument was based on EU law itself, which required the Union 'to give effect to the SC resolutions concerned, within the sphere of its powers.'[53] The Court concluded that it was not empowered to carry out a review of EU acts implementing a UN resolution, for this would be tantamount to an indirect review of the resolution itself, about which the Court has no jurisdiction.

The CFI's conclusion was referred to by the European Court of Human Rights in *Behrami and Saramati*. The Strasbourg Court also relied upon the specific function of the UN in the maintenance of international peace and security to conclude to its lack of jurisdiction. In this line of reasoning, the jurisdiction/attribution question is secondary, because the rationale of the Court's judgment is based on the function and role of the UN. This role is too fundamental to allow for a human rights court to interfere in its workings. This immunity extends to 'voluntary acts of the respondent States' such as 'the contribution of troops to the security mission' which are 'crucial to the effective fulfilment by the UNSC of its Chapter VII mandate and, consequently, by the UN of its imperative peace and security aim.'[54]

3.2 Harmonious interpretation of international obligations

In these cases, the Charter provisions on the UN's aim to promote the respect of human rights and the Security Council obligation to 'act in accordance with the Purposes and Principles of the United Nations'[55] were used to argue that the UN can do no wrong since it is itself bound to respect human rights. However, it can be argued that these provisions entitle Courts to exert a control over the respect by the UN of its own obligations.

The ECtHR's later case-law is based on a supposed lack of contradiction between international obligations of States under the UN Charter and the ECtHR. With this 'harmonious interpretation' of international obligations,

52 Case T-315/01 *Kadi v Council and Commission* [2005] ECR-II 03649 (hereinafter CFI, *Kadi I*), see also Chapter 10 in this book.

53 Cf *Kadi I* (n 52), para. 207.

54 *Behrami and Saramati* (n 41) para. 149.

55 Art. 24 para. 2 United Nations Charter.

the Court tries to avoid a confrontation when it is possible. International obligations have to be reconciled as far as possible to avoid contradiction. The Court found a presumption that the Security Council does in principle not expect States to breach their obligations under other international human rights law when carrying out a resolution[56], and that it would have used a 'clear and explicit language' had it intended to. In interpreting a SC resolution, the Court must choose 'choose the interpretation which is most in harmony with the requirements of the Convention and which avoids any conflict of obligations.'[57] The Court thus avoided any definite pronouncement on supremacy or priority between the Convention and obligations arising from the UN Charter thanks to harmonious interpretation.

States parties to the Convention cannot act in a legal void; they have to abide by all their legal obligations when they act, even under the authorisation of a UNSC resolution. Thus the Court ruled that States parties have to abide by their obligation under the Convention when they carry out operations abroad, even in the framework of the United Nations. This case-law of the ECtHR, in which the Court departs from its earlier deference and accepts to review the conformity with the Convention of acts of a State party committed while taking part in an operation authorised by the United Nations, broadens the 'legal space' of the Convention and at the same time is consistent with general international law. Thus it will spur States parties to improve practices of multinational operations in which they take part.

A State party to the ECHR taking part in a UN-authorised operation retains effective control over its troops and is still bound by its obligations under the Convention. The Court does not assess the conformity with the Convention of the resolution itself, but only of the acts of the State Party. It insists on the fact that the resolution had not explicitly obliged the British forces in Iraq to commit the breaches of the Convention, and that the UK had acted autonomously. This insistence on the autonomy of the State in the context of authorised operation is crucial, because the Court was able to judge the case on the merits, while avoiding any direct confrontation with the UN legal order. There was actually no contradiction between UN and ECHR in this case; while acting under UN authorisation, States are still bound by their remaining obligations under international law, and the UNSC does in principle not demand that Member States disregard the obligations under international law while carrying out its resolutions.

The Court tried to keep the same line of reasoning in the very different context of States' implementation of the sanctions regime adopted against individuals and groups linked to Al-Qaida. However this solution cannot apply to the hypothesis of a clear contradiction between State obligations under the UN Charter and the ECHR, in a case where 'clear and explicit'

56 *Al-Jedda* (n 47) para. 102.
57 Ibid.

language would have been used by the Security Council, making the breach of the Convention unavoidable while implementing the resolution.

4 The shift towards full review over acts of states adopted in application of UNSC resolutions

In his conclusions in the appeal lodged by Kadi against the first instance judgement, Advocate General Poiares Maduro proposed a complete change of approach. Basing his reasoning on the *Van Gend en Loos* judgment, in which the Court affirmed the autonomy of the legal order of the EU and asserted that – in the words of the Advocate General – the 'Treaty has created a ***municipal legal order*** of trans-national dimensions, of which it forms the "basic constitutional charter"'.[58] The Advocate General argued that, given the lack of judicial review of decisions on individual sanctions at the UN level, 'the only option available to individuals who wish to have access to an independent tribunal in order to obtain adequate protection of their fundamental rights is to challenge domestic implementing measures before a domestic court'.[59]

This fundamental shift was confirmed by the ECJ in the Appeal judgment[60], in which it established that 'the obligations imposed by an international agreement cannot have the effect of prejudicing the constitutional principles of the EC Treaty, which include the principle that all Community acts must respect fundamental rights…', while not recognizing any immunity from judicial review to regulations implementing UN Security Council resolutions. The Court judged that the delisting procedure of the sanctions regime 'does not offer the guarantees of judicial protection' because it was 'still in essence diplomatic and intergovernmental'.[61] The Court grounded its judgment on constitutional principles of the EU: the respect of fundamental rights, and thus the duty of courts to review decisions, even if implementing UN resolutions.[62]

The implementation of individual sanctions also came to the fore in the *Nada* case of the ECtHR[63], concerning the application of UNSC sanctions

58 Case C-402/05 *Kadi and Al-Barakaat v Council and Commission* [2008] ECR I-06351, Opinion of AG Poiares Maduro, para. 21.
59 Ibid., para. 38.
60 Case C-402/05 *Kadi and Al-Barakaat v Council and Commission* [2008] ECR I-06351 (hereinafter ECJ *Kadi I*).
61 ECJ *Kadi I* (n 60) para. 323.
62 'the Community judicature must (…) ensure the review, in principle the full review, of the lawfulness of all Community acts in the light of the fundamental rights (…) including review of Community measures which (…) are designed to give effect to the resolutions adopted by the Security Council under Chapter VII of the Charter of the United Nations. Ibid., para. 326.
63 *Nada v Switzerland* (App no 10593/08) 2012 ECHR (GC).

following resolution 1267 by Switzerland against an Egyptian-Italian national who lived in an Italian enclave surrounded by Swiss territory.

Contrary to the case of *Al-Jedda*, the set of resolutions in the *Nada* case obliged them to adopt sanctions against certain persons nominally listed in the annex. Both the measures and the addressees were determined by the resolutions.

The Swiss Federal Tribunal (hereinafter SFT) underlined that the resolutions on sanctions are binding on all States, that they 'are described in detail and afford member States no margin of appreciation in their implementation'[64], and that Switzerland would be in breach of its obligations under the Charter were it not giving effect to restrictive measures against the applicant. The Tribunal decided that Switzerland was bound by the sanctions regime of the UN and as such, could not grant Nada the right to judicial review of the Swiss measures taken against him, for a complete judicial review would entail the possibility for the reviewing Tribunal to annul the Swiss measures implementing the resolutions, and thus lead to a breach of its obligations by Switzerland. It concluded that only the Sanctions Committee can decide upon the delisting of a person or entity. The Tribunal chose a deferential approach towards the UN system, without even trying to reconcile Switzerland's obligations under the sanctions regime on the one hand, and under its own constitution, the ECHR and the ICCPR on the other, even though it acknowledged that the delisting procedure did not meet international human rights standards.[65]

Thereafter, the ECtHR distinguished this case from the *Al-Jedda* case-law, where the resolution left the State some discretion, and judged that the presumption of conformity 'is rebutted in the present case, having regard to the clear and explicit language, imposing an obligation to take measures capable of breaching human rights'.[66] However, the Court found that Switzerland had some leeway and could have applied the sanctions against Nada so as to respect his rights under the Convention. In the Court's view, Switzerland should have tried to take 'all possible measures to the applicant's individual situation.'[67]

Even if the legal context of the case differed in at least one important respect from the *Al-Jedda* precedent – the resolutions on sanctions laid down detailed obligations that the State could not escape, and did not merely authorise the State to act – the Court resorted to the harmonious interpretation of the obligations of the State under the Convention and the Charter, and decided that it dispensed 'from determining the question (…) of the hierarchy between the obligations of the States Parties to the Convention under that instrument, on the one hand, and those arising from the United Nations

64 Ibid., para. 50.
65 Ibid.
66 Ibid., para. 172.
67 Ibid., para. 196.

Charter, on the other. In the Court's view, the important point is that the respondent Government have failed to show that they attempted, as far as possible, to harmonise the obligations that they regarded as divergent.'[68]

The Court avoided addressing the thorny question of the hierarchy of norms and resolution of unsolvable contradictions between UN resolutions and the ECHR at this stage, by artificially finding that Switzerland had had a room for manoeuvre.[69] The Court extended the reasoning of its earlier case-law on *Al-Jedda* to a very different legal context, even though it itself underlined that difference.

However, the Court found that the refusal of the Federal Tribunal to review the legality of the Swiss measures implementing the resolution amounted to a violation of the right to an effective remedy under Article 13 ECHR.[70] In a reference to the *Kadi* Appeal judgment, the ECtHR judged that it belonged to Swiss courts to carry out a judicial review of the administrative acts implementing sanctions against the applicant.[71] The Court decided that the same reasoning as in *Kadi* must be applied, and 'that there was nothing in the Security Council resolutions to prevent the Swiss authorities from introducing mechanisms to verify the measures taken at national level pursuant to those resolutions.'[72]

By this direct reference to *Kadi*, and condemnation of Switzerland for breach of Article 13, the ECtHR judged that it is the duty of States parties to provide addressees of sanctions with an effective remedy.

This judgement has ground-breaking potential, because contrary to the Court of Justice of the EU, the ECtHR has no 'internal' legal order. States parties have the obligation to provide an effective remedy against violations of the Convention, even if these violations arise from measures implementing a resolution of the Security Council which is binding for that State.[73]

5 The influence of the case-law on the UN sanctions regime

The Security Council Sanctions Committee acknowledged the 'challenge' to the sanctions regime made by the case-law of European Courts.[74] At the

68 Ibid., para. 197.

69 See *Nada*, concurring opinion of Judge Malinverni, para. 8–10.

70 Art. 13 ECHR: 'Right to an effective remedy. Everyone whose rights and freedoms as set forth in this Convention are violated shall have an effective remedy before a national authority notwithstanding that the violation has been committed by persons acting in an official capacity.'

71 *Nada* (n 63) para. 212.

72 Ibid.

73 For a detailed account of the mutual influence of Strasbourg and Luxembourg courts, see F Fabbrini, J Larik, 'Global Counter-terrorism Sanctions and European Due Process Rules: The Dialogue between the CJEU and the ECtHR' in M Avbelj, F Fontanelli, G Martinico (eds), *Kadi on Trial – A Multifaceted Analysis of the Kadi Trial* (Routledge 2014) 137.

74 The 2008 report stresses that 'the sanctions regime (is) under challenge' and that the sanctions are at a 'legal crossroads'. Report of the Analytical Support and Sanctions Monitoring

time when the appeals against the CFI judgment before the CJEU were still pending, the conclusions by AG Poiares Maduro raised the interest of the Sanctions Committee, in particular his assertion on the need for a 'genuine and effective mechanism of judicial control by an independent tribunal at the level of the United Nations'.[75]

The Committee reported on the Advocate General's opinion that the European regulation implementing the sanctions infringed the EU's due process and human rights standards, in particular the right to be heard, the right to effective judicial review by an independent tribunal and the right to property. The Committee was concerned that national and European Courts would undermine the efficiency of sanctions. Their review of acts of executive authorities implementing sanctions could lead to their annulment, and thus to gaps in the fight against terrorism.[76]

The Committee considered that it had realised some improvements to its procedures but acknowledged that a 'major issue' – *i.e.* 'the suggestion that listing decisions by the Committee be subject to review by an independent panel' – remained. It also reckoned that it would be almost impossible to secure the Security Council's agreement to such a body which would entail a limitation of its freedom of action.[77]

At the same time, some improvements have been brought to the delisting procedures of the Sanctions Committee. A 'focal point' was created by resolution 1730 (2006) to receive requests for delisting from individuals or entities on the Sanctions Committee's lists.

The creation of Office of the Ombudsperson[78] was a more significant step in the improvement of the status of listed individuals before the Committee. Targeted individuals have the possibility to have their case heard by an independent body. Moreover, if the ombudsperson recommends the delisting of the petitioner to the Sanctions Committee, the petitioner is delisted unless the Committee refuses it by consensus. This rule of negative consensus is favourable to the petitioner. The opposition of one single member of the Committee to his continuing presence on the list is enough to ensure his delisting. However, if there is no consensus a Committee member can ask the petition to be referred to the Security Council for a decision.

Even if this is an improvement in comparison to the earlier situation, this procedure is still not tantamount to a fair trial. The petition is examined and followed upon by the ombudsperson (appointed by the Secretary General,

Team pursuant to resolution 1735 (2006) concerning Al-Qaida and the Taliban and associated individuals and entities, doc. S/2008/324, para. 39.

75 *Kadi I,* Opinion of Advocate General Poiares Maduro (n 60) para. 54.

76 2008 Report (n 74), para. 40.

77 Ibid., para. 41.

78 The Office of the Ombudsperson was created by Security Council resolution 1904, adopted on 17 December 2009. Its mandate was further extended by resolutions 1989 (17 June 2011), 2083 (17 December 2012) and 2161 (17 June 2014).

hence independent from the Member States), but the decision lies with political bodies, the Sanctions Committee and ultimately the Security Council, which can still block a delisting procedure.

The matter came back before EU courts as a new claim against the EU regulations adopted after the Appeals judgement of 2008 was brought. The General Court held in its 2010 *Kadi II* ruling that the Security Council had not established 'an independent and impartial body responsible for hearing and determining, as regards matters of law and fact, actions against individual decisions taken by the Sanctions Committee.'[79] In particular, the fact that the decision to remove a person from the list still lies with the Committee and the Security Council, as well as the limitations on the right of the targeted individual to be informed of the evidence held against him led to the General Court's conclusion that the creation of the focal point and the Office of the Ombudsperson 'cannot be equated with the provision of an effective judicial procedure for review of decisions of the Sanctions Committee.'[80]

However, the General Court's judgment was rendered before the latest amendments to the procedure brought about by resolution 1989 (2011) of 17 June 2012 introducing the rule of negative consensus. These changes raised hopes in the Sanctions Committee for an end to the legal challenge by the ECJ, in particular following the opinion of Advocate General Bot.[81] In his opinion, the Advocate General reckoned that the establishment of the Office of the Ombudsperson 'has made it possible to raise the quality of the list considerably' and that it 'would be paradoxical if the Court failed to take account of the improvements to which it has directly contributed, even though the Office of the Ombudsperson is not a judicial body.'[82]

However, in the *Kadi II*[83] case, the Court rejected the appeal by the Council and confirmed the operative part of the judgment. The Court examined thoroughly the internal legality of the measure.[84] The Court underlined that this full review is made necessary by the inadequacies of the delisting procedure before the Sanctions Committee, despite the improvements. Referring to the *Nada* judgment of the ECtHR[85], the Court held that the procedure does not give the targeted individual the guarantee of effective judicial protection.

The Court considered that the 'essence of effective judicial protection' should 'enable the person concerned to obtain a declaration from a court (…) that the listing of his name, or the continued listing of his name, on

79 Case T-85/09, *Kadi/Commission* [2010] ECR II-05177, para. 128.
80 Ibid.
81 Fourteenth report of the Analytical Support and Sanctions Monitoring Team submitted pursuant to resolution 2083 (2012) concerning Al-Qaida and associated individuals and entities, doc. S/2013/467.
82 Case C-584/10P, *Commission and Others v Kadi*, Opinion of Advocate General Bot, para. 83
83 Case C-584/10P, *Commission and others v Kadi*, 18 July 2013, Electronic Reports 2013 (CJEU *Kadi II*).
84 Ibid., para. 119.
85 *Nada v Switzerland* (n 63).

the list concerned was vitiated by illegality, the recognition of which may re-establish the reputation of that person or constitute for him a form of reparation for the non-material harm he has suffered.'[86]

For the ECJ, full judicial review is indispensable to ensure a fair balance between the maintenance of international peace and security and the protection of the fundamental rights and freedoms of the person concerned, and emphasises that fundamental rights and freedoms are shared values of the United Nations and the European Union.[87]

6 Conclusion

The CJEU and the ECtHR exercised a two-fold influence: a direct influence on the Sanctions Committee and the Security Council, which led them to acknowledge the challenge and the need to improve the procedural guarantees, and an indirect influence via Member States, who had to avoid being caught between contradictory commitments.

However, the destabilising effect of the CJEU case-law on the UN legal order should not be overestimated. The CJEU in the *Kadi I* judgment did not annul the regulation outright but left time to the institutions to react and adopt a new regulation. This new regulation was also annulled, but that did happen only after the name of Mr. Kadi had been erased from the UN list anyway. In practice in the whole *Kadi* case there has been no actual contradiction of obligations for the EU or its Member States.[88] Moreover, the probability of contradiction remains low. This is not least due to the improvement of the delisting procedure under judicial pressure. Indeed, even if the procedure is not equivalent to effective judicial review, *de facto* it works quite well. The probability for a listed person asking for his name to be removed to obtain a positive response is high.[89]

In the case of ECtHR judgment on acts committed by State organs in the framework of an UN-authorised operation, there is no direct contradiction either, as States – the UK in the *Al-Jedda* case – had some freedom of action and were not obliged under the terms of the relevant resolution to perform acts violating the Convention. The Strasbourg Court in *Nada* even avoided finding contradictions in the case of targeted sanctions, resorting to the State's obligation to interpret its obligations under the Convention and the

86 Ibid., para. 133.

87 Ibid., para. 113. For an in-depth analysis of the scope of judicial review, see E de Wet, 'From *Kadi* to *Nada*: Judicial Techniques Favoring Human Rights over United Nations Security Council Sanctions' (2013) 12 *Chinese Journal of International Law* 787, 793–798.

88 J Kokott, C Sobotta, 'The *Kadi* case – Constitutional Core Values and International Law – Finding the Balance?' (2012) 23 *EJIL* 1015, 1017, describing the CJEU as 'dualist, but ready to compromise'. For a critical assessment of this solution, see M Avbelj, 'The Case of Mr. Kadi and the Modern Concept of Law' in Avbelj, Fontanelli, Martinico (n 73), 49, 57.

89 Ex: according to the Sanctions Committee report for 2014 (doc. S/2014/923), the Committee decided on 10 cases; in eight cases delisting was granted, it was refused in two.

UN Charter in a harmonious way, even if it was hardly possible in this case. Both Courts thus attempted to provide a review of EU or State acts without hurting the effectiveness of the UN sanctions regime in practice.

The improvements in the Sanctions Committee were brought about by the challenges of regional constitutional courts to domestic measures adopted to implement the resolutions. Regional constitutionalisation realises some core constitutional functions at a regional level and at the same time challenges the global governance system. This challenge forces in turn the global governance level to adopt at least some 'constitutional' elements, albeit in a rudimentary manner. Even though the review mechanism of the Sanctions Committee is still far from regional-constitutional standards of fair trial, it constitutes the first procedural limitations to the political power of the Security Council.

Regional constitutionalisation is causing a bottom-up spread of constitutional norms and values. The mechanisms for the judicial protection of individual rights are still weak, however necessary. As governmental functions are being exercised by UNSC, judicial checks and balances should exist at this level. Constitutionalisation in the sense of the development of rule of law and judicial review at the global level should be the natural consequence of the increase of executive functions exercised on this level.

This spread of norms between regional and global legal systems invites a parallel with European constitutionalisation and the acceptation of supremacy of EU law by domestic Courts. In both cases, there is no strict hierarchy, relations are not based on provisions giving priority to one or the other system, but the precedence is based on substantive criteria and respect for core constitutional values, such as liberty, democracy and respect for human rights and fundamental freedoms (Article 6(1) TEU)[90] and effective judicial protection.[91]

Constitutionalisation has been evolving in a decentralised way and results in conflicts of hierarchy and precedence caused by contradictory constitutional claims. Indeed, the case-law of European courts shows that to determine precedence, the constitutional norms and values are more important than a supposed hierarchy between global and regional levels. This substantive approach[92], while in some way undermining the authority of the UN, is open to dialogue and accommodation. The hierarchy between orders and institutions is flexible. It is a hierarchy based on the content of norms and their ability to reflect constitutional values more than a vertical hierarchy between universal and regional or federal and State orders.

90 CJEU *Kadi I*, para. 303.
91 CJEU *Kadi II*, para. 133–34.
92 See Paulus (n 17) 87.

6 International constitutionalisation of protection of privacy on the internet

The *Google* case example

Krystyna Kowalik-Bańczyk

1 Introduction

One of the most pressing problems regarding the use of the world wide web or Internet[1] is recently the question of legal protection of the privacy of Internet users[2]. After more than two decades of functioning of this media, there are several strong judicial signals that the Internet cannot be left alone to market powers but requires just the same amount of constitutional protection of individuals as any other media[3]. It has been underlined by the General Assembly of United Nations in its resolution of December 2013[4], however for the time being the main initiative remains in hands of courts and not legislators, giving an impression that the judicial action precedes the legislative response. In this text one decision of the Court of Justice of the European Union (CJEU) that has particular international implications will be exposed, namely the *Google Spain* case[5]. This decision echoes the proposed legislative solution of EU in the form of a new General Data Protection Regulation

1 According to Advocate General Jääskinen the better notion would be "world wide web" but it is at present common to use the word "Internet" – Opinion of AG of 25 June 2013 in case C-131/12 *Google Spain SL, and Google Inc. v Agencia Española de Protección de Datos (AEPD) and Mario Costeja González* ECLI:EU:C:2014:317, para. 1.

2 Cf broadly Oreste Pollicino and Marco Bassini, 'Reconciling Right to be Forgotten and Freedom of Information in the Digital Age. Past and Future of Personal Data Protection in the European Union' (2014) 2 *Diritto Pubblico Comparato Italiano ed Europeo* 640.

3 Case C-131/12 *Google Spain SL and Google Inc. v Agencia Española de Protección de Datos (AEPD) and Mario Costeja González* ECLI:EU:C:2014:317, cf also the joint cases C-293/12 *Digital Rights Ireland Ltd v Minister for Communications, Marine and Natural Resources and Others* and C-594/12 *Kärntner Landesregierung* ECLI:EU:C:2014:238; Stefano Rodotà, 'An Internet Bill of Rights?' *EUTOPIA Ideas for Europe Magazine* 31 May 2014 <http://eutopiamagazine/eu> accessed 17 August 2015. The specificity of harm to constitutional values due to the use of internet are visible in: *Editorial Board of Pravoye Delo v Ukraine* (33014/05) ECtHR judgment 5 May 2011.

4 Resolution of the General Assembly of United Nations of 18 December 2013 'The Right to Privacy in the Digital Age,' UN Doc. A/RES/68/167 <http://www.un.org/en/ga/search/view_doc.asp?symbol=A/RES/68/167> accessed 27 March 2016. This resolution should be perceived as an interpretative declaration that should influence the construction of all existing international treaties and above all the International Covenant on Civil and Political Rights as encapsulating also the right to privacy in the digital means.

5 Case C-131/12 *Google Spain* (n 3).

drafted in 2012[6] that is to be introduced soon[7]. In the Proposal of Regulation the offering of goods or services to data subjects residing in the European Union should be a factor making EU data protection law applicable to third country controllers. This would spread the territorial application of EU legislation to the entities from outside the EU[8]. Whereas the case of *Google Spain* concerns one aspect of privacy protection that is called a right to be forgotten, it has been questioned while preparing the Regulation. In October 2013 the Regulation was discussed to include rather a right to "erasure"[9], but this proposal was not retained in the final version of Regulation. Perhaps one of the reasons for this discussion was a strong criticism expressed by the American doctrine as to the implications of such right for the freedom of expression[10]. The balance between the privacy and freedom of expression is very differently drafted in different parts of the world. The clearest example of very different approach to the balance of privacy versus free speech is the approach of the United States: as Andrej Savin puts it: "what is criminally punishable hate speech in Germany is constitutionally protected in the United States"[11]. In this text we will only focus on one aspect of protection of privacy – namely the possibility of erasing from Internet search engines the possibility of access to data that might put an individual in negative light in his or her perception.

6 The new legislative framework for personal data protection was proposed on 25 January 2012, COM (2012) 9 final, *Safeguarding Privacy in a Connected World A European Data Protection Framework for the 21st Century* <http://eur-lex.europa.eu/LexUriServ/LexUriServ.do?uri=COM:2012:0009:FIN:EN:PDF> accessed 17 August 2015; and COM (2012) 12 final, *Proposal for a Regulation of the European Parliament and of the Council on the protection of individuals with regard to the processing of personal data and on the free movement of such data (General Data Protection Regulation)* <http://ec.europa.eu/justice/data-protection/document/review2012/com_2012_11_en.pdf> accessed 17 August 2015.

7 'Progress on EU Data Protection Reform now irreversible following European Parliament vote', European Commission – MEMO/14/186, 12 March 2014 <http://europa.eu/rapid/press-release_MEMO-14-186_en.htm> accessed 17 August 2015.

8 Opinion of AG of 25 June 2013 in case C-131/12 *Google Spain* (n 1) para. 56. As underlined by Advocate General such extender territorial applicability appears already in cases of cross-border situations in: Directive 2000/31/EC of the European Parliament and of the Council of 8 June 2000 on certain legal aspects of information society services, in particular electronic commerce, in the internal market, [2000] OJ L 178/1 or Directive 2001/29/EC of the European Parliament and of the Council of 22 May 2001 on the harmonisation of certain aspects of copyright and related rights in the information society, [2001] L 167/10.

9 'EU: Right to be Forgotten now the Right to Erasure', <http://www.dataguidance.com/dataguidance_privacy_this_week.asp?id=2119> accessed 17 August 2015. Cf. at present the final proposal of general Regulation <http://www.europarl.europa.eu/RegData/docs_autres_institutions/commission_europeenne/com/2012/0011/COM_COM%282012%290011_EN.pdf> accessed 3 April 2016.

10 J Rosen, 'The Right to be Forgotten' (2012) 64 *Stanford Law Review* 88; S C Bennett, 'The "Right to Be Forgotten": Reconciling EU and US Perspectives' (2012) 30 (1) *Berkeley Journal of International Law* 161.

11 A Savin, *EU Internet Law* (Edward Elgar 2013) 87.

2 The issue of privacy protection in the debate on unification and fragmentation of international law

In order to place this subject in a discussion on unification and fragmentation of international law[12], it is worth underlining, first of all that the protection of privacy should be placed in the context of international human rights protection. However on different judicial forums, this subject is perceived more a subject of international economic law, under the head of free movement of personal data. The recent development of public awareness on the dangers of lack of legal protection of privacy in Internet caused that this issue becomes more a problem of international constitutional law rather than international economic law. Still, any real possibilities to unify the legal solutions in EU-USA relations falls under the hat of Transatlantic Trade and Investment Partnership (TTIP)[13] negotiations. It seems that the "European" approach steers the discussion on privacy in Internet more into human rights context, whereas the "American" approach would be to leave those questions in the sphere of trade law.

In the "fragmentation discussion" it would be worth underlining that the privacy protection on the Internet is strongly linked with the personal data protection rules and it is in this text treated as one issue. However there is as well a strong trend to treat the data protection rules as a separated, fragmented regime, different from the general issues on protection of privacy[14]. This seems to be a wrong approach for several reasons. The personal data is necessary to identify an individual, allow for getting acquainted with someone's life, activity, weaknesses etc., thus therefore they form a necessary part of privacy concerns. It cannot be treated as an issue separated from the question of protection of private life. The privacy, perceived as a protection of one's private life, is a fundamental right that is contained in International Covenant on Civil and Political Rights[15]. Each party to this universal international agreement is obliged to protect it in its own territory and is defining it by its own legislation. There is no unification of the perception of privacy worldwide, yet. Rather the fragmented attitude prevails, with a clear division between the American and European models of protection. The recent *PRISM*[16] scandal has clearly revealed that such a division might be contested

12 As understood in the Report of the Study Group of the International Law Commission, 'Fragmentation of International Law: Difficulties Arising from the Diversification and Expansion of International Law'. UN Doc. A/CN.4/L.702, 18 July 2006, paras 4–9.

13 The latest development of this negotiation was published by the European Commission: Report of the Tenth Round of Negotiations for the Transatlantic Trade and Investment Partnership (Brussels, 13–17 July 2015) <http://trade.ec.europa.eu/doclib/docs/2015/july/tradoc_153667.pdf> accessed 17 August 2015.

14 L A Bygrave, *Data Privacy Law. An International Perspective* (OUP 2014); C Kuner, *Transborder Data Flows and Data Privacy Law* (OUP 2013).

15 Adopted on 16 December 1966, entered into force on 23 March 1976, 999 UNTS 171 and 1057 UNTS 407.

16 PRISM is a mass electronic surveillance data mining program, operated clandestinely by the National Security Agency of the United States from 2007 until its disclosure by Edward

by the international community if one country offers no protection for citizens of other countries. This biggest secret surveillance scandal in the United States showed clearly that the use of the Internet gives privacy infringements an international dimension. The constitutional rights of citizens of different countries in the world have been infringed by another country[17]. The business entities that provided access to the data were obliged to disclose the information to the public services of the US. This case also clearly illustrates that literally anyone using the Internet can be under surveillance, regardless of the national jurisdiction he or she is covered by. In the meantime it is still very difficult to clearly define the applicability of certain jurisdictions to privacy infringements[18].

Therefore it might be presumed that a certain alignment of national legal solutions on protection of privacy in internet will have to occur, either in bottom up development or by top down initiatives (new international agreement). Such agreements on specific issues connected with personal data transfers have already been negotiated and concluded between USA and EU as far as passenger name records or information about money transfers are concerned[19]. Those specific agreements might now be questioned as perhaps not in line with the general requirement to protect private life of individuals.

The new possibility of international use of the right to be forgotten, provided by the case of *Google Spain*, might be a good example of international constitutionalisation of that right. Despite the fact that the right to privacy is naturally subject to constitutional pluralism[20] (it is protected parallelly under different regimes, both national and international), the case of *Google Spain* might bring about a possibility of unification of interpretation of such constitutional rights worldwide. Perhaps in the future it might even bring about an alignment in national and regional legal regimes, thus allowing for overcoming

Snowden on 6 June 2013 in The Guardian and The Washington Post. Cf also: C Bowden, *The US Surveillance Programmes and their Impact on EU Citizens' Fundamental Rights*. Note (Directorate General for Internal Policies, European Parliament's Committee on Civil Liberties, Justice and Home Affaires 2013) 13 <www.europarl.europa.eu/studies> accessed 17 April 2016.

17 See K Kowalik-Bańczyk, 'Les Aspects Transfrontaliers des Infractions à la Vie Privée par la Surveillance de Masse de la Part des Agences Étatiques' (2015) 2 *RGDIP* 383.

18 O Pollicino, M Bassini, 'Internet Law in the Era of Transnational Law' (2011) 24 *EUI RSCA* Global Governance Programme, <http://www.eui.eu/Projects/GGP/Documents/Publications/WorkingPapers/RSCAS201124revOPollicinoMBassini.pdf> accessed 15 April 2016.

19 The Agreement between the United States of America and the European Union on the use and transfer of Passenger Name Records to the United States Department of Homeland Security [2012] OJ L 215/5; the Agreement between the European Union and the United States of America on the processing and transfer of Financial Messaging Data from the European Union to the United States for the purposes of the Terrorist Finance Tracking Program [2010] OJ L 8/11.

20 As it is the case within European Union, cf K Lenaerts, 'EU Values and Constitutional Pluralism: The EU System of Fundamental Rights Protection' (2014) 34 *PYIL* 129.

the fragmentation of international law. The possible collisions between distinct regimes of privacy protection might therefore be better avoided and it might also prevent further erosions within the system of international law. It confirms the theory that the initial fragmentation is a natural step towards a broader coherence[21] and in the presented case it shows how the first draft of the international constitutionalisation of right to privacy might occur[22], leading to what Cançadi Trinidade called "humanization of international law"[23].

3 The privacy versus data protection in EU law

The notion of privacy has different definitions in different legal cultures. For the sake of gaining a quasi-universal approach to this value, it is useful to look at the definition invoked in the Resolution of General Association of United Nations of December 2013, where it is stated that the "human right to privacy" means that "no one shall be subjected to arbitrary or unlawful interference with his or her privacy, family, home or correspondence, and the right to the protection of the law against such interference"[24].

In Europe privacy is perceived through the idea of auto-determination of the information that one would want to deliver to others (to the public)[25]. It is defined as the "ability to withhold information about oneself or, put differently, the ability to have a secluded sphere of life and to select which parts of one's life will be public"[26]. In the legislation of the EU the solutions concerning privacy and protection of personal data reflected the solutions first adopted by the Council of Europe[27], but of course the European Union's *acquis* is much more detailed and modern[28]. The directive 95/46[29] is directly inspired by the Convention no 108 of the Council of Europe of 1981. The

21 R Deplano, 'Fragmentation and Constitutionalisation of International Law: A Theoretical Inquiry' (2013) 6 *EJLS* 67.

22 A Peters, 'Compensatory Constitutionalism, The Function and Potential of Fundamental International Norms and Structures' (2006) 19 *LJIL* 579.

23 A A Cançado Trindade, *International Law for Humankind: Towards a New Jus Gentium* (2nd edn., Nijhoff 2013).

24 UN Doc. A/RES/68/167 (n 4).

25 Starting with the judgment of the German Federal Constitutional Tribunal *Volkszählung (Microcensus)* of 1984, BVerfGE 65, 1. On this line of jurisprudence cf Jacqueline Ross, 'Germany's Federal Constitutional Court and the Regulation of GPS surveillance' (2005) 6 (12) *German Law Journal* 1805, 1809–1810.

26 Savin, EU Internet Law (n 11).

27 Convention for the Protection of Individuals with regard to Automatic Processing of Personal Data no 108, Strasbourg, 28 January 1981 <http://conventions.coe.int> accessed 17 August 2015.

28 J Kokott, C Sobotta, 'The Distinction between Privacy and Data Protection in the Jurisprudence of the CJEU and the ECHR' (2013) 3(4) *International Data Privacy Law* 222.

29 Directive 95/46/EC of the European Parliament and of the Council of 24 October 1995 on the protection of individuals with regard to the processing of personal data and on the free movement of such data [1995] L 281/31.

Charter of Fundamental Rights in its Articles 7 and 8 provides directly effective provisions on the protection of private life and personal data[30]. According to the Court of Justice of the European Union (further: CJEU) the protection of private life under the Charter of Fundamental Rights covers "all information relating to an individual irrespective of whether he acts in a purely private sphere or as an economic operator"[31].

On the other hand, we use the notion of personal data. Some personal information defined as personal data are at present constantly processed by automatic means[32]. As explained by Advocate General Jääskinen in his Opinion to *Google Spain,* there are three situations relating to the use of personal data on the Internet: 1) the publishing of elements of personal data on any webpage (source web page); 2) the provision of search results by the internet search engine, directing to the source web page; 3) performance by internet user of a search using an internet search engine, where the personal data of the seeker is transferred to the internet search engine service provider[33]. The internet search engine is thus just an intermediary in the transmission of possible personal data or in fact any data available[34], however they are "in the unique position of power, with the ability to introduce private control, in the form of filtering or self-cenzoring measures"[35].

There is a natural question on the relationship between the notions of privacy and personal data. It is certain that the introduction of protection of personal data in both US and EU was steered by a need to protect private life of data subject. Therefore the concept of privacy englobes the concept of protection of personal data, even if the legal regime of personal data protection is much more nuanced than the traditional ways of protecting privacy[36]. On the other hand, the personal data possess an important economic value and are even called by the European Commission "the currency of today's digital economy"[37]. Still, in the context of use of internet, the fusion between

30 According to Art. 52.3 of the Charter, those provisions have to be constructed in accordance with the European Convention on Human Rights – cf A Wróbel 'Commentary to Art. 52' in A Wróbel (ed), *Karta Praw Podstawowych Unii Europejskiej. Komentarz* [Charter of Fundamental Rights of the European Union. A Commentary] (C.H. Beck 2013) 1362–1369.

31 Cases C-92/09 and C-93/09 *Volker and Markus Schecke and Eifert*, [2010] ECR I-11063, para. 52; Opinion of AG Jääskinen of 25 June 2013 in case C-131/12 *Google Spain* (n 1), para. 118.

32 Case C-101/01 *Lindqvist* [2003] ECR I-12971.

33 Opinion of AG Jääskinen of 25 June 2013 (n 1) para. 3.

34 Intermediaries are understood as actors that enable the flow of information between those that create the information and those who receive it, cf Savin, *EU Internet Law* (n 11) 104.

35 Savin, *EU Internet Law* (n 11) 106.

36 Kokott, Sobotta (n 28) 222–228; cf Directive 95/46/EC of the European Parliament and of the Council of 24 October 1995 on the protection of individuals with regard to the processing of personal data and on the free movement of such data [1995] L 281/31, para. 10 of the preamble.

37 'The value of European citizens' personal data has the potential to grow to nearly €1 trillion annually by 2020' the European Commission declares in press communication Memo 14–186 of 12 March 2014 *Progress on EU data protection reform now irreversible following European*

the protection of private life and protection of personal data is very visible[38], despite the distinction made between Article 7 and 8 of the Charter. In the opinion of Advocate General in case *Digital Ireland and Seitlinger*[39]:

> 65. There are, however, data which are in a sense more than personal. These are data which, qualitatively, relate essentially to private life, to the confidentiality of private life, including intimacy. In such cases, the issue raised by personal data commences, so to speak, further 'upstream'. The issue which arises in such cases is not yet that of the guarantees relating to data processing but, at an earlier stage, that of the data as such, that is to say, the fact that it has been possible to record the circumstances of a person's private life in the form of data, data which can consequently be subject to information processing.
> 66. It is in that sense that it is possible to argue that, when such data are involved, they raise an issue which essentially precedes that of their processing, relating primarily to the privacy guaranteed by Article 7 of the Charter and only secondarily to the guarantees concerning the processing of personal data referred to in Article 8 of the Charter.

On the international level there is only a very general legal basis for the protection of personal life (in form of the Covenant), with no clear distinction between private life and personal data protection issues. It would be thus advisable to create a new international agreement, named by some authors "digital bill of rights"[40], but it is still just a very vague project of the doctrine.

4 *Google* case as an example of universal judicial influence on solutions worldwide

One of the latest examples of spread of the European way of protecting the privacy, that influences also the developments in other judicial fora is the CJEU *Google Spain* case that can be perceived as a good illustration of a bottom up development – a judicial solution that might in near future influence the development of both national and international regulations. A judicial action rather than a legislative action might influence the way the privacy as a constitutional value is protected worldwide. In the meantime, the privacy

Parliament vote <http://europa.eu/rapid/press-release_MEMO-14-186_en.htm> accessed 17 August 2015.

38 Case C-324/09 *L'Oréal and Others* [2011] ECR I-06011, paras 62 and 63.

39 Opinion of the Advocate General in joint cases C-293/12 *Digital Rights Ireland* and C-594/12 *Seitlinger*, paras 65–66.

40 Suggested by: D. Bigo, S. Carrera, N. Hernanz, J. Jeandesboz, J. Parkin, F. Ragazzi, A. Scherrer, '*National Programmes for Mass Surveillance of Personal Data in EU Member States and their Compatibility with EU Law. Study*' (Directorate General For Internal Policies. Policy Department Citizens' Rights and Constitutional Affaires, September 2013) 9 <www.europarl.europa.eu/studies> accessed 17 August 2015.

is just one of many values that need to be protected on the Internet, next to freedom of expression, freedom of information and freedom to conduct a business[41]. What is interesting in *Google* case is that as its result the balancing of imminently constitutional values are left in hands of business entities and thus the exercise of protection of constitutional values is put on the entities that are not prepared nor interested in such actions. The obligation to undertake this type of balancing is imposed by a court towards undertakings that are not necessarily placed in the European Union. Yet, the internet, unlike any other media, is blurring the divide between the public and private law issues – and this paradoxically has impact on the international level.

The *Google Spain* case concerned a situation where an internet search engine (Google Inc and its Spanish version – Google Spain, further both referred to as: Google) provided search results on Mister Mario Costeja González, that directed any internet user to the source web pages of a Spanish newspaper from 1998. Mister González contested the accessibility of those pages, stating that the information contained therein was no longer relevant and should no longer be displayed[42]. The case occurred in front of CJEU as a preliminary request from Audiencia Nacional (the National High Court of Spain) directed during the proceedings between Google Spain SL and Google Inc and the Agencia Española de Protección de Datos and Mr González. The proceedings concerned the application of the Data Protection Directive[43] to an internet search engine that Google operates as service provider. The Agencia issued a decision ordering Google Spain and Google Inc to withdraw the data from their index and to make further access impossible. Google appealed this decision and the National High Court of Spain decided to ask three questions, concerning 1) the territorial scope of application of EU data protection rules, 2) the legal position of an internet search engine service provider and 3) the right to be forgotten and the problem if data subjects can request that some or all search results concerning them are no longer accessible through search engine. Not all of those questions asked will be relevant for this analysis – we will concentrate on the questions concerning the territorial scope of application of EU data protection rules[44] and the implications of protection of privacy in a form of a right to be forgotten.

41 O Pollicino, M Bassini, 'Freedom of Expression and Defamation in Internet' in A Savin, J Trzaskowski (eds), *Research Handbook on EU Internet Law* (Edward Elgar 2014) 508.

42 It consisted of two announcements in "La Vanguardia" concerning a real-estate auction connected with attachment proceedings prompted by social security debts. The data subject was mentioned as the owner. At a later date an electronic version of the newspaper was made available online by its publisher.

43 Directive 95/46/EC of the European Parliament and of the Council of 24 October 1995 on the protection of individuals with regard to the processing of personal data and on the free movement of such data, [1995] L 281/31.

44 The directive 95/46 that has been object of CJEU interpretation on various occasions, however never on the issues of internet search engines. Cf case C-101/01 *Lindqvist* [2003] ECR I-12971; case C-195/06 *Österreichischer Rundfunk*, [2007] ECR I-08817; case C-73/07

In principle, Google Inc is a Californian firm with subsidiaries in some Member States of the EU (the so called data centres in Ireland, Belgium and Finland). According to Google, no processing of personal data by its search engine does take place in Spain. The firm Google Spain is only a commercial representative of Google for its advertising functions and thus it only processes the personal data relating to its Spanish advertising customers. Google denies performance of any operations on the host servers of the source web pages or collection of information by means of cookies of non-registered users by its search engines. There is therefore a dispute between a Californian firm acting together with its Spanish commercial representative against a Spanish national who requires this company to delete the possibility of finding some particular data by use of the search engine.

In this case an entity from a third country is obliged to protect the privacy of an individual residing in the territory of the European Union, as long as it operates in a way influencing the territory of this individual. The CJEU took a very radical path, departing from a far more moderated opinion of Advocate General. By this judgment the CJEU questioned the judicial *acquis* of ECHR line of judgments on the right to be forgotten as a right that has to step aside in light of the right to information. In cases *Times Newspaper v UK*[45] and later in *Węgrzynowski and Smolczewski v Poland*[46] the ECHR stated that if an information has been published by press, it is not a role of the court to "rewrite history"[47] and improve the online version of the newspaper. The CJEU has not confirmed this position but stated that regardless of the fact that the information is true or false, there should be a possibility to ask for erasure of that information from the results of search on-line. The *Google* case confirms also that the privacy rule of the Charter are of horizontal direct effect[48].

As to the territorial scope of application of directive, it needs first to be understood that the service of Google search is offered worldwide through the website 'www.google.com' with several national versions of this service

Satakunnan Markkinapörssi and Satamedia [2008] ECR I-09831; joined cases C-92/09 and C-93/09 *Volker und Markus Schecke and Eifert* [2010] ECR I-11063. The question of internet search engines appeared in cases on intellectual property rights and jurisdiction of courts: joined cases C-236/08 to C-238/08 *Google France and Google* [2010] ECR I-02417; case C-558/08 *Portakabin Ltd and Portakabin BV v Primakabin BV* [2010] ECR I-06963; case C-324/09 *L'Oréal SA and Others v eBay International AG and Others* [2011] ECR I-06011; case C-323/09 *Interflora Inc. and Interflora British Unit v Marks & Spencer plc and Flowers Direct Online Ltd* [2011] ECR I-08625; case C-523/10 *Wintersteiger AG v Products 4U Sondermaschinenbau GmbH* ECLI:EU:C:2012:220.

45 *Times Newspaper v United Kingdom* (3002/03 and 23676/03) ECtHR judgment 10 March 2009.

46 *Węgrzynowski and Smolczewski v Poland* (33847/07) ECtHR judgment 16 July 2013.

47 Ibid., para. 65.

48 Case C-131/12 *Google Spain* (n 3) para. 69; confirmed recently by the Advocate General and the CJEU in case C-212/13 *Ryneš* ECLI:EU:C:2014:2428.

(like www.google.es). Advocate General Jääskinen proposed to treat the question of territorial applicability of privacy "from the perspective of the business model of internet search engine service providers"[49]. To do this one has to look at keyword advertising as a source of income and the main reason for provision of free information location tool. The entity that is in charge of keyword advertising is usually present on national advertising market. For this reason, Google establishes subsidiaries in EU Member States and provides national web domains, like google.es. Therefore there is an establishment of a controller[50] of data on the territory of a Member State in accordance with Article 4 a) of the directive 95/46. The directive imposes on the Member States an obligation to protect personal data even if "the processing of data is carried out by a person established in a third country"[51]. The CJEU stated that "processing of personal data is carried out in the context of the activities of an establishment of the controller on the territory of a Member State" in cases where the operator of a search engine sets up in a Member State "a branch or subsidiary which is intended to promote and sell advertising space offered by that engine and which orientates its activity towards the inhabitants of that Member State"[52]. Thus it is enough to have a branch or subsidiary that orientates its activity towards a Member State to apply EU law (both directive and the Charter, as it seems). The CJEU stated that given the ease with which an information can be replicated on different sites than the initial one, it would not be effective to ask just the publisher to erase that information from its website[53]. Because the access to information relating to any person is relatively much easier with the list of results displayed by a search engine, such a tool can play a decisive role for dissemination of an information that might interfere with the data subject's fundamental rights[54]. That might be the case even if the publication itself is lawful[55]. The operator of a search engine has been held by the CJEU as obliged to remove from the list of results such links upon a request on an interested person and such a right override both "the economic interest of the operator of the search engine" and "the interest of the general public in finding that information upon a search relating to the data subject's name"[56].

49 Opinion of AG Jääskinen of 25 June 2013 (n 1) para. 64.

50 A "controller" is defined in Art. 2(d) of the Directive 95/46 as "the natural or legal person ... which alone or jointly with others determines the purposes and means of the processing of personal data". The CJEU found that the internet search engine is a controller within the meaning of that provision, cf case C-131/12 (n 3) para. 33.

51 Directive 95/46/EC of the European Parliament and of the Council of 24 October 1995 on the protection of individuals with regard to the processing of personal data and on the free movement of such data [1995] L 281/31, Preamble, para. 20.

52 Case C-131/12 *Google Spain* (n 3) para. 60.

53 Ibid., para. 84.

54 Ibid., para. 87.

55 Ibid., para. 88.

56 (n 52) para. 97.

5 Right to be forgotten applied worldwide?

The Directive 95/46 in its Article 12 (b) provides rights to erasure and blocking of data, accompanied by right to object in Article 14 (a) of the directive. The *Google* case raised the question if the data subject can contact the internet search engine service providers in order to prevent indexing of the information (1) relating to this subject personally, and (2) that has been published on third parties' web pages. The CJEU was to find out whether the right to be forgotten is already contained in the Directive 95/46. As underlined by the Advocate General, the Directive in principle allows for the mechanism, where the data subject claims rectification, erasure and blocking of data that is incomplete or inaccurate[57]. There is therefore no separate, autonomous right to be forgotten in the Directive itself.

The lack of right to be forgotten in the Directive itself led the CJEU and Advocate General to the question whether the provisions of the Charter provide such a right. Two provisions were considered by the Advocate General: Article 7 of the Charter, providing that everyone has the right to respect for his or her private and family life, home and communications and Article 8 of the Charter guarantees everyone the right to the protection of his personal data. What is interesting is that the Advocate General, and further the CJEU have not invoked Article 8 (naturally linked with personal data) but only Article 7 of the Charter[58]. Thus the right to be forgotten is to be perceived as mainly stemming from the right to private life. The interpretation of Article 7 of the Charter needs to be done in light of the jurisprudence of the ECHR, thus particularly the position that "the fundamental right to protection of private life can be invoked even if the information concerned is already in the public domain"[59].

6 Conclusions

The controversies over *Google* case are visible already in the differences between the position of the Advocate General and the Court. Whereas the Advocate was in principle against the admittance that search engines are controlling the data they provide, the CJEU stated that search engines are controlling the personal data. The Advocate was of the opinion that the right to be forgotten should not lead to denial of the right to information by creating a "bowdlerized" version[60] of relevant web pages with information searched by internet user. The CJEU did not consider it any problem. The Advocate was also of the opinion that the "notice and take down procedure" applied to legitimate and legal contents could create a huge burden for the

57 Opinion of AG Jääskinen of 25 June 2013 (n 1) para. 103.

58 Ibid., paras 126–137.

59 *Aleksey Ovchinnikov v Russia* (24061/04) ECtHR judgment 16 December 2010, cited in the Opinion of AG Jääskinen of 25 June 2013 (n 1) para. 127.

60 Opinion of AG Jääskinen of 25 June 2013 (n 1) para. 131.

most popular internet search engine service providers[61] (he even said that they would be saddled with this obligation[62]). The CJEU took an opposite position and imposed this burden on the providers.

The differences between European and American legal approaches to privacy protection are one of the main sources of possible "misuses" of the Internet. The United States stands at the forefront of Internet development. As Andrej Savin writes: "Most of what other jurisdictions do can be interpreted as a response or reaction to a trend that comes from the US"[63]. The contrasts between the US and European approach to privacy and data protection can also show how difficult it is (and probably will remain) to find a common denominator for regulating privacy issues worldwide. The European Union is possibly the only actor able to respond to the American vision for the Internet with its own ideas and solutions (this was plain with the EU's introduction of the e-commerce directive of 2000). Therefore, all initiatives undertaken in the EU have to be contrasted with what is happening on the other side of the globe. The *Google* case, concerning an American undertaking, will certainly raise an echo in US approach to the privacy issues, leading perhaps to working out a common US/EU denominator at least for the issue of the right to be forgotten. It might be a first step towards an international consitutionalisation of rights of Internet users.

61 Ibid., para. 133.
62 Ibid., para. 134.
63 Savin, *EU Internet Law* (n 11) X.

7 The "revival" of sovereignty via the complementarity regime and the "doctrinal" idea of responsibility to protect; what about constitutionalisation?

Maria Varaki

The so called "S" word – sovereignty – has been attacked during the last decades as an impediment to the further realization of a globalized world, sharing common values and promoting universal goals.[1] Scholars tend to abandon the traditional normative understanding of state sovereignty towards a functional one.[2] Within this context, the ontological concept of state sovereignty is conditional upon the fulfillment of certain goals, such as the protection of its own people or otherwise humanity.[3] Concepts like justice, accountability and peace appear to obtain a liberal cosmopolitan normative content accepted by the "international community as a whole" and function as a vehicle of constitutionalisation of international law against the peril of fragmentation.[4]

1 M Reisman, 'Sovereignty and Human Rights in Contemporary International Law' (1990) 84 *AJIL* 866, L Henkin, 'That "S" Word: Sovereignty, and Globalisation, and Human Rights et cetera' (1999–2000) 68 *Fordham Law Review* 1.

2 M Koskenniemi, 'What use for sovereignty today?' (2011) 1 *Asian Journal of International Law* 61.

3 See e.g. A-M Slaughter, 'Security, Solidarity, and Sovereignty: The Grand Themes of UN Reform' (2005) 99 *AJIL* 619, J Waldron, 'Are Sovereigns Entitled to the Benefit of the International Rule of Law?' (2011) 22 *EJIL* 315, A Peters, 'Humanity as the A and Ω of Sovereignty' (2009) 20 *EJIL* 513, T G Weiss, J Chopra, 'Sovereignty under Siege: From Intervention to Humanitarian Space' in Lyons, Mastanduno (eds), *Beyond Westphalia, State Sovereignty and International Intervention* (Johns Hopkins University Press 1995).

4 See e.g., UN Doc. A/CN.4/L.682 (April 13, 2006), M Koskenniemi, P Leino, 'Fragmentation of International Law? Postmodern Anxieties' (2002) 15 *LJIL* 553–579, M Koskenniemi, 'Global Legal Pluralism: Multiple Regimes and Multiple Modes of Thought' *Harvard* 7 (Mar. 5, 2005), E De Wet, 'The Emergence of International and Regional Value Systems as a Manifestation of the Emerging Constitutional Order' (2006) 19 *LJIL* 3, 6–13, and the contributions in the 25th Anniversary Symposium of the *Michigan Journal of International Law* on *Diversity or Cacophony? New Sources of Norms in International Law?* especially by Teubner and Lescano, Hafner; E Benvenisti, G W Downs, 'The Empire's New Clothes: Political Economy and the Fragmentation of International Law' (2007) 60 *Stanford Law Review* 595 and more recently J Klabbers, A Peters, G Ulfstein (eds), *The Constitutionalization of International Law* (OUP 2009), N Krisch, *Beyond Constitutionalism, The Pluralist Structure of Postnational Law* (OUP 2010), JL Dunoff, JP Trachtman, 'A Functional Approach to International Constitutionalization' in Dunoff & Trachtman (eds) *Ruling the World? Constitutionalism, International Law and Global Governance* (CUP 2009).

Yet, both the complementarity regime of the Rome Statute (art.17) and the so called "doctrine" of responsibility to protect, refocus on the concept of state sovereignty as a source of primary responsibility and action in the field of accountability and prevention of gross violations of human rights and humanitarian law where the state carries the primary responsibility of intervention/protection and the international community the residual one.[5] Both concepts are based on the principle of sovereignty as a source not only of rights but also of obligations,[6] where the initial residual responsibility of the international community is translated into enabling others to act in order to rescue those in need or punish the perpetrators of atrocities.[7]

One could argue that there is a well founded consensus that those crimes shock the consciousness of the international community as a whole and the perpetrators of genocide, war crimes, crimes against humanity and ethnic cleansing are considered to be *hostis humanis generis*.[8] This rationale is the drive behind a strong advocacy for impartial and consistent application of the international rule of law in every context irrespective of other important players of the system, mainly state sovereignty and the limits of law against power.[9] Professor Bassiouni, while developing his theory on punishment for *jus cogens* international crimes, refers to a *civitas maxima* which "transcends the interests of the singular" on a common interest in "repressing certain international crimes."[10] This theory carries the common characteristic of a

5 For a comprehensive introduction to both concepts see J T Holmes, 'The Principle of Comlementarity' in R S Lee (ed), *The International Criminal Court: The Making of the Rome Statute Issues, Negotiations, Results* (Nijhoff 1999) and for the development of the principle of complementarity see M. El Zeidy, 'The Principle of Complementarity: A New Machinery to Implement International Criminal Law' (2002) 23 *Michigan Journal of International Law* 869, JK Kleffner, *Complementarity in the Rome Statute and National Criminal Jurisdictions* (OUP 2008) and G Evans, 'From Humanitarian Intervention to the Responsibility to Protect' (2006) 24 *Wisconsin International Law Journal* 703, C Stahn, 'Responsibility to Protect: Political Rhetoric or Emerging Legal Norm?' (2007) 101 *AJIL* 99; for a critical perspective A Orford, *International Authority and the Responsibility to Protect* (OUP 2011).

6 The re-conceptualization of sovereignty as responsibility is attributed to Francis Deng, former Representative of the Secretary-General on internally displaced persons, F Deng et al., *Sovereignty as Responsibility: Conflict Management in Africa* (Brookings Institution Press 1996).

7 It is beyond the scope of this piece, the critique that this maximalist conception of sovereignty suffers from a dramatic unevenness since the emerging responsibility is restricted to a particular understanding of global justice, as an antidote solely to gross violations of human rights escalating to the level of hard core crimes.

8 See e.g., D Luban, 'A Theory of Crimes against Humanity' (2004) 29 *Yale Journal of International Law* 85 and L May, *Crimes Against Humanity* (CUP 2005).

9 B Broomhall, *International Justice & the International Criminal Court, Between Sovereignty and the Rule of Law* (OUP 2003) 54–62, M Koskenniemi, 'Hersch Lauterpacht and the Development of International Criminal Law' (2004) 2 *JICJ* 823–825, see also JL Goldsmith & EA Posner, *The Limits of International Law* (OUP 2005) and the critique by ME O'Connell, *The Power & Purpose of International Law* (OUP 2008).

10 MC Bassiouni, *Introduction to International Criminal Law* (Brill 2003) 33.

shared sense of humankind, which serves as a rigid threshold delineating what is morally acceptable and what has to be condemned.[11]

Both the principle of complementarity and the RtP concept promote a globalist understanding of state sovereignty that repudiates as anachronistic the traditional statist conceptualization.[12] The globalist position contains elements of a Kantian vision of international law and varies from hard versions of global responsibility to softer ones that advocate for the wither of sovereignty only in extreme situations such as the case of mass atrocities.[13] Fernando Teson for example promulgates a liberal theory of international law that evolves around the principle of normative individualism; the individual is the primary unit and the legitimacy of state sovereignty is directly linked to the protection of justice.[14] Similarly, Anne Peters supports:

> It has become clear that the normative status of sovereignty is derived from humanity, understood as the legal principle that human rights, interests, needs, and security must be respected and promoted, and that this humanistic principle is also the telos of the international legal system. Humanity is the A and Ω of sovereignty.[15]

In a more restricted version, Larry May, justifies the infringement of sovereignty under the moral minimalist principle that operates together with the security and the international harm principle. According to his theory, only when the security and subsistence of people is in danger, and the crimes carry a group character, the toleration of sovereignty fades away.[16] This latter form of state sovereignty reflects what David Held calls, the liberal international sovereignty between the classic and cosmopolitan one. For him, the liberal cosmopolitan sovereignty resides between the law of states and the law of peoples and mirrors the dramatic transformations

11 D Luban, 'Fairness to Rightness: Jurisdiction, Legality and the Legitimacy of the International Criminal Law' in S Besson, J Tasioulas (eds), *The Philosophy of International Law* (OUP 2010) 577–579, May (n 8) 89–90.

12 Jose Alvarez talks of globalists v. sovereigntists in JE Alvarez, 'State Sovereignty is not Withering Away: A few Lessons for the Future' in A Cassese (ed), *Realizing Utopia, The Future of International Law* (OUP 2012) 27, see also B Kingsbury, 'Sovereignty and Inequality' (1998) 9 *EJIL* 599.

13 F Teson, 'The Kantian Theory of International Law' (1992) 92 *Columbia Law Review* 53.

14 Ibid., also F Teson, *Humanitarian Intervention: An Inquiry into Law and Morality* (3rd ed. Transnational Publishers, 2005) where he attacks the so called Hegelian Myth of the autonomous moral standing of the state. Allen Buchanan also proposes a moral theory of international law, that is linked to the promotion of justice and human rights both in a normative but also institutional perspective and the latter justifies the infringement of sovereignty under the moral minimalist principle that operates together with the security and the international harm principle, A Buchanan, *Justice Legitimacy and Self Determination: Moral Foundation for International Law* (OUP 2004).

15 A Peters, 'Humanity as the A and Ω of Sovereignty' (2009) 20 *EJIL* 513, 514.

16 May (n 8), Peters (n 15).

that took place in the law of warfare, the expansion of human rights and the enhancement of the right to self-determination and democratic governance.[17]

Since the end of the Cold War, a number of scholars have proclaimed the withering, dethroning and erosion of state sovereignty since it was, an "organized hypocrisy",[18] an "illegitimate offspring",[19] a hinder to the rule of law,[20] an enemy to the "collective conscience of humanity".[21] This deontological liberal messianism supports an extreme anti-sovereigntism, while promoting the *telos* of international law to end impunity for gross violations of human rights via the channels both of criminal prosecution and use of force.[22] Yet both the complementarity principle in the Rome Statute and the RtP concept reveal a more complicated and diverse image of state sovereignty challenging the funeral of the S word. To the contrary, the developments in both fields emphasize a persistent preservation of state sovereignty that resists its normative death. The following chapter will address some critical characteristics of the Rome Statute and the responsibility to protect concept for the purposes of the current contribution.

1 Some critical thoughts on the Rome Statute and RtP

Since its adoption the Rome Statute[23] has been characterized "a gift of hope for future generations",[24] the United Nations' "most significant accomplishment since its establishment in 1945",[25] "an uneasy revolution",[26] "a seismic shift in international criminal law generally and in the context of conflict resolution in particular",[27] whereas most recently the Secretary General of the United

17 D Held, 'Law of States, Law of Peoples: Three Models of Sovereignty' (2002) 8 *Legal Theory* 1.
18 S D Krasner, *Sovereignty: Organized Hypocrisy* (Princeton University Press 1999).
19 Henkin (n 1).
20 A Cassese, 'On the Current Trends towards Criminal Prosecution and Punishment of Breaches of International Humanitarian Law' (1998) 9 *EJIL* 2.
21 A Orford, 'Moral Internationalism and the Responsibility to Protect' (2013) 24 *EJIL* 83, 104.
22 B R Roth, 'Anti-Sovereigntism, Liberal Messianism, and Excesses in the Drive against Impunity' (2001) 12 *Finnish Yearbook of International Law* 17.
23 Rome Statute of the International Criminal Court, July 17, 1998, 2187 UNTS 90 [hereinafter Rome Statute], see also Chapters 8 and 9 of this book.
24 Kofi Annan, Former Secretary General of the United Nations, Address at the Rome Conference (July 18, 1998).
25 M Cherif Bassiouni, 'Preface', in O Triffterer (ed.), *Commentary on the Rome Statute of the International Criminal Court: Observers' Notes Article By Article* (2nd edn, C.H. Beck, Hart, Nomos 2008) 39.
26 L N Sadat, *The International Criminal Court and the Transformation of International Law: Justice for the New Millennium* (Transnational Publishers 2002) 1.
27 P Seils, *The Impact of the ICC on Peace Negotiations*, Speech at International Conference 'Building a Future on Peace and Justice' Nuremberg (June 2007).

Nations supported that the "[t]he Rome Statute represents the best that is in us, our most noble instinct … the instinct for peace and justice."[28]

At the same time the Rome Statute is the product of compromises among states, reflecting the political realities of its era.[29] In particular, the principle of complementarity, the *proprio motu* powers of the Prosecutor and the active role of the Security Council reflect this compromised politico-legal reality.

Cherif Bassiouni emphasizes that the Court is the product of the tension between the Westphalian system of state sovereignty and the Hobbesian anarchical nature of international relations, which still allow a wide degree of unilateral exceptionalism.[30] For him, the Court was never intended to be a supranational legal institution, because, as he observes, that would not be acceptable.[31] Instead because it is designed to act as "an international jurisdictional safety net" the court is "more a utilitarian institution than a utopian one".[32]

Yet, the issue that has to be addressed first is twofold and pertains to the nature of the Court while functioning in the current international system of sovereign states, as it has already been observed by Professor Bassiouni. As far as concerns the nature of the Court, the former Prosecutor of the Court, Mr. Luis Moreno Ocampo repeatedly set the parameters of his action saying that:

> [t]he Court is a judicial institution operating in a highly political environment. I shall not be involved in political considerations. I have to respect scrupulously my legal limits. Our policy is never to stretch the interpretation of the norms adopted in Rome. This is the only way to build a judicial institution.[33]

The speech of the former Prosecutor seems to be an unconscious reflection of the principal characteristics of the discussions in legal and international relations disciplines about the creation, nature and scope of the permanent International Criminal Court. As Luis Moreno Ocampo noted, the answer in todays politics is institutions. The legalization process of politics has been

28 The Secretary General, An Age of Accountability, Address at the Review Conference on the International Criminal Court Kampala (May 31, 2010) available at: http://www.icc-cpi.int/iccdocs/asp_docs/RC2010/Statements/ICC-RC-statements-BanKi-moon-ENG.pdf, accessed on 12 November 2015.

29 A Bos, 'The International Criminal Court: Recent Developments' in H A M von Hebel, J G Lammers, J Schukking (eds), *Reflections on the International Criminal Court, Essays in Honor of Adriaan Bos* (The Hague, T.M.C Asser Press 1999) 40, M C Bassiouni, *The Legislative History of the International Criminal Court: Introduction, Analysis and Integrated Text*, vol. I (Brill 2005) 191.

30 M Cherif Bassiouni, 'The ICC-Quo Vadis?'(2006) 4 *JICJ* 421.

31 Ibid., 422.

32 Ibid.

33 Mr. Luis Moreno Ocampo, *Prosecutor of the International Criminal Court, Keynote Address at the Council on Foreign Relations*, Washington DC (Feb. 4, 2010).

examined by prominent theorists of both disciplines trying to explain and clarify its content.[34]

However, the current trend of persistent institutionalisation of justice, encounters suspicions and even hostility by many people. The shadow of the Court,[35] as depicted by the former Prosecutor, has been challenged in an exchange of aphorisms; in particular the principle of complementarity and the interests of justice clause, triggered a schism between those who support the Court and those who question its utility. Under both auspices the primacy of international law v. domestic law, the preference of criminal trials over other forms of accountability and the focus on justice rather than peace, summarize the debate.[36] Especially in northern Uganda, Darfur, Kenya and Libya those issues retain a vivid debate, revealing a normative gap between legal scholars and scientists from other disciplines.

Furthermore, the International Criminal Court is not a supranational legal institution which operates independently of state sovereignty. To the contrary, the Court is a treaty based inter-state institution and therefore, its smooth and efficient function depends on the political will for cooperation of the states within the limits of state sovereignty.[37] Eighty years almost after the characterization of state sovereignty as a volcano, this basic notion of international relations retains its significance, despite persistent propositions for the opposite.[38] This reality has been unfolded before the Court in all situations, but mostly in the case of Darfur, where, despite the commitment of the international community to combat impunity, the referral of the Security Council was not escorted with the necessary political strengthening.

However, the demonization of the notion of politics by legal scholars and legal activists has overlooked reality while producing unrealistic public expectations and disappointing outcomes. In that sense we all appear to be utopians. On the other hand, the actual prosecutorial action or inaction up until now is subjected to criticism that the Court tends to be too apologetic serving the interests of specific states. The so called sweeping moral internationalism appears to marginalize even the realist idealism that was advanced by the pioneer work of Michael Walzer many decades ago.[39]

34 See K W Abbott, R O Keohane, A Moravcsik, A-M Slaughter, D Snidal, 'The Concept of Legalization' in Goldstein, Kahler, Keohane, Slaughter (eds), *Legalization and World Politics* (MIT Press 2001) 17–18.

35 Mr. Luis Moreno Ocampo, *Prosecutor of the International Criminal Court, Keynote Address at the Council on Foreign Relations*, Washington DC (Feb. 4, 2010).

36 See e.g. K M Clarke, *Fictions of Justice, The International Criminal Court and the Challenge of Legal Pluralism in Sub-Saharan Africa* (CUP 2009).

37 See E A Posner, *The Perils of Global Legalism* (The University of Chicago Press 2009) 198–206.

38 H G Niemeyer, 'International Law is an Edifice Built on a Volcano – State Sovereignty' in H G Niemeyer, *Einstweilige verfungen des Welt Gerichtshofs ihr Wesen und ihre Grenzen* (Noske 1932) 3.

39 Orford (n 21) 104 analyzing extensively the book of Walzer, *Just and Unjust Wars* (Basic Books 1977).

2 Introduction to the concept of the *responsibility to protect*

One of the most controversial issues within the international arena until the events of September 11, has been the so called phenomenon of humanitarian intervention, when states undertake forceful measures against another state in order to protect its citizens from gross violations of human rights.

After the end of the Cold War and the reactivation of the Security Council, one of the main pillars of the UN Charter, the collective security foundation has been challenged severely with events like Rwanda, Somalia, Bosnia and Kosovo.[40] Especially in the aftermath of the unauthorized NATO campaign in Kosovo, the controversy regarding the frequently mentioned humanitarian intervention became quite intense, for the future of the collective security system. In particular, predominant were the following characteristic questions of whether there is a right to humanitarian intervention to protect people from "democide"- the extended killing of civilians by their state apparatus itself?[41] If yes, under which circumstances? Who should decide about the existence or not of the need? Who should act and under whose authority? Most significantly, what is the role of the UN and in particular of the Security Council, assigned with "the primary responsibility for the maintenance of international peace and security."[42]

Within this context, the Government of Canada, responded to the request of the Secretary General for a *new consensus* to "forge unity" concerning the main problems upon the *principle and process involved*.[43] Together with a group of scholars and foundations, Canada announced before the General Assembly in September 2001, the establishment of the so called *The International Commission on Intervention and State Sovereignty* (ICISS).[44] The Commission was assigned to deal with a variety of questions including legal, moral, political dimensions of the humanitarian intervention phenomenon and subsequently come up with a common ground after wide consultation with the international community.[45]

The report of the Commission, which was completed before the terrorist attacks of September 11, 2001, was unanimously adopted by the 12th Commissioners and it was titled: "The Responsibility to Protect".[46] According to the Report the central idea is that:

40 See P-M Dupuy, 'The Place and Role of Unilateralism in Contemporary International Law' (2000) 11 *EJIL* 1.

41 See K Simons, 'The Sovereignty and Responsibility to Protect' (Jan-Mar 2003) *Peace Magazine* 23.

42 See Art. 24 of UN Charter.

43 See The Responsibility to Protect, Report of the International Commission on Intervention and State Sovereignty (ICISS), December 2001, available at: http://www.iciss.ca/report-en.asp, accessed on April 15, 2016.

44 Ibid.

45 Ibid.

46 Ibid.

> [s]overeign states have a responsibility to protect their own citizens from avoidable catastrophe – from mass murder and rape, from starvation – but that when they are unwilling or unable to do so, that responsibility must be borne by the broader community of states.[47]

Based on the ICISS report in September 2003, the Secretary General announced before the General Assembly his intention to appoint a High-Level Panel consisted by prominent members of the international community, assigned to examine the new challenges in peace and security and provide proposals for the strengthening of the collective security system, via institutional reforms.[48]

A year later, in September 2004, the Secretary General presented before the General Assembly the report prepared by the High Level Panel on Threats, Challenges and Changes. The Report was titled: "A more secure world: our shared responsibility".[49] In particular, paragraph 203 of the Report summarizes the main aspects of the emerging norm of the so called *collective responsibility to protect*, via Security Council's authorization of military intervention as last resort, in cases of genocide, ethnic cleansing or serious violations of humanitarian law, where sovereign governments are unwilling or powerless to prevent.[50]

Subsequently, in March 2005, the Secretary General presented before the General Assembly a new follow up report, to the outcome of the Millennium Summit titled: "*In Larger Freedom, towards development, security and human rights for all*".[51] Under Chapter IV of the Report, entitled "*Freedom to live in Dignity*" and in specific under sub-title "*Rule of Law*", the Secretary General reaffirmed the *emerging norm* (as emphasized in the previous report of the High Level Panel, para. 203) of the *responsibility to protect* primarily by the state concerned and subsidiary by the international community which should act under the UN auspices.[52]

Finally, in September 2005 the General Assembly issued the World Summit Outcome.[53] There, in paragraphs 138–139 the General Assembly repeats the same focal points of the primary responsibility conferred upon the State and the secondary one being undertaken by the International Community, which has to operate via the regulations of the UN Charter.[54] Almost four years later

47 Ibid.

48 See The Secretary General, *Report of the Secretary-General on the Work of the Organization, delivered to the General Assembly*, UN Doc. A/58/1 (August 28, 2003).

49 The Secretary General, *Report of the High-Level Panel on Threats, Challenges and Changes: "A more secure world: 'our shared responsibility'*, UN Doc. A/59/565 (December 2, 2004).

50 Ibid., para. 203.

51 The Secretary General, *Report of the Secretary General "In larger freedom, towards development, security and human rights for all", delivered to the General Assembly,* UN Doc. A/59/2005 (Mar. 21, 2005).

52 Ibid., para. 135.

53 See UN Doc. A/RES/60/1 (Oct. 24, 2005).

54 Ibid., paras 138–139; see para. 138: 'Each individual State has the responsibility to protect its populations from genocide, war crimes, ethnic cleansing and crimes against humanity.

in January 2009, the Secretary General published his report on the implementation of the RtP concept where he outlined a three pillar strategy; Pillar one: the protection responsibilities of the State (sect. II), Pillar two: international assistance and capacity-building (sect. III), Pillar three: timely and decisive response (sect. IV).[55]

The first pillar reflects the first three sentences of paragraph 138 of the Outcome document that:

> Each individual State has the responsibility to protect its populations from genocide, war crimes, ethnic cleansing and crimes against humanity. This responsibility entails the prevention of such crimes, including their incitement, through appropriate and necessary means. We accept that responsibility and will act in accordance with it.

Here, the role of the International Criminal Court and particularly of the complementarity principle are of paramount importance for the fulfillment of the protection responsibilities the State carries. Additionally, the role of Court reappears in pillar three (timely and decisive response), via the referral option of a situation to the ICC. Since 2006 there is reference of the RtP concept in 23 SC resolutions and 6 presidential statements. SC Resolution 1674, in April 2006, on the Protection of Civilians in Armed Conflict (POC), was the very first official inclusion of the RtP concept by the Security Council, whereas the landmark 2150 Security Council resolution on the Prevention and Fight against Genocide, highlights the importance of the RtP concept. Similarly the General Assembly adopted its first resolution on RtP in

This responsibility entails the prevention of such crimes, including their incitement, through appropriate and necessary means. We accept that responsibility and will act in accordance with it. The international community should, as appropriate, encourage and help States to exercise this responsibility and support the United Nations in establishing an early warning capability.

> 139. The international community, through the United Nations, also has the responsibility to use appropriate diplomatic, humanitarian and other peaceful means, in accordance with Chapters VI and VIII of the Charter, to help to protect populations from genocide, war crimes, ethnic cleansing and crimes against humanity. In this context, we are prepared to take collective action, in a timely and decisive manner, through the Security Council, in accordance with the Charter, including Chapter VII, on a case-by-case basis and in cooperation with relevant regional organizations as appropriate, should peaceful means be inadequate and national authorities are manifestly failing to protect their populations from genocide, war crimes, ethnic cleansing and crimes against humanity. We stress the need for the General Assembly to continue consideration of the responsibility to protect populations from genocide, war crimes, ethnic cleansing and crimes against humanity and its implications, bearing in mind the principles of the Charter and international law. We also intend to commit ourselves, as necessary and appropriate, to helping States build capacity to protect their populations from genocide, war crimes, ethnic cleansing and crimes against humanity and to assisting those which are under stress before crises and conflicts break out.

55 The Secretary General, *Report of the Secretary General "Implementing the responsibility to protect", delivered to the General Assembly,* UN Doc. A/63/677 (January 12, 2009).

June 2009, whereas the mandate of a special adviser on RtP was established in 2007. Since 2006 there is a call for the application of the RtP concept in several crisis situations starting from Darfur, Central African Republic, Burma, Kenya, Mali, Nigeria, Sri Lanka, Zimbabwe, Libya, Syria and Gaza. Especially with regard to Libya and Syria, the Human Rights Council also emphasized the role of the RtP concept. Those two cases are also the ones that present an interesting comparative perspective, wherein the role of the ICC and the concept of RtP were brought on the table.

Regarding Libya, it is well known that there was a SC referral before the ICC and the OTP decided expeditiously to open an investigation in March 2011 and issue subsequently three arrest warrants. The Libya situation triggered an interesting debate about the meaning and limits of the complementarity principle both from a legalistic perspective but also a normative one.[56] The principle of state sovereignty, local ownership and fair trial standards questions revealed the dynamics and limits of the global justice language.[57] Similarly, the SC resolution on Libya, tested the limits of RtP concept regarding the width of the protection of civilians and its implication for a legal "right" of regime change beyond the strict idea of security.[58]

The Syria situation on the other hand, reflects the old debate on the morality of the veto powers before the Security Council and the alternative responsibility to bypass those impediments in situations of gross violations of human rights that reach the threshold of core international crimes such as genocide, crimes against humanity, ethnic cleansing and war crimes.[59] There, the juxtaposition of *jus ad bellum* and *jus in bello* rhetoric and the call for international criminal intervention as a tool to end impunity but also contribute to regime change, revealed an interesting normative trend, where the usage of criminal justice obfuscates political motives and interests in the name of humanity.[60] Both Syria and Libya indicated that the relationship between law and politics is far more nuanced, revealing a considerable transformation of state sovereignty, where state consent remains paramount and the state continues to play a contradictory but imminent role in the terrain of global governance when human rights and international crimes are at stake. As Robert Cryer noted:

56 C Stahn, 'Libya, the International Criminal Court and Complementarity, A Test for "Shared Responsibility"' (2012) 10 *JICJ* 325.

57 F Megret, M Giles Samson, 'Holding the Line on Complementarity in Libya: The Case for Tolerating Flawed Domestic Trials' (2013) 11 *JICJ* 571.

58 See A Bellamy, 'Libya and the Responsibility to Protect: The Exception and the Norm' (2011) 25 *Ethics & International Affairs* 3, S Zifcak, 'The Responsibility to Protect after Libya and Syria' (2012) 13 *Melbourne Journal of International Law* 1; B Pommier, 'The Use of Force to Protect Civilians and Humanitarian Action: The Case of Libya and Beyond' (2011) 93 *International Review of the Red Cross* 1063.

59 Zifcak (n 58).

60 See C Stahn, 'Syria and the Semantics of Intervention, Aggression and Punishment: On "Red Lines" and "Blurred Lines"' (2013) 11 *JICJ* 955.

> [i]n some ways this maps on to the ambivalent role that sovereignty plays in international criminal law. An excess of sovereignty and state power can lead to international crimes, as in the Holocaust, but so can a lack of sovereign authority, as in Somalia or Sierra Leone. Ironically, we act through state sovereignty in order to restrict actions justified in the name of state sovereignty. Sovereigns need limitation, but then maybe we all do. Either way, as it is hoped has been shown, whatever human nature, sovereignty is still part of the society in which we find ourselves, and its relationship to international criminal law is multifaceted and not easily reducible to shibboleths on either side. And so it is likely to stay.[61]

3 What use for the sovereignty then?[62]

Martti Koskenniemi claims that state sovereignty has lost part of its normative content in the era of globalization and massive interdependence.[63] States, are overshadowed by networks of regimes and norms where expertise has replaced the traditional operation of statehood.[64] The managerial language of global governance such as regime interaction, compliance, effectiveness and legitimacy has replaced the "obsolete" for the network of experts vocabulary of state sovereignty.[65] Similarly the so-called "reduction to purpose" normative shift presupposes a consensus on the normative content of the principles of justice, security and peace.[66] This "hegemonic" behavior articulates an absolutist manihaistic understanding of truth; what it reflects, is the preferences and interests of the international community.[67] Similarly, this "transcendent justice" position accepts no challenge since it represents universal values on behalf of humanity.[68] Yet, this "oceanic feeling" of common shared values, interests and preferences is far from uncontested.[69] The mainstream idea advocating for the universality of humanity, has been severely criticized as a "cosmopolitan dream" or as a hegemonic project of

61 R Cryer, 'International Criminal Law vs State Sovereignty: Another Round?' (2005) 16 *EJIL* 100.
62 Koskenniemi (n 2).
63 Ibid.
64 Ibid., 62–63.
65 Ibid., 65, see also M Koskenniemi, 'The Politics of International Law – 20 Years Later' (2009) 20 *EJIL* 1, M Koskenniemi, 'The Fate of Public International Law: Between Technique and Politics' (2007) 70 *Modern Law Review* 1; M Koskenniemi, 'Hegemonic Regimes' in Young (ed), *Regime Interaction in International Law: Facing Fragmentation* (CUP 2012).
66 Koskenniemi (n 2) 66–67.
67 Koskenniemi, 'Hegemonic Regimes' (n 65).
68 B R Roth, 'State Sovereignty, International Legality and Moral Disagreement' in Broode & Shany (eds), *The Shifting Allocation of Authority in International Law, Considering Sovereignty, Supremacy and Subsidiarity* (Hart 2008) 125.
69 M Koskenniemi, 'Projects of World Community' in Cassese (ed.), *Realizing Utopia, The Future of International Law* (OUP 2012) 3.

the West to "civilize" the rest of the world.[70] In the field of international criminal law, for example, Antony Duff responding to David Luban has questioned the content and legality of *hostis humani generis* raising two concerns.[71] The first one pertains to the problematic contention of the existence of a political community (humanity) to which the perpetrators are accountable. The second challenges the authoritative basis of the ICC to act on behalf of this community. Duff rejects the harm principle to humanity, developed by Arendt and May.[72] Instead he supports that "[c]rimes are 'public' wrong in the sense not that they harm 'the public' but they properly concern 'the public'....[A] crime against humanity should be one that properly concerns us all in virtue simply of our shared humanity."[73] But even if it is accepted that there is this humanity, which shares common moral aspirations, then as Mark Drumbl observes, "[i]t is one thing to agree to the universal repudiation of the great evils and to agree that victims are entitled to accountability. It is another matter to accept the universality of categorizing the great evils as crimes."[74]

The real issue that gradually comes into surface is the question of authority; who decides about the universal validity of those values and preferences and who prevails in this "hegemonic contestation"?[75]

Similarly in the RtP spectrum, the so called "hegemonic contestation" evolves around the issue of authority that new actors and states proclaim in the name of humanity.[76] Who is entitled to invoke legitimate authority when this invocation implies normative preferences regarding the content and modalities of protection?[77] Is the actual issue a problem of authority at the very end? Critical legal scholars emphasize the interrelation between the content of normative claims and the source of those claims. They highlight the ideological projects that particular actors and institutions carry, preferably of a liberal nature, that are presented as universally accepted common normative and political ground. The actors define the project and the project legitimizes the actors, since there is only one way for the international community as a whole.

70 See e.g. D Kennedy, *One, Two, Three, Many Legal Orders: Legal Pluralism and the Cosmopolitan Dream*, Speech delivered at the International Law Association, British Branch, University College London and School of Oriental and African Studies (Mar. 2006), M Koskenniemi, *The Gentle Civilizer of Nations* (CUP 2001), see also C Douzinas, *Human Rights and Empire, The Political Philosophy of Cosmopolitanism* (Routledge 2007).

71 A Duff, 'Authority and Responsibility in International Criminal Law' in Besson, Tasioulas (eds), *The Philosophy of International Law* (OUP 2010) 597–604.

72 H Arendt, *Eichmann in Jerusalem* (Penguin Books 1994) 269 and L May, *Crimes Against Humanity* (CUP 2005).

73 Duff (n 71) 600.

74 M Drumbl, *Atrocity, Punishment and International Law* (CUP 2007).

75 Koskenniemi, 'Hegemonic Regimes' (n 65) 312–313.

76 Orford (n 21), JE Alvarez, 'The Schizophrenias of R2P' in P Alston, E MacDonald (eds), *Human Rights, Intervention and the Use of Force* (OUP 2008).

77 Alvarez (n 76) 105.

The problem of authority has attracted a variety of responses diverging between pluralism and relativism especially in the field of human rights and criminal justice. For Koskenniemi, state sovereignty mirrors the ideal of self hood, since it allows active decision making participation.[78] As he supports:

> [s]overeignty articulates the hope of experiencing the thrill of having one's life in one's own hands.[...]Today, it stands as an obscure representative of an ideal against disillusionment with global power and expert rule. In the context of war, economic collapse, and environmental destruction, in spite of all the managerial technologies, sovereignty points to the possibility, however limited or idealistic, that whatever comes to pass, one is not just a pawn in other people's games but, for better or for worse, the master of one's life.[79]

Still one could argue that this ideal type of sovereignty does not entirely reflect reality where the formal sovereign equality of states is not translated into a substantial one. In the era of globalization and intense interdependence, less powerful states may find their role marginalized and their voice excluded, when they do not participate in the new global terrain. State sovereignty remains one of the cornerstones of the international law but it has been subjected to a series of transformations.[80] It is definitely important to acknowledge the connotations this new moral internationalism carries for the question of authority, yet, it could be problematic to insist on the revival of a statist paradigm of sovereign authority that neglects the current multilayer levels of authoritative decision process. Especially, since the debates about the purpose, limits and prospect of international justice and RtP carry already a polarized content. A more sociologically sensitive format of responsive governance to the concerns and interests of the affected populations could provide an alternative model of legitimate authority.[81] This proposition does not argue that the alternative way is a non controversial one. Instead it opts for a dialectic and communicative understanding of governance where the limits and dynamics of the various actors are taken under consideration. This process touches upon the question of legitimacy of the overall project of international justice (criminal prosecution and responsibility of protection). It presupposes tolerance for the different one and it has to be a two-way communication. The success or failure of this normative project will be

78 Koskenniemi (n 2) 69.
79 Ibid., 70.
80 L Condorelli, A Cassese, 'Is Leviathan Still Holding Sway over International Dealings' in Cassese (ed.), *Realizing Utopia, The Future of International Law* (OUP, 2012) 14, referring to human rights spread, globalization and internal strifes.
81 T M Franck, 'The Centripede and the Centrifuge: Principles for the Centralisation and Decentralisation of Governance' in T Broode & Y Shany (eds), *The Shifting Allocation of Authority in International Law, Considering Sovereignty, Supremacy and Subsidiarity* (Hart 2008) 28, Condorelli, Cassese (n 80) 25.

decisive for the depolarization or not of the authority question about state sovereignty. This third way between statists and globalists does not mean necessarily moderation. To the contrary, this dialectic process will unavoidably result in concrete choices and preferences, reflecting the necessities of their era. Predetermined absolutist policies in the name of humanity and nihilistic critical denunciations in favor of a monolithic sovereignty have no place in this process. This is an open-ended dialogue, where concepts such as justice, peace, security and protection have to be contextualized and mutually applied even to the detriment of well-established understandings. State sovereignty is still alive, still central and surprisingly adaptable to the new challenges. The case studies of Syria and Libya, highlight the implications by the key question about the authority of international law, that is produced by various actors and functions in several levels, casting serious doubt on the predetermined normative project of the constitutionalisation of international legal order.

8 Fragmentation of the law of targeting

A comfortable excuse or a dangerous trap?[1]

Patrycja Grzebyk

1 Introduction

In order to assess the rules of targeting in armed conflicts (selection of targets and methods of their elimination), at least two main regimes of international law must be taken into account. The first one is International Humanitarian Law, IHL, which applies only during armed conflicts and describes who/what and how can be attacked. The second is Human Rights Law, HRL, which applies both in times of peace and in armed conflicts. It includes e.g. the right to life, prohibition of torture, the right to possession etc., and thus also covers the question of who/what and how can be attacked. Additionally, International Criminal Law (which e.g. defines war crimes such as attacks on unlawful targets, and outlines the principles of responsibility for them) should be evaluated too. Even if it plays a secondary role towards IHL and HRL, and even if in theory international criminal courts only apply appropriate provisions of IHL and HRL in interpretation of their statutes defining particular crimes, the specific approach of courts (as they are rightly focused on the goal of determining individual criminal responsibility) impacts the understanding of main principles of the law of targeting derived from IHL and HRL. In addition, the law of particular organizations should be taken into account, as should national laws, because both of these also frame the law of targeting of particular states.

In consequence, the above-mentioned regimes might indicate what kinds of attacks are lawful in armed conflict, as well as which are unlawful. Unfortunately, these regimes vary in terms of principles related to targeting. Thus an act which could be perceived as lawful according to International Humanitarian Law is not acceptable from the point of view of Human Rights Law. There is another difficulty, too. Due to the absence of hierarchy between international tribunals, HRL tribunals are not bound by criminal tribunals' judgments and *vice versa*, so the jurisprudence is by necessity plagued by lack of coherence.

1 The project was financed from the means of the Polish National Center of Science based on the decision no. DEC-2013/11/D/HS5/01413.

The problem of fragmentation of the law of targeting is not just an abstract issue to be considered by legal theorists, a mere intellectual game. On the contrary, it has tremendous importance for day-to-day application of the law of targeting. All those engaged in hostilities expect clear rules as to how they should perform their tasks. Yet the issue of fragmentation of law applied in armed conflicts complicates the legal framework in which they act. Paradoxically, from an individual perspective, the blurred rules on targeting can result in greater freedom of action. Perhaps therefore this fragmentation is welcomed by attackers – but not necessarily by their victims.

This chapter focuses on the problem of fragmentation of the law of targeting and its consequences in the practice of conducting hostilities. The first part discusses the fragmentation of the rules on targeting and the relations between the various regimes which specify the rules of targeting. In the second part, the focus is on the practical implications of the fragmentation of the law on targeting. The following questions will be answered: is this fragmentation a blessing or a curse? For whom? The third part of the chapter ponders what remedies might be used (including the process of constitutionalisation) to deal with the faults of law on targeting.

2 Fragmentation

The relation between IHL and HRL is a classic example of fragmentation of international law pointed out in the works of the International Law Commission[2] which defined fragmentation as "the emergence of specialized and relatively autonomous rules or rule-complexes, legal institutions and spheres of legal practice"[3]. These branches of public international law differ in a great number of aspects: their origins, subject matters, self-executive character, aims, principles, rules of interpretation, and systems of control[4]. In

2 International Law Commission, Fifty-eighth Session Geneva, 1 May–9 June and 3 July–11 August 2006, 'Fragmentation of International Law: Difficulties Arising from the Diversification and Expansion of International Law', Report of the Study Group of the International Law Commission Finalized by Martti Koskenniemi, UN Doc. A/CN.4/L.682, 13 April 2006, 104, hereafter 'Koskenniemi Report'.

3 Ibid., 8.

4 Summary of the debate on relations between IHL and HR, see K Bennoune, 'Toward a Human Rights Approach to Armed Conflict: Iraq 2003' (2004–2005) 11 *U. C. Davis Journal of International Law and Policy* 171, 179 ff; R Kolb, 'Aspects Historiques de la Relation entre le Droit International Humanitaire et les Droits de l'Homme' (1999) 37 *Canadian Yearbook of International Law* 57 ff; F J Hampson, 'The Relationship between International Humanitarian Law and Human Rights Law from the Perspective of a Human Rights Treaty Body' (2008) 90 *International Review of the Red Cross* 549, 559 ff; H-J Heintze, 'On the Relationship between Human Rights Law Protection and International Humanitarian Law' (2004) 86 *International Review of the Red Cross* 789. On basic differences between two regimes see: M A Hansen, 'Preventing the Emasculation of Warfare: Halting the Expansion of Human Rights Law into Armed Conflict' (2007) 194 *Military Law Review* 1, 6; B A Feinstein, 'The Applicability of the Regime of Human Rights in Times of Armed Conflict and Particularly to Occupied Territories: The Case of Israel's Security Barrier' (2005–2006) 4

the period 1948–1949, when the fundamental instruments of IHL and HRL were created, they provided no mutual inspiration. Both branches are now expanding their geographic scope of application, i.e. claims are being made to the effect that HRL is extraterritorially applicable[5] and also that IHL is to be applied to conflicts which theoretically encompass the whole globe (such as the infamous war on terror announced by the US)[6]. Thus the tension between the two regimes is growing[7]. The conflict between IHL and HRL is particularly strong in the case of rules on targeting: HRL is extremely prohibitive where it concerns possible deprivation of life[8], while IHL is in comparison extremely

Northwest Journal of International Human Rights 238, 245 ff; L Doswald Beck, 'International Humanitarian Law: A Means of Protecting Human Rights in Time of Armed Conflict' (1989) 1 *African Journal of International and Comparative Law* 595, 615; C Droege, 'Elective Affinities? Human Rights and Humanitarian Law' (2008) 90 *International Review of the Red Cross* 501, 521 ff.

5 Convention for the Protection of Human Rights and Fundamental Freedoms, hereafter European Convention for Protection of Human Rights, ECHR, 4 November 1950 (213 UNTS 222) secures respect of HR "to everyone within their jurisdiction" (Article 1) thus its literal meaning allows application of the Convention out of the territory of member states which was confirmed in several judgments of European Court of Human Rights (ECtHR), see e.g. *Al-Skeini and Others v the United Kingdom*, App no 55721/07 (ECtHR, 7 July 2011), *Catan and Others v The Republic of Moldova and Russia*, App nos 43370/04, 8252/05 and 18454/06 (ECtHR, 19 October 2012). According to Article 2 (1) International Covenant on Civil and Political Rights (ICCPR), 16 December 1966 (999 UNTS 171) states parties agree to respect HR "to all individuals within its territory and subject to its jurisdiction", in theory it means that ICCPR excludes extraterritorial application of the Covenant but Human Rights Committee's decisions prove that also ICCPR according to the HRC can be applied extraterritorially, see e.g. *Lopez Burgos v Uruguay, Saldias de Lopez (on behalf of Lopez Burgos) v Uruguay*, Merits, Communication No 52/1979, UN Doc. CCPR/C/13/D/52/1979, IHRL 2796 (UNHRC 1981), 29 July 1981, Human Rights Committee. See more in M Milanowic, *Extra-territorial Application of Human Rights Treaties: Law, Principles, and Policy* (OUP 2011); K da Costa, *The Extraterritorial Application of Selected Human Rights Treaties* (Brill 2013). The practice of extraterritorial application of HRL is opposed mainly by the US and Israel, see e.g. Hansen (n 4), B Van Schaack, 'The United States' Position on the Extraterritorial Application of Human Rights Obligations: Now is the Time for Change' (2014) 90 *International Law Studies* 20.

6 See e.g. N Lubell, N Derejko, 'A Global Battlefield? Drones and the Geographical Scope of Armed Conflict' (2013) 11 *JICJ* 65.

7 Charles Garraway commented on the relation between HRL and IHL in the following way: "As the nature of conflict changed so that the majority of armed conflicts took place within the territorial boundary of a single State, so the law of armed conflict and human rights law began to rub up against each other like two tectonic plates." C Garraway, Chatham House, "The 'War on Terror": Do the Rules Need Changing?' (2006) 6(02) *International Law Briefing Paper* 1, 4.

8 The ICCPR, under Article 6, (as also American Convention on Human Rights (ACHR) 22 November 1969 (1144 UNTS 123, Article 4) uses a non-definite standard of arbitrariness in assessment of legality of deprivation of life, where the ECHR, Article 2, names strict conditions in which a person can be deprived of life: execution of a sentence of a court following conviction of a crime for which capital punishment is provided by law; in case the absolutely necessary use of force in three situations: (a) in defence of any person from unlawful violence; (b) in order to effect a lawful arrest or to prevent the escape of a person lawfully detained; (c) in action lawfully taken for the purpose of quelling a riot or insurrection.

permissive in that it gives great freedom to combatants to kill indicated categories of persons during an armed conflict (only placing limits on killing those who are not engaged in hostilities, who are *hors de combat*)[9]. It must be added that there is no possibility of derogation of some human rights in an emergency situation (e.g. in an armed conflict). This is true, for instance, with regard to the right of life or the prohibition of torture. Thus the states failed to eliminate in advance a conflict of HRL and IHL norms by appropriately broadening the derogation clauses[10]. Admittedly, the European Convention on Human Rights (Article 15) directly refers to the exception concerning "deaths resulting from lawful acts of war" in times of war or other public emergency. Yet states are unwilling to act based on this provision and to take measures derogating from their obligations derived from Convention. Perhaps the reason of this unwillingness lies in the reluctance to admit that a state is involved in armed conflict or it is forced to apply special procedures in order to crash a rebelling party. On the other end of the spectrum, IHL does notice the possible application of HRL standards, but it rarely refers to them directly[11].

The relationship between IHL and HRL was discussed a few times in the jurisprudence of the International Court of Justice. In the advisory opinion concerning legal consequences of the construction of a wall in the occupied Palestinian territory dated 9 July 2004, the ICJ stated:

> As regards the relationship between IHL and HR law, there are thus three possible situations: some rights may be exclusively matters of IHL; others may be exclusively matters of HR law; yet others may be matters of both these branches of international law. In order to answer the question put to it, the Court will have to take into consideration both these branches of international law; namely HR law and, as *lex specialis*, IHL[12].

The Court had used a term *lex specialis* in reference to the relationship between HRL and IHL also in its previous advisory opinion on the legality of

9 See Article 13 of the Geneva Convention on Wounded and Sick in Armed Forces in the Field, I GC; Article 13 of the Geneva Convention on the Wounded, Sick and Shipwrecked of Armed Forces at Sea, II GC; Article 4 of the Geneva Convention Relative to the Treatment of Prisoners of War, III GC; Article 4 of the Geneva Convention Relative to the Protection of Civilian Persons in Time of War, IV GC, all four Geneva Conventions were adopted on 12 August 1949, and entered into force on 21 October 1950, 75 UNTS 287.

10 See Article 4 ICCPR, Article 15 ECHR, Article 27 ACHR.

11 See e.g. Article 72 III GC referring to the treatment of persons in the power of a party to the conflict: "The provisions of this Section are additional to the rules concerning humanitarian protection of civilians and civilian objects in the power of a Party to the conflict contained in the Fourth Convention, particularly Parts I and III thereof, as well as to other applicable rules of international law relating to the protection of fundamental human rights during international armed conflict".

12 Advisory Opinion, *Legal Consequences of the Construction of a Wall in the Occupied Palestinian Territory*, ICJ Reports 2004, p. 136, para. 106.

the threat or use of nuclear weapons (dated 8 July 1996). That opinion refers directly to the issue of targeting in armed conflicts. According to the Court:

> … the protection of the International Covenant on Civil and Political Rights does not cease in times of war, except by operation of article 4 of the Covenant … The test of what is an arbitrary deprivation of life, however, then falls to be determined by the applicable *lex specialis*, namely, the law applicable in armed conflict which is designed to regulate the conduct of hostilities. Thus whether a particular loss of life, through the use of a certain weapon in warfare, is to be considered an arbitrary deprivation of life contrary to article 6 of the Covenant, can only be decided by reference to the law applicable in armed conflict and not deduced from the terms of the Covenant itself[13].

The use of the notion of *lex specialis* provoked much discussion among scholars. They argued that not only does it fail to clarify the problem of the relationship between the two regimes, but actually creates confusion[14]. Perhaps this criticism led to the avoidance of the term in subsequent judgments of the ICJ.[15] However, in the case of assessment of arbitrariness of killing anyone in international armed conflict, there seemed to be a consensus that IHL should in fact prevail as text. *Travaux préparatoires* of HR conventions confirm that states did not want to eliminate the possibility of killing enemy combatants during armed conflict, if it were done according to the law of war[16]. The provisions on conduct of hostilities in international armed conflicts included in Geneva Conventions of 12 August 1949 and the First Additional Protocol of 8 June 1977 are much more precise in comparison to the usually general statements on protection of life included in HRL documents. Therefore, they fit very well the description of a *lex specialis,* as they are "more to the point"[17].

A problem arises in the analysis of the rules on targeting in a non-international armed conflict. IHL rules (Article 3 common to the Geneva Conventions, with Second Additional Protocol and customary law) are extremely rudimentary, and so the argument that IHL rules are in this case more concrete

13 Advisory Opinion, *Legality of the Threat or Use of Nuclear Weapons*, ICJ Reports 1995, p. 226, para. 25.

14 See e.g. C Droege, 'The Interplay between International Humanitarian Law and International Human Rights Law in Situations of Armed Conflict' (2007) 40 *Israel Law Review* 310, 335 ff.

15 See Judgment on *Armed Activities on the Territory of the Congo (Democratic Republic of the Congo v Uganda)*, ICJ Reports 2005, p.168, para. 216.

16 Report of the Secretary General, *Respect for Human Rights in Armed Conflicts,* 18 September 1970, UN Doc. A/8052, para. 46. See also M Milanovic, 'The Lost Origins of Lex Specialis: Rethinking the Relationship between Human Rights and International Humanitarian Law', in JD Olin (ed.) *Theoretical Boundaries of Armed Conflict and Human Rights* (Cambridge University Press, Forthcoming), available at SSRN: http://ssrn.com/abstract=2463957.

17 Koskenniemi Report, para. 60.

loses its validity (unless we agree that all rules concerning targeting applied in international armed conflict are also binding in non-international ones as customary law – but such a claim would be questionable)[18]. Other questions for which IHL provides no answers pertain to lawfulness of attacks that are likely to unintentionally kill persons not taking part in hostilities, or the application of shoot-to-kill tactics against lawful targets ("capture or kill" dilemma)[19]. Therefore, the option of application of HR standards of e.g. graduate use of force could also be raised[20].

The mere application of the rule *lex specialis derogat legi generali* is not a solution in these cases as there are no clear indications which branch of law should be treated as *lex specialis* (i.e. there is no clarity as to which norms are more specific).

The ILC stated:

> Generality and speciality are thus relational. A rule is never "general" or "special" in the abstract but in relation to some other rule. This relationality functions in two registers. A rule may be general or special in regard to its subject-matter (fact-description) or in regard to the number of actors whose behaviour is regulated by it.

If the subject matter offers no clue with regard to non-international armed conflict, perhaps the personal scope of application should be a signpost as to which norms should prevail. IHL and HRL have different personal scope of application: IHL must be applied by each party to the conflict (and thus also by non-state actors)[21], while HRL, in general terms, imposes obligations only on states[22]. In consequence, application of only HRL in internal armed conflict would give a great advantage to non-state actors, as only states would be bound by its restrictive rules on targeting. This is not acceptable from the

18 As W Abresch rightly points out: "In most internal conflicts, the only applicable treaty law is Common Article 3 of the Geneva Conventions of 1949, a legal regime consisting of 263 words", see W Abresch, 'A Human Rights Law of Internal Armed Conflict: the European Court of Human Rights in Chechnya' (2005) 16 *EJIL* 741, 747.

19 About dilemmas related with "shoot to kill" or "kill or capture" tactic, see J Pictet, *Development and Principles of International Humanitarian Law* (Nijhoff 1985) 751; and 'Interpretive Guidance on the Notion of Direct Participation in Hostilities under International Humanitarian Law' (2008) 90 *International Review of the Red Cross* 991, 1040. Compare with: T M McDonell, 'So What You Reap? Using Predator and Reaper Drones to Carry Out Assassinations or Targeted Killings of Suspected Islamic Terrorists' (2012) 44 *George Washington International Law Review* 243, 273; R S Taylor, 'The Capture versus Kill Debate: Is the Principle of Humanity Now Part of the Targeting Analysis When Attacking Civilians Who Are Directly Participating in Hostilities?' (2010) 6 *Army Lawyer* 103.

20 See e.g. *McCann and Others v The United Kingdom*, App no 18984/91 (ECtHR, 27 September 1995) 146–150 and 192–214; see also *Nachova and Others v Bulgaria*, App no 43577/98 and 43579/98 (ECtHR, 6 July 2005) 95.

21 See common Article 3 of GC of 1949.

22 See Article 2 of the ICCPR; Article 1 of the ECHR and of the ACHR.

point of view of states. On the other hand, the decision to apply only IHL is hardly understandable from the point of view of non-state actors: IHL is far more favourable to states. Despite the fact that it must be applied by all parties to the conflict, in situations of non-international armed conflict it differentiates between members of armed forces of states and of non-state actors, as it does not give a right to take part in hostilities to the latter[23]. States, the main subjects and creators of international law, are certainly satisfied with this solution. However, they do not notice that non-state actors have no interest to apply IHL, as members of non-state armed groups cannot gain any combatant privileges even if they comply perfectly with IHL, and thus the state's citizens are at risk. Moreover, from the perspective of civilians who are not engaged in any way in hostilities, application of IHL during an armed conflict which takes place in their own country, where they are often forced to stay due to the absence of alternatives, is less understandable: the law of war tolerates killing and wounding of innocent people (if it is not excessive in relation to the concrete and direct military advantage anticipated)[24]. Not surprisingly, in recent years we could observe an increasing influence of HRL on the conduct of hostilities which was a result of a significant number of judgments by HRL courts in cases concerning non-international armed conflicts, brought by citizens against their own states (for example in numerous Chechen cases against Russia)[25].

Involvement of HRL courts in judging the lawfulness of actions undertaken during armed conflict resulted in e.g. introducing by HRL tribunals *ius ad bellum* issues[26]. This is hardly acceptable from IHL perspective. One of the basic principles of International Humanitarian Law is a complete division between *ius in bello* (law of war) and *ius ad bellum* (law on use of force). Consequently, the reason why force was used is completely irrelevant for the assessment of actions taken by those engaged in hostilities from the point of view of IHL, as long as these actions were necessary from a military point of view (and in conformity with other principles of IHL)[27]. This separation

23 Even if members of armed groups respect norms of IHL, they can be still prosecuted and even sentenced to capital punishment for mere taking part in hostilities. See Article 6 of the Protocol Additional to the Geneva Conventions of 12 August 1949, and relating to the Protection of Victims of Non-International Armed Conflicts (Protocol II), 8 June 1977 (1125 UNTS 609) which only encourages a state to grant amnesty to persons who have participated in the armed conflict.

24 See Article 51 (5) (b) of the Protocol Additional to the Geneva Conventions of 12 August 1949, and relating to the Protection of Victims of International Armed Conflicts (Protocol I), 8 June 1977 (1125 UNTS 3) and Rule 14 of Customary IHL (available at http://www.icrc.org/customary-ihl/eng/docs/v1_rul, accessed on 18 April 2016).

25 See e.g. *Esmukhambetov and Others v Russia*, App. no 23445/03 (ECtHR, 29 March 2011), *Isayeva v Russia*, App. no 57950/00 (ECtHR, 24 February 2005); *Isayeva, Yusupova and Bazayeva v Russia*, App no 57947/00, 57948/00, 57949/00 (ECtHR, 24 February 2005).

26 See e.g. *Isayeva v Russia* (2005) (n 25) 180–181.

27 See Preamble of the Protocol I; M Sassòli, A A Bouvier, *How Does Law Protect in War?* vol. I (2nd edn, ICRC 2006) 102 ff.

guarantees that all parties to the conflict (aggressors and those acting in self-defence) have the same obligations and rights which in fact cannot be separated from each other[28]. However, from the point of view of HRL, the reasons of using force have great importance and are essential to judging the lawfulness of use of force against other people[29]. HRL cannot be neutral to the question of aggression: peace is a *sine qua non* condition if right to life is to be fully respected[30]. In consequence, IHL cannot be treated as *lex specialis* in relation to HRL which would mean that the provisions of the law on use of force may be disregarded in assessment of lawfulness of targeting, as doing so would frustrate the purpose of HRL[31].

On the margin of growing involvement of HR tribunals in the assessment of lawfulness of actions undertaken during armed conflict, an additional question arises. Are HR tribunals entitled to take into account not only HR conventions, but also IHL sources? The approach of the European Court of Human Rights has been very cautious. The Court has referred to the IHL instruments in its reasoning, but has always based its final conclusions only on the Convention for the Protection of Human Rights and Fundamental Freedoms[32]. Despite some references to IHL and ICL, the analyses of the entire legal frameworks applied in a specific situation made by the HRL courts are usually rather poor. Some ECtHR's judgments have unfortunately proved that judges of HR law courts are not necessarily accustomed with IHL or ICL and have problems with fundamental terminology usage[33].

A different solution was chosen in the case of the International Criminal Court, which should take into account in its deliberation "applicable treaties and the principles and rules of international law, including the established principles of the international law of armed conflict"[34]. In addition, "[t]he application

28 F Bugnion, 'Just Wars, Wars of Aggression and International Humanitarian Law' (2002) 84 *International Review of the Red Cross* 3, 16 ff.

29 See e.g. *Isayeva v Russia* (2005) (n 25) 180–181. See also W Schabas, 'Lex specialis? Belt and Suspenders? The Parallel Operation of Human Rights Law and the Law of Armed Conflict, and the Conundrum of ius ad bellum' (2007) 40 *Israel Law Review* 592, 607.

30 See works on the right to peace within Human Rights Council, extensive analysis available in P Grzebyk 'Prawo do Pokoju [Right to peace]' (2013) 48 *Stosunki Międzynarodowe – International Relations* 67 ff.

31 Koskennienni Report, para. 281. See also Article 41 (b) of the Vienna Convention on the Law of Treaties, 23 May 1969 (1155 UNTS 331) and ILC, 'Conclusions of the Work of the Study Group on the Fragmentation of International Law: Difficulties arising from the Diversification and Expansion of International Law', 10 (published in the *Yearbook of the International Law Commission*, 2006, vol. II, Part Two), hereafter ILC, 'Conclusions on Fragmentation'.

32 See e.g. *Isayeva v Russia* (2005) (n 25) 175–176.

33 See e.g. *Kononov v Latvia*, App no. 36376/04 (ECtHR 24 July 2008) in which Court wrongly distinguished in IAC a third status (apart from civilian and combatant status) not protected by the law of war; or *Korbely v Hungary*, App no 9174/02, (ECtHR 19 September 2008), in which Court wrongly qualified violations of the Article 3 common to GC of 1949 as "crime against humanity".

34 Article 21 of the Rome Statute of the International Criminal Court, 17 July 1998 (2187 UNTS 90), see also Chapters 7 and 9 of this book.

and interpretation of law pursuant to this article [i.e. article 21] must be consistent with internationally recognized human rights"[35]. In result, the Court's judges are entitled and even obliged to assess norms of all branches of international law as they may be applied to targeting. It must be stressed here that international criminal courts have a different perspective on targeting than IHL. They use stricter standards, as their goal is to determine whether a person is or is not guilty beyond reasonable doubt of a violation of e.g. law applied in armed conflicts. A good example is the issue of proportionality of attacks. According to the IHL, it is prohibited to perform attacks "which may be expected to cause incidental loss of civilian life, injury to civilians, damage to civilian objects, or a combination thereof, which would be excessive in relation to the concrete and direct military advantage anticipated."[36] However, ICL only penalizes attacks which are "clearly excessive in relation to the concrete and direct overall military advantage anticipated"[37]- i.e., the threshold is higher. In consequence, the proportionality principle is stretched in order to qualify as many attacks as possible as completely lawful, and give greater freedom to states engaged in conflict in contravention to the letter of the IHL instrument. Taken to the extreme, this could deprive the principle of proportionality of any meaning.

Another complication lies in the proliferation of international tribunals and the absence of hierarchy between them. This creates the potential for inconsistency in interpretation of terms of HRL or IHL, especially that international tribunals do not establish binding precedents. Among international criminal tribunals, this problem is addressed at least to a degree, in that the International Criminal Tribunal for the former Yugoslavia and International Criminal Tribunal for Rwanda had a common appeal chamber in order to avoid contradicting judgments. There has also been a practice of exchanges of experience between judges of *ad hoc* tribunals and the ICC (even if none of them are bound by the principles established by the others). In case of HRL courts, these courts refer to each other's judgments, but none of them is bound to follow the reasoning of the others. Certainly, the purposes of International Criminal tribunals and Human Rights Law tribunals are different. The former must establish individual criminal responsibility whereas the latter (as well as International Criminal Justice) refers to state responsibility. That is why they use e.g. different tests of attribution and not necessarily are willing to take into account other courts' perspective which sometimes is criticized as a "dialogue des sourds"[38]. Even if we agree that different purposes must be combined with different tests and different understanding of some terms[39], the courts should not neglect their legacy and they should justify

35 Ibid.

36 See n 23.

37 See Article 8(2)(b)(iv) of the Rome Statute.

38 B Simma, 'Universality of International Law from the Perspective of a Practitioner' (2009) 20 *EJIL* 265, 280.

39 K Del Mar, 'The Requirement of "Belonging" under International Humanitarian Law' (2010) 21 *EJIL* 105.

broadly any departure of a line of reasoning proposed by other international courts (even if they are not legally bound to do it). This judicial exchange of argument can help to clarify vague terms and keep coherence of IL. It must be kept in mind that any incoherence can be used by defendants in order to invoke lack of clear rules and in consequence demand qualification of their behavior as actions taken in mistake of law.

3 A trap or an excuse

To illustrate the practical problems with appropriate application of the law of targeting in armed conflicts, two problems can be discussed. Firstly, a soldier in the battlefield needs clear guidance as to which categories of persons can be attacked. The soldier must also know whether these persons can be killed, or whether perhaps they must be captured, if possible, instead of being killed. IHL specialists emphasize that in the fervor of fights, expectations to arrest anyone are unrealistic[40]. However, even in situations when capture is possible and action takes place a considerable distance from the actual battlefield, soldiers prefer to kill and avoid problems related to transfer and appropriate treatment of captured persons (as illustrated by the killing of Osama bin-Laden). Some states point out that IHL allows that solution. Secondly, IHL does not offer a precise definition of "direct participation of hostilities"[41], and thus there is no precise indication of who can be legally attacked in armed conflicts (especially in situation of non-international armed conflict in framework of which there is no combatant status). In consequence, states such as the US prefer to broaden the term of participation in hostilities to the extreme. For example, they qualify financial officers of armed groups or drug lords (as they provide financial support to armed organization and enable them to function) as lawful targets[42]. However, in light of the traditional understanding of this term in the IHL or from the HR perspective, such persons may not be treated as lawful targets, i.e. as those who can be lawfully killed.

40 See e.g. M Sassòli, L M Olson, 'The Relationship Between International Humanitarian and Human Rights Law Where it Matters: Admissible Killing and Internment of Fighters in Non-international Armed Conflicts' (2008) 90 *International Review of the Red Cross* 599, 613.

41 To clarify this issue the Assembly of the International Committee of the Red Cross adopted 'Interpretive Guidance on the Notion of Direct Participation in Hostilities under International Humanitarian Law' on 26 February 2009, see n 19. Reference to Interpretive Guidance can be found e.g. in the UN's official documents such as the Report of the Special Rapporteur (Ben Emmerson) on the promotion and protection of human rights and fundamental freedoms while countering terrorism, 18 September 2013, A/68/389, *passim*.

42 See Report to the Committee on Foreign Relations, United States Senate, One Hundred Eleventh Congress, First Session, 10 August 2009, available at http://www.gpo.gov/fdsys/pkg/CPRT-111SPRT51521/html/CPRT-111SPRT51521.htm accessed 8 April 2016.

The fragmentation of law of targeting definitely complicates the legal assessment of lawfulness of military actions. Importantly, the law of targeting is to be applied by non-lawyers (such as soldiers), who are not expected to have a profound legal background, including knowledge about the potential contradictions resulting from the fragmentation of law. From their perspective, law cannot be clarified *ex post facto* by lawyers. Rather, the law must be clear when the actual combat takes place.

In Poland, a judge deciding a case concerning war crimes is obliged to apply international law as such. It is not specified whether it should be IHL or HRL. A clear solution is therefore necessary to rightly judge a person, especially given that war crimes are punished with imprisonment (for a duration up to life imprisonment). If the judge applies a wrong standard, the final judgment may be too severe or too lenient. In the above-mentioned example concerning the killing of a financial officer, the standard can be clarified by the court. Yet it seems unfair to sentence a person who had clear guidance on the part of their state (command) to the effect that the accountant was a lawful target; the person may now be surprised by the different interpretation of law. However, a prosecuted person can always defend her/himself by claiming that the standard applied by the court was too high and that it had not been revealed to her/him before the fights. The person may then argue that she/he had acted in mistake of law. Thus, a ground excluding responsibility can be raised[43].

The burden of blurred rules applied in armed conflict cannot be put on the prosecuted person. Yet in result, it is put on the victims of an attack – which is also hard to accept. Certainly it can be argued that a person who remains uninvolved in armed conflict can feel completely safe. The problem is that when someone is living on the territory where hostilities are taking place, that person is always in some way involved. The issue is what kind of involvement and what extent of involvement is treated as sufficient reason to kill that person. Recent developments of IHL (concerning distinction of separate group of members of organized armed groups) show that the pool of possible targets is dangerously broadening; IHL is going towards expanding the permission with regard to killings. Thus a mere application of IHL might not be in the interest of victims of armed conflict.

Blurred lines between the application of IHL and HR, and the more lenient standards in ICL, can become an excuse for perpetrators of violations of IHL as doubts on what standards should be applied in specific situations must result in finding an accused innocent in light of *in dubio pro reo* principle. At the same time, the unclear rules on targeting can become a trap for

43 See e.g. Article 30 of the Polish Penal Code, 6 June 1997 (Polish Official Journal 1997 no. 88, item 553 with amend., available at http://www.legislationline.org/documents/section/criminal-codes/country/10 accessed 8 November 2015) and Article 32 of the Rome Statute.

states judged by HR courts such as the ECtHR, as those courts can decide on state's responsibility despite the lack of an individual guilt of an individual person. This can result in implementation by states of more HR-focused approach to targeting in armed conflicts in order to avoid payments of considerable indemnities, along with condemnation of international public opinion. The recent (2014) conflict in Gaza demonstrates that killing of every "civilian" raises outrage (no matter if it can be qualified as a war crime or not), and that explanations in terms of protection of security and conformity with the IHL fail to convince the world of the legitimacy of such actions.

4 Constitutionalisation or unification

According to the ILC: "A norm may assist in the interpretation of another norm for example as an application, clarification, updating, or modification of the latter. In such situation, both norms are applied in conjunction."[44]

In this light, it may be stated that the solution to the problem of fragmentation of the law of targeting, i.e. the elimination of possible contradictions between different legal regimes, is not to decide which norms prevail but rather to attempt to apply them in conjunction, to attempt to harmonize them in order to establish "a single set of compatible obligations"[45]. If states ratified basic instruments of IHL, HRL and ICL[46], we assume that there is no contradiction. Perhaps states did not expect that they will be forced to apply Human Rights Law in armed conflicts in which they are engaged abroad (and so when the security of their citizens is not at risk). However, public opinion nowadays cannot understand why the law could allow the killing of civilians in any part of the world. The obsolete IHL distinctions of different types of conflicts only complicate the legal perspective and obstruct training in IHL and HRL applied in armed conflicts. Perhaps the solution lies in the application of the same rules on targeting in all types of armed conflicts, while accepting the great impact of HRL in the clarification of appropriate standards? If there were doubts in IHL doctrine whether a shoot-to-kill doctrine can be applied during armed conflict, the existence of different standard in HRL would have to be taken into account in order to fill the gap, to complement the apparently insufficient IHL rules. The issue of indication of lawful human targets in non-international armed conflict, and application of stricter standards of proportionality concerning assessment of lawfulness of

44 ILC, 'Conclusions on Fragmentation' (n 31) 2.
45 Ibid., 4.
46 The current (as of 8 November 2015) numbers of ratifications of basic IHL, HRL, ICL instruments are as follows: Geneva Conventions of 1949 – 196 states members; Additional Protocol I to GC of 1949 – 174 states parties; Additional Protocol II to GC of 1949 – 168 states parties; ICCPR – 168 states parties, ICESCR – 162 states parties, Rome Statute – 123 states parties.

killings of innocent people in an attack on military object, may be dealt with in the same manner. It is desirable for all kinds of courts to apply stricter and unified standards of proportionality (no matter if in assessment of state's or individual's responsibility) in order to protect possible innocent victims and to provide clear guidance to those who are undertaking military actions. All courts (whether or not they have direct entitlement in their statutes) should take into account different branches of international law. This principle must be applied also to HRL courts; they cannot pretend to act in a legal vacuum filled only with HRL.

Harmonization of standards applied in armed conflicts is also desirable from the point of view of constitutionalisation of international law[47], especially if we agree that the goal of constitutionalisation is to better serve the interest of humanity (thus states' interest must be conforming with it), or to create a new type of law, such as for example Humanity Law[48]. The law which is not clear, which blurs the rules deciding about life and death of innocents, cannot be treated as law protecting the interest of humanity. Moreover, if we tolerate a situation where the fragmentation of law makes it possible to interpret the law always in favour of states, we can never expect a real improvement of protection standards of mere citizens. It should be also noticed that peremptory norms (*jus cogens*) as prohibition of genocide, crimes against humanity and war crimes (at least of some of them)[49] are treated as rudiments of a world constitution. Yet without a clarification of the law of targeting, it is impossible to state what kind of activities can be treated as war crimes in hard cases. The existing contradictions in law of targeting, if not solved by the application of HRL – thus filling significant gaps in IHL – may undermine the opinion about international law as a system. The fact that the UN Charter, treated by some as a constitution of the international community, mentions several times the role of HRL[50], can also be a guidance about the necessity of humanization of the entirety of the law applied in armed conflicts. Clarification of the law of targeting would also be useful from the point of view of so-called constitutionalisation of particular branches of law. This can be treated as an argument in fostering discussion among different specialists of law on the amendment of existing documents or adoption of new ones in light of the entirety of law applied in armed conflicts, mainly IHL, HRL, ICL.

47 Concerning definition of constitutionalisation, see J Klabbers, 'Setting the Scene', in J Klabbers, A Peters, G Ulfstein (eds), *The Constitutionalization of International Law* (OUP 2009) 10, where it is described as "a process, inspired by constitutionalist thought".

48 J Zajadło, 'Konstytucjonalizacja Prawa Międzynarodowego [Constitutionalisation of International Law]' (2011) 3 *Państwo i Prawo* 6, 12.

49 See e.g. Trial Chamber II, Judgment, *Prosecutor v Kupreskic* (ICTY 14 January 2000, Case No. IT-95-16) 520 where the Tribunal stated: "most norms of international humanitarian law, in particular those prohibiting war crimes, crimes against humanity and genocide, are also peremptory norms of international law or jus cogens, i.e. of a non-derogable and overriding character".

50 See e.g. Preamble, Articles 1 (3), 55 and 56 UN Charter, 26 June 1945 (1 UNTS XVI).

5 Conclusions

Fragmentation of the law of targeting is particularly dangerous: the focus here is on norms which determine who can be killed in armed conflicts. We expect that this kind of law has to be clear, leaving no room for doubt in order to avoid abuse. Unfortunately, there are many grey areas, particularly in internal armed conflicts, which constitute the majority of conflicts nowadays. In result, both individuals and states avoid responsibility. A layperson may believe that law applied in armed conflicts is often violated. In consequence, it is often believed to be non-existent. This is a result of blurred rules and of the legal argumentation of states being able to justify almost every military action in light of international law. It is not without reason that prosecution of war crimes is considered "mission impossible"[51]. However, having in mind the conclusions of work of the International Law Commission on the question of fragmentation of IL and meaning of VCLT, there seems to be one obvious solution to the problem of fragmentation: attempt to interpret IHL, HRL or ICL in light of the remaining branches of law in order to produce a coherent set of obligations. If the territorial scope of application of a particular branch of law is subject of the debate, as it is in the case of HRL or IHL, the argument of necessity of humanization of international law must be raised – this is the pathway indicated in the UN Charter. International judges must be expected to have profound knowledge of all these areas of law if they wish to discuss issues related to armed conflicts. Proliferation of courts and the absence of hierarchy among them, as something which cannot be avoided, can be seen as a value. Judges can make good use of arguments presented by their colleagues if they decide to listen to each other. Having in mind the goal of keeping coherence of IL as a system, they must always broadly justify any departure from the lines of reasoning previously established in other courts. In addition, more fora available to states and individuals means more instruments to force the states to respect the law of targeting.

51 C Wuerzner, 'Mission Impossible? Bringing Charges for the Crime of Attacking Civilians or Civilian Objects before International Criminal Tribunals' (2008) 90 *International Review of the Red Cross* 907.

9 The Rome Statute and the debate surrounding the constitutionalisation, fragmentation and pluralisation of international criminal law

Karolina Wierczyńska

1 Introduction

The debate over International Criminal Law (ICL) is characterized by the use of three major narratives concerning its role in the international legal order. These narratives refer to: 1) the constitutionalisation of international law; 2) the fragmentation and/or diversification of international law; and 3) the pluralisation of international law. Since the fall of the "iron curtain" international law has experienced an unprecedented development, resulting in the establishment of many international organizations and judicial institutions and the ratification of hundreds of international covenants. The use of different narratives in relation to ICL is one way to deal with the convergences and divergences in international legal relations, a way to present the complex reality of international criminal justice.

It would seem that all three narratives properly capture and describe the nature of ICL, and particularly the Rome Statute (RS) and the resulting International Criminal Court (the Court or ICC), as well as ICL as the field of international debate on which all these narratives are focused. As will be examined in this chapter, certain features of the ICC's legal regime have a constitutional character, while certain provisions could be definitely viewed through the lenses of fragmentation and/or diversification of international law, especially when we refer to the decentralization of ICL; and finally we can also take into account the pluralist perspective, as the Rome Statute not only can be seen as linking criminal justice with, for example, human rights values, but also because its complementary character demands deference towards national systems of justice and some leniency in the context of national procedures.

Thus instead of interpreting constitutionalisation/fragmentation/pluralisation as theories, trends, phenomena,[1] processes[2] or analytical devices or

1 Like for example F Lattanzi's 'Introduction' in L van den Herik, C Stahn (eds), *The Diversification and Fragmentation of International Criminal Law* (Nijhoff 2012) 1.

2 Like for example C Walter's 'Progress in International Organization: A Constitutionalist Reading' in R Miller, R Bratspies (eds), *Progress in International Law* (Brill 2008) 142.

mechanisms, and characterizing them broadly,[3] I would rather take a different approach and focus on them as narratives[4] which assist in properly describing and analyzing the realm of the Rome Statute.

In this chapter I draw particular attention to the overlap between these narratives, taking into account the Rome Statute and the practice of the ICC. Going beyond the issue of state sovereignty, I refer to the developments of international criminal law in the context of the multitude of jurisdictions and the international legal order in the era of globalization.

The first section of this chapter focuses on the ICC and its powers. More specifically I attempt to demonstrate the unique features of the International Criminal Court and its role, as foreseen in its constitutive document, the Rome Statute. The second section is devoted to the context of constitutionalisation, seen as a "process inspired by constitutionalist thoughts."[5] Consequently the constitutional features of the Rome Statute will be underlined, aiming to demonstrate how the organization of the ICC's powers can inspire the constitutional narrative. However I do not refer to the concept of domestic constitutionalism, as the 'constitutional idea' of international law must be seen as an autonomous concept,[6] not mirroring or replicating any specific national system. Subsequently I endeavour to reconstruct responses beyond the realm of state sovereignty, or as Habermas puts it, in a "post national constellation".[7] Thus the Rome Statute will not be presented as a constitution or the *Grundnorm*, but rather attention will be paid to particular features which allow for analyzing the RS in the context of the constitutionalisation of international law. The third section of the chapter provides a short introduction into the fragmented nature of the Rome Statute "as a specialized and relatively autonomous sphere"[8] and to the ICC practice in the broader context of international criminal justice. The notion of fragmentation will refer here to the emergence of specialized fields in international

3 Which is actually developed in the literature and reports. See: A Stone Sweet, 'Constitutionalism, Legal Pluralism, and International Regimes' (2009) 16(2) *Indiana Journal of Global Legal Studies* 621; S Roberts, 'Against Legal Pluralism. Some Reflections on the Contemporary Enlargement of the Legal Domain (1998), 30: *The Journal of Legal Pluralism and Unofficial Law* 95; Fragmentation of International Law: Difficulties Arising From The Diversification And Expansion of International Law, Report of the Study Group of the International Law Commission, Finalized by Martti Koskenniemi, UN Doc. A/CN.4/L.682, 13 April 2006 (hereinafter referred to as the 'Report on Fragmentation'); J Klabbers, A Peters, G Ulfstein (eds), *Constitutionalization of International Law* (OUP 2011); L van den Herik, C Stahn (eds), *The Diversification and Fragmentation of International Criminal Law* (Nijhoff 2012); P Webb, *International Judicial Integration and Fragmentation* (OUP 2013); as well as the literature cited below.

4 By 'narratives' I mean the denotation of certain contexts relating to the constitutionalisation, fragmentation or pluralisation of international law, depending on how the story is told.

5 J Klabbers, 'Setting the scene' in J Klabbers, A Peters (n 3) 10.

6 As noted by B Fassbender, *The United Nations Charter as the Constitution of the International Community* (Nijhoff 2009) 170.

7 J Habermas, *The Postnational Constellation* (Polity Press 2004).

8 See Report on Fragmentation (n 3) para. 7.

law[9] and its diversification.[10] The fourth section of this chapter deals with the question of legal pluralism and its relevance to describing the ICC's regime. In my conclusions I discuss the interdependence of these contexts in light of the provisions of the RS and the ICC's practice.

2 The Rome Statute and ICC's competences

The ICC, established under the Rome Statute,[11] is the first permanent and independent institution with "jurisdiction over the most serious crimes of concern to the international community as a whole."[12] The powers of the Court are strictly limited. As to the competence *ratione materiae*, the Court can only exercise jurisdiction with respect to genocide, crimes against humanity, war crimes, and the crime of aggression.[13] Jurisdiction *ratione temporis* is limited to the crimes committed after the entry into force of the Statute for all state parties of the RS, and the jurisdiction of the Court commences at the moment of becoming a state party for those which became state parties after the entry into force of the Statute, unless a declaration was made by that state accepting the jurisdiction of the Court from the entry into force of the RS, even if such state is not a party to the RS.[14] Jurisdiction *ratione personae* relates to persons responsible for the most serious crimes of international concern and is limited to the citizens of state parties, or criminals who commit the crimes on the territory of state parties; however a person can also be prosecuted by the ICC in the situation in which crimes were committed and referred to the prosecutor by the Security Council (SC) acting under Chapter VII of the UN Charter. Basically, jurisdiction *ratione loci* is also limited to state parties, unless the SC referred a situation to the prosecutor as described above. Existing practice shows that Security Council referrals concern those states not parties to the RS.[15]

In addition, the jurisdiction of the Court is complementary to national criminal jurisdictions, which means that the Court will apply its jurisdiction only

9 Ibid. 15; similarly, R Deplano, 'Fragmentation and Constitutionalisation of International Law: A Theoretical Inquiry' (2013) 6(1) *EJLS* 67, 69.
10 F Lattanzi, 'Introduction' (n 1) 1.
11 Rome Statute of International Criminal Court, adopted 17 July 1998, entered into force 1 July 2002, 2187 UNTS 3; also see Chapters 7 and 8 in this book.
12 See the Preamble of the Rome Statute.
13 Arts 5–8 bis of the RS. It is worth mentioning that the crime of aggression will be prosecuted after the coming into force of the amendments to the Statute adopted during the Kampala conference in 2010. Amendments on the crime of aggression to the Rome Statute of the International Criminal Court, 11.06.2010, Resolution RC/Res.6 of the Review Conference of the Rome Statute.
14 Arts 11, 12 (3) of the RS. This, for example, is the case for Ukraine, which is not a state party of the Statute but lodged two declarations accepting the jurisdiction of the ICC.
15 So far there have been two referrals by the SC, concerning the situation in Sudan/Darfur and Libya.

when a case is admissible according to the provisions of Article 17 of the RS. Beside such a restricted jurisdiction and the Court's rather rudimentary significance (according to the number of prosecuted persons),[16] the ICC is nevertheless, because of its universal character, the point of reference in every discussion referring to international criminal law and international justice. It is simply a central institution of international criminal justice, in the same way as the Rome Statute is a key document of ICL.[17]

3 Constitutionalisation and constitutional features of the Rome Statute

Prior to the signing of the RS, the constitutional architecture of international criminal law (in the context of institutional and substantive constitutionalism[18]) was almost never legitimized by the process of implementing international agreements specifying ICL principles or values, and never before had any constitutional rank document been accepted by the international community, although some attempts had been previously undertaken – for example formulation of the Nuremberg principles; signing of the Genocide Convention; or works concerning an international criminal code.[19] But before the establishment of the ICC there certainly had never been any such permanent, universal court with such a broad mandate, as reflected in the global engagement of states in drafting the Statute or the number of states that ratified it (it could also be argued with respect to the number of states which have accepted compulsory jurisdiction of the International Court of Justice[20] – with their acceptance referring to the jurisdiction of the ICC[21,22]). Bardo Fassbender, in propagating the Charter of the United Nations as the "constitution of the international

16 Up until this moment (September 2015), only two persons have been sentenced to imprisonment, and one acquitted.

17 In this context S Nouwen, W Werner sketch a portrait of a monopolized global justice; see their paper: 'Monopolizing Global Justice: International Criminal Law as Challenge to Human Diversity' (2014) *University of Cambridge Faculty of Law Research Paper* No. 63/2014, available at SSRN: http://ssrn.com/abstract=2531638 or http://dx.doi.org/10.2139/ssrn.2531638.

18 C E J Schwöbel, *Global Constitutionalism in International Legal Perspective* (Nijhoff 2011) 13.

19 Compare: Draft Code of Offences against the Peace and Security of Mankind, *Yearbook of the International Law Commission*, 1951, vol. II, at para. 59 et. seq.; as well as the Draft Code of Crimes against the Peace and Security of Mankind, *Yearbook of the International Law Commission*, 1996, vol. II, Part Two.

20 Seventy-two states accepted the compulsory jurisdiction of the ICJ. See: <http://www.icj-cij.org/jurisdiction/index.php?p1=5&p2=1&p3=3> (accessed 10.09.2015).

21 The RS is ratified by 124 States. See: <http://www.icc-cpi.int/en_menus/asp/states%20parties/Pages/the%20states%20parties%20to%20the%20rome%20statute.aspx>, (accessed 5 April 2016).

22 See the analysis of E J Powell, 'Two Courts – Two Roads? Domestic Rule of Law and Legitimacy of International Courts' (2013) 9(4) *Foreign Policy Analysis* 349.

community"[23] referred to some international documents, including the Rome Statute, as "constitutional by-laws",[24] suggesting that the UN Charter is in that context the "framework constitution" and the other documents supplement and fulfil it.[25] Viewed in such a light, one can ask whether the Rome Statute can be seen as fitting into the constitutional narrative.

The universal nature of the ICC is not its most important constitutional feature. Rather its constitutional character should be analyzed through more typical constitutional features or elements of constitutional order, although it must be underlined that there is no "check list" containing the elements of the ideal constitution. But the discussions concerning constitutionalisation have reached the point where certain propositions of functional perspectives can be gathered and compiled. Fassbender, for example, refers to the "constitutional moment", in context of the UN Charter, as marking a special moment in history.[26] Leyla Sadat and Richard Carden make a similar assertion, but they refer to the establishment of the ICC as the "constitutional moment"[27] – underlining the fact that 120 States decided to move forward the idea of prosecuting individuals, not abstract entities.[28]

Fassbender additionally mentions other constitutional elements, such as: system of governance (relating to the system introduced by the UN Charter concerning the making and application of the law as well as adjudicating claims); definition of membership (relating to its members); hierarchy of norms; its eternal nature and amendment (the former relating to possible termination of the UN Charter);[29] the name (regarding use of the term "Charter" which was Fassbender's point of reference); constitutional history; and finally universality and sovereignty.[30] Unlike Fassbender, Jeffrey Dunoff and Joel Trachtman referred to a "constitutional matrix" as appropriate to classify and identify the constitutional order, including such constitutional mechanisms as: creation of governance institutions and allocation of governance authority in a horizontal context; allocation of governance authority in a vertical context (which is similar to Fassbender's system of governance); supremacy (Fassbender's hierarchy of norms); stability (Fassbender's eternity and amendment); fundamental rights (Fassbender refers to constitutional history mentioning fundamental rights

23 Fassbender, *The United Nations Charter* (n 6) 1.
24 Ibid., 169.
25 Ibid., 170.
26 B Fassbender, 'The U.N. Charter as Constitution' (1998) 36 *Columbia Journal of Transnational Law* 530, 573.
27 L N Sadat, S R Carden, 'The New International Criminal Court: An Uneasy Revolution' (1999–2000) 88 *Georgetown Law Journal* 381, 395.
28 Many others also make this observation, such as J Kleffner, *Complementarity in the Rome Statute and National Criminal Jurisdictions* (OUP 2008) 3; or E Mendes, *Peace and Justice at the International Criminal Court: A Court of Last Resort* (Edward Elgar Publishing 2010) 22.
29 Fassbender, 'The U.N.Charter as Constitution' (n 26) 570–80.
30 Ibid., 581.

and other debates, for which the UN was the "natural forum"[31]); review; and accountability/democracy.[32]

Analyzed in the context of some of the above-mentioned constitutional features or the "constitutional matrix", the Rome Statute can be viewed as a document with constitutional features. The first argument relates to the system of governance of the Rome Statute as well as the allocation of governance authority. Definitely the ICC falls in the category of public authority, but clearly is not a typical institution such as the United Nations, embodying the classical attitude to main bodies and their competences. The Statute delineates the powers of its main organs (see Part IV of the Statute, Arts 34–52), but it must be noted that the ICC's main goal is to prosecute individuals and that it is complementary to national jurisdictions. These two characteristics play a key role in the division of powers between its "main bodies", consequently only a rough analogy can be made in that context. Interestingly, we might consider the Assembly of State Parties as a legislator,[33] the prosecutor as enforcing power, and the court as exercising adjudicative power.[34] But as some scholars argue we can also recognize in the RS some features referring to a state's criminal jurisdiction, such as jurisdiction to prescribe (citing Sadat, the "Rome Statute does this by embodying prescriptive norms for the international community as a matter of substantive criminal law"[35]), to adjudicate (when implementing its judicial functions), and to enforce the law (although these functions of the ICC must be assessed as limited; for example Sadat mentions only Arts 56 and 99 (4) of the Statute as reflecting the enforcing powers of the Court).

As to the issue of hierarchy of norms or supremacy, there is no equivalent in the Rome Statute of Article 103 of the UN Charter, but its provisions regulate breaches of *jus cogens* norms (see for example Arts 5 and 6 of the Statute, also Art. 21 relating to the applicable law, which does not have an equivalent in other international criminal courts' statutes) could definitely be understood as being ranked higher than ordinary international law. Supremacy can also be considered in relations with states, although the Court's supremacy is conditional in that it can exercise its adjudicative powers only if a case is admissible before the ICC, which means that a state has priority to prosecute

31 Ibid., 580.

32 J L Dunoff, J P Trachtman, 'A Functional Approach to Global Constitutionalism' in J L Dunoff, J P Trachtman (eds), *Ruling The World? Constitutionalism, International Law And Global Governance* (CUP 2009) 16–20.

33 Although certain doubts could be raised in this context inasmuch as the Assembly is not mentioned as an organ of the Court, but rather the Statute refers to the Assembly in Part XII on financing.

34 See D Raab, H Bevers, 'The International Criminal Court and the Separation of Powers' (2006) 3 *International Organizations Law Review* 93; M Ajevski, 'International Criminal Law and Constitutionalisation. On Hegemonic Narratives in Progress' (2013) 1 *Erasmus Law Review* 50, 53.

35 L N Sadat, 'Redefining Universal Jurisdiction' (2001) 35 *New England Law Review* 541, 545.

the crimes and the ICC can act only when the state is not acting to prosecute an international crime, or is acting but in fact is unwilling and unable to genuinely prosecute (Art. 17 of the Statute). In this context we can also postulate a constitutional function of the Court, as it interacts with national constitutional organs, partly coordinating their activities if they lodge an 'effective' admissibility challenge, i.e. the ICC assesses the actions of domestic powers by determining the admissibility issues before it.

Another argument relates to the stability/eternity/amendment/review aspect of the Statute. The Statute does not contain any provisions concerning the termination of the agreement, nor does it grant the possibility of making reservations to the Statute (Art. 120), but a State can withdraw from the Statue with immediate effect (Art. 121). Amendments can be made only after seven years from the entry into force of the Statute, and involve a complex procedure which include convocation of a Review Conference, and in addition different amending procedures apply to different provisions of the Statute. This however may not only demonstrate its stable character, but also reflect the will of its drafters to grant the Statute a special perennial meaning, as they did not provide the possibility to conclude a treaty.

With respect to fundamental rights, the Statute reflects and embodies major principles of international criminal law. Its jurisdiction *ratione materiae* refers to the core international crimes. Furthermore, it may and it indeed does constitute a pattern (model) for national legal systems. National legislators tend to incorporate the crimes identified in the RS or adopt penal provisions identical to those provided by the Statute, and their courts follow the ICC's interpretations.[36] The ICC is pushing state parties towards implementing the exact provisions of the RS.[37]

In addition Dunoff and Trachtman note that the acceptance of an authoritative meaning of the document as a constitution is not necessarily linked to features such as supremacy or hierarchy of norms, but is connected with some other questions, external to a constitution,[38] which can be analyzed taking into account historical, political or sociological perspectives, which in turn makes Fassbender's assertion of a "constitutional moment" quite appropriate in the context of the ICC.

36 See, for example, Kleffner, *Complementarity in the Rome Statute* (n 28) 334–39, and cited literature; A Katz, 'An Act of Transformation. The Incorporation of the Rome Statute of the ICC into National Law in South Africa' (2003) 12(4) *African Security Review* 25. However, it must be underlined that still there are state parties of the RS with provisions relating to international crimes which strongly differ.

37 See, for example, the keynote speech of the president of the Court, Judge Sylvia Fernandez de Gurmendi: 'From Ratification to Action: The Importance of Full Implementation of the Rome Statute', 16.09.2015, online: <http://www.icc-cpi.int/iccdocs/presidency/150916_Keynote_remarks_at_seminar_on_full_implementation_of_RS.pdf>, accessed 17.09.2015; although it can be doubted whether state parties are obliged to implement provisions of the Rome Statute into their penal codes.

38 Dunoff, Trachtman, 'A Functional Approach' (n 32) 21.

To sum up this section, we definitely have to agree that one can recognize certain constitutional features in the Rome Statute. However closer scrutiny reveals the fact that such a perspective also has substantial weaknesses, and that what we assess as a "constitutional feature" could be also treated as an argument against the constitutional nature of the Rome Statute, or even an argument for its fragmentation. As Martti Koskenniemi noted, "[F]ragmentation and unity are matters of narrative perspective."[39] Taking this into account, certain concerns appear which lead to the following questions: Why do we even discuss the separation of powers in that context if in a national system this separation of powers was designed to protect the rule of law and democracy, while the goal of the ICC is completely different? Why do we discuss the constitutional character of the Statute if it is not the sole organ of international criminal justice? Why does the RS deal with such a limited number of international crimes, and why do so many core international crimes remain outside its scope if it is supposed to be a "constitution" of ICL? In consequence it can hardly be perceived as the symbol of a constitutionalized order as such. Viewed from such a perspective the RS has also been analyzed within the broader debate on the fragmentation and diversification of international law, concerning, *inter alia*, the proliferation of international courts and viewing the broad scope of their legal discourses as posing a risk to the unity of international criminal law.

4 Fragmentation as a risk to the unity of international criminal law?

If one asks: has ICL ever been unified?[40]; it must surely be concluded that it has not been and that it could not be. There was never any universal "criminal code" ratified by states. Additionally, starting from the IMT (as the 'current debate' refers to last 70 years), the IMTFE and through to the ICTY, ICTR,[41] the international criminal courts (ICTs) were always created as having different *ratione personae*, *ratione temporis*, *ratione loci* and partly different *ratione materiae*. This was a result of the fact they were established for different reasons and purposes. In addition their jurisprudence could also differ, as the justices were never bound by previous judgments and the interpretations of other courts. However, despite the fact that the international courts were always autonomous regimes,[42] they were created within certain

39 M Koskenniemi, 'The Fate of Public International Law: Between Technique and Politics' (2007) 70 *The Modern Law Review* 1, 25.

40 See, for example, D Jacobs, 'The Mythical Unities of International Criminal Law: Some Thoughts on Perisic, Taylor and Sainovic' (2014) 3 *QIL, Zoom-in* 23–39.

41 These shortened forms and abbreviations refer to: the International Military Tribunal at Nuremberg, International Military Tribunal for the Far East, International Criminal Tribunal for the former Yugoslavia, and International Criminal Tribunal for Rwanda.

42 As termed by Lattanzi, 'Introduction' (n 1) 1–20.

frameworks of international law, referring to common principles and core legal values, based on individual responsibility and the principles of *nullum crimen sine lege*, non-retroactivity, etc.

But even though the establishment of the ICC was in part a definite call by the world for unity,[43] it also reintroduced the debate relating to the fragmentation of international law, and in particular the proliferation of international courts and tribunals[44] (coined "institutional fragmentation" by Lattanzi[45]). In addition to the negative connotations and/or pejorative meaning of the notion "fragmentation,"[46] the provisions of the RS and the practice of the Court also provide a different basis to doubt the existence of a unified system of international criminal law.

In the first instance we might refer to the provisions of Art. 21 (1) of the Statute referring to "Applicable law". The Statute enumerates the primary sources to be applied by the Court as: the Statute, Elements of the crimes, its Rules of procedure and evidence. It does not expressly regulate the application of customary law, nor more specifically the jurisprudence of other international tribunals, unlike for example Art. 20 (3) of the Statute of Special Court for Sierra Leone (SCSL), which expressly provides that: "The judges of the Appeals Chamber of the Special Court shall be guided by the decisions of the Appeals Chamber of the International Tribunals for the former Yugoslavia and for Rwanda (…),[47]" which refers to the single appeal chamber for both for ICTY and ICTR and which in turn ensures consistent jurisprudence and judicial dialogue in the *ad hoc* tribunals. And although Judge Kaul noted that: "the ICC does not exist in autistic isolation from developments in international criminal law (…) and the Court may resort to the jurisprudence of other courts and tribunals," he subsequently added that "[t]he jurisprudence of the ad hoc tribunals, as critical and significant as it has been in the development of international criminal law, may serve as a source of inspiration but may be only of limited value for the ICC."[48]

Clearly the ICC is not obliged to take into account the jurisprudence of other courts and tribunals, and there are no institutional links between those

43 See the Preamble (n 11): "Conscious that all peoples are united by common bonds, their cultures pieced together in shared heritage…"; "resolved to guarantee lasting respect for and the enforcement of international justice…", which promotes cultural diversity but at the same time underlines the question of common bonds and shared heritage.

44 See, for example, Y Shany, *The Competing Jurisdiction of International Courts and Tribunals* (OUP 2003) 1.

45 Lattanzi (n 1) 5.

46 L van den Herik, C Stahn, '"Fragmentation", Diversification and "3D" Legal Pluralism: International Criminal Law as the Jack-in-the-Box?' in L van den Herik, C Stahn (eds), *The Diversification* (n 1) 26; E van Sliedregt, S Vasiliev (eds), *Pluralism in International Criminal Law* (OUP 2014) 9.

47 On line at:<http://www.rscsl.org/Documents/scsl-statute.pdf> (accessed 22.09.2015).

48 PTC II, Decision Pursuant to Art. 15 of the Rome Statute on the Authorization of an Investigation into the Situation in the Republic of Kenya, Dissenting Opinion of Judge Hans-Peter Kaul, ICC-01/09-19, 31.03.2010, para. 30.

institutions. A good argument on the fragmentation of ICL could be made if the courts and tribunals were interlinked somehow, particularly by concurrent jurisdiction.[49]

My second argument refers to the definitions used in the statutes of ICTs. For example, the definition of crimes against humanity (CAH) can be analyzed as a symbol of the fragmentation of international criminal law (although this could also relate to the definition of war crimes). CAH were to be prosecuted as offences in the Nuremberg Charter and in the Statutes of the ICTY, ICTR, SCSL, but because they were never defined in a uniform manner we cannot speak about a unified definition used in international customary law in this context. For this reason the potential reliance of the ICC on the jurisprudence of *ad hoc* tribunals and other courts must in fact be limited and cautious.

The definition of CAH contained in the RS was aimed at reconciling the trends concerning interpretations before other Courts in their practice[50] and to reflect international customary law to the extent possible,[51] but at the same time it seems clear that the intent was most likely not to fill the gap relating to the lack of a definition of the crime in international customary law, because the definition used in the RS starts with the proviso that "for the purpose of this Statute CAH means...". This actually limits the impact of the RS and positions it outside the scope of customary law.[52]

Considered in a vacuum, the analyzed provisions concerning the sources of law and definitions of the crimes could give the impression that the ICC will in practice constitute a fragmented, inconsistent jurisdiction, not comparable to the jurisdiction of other ICTs, being a result of the lack of judicial dialogue, with no common grounds as a point of reference. This in consequence could lead to a kind of anarchy created by different autonomous judicial regimes and their "self-contained" practices. Without doubt the RS,

49 The recently established Special Criminal Court for CAR might be an example – it was established not to compete with the ICC but to complement the ICC, and the most responsible persons will be sent to the Hague.

50 The definition is much broader than this used before ad hoc tribunals, as it contains for example forced pregnancy, absent in the statutes of the ad hoc tribunals, but recognized and interpreted in their practice.

51 M H Arsanjani, 'The Rome Statute of the International Criminal Court' (1999) 93 *AJIL* 22, 25; L N Sadat, 'Crimes Against Humanity in the Modern Age' (2013) 107 *AJIL* 334.

52 On the other hand, if we take a broader perspective – beyond the limited provisions of the RS – it can be considered as representing a codification of customary international law, especially taking into account the fact that the draft Convention on CAH, prepared by the Crimes Against Humanity Initiative, repeats the definition of CAH from the RS and draws heavily upon many of its provisions, which can be explained as a growing acceptance of the definitions contained in the RS and their undisputed position among other ICL norms, being also at the same time an argument in favor of the constitutionalisation narrative. The draft can be seen at: http://law.wustl.edu/harris/cah/docs/EnglishTreatyFinal.pdf, and the report prepared of the given initiative here: http://law.wustl.edu/harris/documents/Final-CAHGenevaReport-071714.pdf.

if examined in isolation from the works of *ad hoc* tribunals, falls within the scope of the fragmentation of ICL narrative. But as noted, the ICC does not operate in "autistic isolation" and in fact its judgments and decisions contain numerous references to the existing jurisprudence of ICTs,[53] so this may be more a problem of the coherence of this judicial dialogue than its actual existence.

The argument concerning the risk of the fragmentation of ICL can also be raised in the context of the duty to prosecute and the ICC's principle of complementarity, which gives states the priority to prosecute individuals, at the same time putting on a state (although only in the Preamble) a duty to exercise its criminal jurisdiction over individuals responsible for international crimes. Every state has its own system of justice, its own criminal laws and criminal codes. The RS does not oblige[54] the state to implement unified definitions of the core international crimes. In consequence, a State can prosecute differently defined crimes and apply different interpretations than those used by the Court. The situation becomes even more complicated when a state introduces limitations on criminal sanctions, such as amnesties or pardons, or establishes a Truth Commission, which is not recognized in the RS but at the same time is not illegal or forbidden by ICL.[55]

Such a fragmented reality, which includes both the fragmentation of substantive law and institutional fragmentation, is however in a way justified by the fact that every state has autonomy to determine its own jurisdiction, which must be perceived in the perspective of a state's historically-motivated legal culture, specific language, and particular context in approaching international law. So is the ICC a forum about which one may make a claim for the fragmentation narrative? By its very nature the complementarity principle demands a comparative approach to criminal justice, undermining both domestic and international justice. When we focus on complementarity, the discussion leads us towards cooperation with states, deference to their jurisdiction, granting a margin of appreciation with respect to a state's action and so on,[56] until it reaches the point of acceptance of legal diversity, different legal traditions, and differing perspectives. When we consider such different domains, systems and discourses and their mutual co-existence, the issue of the relationship between them becomes crucial, which in turn leads to the discussion concerning the pluralisation of ICL.

53 See, for example, PTC II, Decision Pursuant to Art. 15 of the Rome Statute on the Authorization of an Investigation into the Situation in the Republic of Kenya (n 48), paras 81–82, etc.

54 Although it may be said it pushes in that direction; see (n 37).

55 D Jacobs, 'Puzzling over Amnesties: Defragmenting the debate for International Criminal Tribunals' in L van den Herik, C Stahn (n 1) 306.

56 For more, see: K Wierczyńska,'Deference in the ICC Practice Concerning Admissibility Challenges Lodged by States' in L Gruszczynski, W Werner (eds), *Deference in International Courts and Tribunals: Standard of Review and Margin of Appreciation* (OUP 2014) 355.

5 Legal pluralism and its usefulness in describing the ICC's regime

Legal pluralism, whether understood as a system for "granting of recognition to different forms and forums of dispute-resolution"[57] and/or a system which "accepts a range of different and equally legitimate normative choices by national governments and international institutions and tribunals, but does so within the context of a universal system,"[58] means the acceptance of different legal traditions, multiple legal regimes, different judicial institutions (and consequently different judicial interpretations) and the possibility of their co-existence.[59] At first glance it might be argued that it is the equivalent of fragmentation, and that both notions are synonyms, and Elies van Sliedregt and Sergyey Vasiliev explain the choice of vocabulary as a "matter of perspective".[60] While lacking any legal definition of these notions, I would nevertheless treat them separately, as fragmentation is a narrative connected with the existence of multiple different authorities with different regimes (not seen as good or bad), while pluralisation is a narrative aimed at reconciling such a diversified reality. Both of them seem adequate, however, to refer to different phases of development of such an international reality.

Ironical as it may be to make such an assumption towards the community of states, the provisions of the RS seem to be a piece of legal pluralism, as it aims at compromise and seeks to strike a balance between different legal regimes, i.e. between national and international jurisdiction. This can be seen in a number of statutory provisions, such as: "cultures pieced together in a shared heritage" (Preamble); the principle of complementarity; issues of admissibility and challenges of admissibility (Arts 17–19 of the RS); the *ne bis in idem* principle (Art. 20); recognition of the fact that general rules of state law can be applied by the ICC (Art. 21(b)); and also including the execution of sentences, cooperation with states, etc.

In addition to the statutory provisions, the practice of the ICC also seems to confirm such a pluralistic tendency. This is visible mainly in the context of procedures concerning admissibility challenges of states, whereby the ICC must assess domestic procedures and decide whether a state is prosecuting the same person for the same conduct.[61] The situation in Libya (referred to the Court via a resolution of the Security Council) may serve as an example. Libya is a state which has not incorporated international crimes into its domestic system and is not a state party of the RS, yet the ICC found that

57 D Nelken, 'Eugen Ehrlich, Living Law, and Plural Legalities' (2008) 9(2) *Theoretical Inquiries in Law* 443.

58 W W Burke-White, 'International Legal Pluralism' (2004) 25 *Michigan Journal of International Law* 977.

59 See K M Clarke, *The International Criminal Court and the Challenge of Legal Pluralism in Sub-Saharan Africa* (CUP 2009) 24.

60 Sliedregt, *Pluralism* (n 46)12–13.

61 Wierczyńska, 'Deference in the ICC' (n 56) 366.

its domestic investigation or prosecution for "ordinary crimes could, to the extent that it covered the same conduct, be considered sufficient."[62] While this approach is inconsistent with the provisions of the ICTY and ICTR statutes,[63] nevertheless the ICC respected the domestic assessments and accepted the fact that the domestic proceedings can actually differ from the potential proceedings before the ICC, in essence demonstrating a pluralistic approach to criminal justice.

Unfortunately the picture sketched above is not as ideal as it might appear. The ICC is also criticized for its hegemonic attitude towards states' systems of justice. While it has accepted states' policy of lodging self-referrals[64] (considering referred situations even when a state was actually willing or able to prosecute), out of a dozen of admissibility challenges lodged by states so far only one has been considered positively (the case of Al-Senussi). This may signify a problem of granting too small a margin of appreciation left to states, or a real problem on the part of states to fulfil certain standards of criminal justice. The problem can also be a result of the fact that the ICC is a body charged with simultaneously assessing the activities of states and deciding on the admissibility of cases before itself. In this context it is both the first and final authority, the arbiter, not just – as declared in the RS Statute – the court of last resort,[65] established to prosecute those most responsible for international crimes. As a court of last resort it should act only when there is no other forum to prosecute, not in a situation in which a state is acting but in the Court's view its proceeding is not a genuine prosecution.

One telling example of the ICC's hegemonic attitude is the case of Thomas Lubanga Dyilo, extensively discussed in the literature.[66] Dyilo was charged by the Democratic Republic of Congo (DRC) for CAH and genocide, but the fact that those proceedings did not include the war crime of specifically enlisting and conscripting children under the age of 15 to participate in hostilities was deemed sufficient to assess the case as admissible before the ICC,[67]

62 PTC I, Decision on the Admissibility of the Case Against Saif Al-Islam Gaddafi, ICC-01/11-01/11, 31.05.2013, para. 88.

63 Art. 10 (2)(a) of the ICTY statute and 9 (2)(a) of ICTR Statute provides the possibility for subsequently trying a person by the ICTY/ICTR even if the person was already tried by a domestic court, but the crime was characterized as an ordinary crime.

64 W Schabas, 'Complementarity in Practice: Some Uncomplimentary Thoughts' (2008) 19 *Criminal Law Forum* 5, 22.

65 Summary records of the plenary meetings in United Nations Diplomatic Conference of Plenipotentiaries on the Establishment of an International Criminal Court, Rome, 15 June – 17 July 1998, A/CONR183/13 (Vol II), 67–68.

66 W Schabas, 'Complementarity in Practice: Creative Solution or a Trap for the Court?' in Politi, F Gioia (eds), *The International Criminal Court and National Jurisdictions* (Ashgate 2008) 25, 42; B Olugbuo, 'Positive Complementarity and the Fight against Impunity in Africa' in C Murungu, J Biegon (eds), *Prosecuting International Crimes in Africa* (Pretoria University Law Press 2011) 249, 255; N N Jurdi, *The International Criminal Court and National Courts: A Contentious Relationship* (Ashgate 2011) 180.

67 PTC I, *The Prosecutor v Thomas Lubanga Dyilo*, Decision on the Prosecutor's Application for a warrant of arrest, Art. 58, ICC-01/04-01/06, 10.02.2006, paras 35, 40.

even though the domestic charges were much stronger. Dyilo was sentenced by the ICC and is now imprisoned. The case has raised much controversy, as the dilemma was not between justice and impunity, but between the different scopes of the national and international proceedings. The ICC is supposed to be complementary and act when the state is inactive or is unwilling or unable to genuinely prosecute. It seems that the DRC was willing and able, but the ICC deemed the charges were not adequate to the type of proceedings it envisioned, which clearly reflects a hegemonic attitude on the part of the Court towards international criminal justice, and its penchant for supremacy and for exercising power. In this instance it did not engage in judicial dialogue, but rather in a turf war. This could discourage states from providing their own domestic prosecutions if a core international crime is at stake, which is precisely the opposite to the idea of positive/proactive complementarity advocated by some scholars.[68] It must be noted that legal pluralism is not a proper tool to analyze the system of criminal justice without a recognized coexistence of different legal systems and mutual acceptance of diversity. Until the ICC begins to grant a more lenient margin of appreciation towards states' actions, legal pluralism will not be a proper tool to describe the existing reality and we will have to go back to the discussion relating to the fragmentation of ICL, or more specifically the negative connotations it raises.

6 "One ring to rule them all"[69] or three pairs of glasses? Conclusions

Much concern has been expressed over whether "constitutionalisation" is the proper term/narrative to describe the realm of international criminal justice; over the potential dangers of fragmentation due to the multiplication of ICTs; and whether legal pluralism could reconcile them. In this chapter I have attempted to demonstrate that these three narratives properly capture and describe the reality of the RS and the ICC, although they do not provide any definitive answers to the dilemmas associated with them.

The Court is yet another autonomous island in the sea of ICL. From the fragmentation perspective we can see many islands, different cultures, and some contours of a hierarchy between them (even if limited only to the sole recognition of peremptory norms). The constitutional perspective comes into being if, in this sea, we can observe the ICC operating as an independent and permanent institution with in a complementary way vis-à-vis national

68 Such as, for example, W W Burke-White, 'Proactive Complementarity: The International Criminal Court and National Courts in the Rome System of International Justice' (2008) 49 *Harvard International Law Journal* 53; C Stahn, 'Taking Complementarity Seriously: On the Sense and Sensibility of "Classical", "Positive" and "Negative" Complementarity' (30 June 2011). Available at SSRN: http://ssrn.com/abstract=2321844 (accessed 17.09.2015).
69 Paraphrased from J R R Tolkien, *Lord of the Rings* (Houghton Mifflin 2003).

jurisdictions, and with multiple international jurisdictions on the horizon, all governed by common rules and values. Pluralists will tend to see this reality as coordinated and co-existing, containing the contours of a recognized hierarchy.

The storm wreaking havoc on the islands is the result of a lack of judicial dialogue, inconsistent jurisdiction, as noted by Webb a "significant divergence in reasoning on the same/similar legal issues,"[70] and the lack of cooperation and/or hegemonic aspirations by one of the key actors in this judicial landscape. The landscape is neither fully divergent (fragmented) nor completely unified (constitutionalised); rather it is pluralism that reconciles the trends by accepting the diversity of the systems on the one hand and the existence of the powers tending to unify it on the other. As Burke-White has noted: "[S]uch diversity or legitimate difference may then promote compliance, resulting in a more effective, more active, and more robust international legal system."[71]

The three narratives discussed focus on different aspects of the development of international law, thus they may be simultaneously applied in interpreting and analyzing the RS and the realm of the ICC. It seems that none of them can refer to it alone. Until all three are governed by common values and principles, which in the context of ICL means individual criminal responsibility for perpetrating international crimes, the perspective taken seems quite proper.

70 Webb, *International Judicial Integration* (n 3) 6.
71 Burke-White, 'International Legal Pluralism' (n 58) 979.

Part III

Constitutionalisation through fragmentation

10 Justifying 'fragmentation' and constitutional reforms of international law in terms of justice, human rights and 'cosmopolitan constitutionalism'

Ernst-Ulrich Petersmann

1 'Constitutionalisation' through 'fragmentation' of legal systems

Similar to the progressive 'constitutionalisation' of monarchical and feudal governance powers inside states through the evolution of 'republican constitutionalism' since the ancient Greek and Italian city republics more than 2000 years ago, globalization and its transformation of *national* into *transnational PGs (res publica)* have prompted governments to conclude ever more international treaties for the collective supply of transnational PGs demanded by citizens. The universal recognition of human rights by all UN member states, their adoption of national (big C) Constitutions (written or unwritten), and international treaties constituting, limiting, regulating and justifying multilevel governance of transnational 'aggregate PGs' (like the international monetary, trade, environmental, communications, health, security, human rights and related legal systems) entail multilevel legal obligations to protect human and constitutional rights and related PGs through democratic governance, judicial remedies and other 'constitutional reforms' of the power-oriented 'Westphalian international law among states'. The more globalization supplements the 'international community of states' (Article 53 Vienna Convention on the Law of Treaties, VCLT) by global communications and cooperation among citizens, the stronger does the emerging 'global civil society' require cosmopolitan and 'constitutional re-interpretations' of international law rules and 'principles of justice' for the benefit of citizens and their constitutional and cosmopolitan rights. This contribution asks how the *existing IEL* should be construed in the light of the changing 'principles of justice' so as to protect human rights and other PGs more effectively.

Similar to the 'trials and errors' during centuries of struggles for 'republican constitutionalism' and to the dialectic evolution of 'public reason' inside states (e.g. through civil struggles among citizens with often different conceptions for a good life and social justice), the decentralized international legal system evolves through 'legal fragmentation' due to, *inter alia*, (1) the power-oriented relations among sovereign states with diverse national interests; (2) the multilevel legal protection of individual and democratic diversity through national and international human rights law (HRL) and related constitutional principles of law; and (3) the diverse rationalities of civil, political, economic, social and cultural legal systems which, as explained by Nobel Prize economist Jan Tinbergen, call for 'separation of policy instruments' for the optimal pursuit of separate policy objectives. HRL and related 'constitutional principles of law' (like rule of law, limited delegation and separation of legislative, executive and judicial powers, democracy, subsidiarity, proportionality, judicial administration of justice) protect 'struggles for justice' aimed at limiting power politics (like colonialism, imperialism) through 'constitutionalisation' of multilevel legal systems, for instance by impartial, judicial interpretation and justification of international rules as protecting rights of citizens. Fragmentation and constitutionalisation are interlinked dimensions of the changing structures of multilevel legal regulation; they are illustrated and 'contextualised' in this contribution by recent developments in IEL. Fragmentation may be based on power-oriented models of legal reasoning; more often, rules-based fragmentation is an inevitable instrument for 'piecemeal constitutionalisation' of power politics in bilateral, regional or functional relations, for instance through bilateral investment treaties (BITs), regional free trade agreements (FTAs) or human rights treaties like the European Convention on Human Rights (ECHR) if states disagree on worldwide constitutional reforms in the United Nations (UN) and the World Trade Organisation (WTO). The 'fragmented evolution' of 15 UN Specialised Agencies and of the General Agreement on Tariffs and Trade (GATT) through dozens of specialised treaty regimes confirms this reality of 'legal fragmentation' and the 'constitutional challenges' resulting therefrom.

Since the emergence of human rights revolutions and democratic Constitutions in the 18th century and the universal recognition of 'inalienable' human rights by all UN member states during the 20th century, citizens increasingly challenge the legitimacy of the power-oriented Westphalian system of 'international law among sovereign states' by insisting on justification of law and governance in terms of human rights, constitutional rights of citizens and other 'principles of justice'. Not only have monarchical powers inside states been progressively limited or abolished through 'glorious revolutions' (e.g. in England in 1688) limiting 'state sovereignty' and foreign policy powers by democratic conceptions of 'parliamentary' or 'popular sovereignty', 'inalienable human rights', and constitutional rights of citizens that often transformed domestic legal traditions progressively through 'legal fragmentation' (e.g. limiting feudal powers of the King and the 'House of Lords' in the English Parliament). The emergence of regional and UN HRL and related institutions (like international parliaments, courts of justice) also limit 'horizontal conceptions' of 'international law among states' by 'vertical conceptions' of international law and institutions committed to protection of human rights and other cosmopolitan rights of citizens (e.g. *EU citizenship rights* to participate in elections of the European Parliament, thereby 'fragmenting' formerly exclusively *national citizenship rights*). 'Struggles for justice', both inside and among states, use 'legal fragmentation' as an instrument for constituting new rights and governance institutions (like regional economic and human rights courts) and for limiting, regulating and justifying multilevel governance powers. For instance, modern HRL is composed of hundreds of national, regional and UN human rights instruments and implemented through multilevel legislative, administrative and judicial institutions. Modern IEL dynamically evolves through thousands of bilateral and regional trade, financial, investment, double taxation and environmental agreements and related adjudication by national and international courts and transnational arbitration. 'Legal fragmentation' is occasionally abused by government executives in order to evade constitutional restraints (e.g. by means of non-transparent 'voluntary export restraints' evading parliamentary control). Yet, it remains indispensable for decentralized reforms of international law, for instance by circumventing abuses of 'veto-powers' in UN and WTO legal regimes through 'constitutional reforms' at regional or bilateral levels of governance that remain opposed in worldwide UN and WTO institutions. *Section 2* illustrates and contextualises these interrelationships between fragmentation and constitutionalisation of international law by examples from IEL.

In many UN member states, the national and international legal commitments to 'constitutional principles of justice' (like human rights) have not been effectively transformed into democratic legislation, administration, judicial protection of human rights, additional constitutional rights of citizens, and participation in international treaties and institutions for collective supply of international PGs. This 'incomplete constitutionalisation' of power politics inside and beyond national legal systems is aggravated by 'globalization' and its transformation of *national PGs* into *transnational 'aggregate PGs'*. National Constitutions reveal themselves as 'partial Constitutions' that can no longer protect most PGs demanded by citizens without international law and institutions for the collective supply of transnational 'aggregate PGs'. *Section 3* discusses why also most international treaties for collective supply of international PGs are based on 'incomplete' and 'under-theorized' treaty provisions that must be interpreted and clarified 'in conformity with the principles of justice and international law', including 'human rights and fundamental freedoms for all', as recalled in the customary rules of treaty interpretation and related adjudication as codified in the VCLT (cf its Preamble and Articles 31–33). Legal and judicial re-interpretation of 'treaties among states' in order to protect constitutional rights, human rights and other cosmopolitan rights of citizens – even if carried out through 'fragmented legal reforms' (e.g. limited to regional agreements implementing UN HRL and WTO trade rules) – is no less important for 'constitutionalising' international law than new international treaties protecting rights of citizens.

Both 'legislative' and 'judicial constitutionalisation' of international law aim at enhancing citizen-oriented 'public reason' and 'democratic capabilities' for 'republican constitutionalism' protecting PGs beyond state borders for the benefit of citizens.

2 'Fragmentation' and 'constitutionalisation' in IEL and adjudication

All states have made the historical experience that effective *democratic protection of national PGs* has been possible only in the framework of constitutional democracies providing for constitutional, legislative, administrative and judicial protection of human rights and democratic 'public reason'. Yet, the prerequisites for national constitutional democracies – a *demos* asserting constituent powers, often as a result of democratic revolutions ushering in a 'constitutional moment' and democratic approval of a comprehensive (big C) Constitution – do not exist at the transnational level. European economic law was transformed into multilevel constitutional orders – as protected by the EU Court of Justice (CJEU), the European Free Trade Area (EFTA) Court and the European Court of Human Rights (ECtHR) in cooperation with national courts in the 31 member states of the European Economic Area (EEA) and 47 member states of the ECHR – only through successive treaties that first 'fragmented' worldwide legal regimes (e.g. UN law, GATT 1947) and then progressively 'constitutionalised' multilevel governance of transnational PGs like human rights and the common market in Europe. *Section 2.1* uses the example of five different narratives of IEL in order to illustrate how the 'fragmented' conceptions of economic regulation progressively reformed IEL. *Section 2.2* explains the important role of multilevel judicial protection of individual rights in constitutional reforms and 'cosmopolitan interpretations' of IEL rules for the benefit of citizens.

2.1 Competing conceptions, fragmentation and 'constitutionalisation' of IEL

The UN Charter principles of 'sovereign equality of states' (Article 2) and 'self-determination of peoples' (Articles 1, 55) aim at protecting international peace by legally recognizing the territorial *status quo* (e.g. in terms of governmental and popular control over a territory) even if the related distribution of natural resources may be as arbitrary from a moral point of view as the distribution of natural human capacities among individuals. The UN legal obligations to respect, protect and fulfill 'human rights and fundamental freedoms for all' (cf Articles 1, 55, 56) limit injustices deriving from such power-oriented allocation of rights (e.g. to the rulers controlling a national territory) and from natural inequalities among individuals by protecting individual and popular rights to liberty and self-development so as 'to establish conditions under which justice and respect for the obligations arising from treaties and other sources of international law can be maintained' (Preamble UN Charter). These tensions – between power politics aimed at protecting *order* (e.g. as defined by government executives claiming to remain the 'masters of international treaties') and *justice* aimed at protecting human rights (e.g. as defined by constitutional courts limiting national implementation of international rules so as to protect constitutional rights of citizens) – must be limited by interpreting treaties and settling related disputes 'in conformity with principles of justice' and 'human rights and fundamental freedoms for all' (Article 1 UN Charter, Preamble and Article 31 VCLT) so as to promote constitutional reforms extending the 'trias' of democratic constitutionalism (human rights, democracy, rule of law) – as universally recognized in UN HRL – beyond state borders to multilevel governance of transnational 'aggregate PGs'. UN HRL recognizes human rights to justification and to judicial review of governmental restrictions of human freedom.[1] Yet, citizens and rulers often disagree on how international law and institutions should be justified and regulated. Both from historical and normative perspectives, five competing conceptions of IEL and their progressive 'constitutionalisation' can be distinguished:[2]

2.1.1 IEL as international order protected by power politics (e.g. GATT 1947)

National '*political realism*' focuses on states as main international actors in a 'billiard ball model' of 'international law among egoist states' driven by power-politics so as to maximize national security and other 'state interests'. Realists claim that, as state-centred international law reflects the *status quo* distribution of power rather than 'principles of justice', also international adjudication is unable to impose effective restraints upon the struggle for power on the international scene. For instance, the General Agreement on Tariffs and Trade (GATT 1947) was negotiated among government executives and applied, since 1 January 1948, on the basis of a 'Protocol of Provisional Application' that was not ratified by national parliaments in most GATT member states and 'grandfathered' existing national legislation inconsistent with GATT provisions. Colonial and intergovernmental power politics in the context of GATT 1947 prior to the establishment of its Legal Office in 1982/83 illustrated the IEL dimensions of 'political realism'. Many GATT rules and GATT dispute settlement rulings were not effectively implemented inside domestic legal systems (e.g. in the context of import restrictions on cotton and textiles from less-developed countries) in response to domestic interest groups pressures and power-oriented majority politics.

1 Cf A A Cançado Trindade, *The Access of Individuals to International Justice* (OUP 2011); R Forst, *The Right to Justification. Elements of a Constructivist Theory of Justice* (Columbia University Press 2012).

2 Cf E U Petersmann, *International Economic Law in the 21st Century. Constitutional Pluralism and Multilevel Governance of Interdependent Public Goods* (Hart 2012) chapter I.

The first and second Directors-General of GATT 1947 (Wyndam White and Olivier Long) had been lawyers by training; yet, they avoided establishing a GATT Office of Legal Affairs up to the 1980s. GATT dispute settlement procedures remained dominated by 'diplomats jurisprudence' that often disregarded the customary rules of treaty interpretation and prevented adoption of GATT dispute settlement reports if domestic interest groups objected to rule-compliance and the related adjustment costs.[3] GATT diplomacy aimed at remedying some injustices of colonial politics (e.g. by adding Part IV on 'Trade and Development' to GATT 1947). Yet, trade diplomats continued expressing the view of *Thrasymachos* in Plato's *Republic* that justice is merely whatever the powerful say it is. Realist conceptions of foreign power politics in a 'society of states' fail to protect justice vis-à-vis individuals, including domestic citizens participating in the global division of labour without effective judicial remedies against violations of UN and WTO agreements and 'disconnected UN/WTO governance' that failed to protect international PGs effectively.

2.1.2 'Constitutionalisation' of GATT law through parliamentary ratification and implementation of the Kennedy and Tokyo Round agreements?

The law of GATT 1947 was progressively developed and 'constitutionalised' through 8 'GATT Rounds' of multilateral trade negotiations (MTN) ushering in additional trade agreements limiting some of the 'constitutional failures' of GATT law. For example, the 1967 Kennedy Round and 1979 Tokyo Round Agreements were ratified by national parliaments and implemented through domestic legislation in most constitutional democracies. Yet, as many less-developed GATT contracting parties did not join these 'MTN agreements' (e.g. on agricultural and textiles trade, anti-dumping and safeguard measures, subsidies and countervailing duties, technical barriers to trade, customs valuation, government procurement), GATT law was transformed into a fragmented 'GATT/MTN legal system' limiting the agreed 'constitutional reforms' (e.g. in terms of parliamentary ratification and implementation of MTN agreements) to 20–30 GATT contracting parties. The parliamentary legislation and control of both *domestic* and *transnational monetary, trade and financial regulations* (e.g. based on the 1944 Bretton Woods agreements) reflected a constitutional 'integrity principle'[4] – as explained by the 'democratic New Haven approach' in US foreign policies exercising leadership for democratic ratification of international 'PGs agreements' on the basis of drafts prepared by the US government (e.g. US

3 On my experiences as first 'legal officer' ever employed by the GATT Secretariat since 1981 see E U Petersmann, 'The Establishment of a GATT Office of Legal Affairs and the Limits of "Public Reason" in the GATT/WTO Dispute Settlement System' in: *EUI Working Papers Law* 2013/10.

4 Cf F J Garcia, *Global Justice and International Economic Law. Three Takes* (CUP 2013) 67 ff.

congressional control of financial assistance by the Bretton Woods institutions, US 'fast track authority' for negotiating and ratifying the 1979 Tokyo Round Trade Agreements)[5]; yet, due to domestic interest group politics, human rights, justice and PGs were not effectively protected across national borders. For instance, the cotton and textiles agreements continued to systematically discriminate against less-developed GATT contracting parties; and GATT anti-dumping rules responded to protectionist pressures without correcting 'market failures' through non-discriminatory competition rules. Also proposals for limiting protectionist interest group politics by 'global administrative law' (GAL) as a means of promoting transparency, legal and judicial accountability and 'good governance' in multilevel governance of IEL tend to be based on US administrative law principles without effective 'constitutional limitations' on welfare-reducing trade protectionism.[6]

2.1.3 Multilevel constitutionalisation of regional free trade agreements in Europe

Multilevel governance institutions effectively empowering citizens have been established so far only through some regional economic and human rights conventions like the ECHR – adopted by now 47 'European countries ... to take the first steps for the collective enforcement of certain of the rights stated in the Universal Declaration' based on 'their profound belief in those fundamental freedoms which are the foundation of justice and peace in the world' (Preamble ECHR). EU law and EEA law used the common GATT commitments of their member states regarding customs unions and free trade agreements (cf Article XXIV GATT) for designing free trade and common market regulations among the 31 EEA member states. The CJEU and the EFTA Court construed these free trade and common market rules as justifying and protecting individual 'fundamental freedoms' and related judicial remedies in national and European courts of justice. The legislative, administrative and judicial EU and EEA institutions differ considerably and respect legitimate 'constitutional pluralism' at national and European levels of governance. Yet, both EU law and EEA law have become progressively 'constitutionalised' on the basis of constitutional principles common to EU and EEA member states, as reflected in the ECHR and the EU Charter of Fundamental Rights (EUCFR). The regional treaties establishing the EU, the EEA and the ECHR are interpreted and enforced by national and European courts as 'constitutional instruments' protecting regional PGs – like

5 For a modern presentation of the 'New Haven school' see: W M Reisman, *The Quest for World Order and Human Dignity in the 21st Century: Constitutive Process and Individual Commitment* (Hague Academy of International Law 2012) 433–454.

6 Cf R Stewart, R M Ratton Sanchez Badin, 'The WTO and Global Administrative Law' in: C Joerges, E U Petersmann (eds), *Constitutionalism, Multilevel Trade Governance and International Economic Law* (Hart 2011) 457–494.

the European common market, human rights, fundamental freedoms and transnational rule of law for the benefit of citizens – for instance through 'constitutional interpretations' (e.g. of 'common market freedoms' in the EU and EEA) protecting cosmopolitan rights of citizens and democratic and judicial accountability of governments through 'evolutionary interpretations' and clarification of fundamental rights in their European context.[7]

The North American Free Trade Agreement (NAFTA) among Canada, Mexico and the USA, by contrast, remains based on 'constitutional nationalism'; NAFTA institutions lack independent legislative, administrative and judicial powers and remain dominated by US hegemonic policies (e.g. preventing intergovernmental dispute settlement proceedings pursuant to Chapter 20 of NAFTA). Investor-state arbitration pursuant to Chapter 11 NAFTA and anti-dumping dispute settlement procedures pursuant to Chapter 19 NAFTA aim at strengthening individual and judicial remedies on the basis of 'GAL principles' rather than of 'constitutional restraints' of national trade and investment policy-making. Beyond *regional* treaty law and institutions, there are only few *worldwide* 'treaty constitutions' (*sic*) constituting individual rights and limiting, regulating and justifying multilevel governance institutions. For instance, the Peace Treaty of Versailles included the 'Constitution of the International Labour Organisation' (ILO, 1919) so as 'to secure the permanent peace of the world' proceeding from the recognition that 'lasting peace can be established only if it is based upon social justice', and 'the failure of any nation to adopt humane conditions of labour is an obstacle in the way of other nations which desire to improve the conditions in their own countries' (Preamble). Just as the more than 180 ILO conventions adopted by the ILO were justified in terms of protecting social and labour rights and peace, so were the post World War II 'constitutions' (*sic*) establishing the Food and Agriculture Organization (FAO, 1945), the United Nations Educational, Scientific and Cultural Organization (UNESCO, 1945) and the World Health Organization (WHO, 1946) justified in terms of fundamental rights like:

- 'ensuring humanity's freedom from hunger' (Preamble of the FAO Constitution);
- 'to further universal respect for justice, for the rule of law and for the human rights and fundamental freedoms which are affirmed for the peoples of the world without distinction of race, sex, language or religion, by the Charter of the United Nations' (Article 1 UNESCO Constitution); and

7 For a comparison of the judicial methodologies of the CJEU, the EFTA Court and the ECtHR see: E U Petersmann, 'Multilevel Judicial Governance in European and International Economic Law' in: S Besson, A Ziegler (eds), *Le Juge en Droit Européen et International* (Schulthess 2013) 45–64.

- 'the enjoyment of the highest attainable standard of health (as) one of the fundamental rights of every human being without distinction of race, religion, political belief, economic or social condition' (Preamble and Article 1 of the WHO Constitution).

Such functionally limited treaty constitutions are fundamentally different from national democratic Constitutions. Yet, they share the 'constitutional functions' of constituting, limiting, regulating and justifying limited governance powers in terms of equal rights of citizens and other PGs. Due to the domination of UN decision-making processes by governments interested in limiting their legal accountability towards citizens, UN law – including the law of UN Specialized Agencies like the ILO, FAO, UNESCO and WHO – continues to prioritize rights of governments without effectively protecting rights and judicial remedies of citizens inside states.

2.1.4 'Constitutional justice' and 'commutative justice' in WTO law?

The termination of GATT 1947 by the end of 1995 and its replacement by the global WTO legal and dispute settlement system introduced new 'constitutional reforms' of the world trading system, for instance due to:

- the establishment of legislative, administrative and judicial WTO institutions governing international trade among 161 WTO members (2015);
- the compulsory nature of the WTO legal and dispute settlement system based on international panel, appellate and arbitration procedures and complementary WTO legal guarantees of *individual access* to domestic legal and judicial remedies; and
- the reciprocal liberalization and regulation of international trade on the basis of mutually agreed '*commutative justice principles*'[8], like reciprocal market access commitments (cf GATT Articles II, XXVIII) subject to sovereign rights to protect non-economic PGs (cf Articles XIX-XXI GATT).

Following the establishment of a GATT Legal Office in 1983, the progressive transformation of the multilevel GATT dispute settlement system into a compulsory worldwide jurisdiction for the settlement of trade disputes through panel, appellate, arbitration and domestic judicial procedures promoted constitutional 'checks and balances' between the political and judicial branches of multilevel trade governance. Yet, similar to UN law, WTO law remains dominated by 'inter-governmental decision-making' and

8 The Latin term '*commutare*' means 'to exchange'; 'commutative justice' refers to mutually agreed 'principles of justice' protecting the 'balance of reciprocal market access commitments', for instance through 'violation' and 'non-violation complaints' pursuant to GATT Article XXIII and the WTO Dispute Settlement Understanding.

fails to effectively protect its treaty objectives (like 'sustainable development') due to inadequate regulation of 'market failures', 'governance failures' and of legal, democratic and judicial 'accountability mechanisms'. WTO dispute settlement bodies recognize that WTO law does not constitute a 'self-contained regime'; treaty-based IEL systems remain embedded into general and treaty law, as illustrated by the WTO provisions for cooperation with other treaty regimes (e.g. IMF law) and regulatory agencies (e.g. national and non-governmental risk assessment institutions in the field of technical and sanitary regulation). WTO law provides for a multilevel legal and dispute settlement system protecting also individual 'access to justice' in domestic courts (e.g. in GATT Article X and similar WTO provisions); yet, many governments limit their domestic legal and judicial accountability for harmful violations of their WTO obligations by insisting that domestic courts should *not* protect domestic citizens against violations of WTO obligations and WTO dispute settlement rulings, thereby impeding adversely affected citizens to obtain judicial remedies in domestic courts. Many FTAs (e.g. by the USA) remain dominated by hegemonic power politics rather than liberal and constitutional 'principles of justice'.[9] The WTO agreements adopted at the 2013 WTO Ministerial Conference (e.g. on trade facilitation for less-developed countries, public stockholding for food security purposes, preferential treatment of least-developed countries) confirm that 'commutative justice' based on voluntarily agreed transactions must include 'communitarian principles of justice' justifying and complementing consensus-based decision-making among 161 WTO members by empowering citizens and governments to make better use of the mutually beneficial opportunities of international trade.

2.1.5 'Cosmopolitan justice regimes' in commercial and investment law

Cosmopolitan constitutionalism[10] and cosmopolitan conceptions of IEL and HRL aim at multilevel legal and judicial protection of cosmopolitan rights (e.g. human, commercial, property rights, labour and social rights) of citizens so as to protect transnational rule of law for the benefit of citizens through institutionalized networks of national and transnational courts and arbitral tribunals. The WTO Agreement on Preshipment Inspection, for example, protects individual access of 'preshipment inspection' companies and exporters to submit disputes over preshipment inspections to

9 Cf Garcia (n 4), 260 ff (describing US abuses of power in NAFTA and CAFTA dispute settlement procedures as illustrating 'how US trade policy is not always consistent with notions of justice', 257, 324).

10 The Greek term 'cosmopolite' refers to a 'citizen of the world' recognizing all human beings as morally equal and constituting a single world community. On 'cosmopolitan constitutionalism' (e.g. in terms of multilevel constitutional and judicial protection of human rights, rule of law and democratic governance across national frontiers in European HRL and economic law) see Petersmann (n 2), chapters III and VIII.

commercial arbitration in the WTO (cf Article 4), thereby decentralizing and depoliticizing related disputes among the importing and exporting countries concerned. Similarly, Article XX of the WTO Agreement on Government Procurement protects individual access to domestic courts reviewing the legal consistency of domestic government procurement proceedings with the WTO Agreement. Some 3,000 bilateral and regional investment agreements replace 'diplomatic protection' of foreign investors by their home states – which has proven to be politically controversial (e.g. due to the absence of individual rights to diplomatic protection) and legally inadequate, for instance in ICJ dispute settlement proceedings among states ushering in judgments only more than 25 years after prior exhaustion of local remedies in domestic courts and intergovernmental diplomatic and judicial protection of foreign investors – by legal guarantees of individual access to investor-state arbitration. Comparative legal and institutional analyses confirm the insight from economic theory that cosmopolitan legal regimes – like transnational commercial and investment law and arbitration, rights-based free trade agreements like the EEA, the EU common market and competition law agreements, co-operation among national and international criminal courts in holding individuals accountable under international criminal law – use more efficient 'optimal policy instruments' that correct 'governance failures' directly at their source (e.g. by protecting 'countervailing rights' of adversely affected citizens); they protect international PGs (like transnational rule of law, fundamental rights) more effectively than 'Westphalian regimes' that lack effective legal, democratic and judicial accountability of governments vis-à-vis adversely affected citizens.[11] Multilevel judicial administration of justice and protection of individual rights have contributed to 'civilizing', de-politicizing and 'constitutionalizing' international law and transnational rule of law for the benefit of citizens, for instance through:

- cooperation between national courts and arbitral tribunals in the recognition, surveillance and enforcement of arbitral awards pursuant to the 1958 New York Convention on Recognition and Enforcement of Foreign Arbitral Awards;
- cooperation among national and regional economic and human rights courts protecting transnational rule of law for the benefit of more than 500 million citizens protected by EU law, EEA law and the ECHR in domestic and European courts;
- the arbitration and annulment procedures of the International Center for the Settlement of Investment Disputes (ICSID) in cooperation with national courts; or
- the more than half a dozen of international criminal courts complementing national criminal jurisdictions and protecting individual rights and legal accountability through multilevel judicial cooperation.

11 Cf Petersmann (n 2), 145 ff.

2.2 *'Struggles for justice' in international treaty interpretation and adjudication*

As briefly explained in *section 1*, positive law (e.g. in the sense of authoritative issuance of 'primary rules of conduct' and 'secondary rules' of recognition, change and adjudication and their social effectiveness[12]) and 'principles of justice' (e.g. in terms of procedural, constitutional, distributive, corrective, commutative and equity principles of justification of law and governance vis-à-vis citizens) interact in dialectic ways, as illustrated by the customary law requirement of interpreting treaties and settling related disputes 'in conformity with the principles of justice and international law', including also 'human rights and fundamental freedoms for all' (Preamble and Article 31 VCLT). Many national Constitutions (like the Preamble of the US Constitution) and international treaties (like the UN Charter, human rights conventions, the 2009 Lisbon Treaty on the EU) are explicitly justified in terms of 'principles of justice'; they call on legislative, administrative and judicial institutions to implement and protect such principles through democratic legislation, administration and judicial protection of human rights and constitutional rights of citizens. If rulers and 'diplomatic realism' resist such legal reforms, independent courts of justice are often the only institutions that have to impartially justify their dispute settlement findings in terms of 'administration of justice'.

Yet, UN member states, their citizens and also courts of justice often disagree on how to define indeterminate 'principles of justice' mentioned in numerous treaties (e.g. the UN Charter, human rights treaties); also the 'balancing' of such principles in national Constitutions and in jurisprudence of national and international tribunals remains contested. For instance, the 1982 Constitution of the People's Republic of China is based on the democratic principle that 'all power belongs to the people' (Article 2). *Democratic constitutions* derive from this principle the need for protecting human rights and delegation of limited powers to democratically elected legislative, executive and judicial government branches so as to protect constitutional, participatory, representative and deliberative self-government by citizens and peoples. China's Constitution, however, emphasizes the need for 'dictatorship by the proletariat' (Preamble) and the 'people's democratic dictatorship led by the working class' (Article 1), as postulated by Karl Marx based on his claims to know 'historic truth' about the domination of the human condition by materialism. Human rights and democratic constitutionalism, by contrast, proceed from the 'Kantian premise' that – because the limits of cognitive human reason (e.g. in terms of time, space, causality, subjective human senses) exclude knowledge of 'absolute truth' – democratic constitutions must protect individual autonomy rights (e.g. to choose one's own conceptions of a 'good life' and 'social justice',

12 Cf H L A Hart, *The Concept of Law* (OUP 1994), chapter V.

freedom to 'falsify' claims of truth) and respect for legitimate 'constitutional pluralism'. As discussed in *section 3*, also worldwide, regional and national courts increasingly insist that the 'horizontal dimensions' of 'international law among states' must remain justifiable in the vertical relations among governments and citizens in terms of human rights, democratic governance and other 'principles of justice'. Apart from multilevel adjudication by national and international economic courts, even the jurisprudence of UN tribunals reflects such re-integration of fragmented national and international legal regimes, for instance:

- by increasing references in ICJ jurisprudence to other international, regional and also national courts of justice 'as subsidiary means for the determination of rules of law' (Article 38:1(d) ICJ Statute) in order to justify, e.g., why state practice continues to support and accept as law (*opinio juris*) the jurisdictional immunity of states even if *jus cogens* is involved;[13]
- by emphasizing that the settlement of disputes among states must remain in conformity with their human rights obligations;[14]
- by evolutionary interpretation and development of international environmental law in ICJ judgments like *Gabcikovo-Nagymaros*, *Pulp Mills* and *Whaling in the Antarctic*;[15]
- by ascertaining international legal practice no longer only in terms of state consent, but recognizing also individuals, corporate actors and international organizations as legal subjects of ever more fields of international law; individual rights increasingly limit traditional principles of 'international law among states' (e.g. lack of reciprocity as *not* limiting the application of human rights treaties; recognition of *erga omnes* and *jus cogens* obligations limiting the legal relevance of state consent and enlarging the scope of rights of diplomatic protection against foreign human rights violations; different allocation of burden of proof in case of human rights violations by authoritarian governments; award of damages in the 2012 ICJ judgment as reparation for the violation of the human rights of *Diallo*).[16]

13 Cf *Jurisdictional Immunities of the State*, *Germany v Italy*, ICJ Reports 2012, p. 99.

14 Cf *Arctic Sunrise*, *Netherlands v Russia*, International Tribunal on the Law of the Sea, Case No. 22, Order of 22 November 2013.

15 See the overview of international environmental adjudication and of human rights courts identifying human rights provisions with environmental content in: P-M Dupuy, J E Vinuales, *International Environmental Law* (CUP 2015) 244 ff, 307 ff.

16 For a discussion of the relevant ICJ judgments in *Congo v Uganda* (2005), *Diallo* (2010) and *Belgium v Senegal* (2012) see: M Andenas, 'Reassertion and Transformation: From Fragmentation to Convergence in International Law' (2015) 46 *Georgetown Journal of International Law* 685, 712 ff.

3 Interpreting and justifying 'incomplete treaties' and 'indeterminate IEL rules' in conformity with 'principles of justice' and 'human rights and fundamental freedoms for all'

This section briefly discusses examples from investor-state arbitration, WTO and EU adjudication as illustrations of citizen-oriented 're-interpretations of treaty rules among states' protecting individual rights on the basis of 'proportionality balancing' and other constitutional 'principles of justice'. The ICJ takes it for granted that:

> 'Whatever the legal reasoning of a court of justice, its decisions must by definition be just, and therefore in that sense equitable.'[17] 'Equity as a legal concept is a direct emanation of the idea of justice. The Court whose task is by definition to administer justice is bound to apply it.'[18]

Yet, also ICJ judges have criticized the ICJ jurisprudence for neglecting human rights and other citizen-oriented 'principles of justice'; the ICJ judgment of November 2010 in the *Diallo Case (Guinea v Congo)* seems to be the first economic dispute in which the ICJ assessed breaches of human rights treaty obligations by referring to the jurisprudence of UN and regional human rights bodies; in 2012, it awarded for the first time financial damages as reparation for the violation of the human rights of *Diallo*.[19] In trade, investment and other economic courts protecting also *individual access* to judicial remedies, the need for reconciling rules and principles for relations among states with rules and principles protecting rights of citizens is more obvious than in ICJ disputes among states, for instance because private complainants invoke their human, constitutional and other rights as legal restraints on governmental interferences and courts interpret international trade, investment and economic treaties as protecting individual trading rights, investor rights, intellectual property rights or fundamental rights.

3.1 Citizen-oriented 'proportionality balancing' in investor-state arbitration

Most international trade and investment agreements include 'general exceptions' or 'non-precluded measures' provisions like Article XI of the

17 *North Sea Continental Shelf Judgment*, ICJ Reports 1969, pp. 48–49, para. 88.
18 *Continental Shelf (Tunisia v Libyan Arab Jamahiriya) Judgment*, ICJ Reports 1982, para. 60, para. 71.
19 Cf (n 16) and the analyses of the ICJ jurisprudence on human rights by Judge B Simma, 'The ICJ and Human Rights' and by Judge A Yusuf, 'The ICJ and the Development of Human Rights Law' in: Società Italiana di Diritto Internazionale (ed), *La Tutela Dei Diritti Umani e il Diritto Internazionale* (Editoriale Scientifica: Napoli 2012) 3–30, 573–581.

Argentina-USA BIT: 'This Treaty shall not preclude the application by either party of measures necessary for the maintenance of public order, the fulfilment of its obligations with respect to the maintenance or restoration of international peace or security, or the protection of its own essential security interests'. The deliberate use of indeterminate treaty terms (e.g. 'necessity') and the treaty provisions for interpretation and adjudication entail that judges have to take into account the 'relevant rules of international law applicable in the relations between the parties' (Article 31:3(c) VCLT) in their treaty interpretations and judicial administration of justice. In investor-state dispute settlement, a number of arbitral awards interpreting such treaty provisions on 'necessity' in the light of the restrictive customary rules on state responsibility (e.g. precluding invocation of 'necessity' if 'the State has contributed to the situation of necessity')[20] have been criticised or annulled by ICSID annulment committees on the ground that 'proportionality balancing' as a 'general principle of law' (in terms of Article 38:1(c) ICJ Statute) offers a more appropriate legal methodology for balancing all interests involved on the basis of 'suitability', 'necessity' and 'proportionality *stricto sensu*' principles as practiced by ever more national and international courts throughout the world.[21] As a general principle of HRL (e.g. as codified in Article 29 UDHR) and of constitutional law (e.g. as codified in Article 52 of the EUCFR), the 'proportionality principle' requires transparent, systemic balancing not only of competing 'state interests' and of reciprocal rights and obligations among states; also civil, political, economic, social and cultural human rights and other rights of citizens and non-governmental organizations must be taken into account, including property rights of companies. Especially in economic and social crisis situations (as in Argentina 1999–2002, Greece since 2010) leading to 'regulatory takings' of foreign property rights protected under international investment law, or to international financial assistance conditional on 'austerity measures' limiting social rights of citizens, national and international judgments continue to clarify the controversial, legal 'borderlines' between 'necessary' governmental restrictions of rights of *domestic citizens* (e.g. social rights exceeding national budgetary resources) and 'disproportionate' restrictions of *foreign property rights*.[22] The more complainants, respondent states, third parties and judges invoke individual rights and other 'principles of justice' as applicable law in investment disputes, the more can judicial rule-clarification and adjudication on the basis

20 Cf J Crawford, *The International Law Commission's Articles on State Responsibility. Introduction, Text and Commentaries* (CUP 2002) 178 ff.

21 Cf A Stone Sweet, G della Cananea, 'Proportionality, General Principles of Law, and Investor-State Arbitration: A Response to José Alvarez' (2014) 46 *New York University Journal of International Law and Politics* 911–954.

22 On the different cultures and legal understandings of judicial 'balancing' and 'proportionality review' see: G Huscroft, B W Miller, G Webber (eds), *Proportionality and the Rule of Law. Rights, Justification and Reasoning* (OUP 2014).

of general principles of law limit incoherencies among fragmented treaty regimes, especially if they are dominated too one-sidedly by 'state interests' and government executives eager to limit their own legal, democratic and judicial accountability vis-à-vis citizens adversely affected by harmful treaty violations.

3.2 Citizen-oriented 'proportionality balancing' in trade adjudication

The clarification of indeterminate and incomplete rules and principles by national, regional and WTO dispute settlement bodies in international trade and regional economic integration agreements has given rise to hundreds of judgments interpreting treaty rules among states as conferring and protecting also rights of non-governmental economic actors. By clarifying general principles of law resulting from 'the constitutional traditions common to the Member States', including fundamental rights (cf. Article 6 TEU), national and regional courts have cooperated in strengthening the effectiveness and legitimacy of fragmented legal regimes by clarifying 'principles of justice' justifying IEL vis-à-vis citizens and peoples. Often building on national 'due process of law' guarantees (e.g. in French and Swiss law, according to which 'the judge who refuses to judge, on the pretext of the silence, the obscurity, or the adequacy of the law, may be prosecuted as one guilty of denial of justice'), the judicial task of clarifying and developing the applicable law (e.g. through 'dynamic interpretations') is explicitly recognized in regional economic and human rights jurisprudence. As customary law requires interpreting treaties and settling related disputes 'in conformity with the principles of justice and international law', including 'human rights and fundamental freedoms for all' (cf. the Preamble and Article 31 VCLT), ever more regional economic courts follow the jurisprudence of the CJEU and of the EFTA Court that 'the fact that certain provisions of the Treaty are formally addressed to the Member States does not prevent rights from being conferred at the same time on any individual who has an interest in compliance with the obligations thus laid down.'[23] Hence, European courts interpret FTA and common market rules of the EU Treaty as conferring fundamental rights on individuals. Governmental limitations of such 'market freedoms' – e.g. in case of imported laser games that simulate killing of peoples and were prohibited in the German town of Bonn as offending 'human dignity' and public order – were accepted by the CJEU as legally justifiable and

23 See Case 43/75 *Defrenne v Sabena* [1976] ECR 455, para. 31. 'Such consideration must, *a fortiori*, be applicable to Article 48 of the Treaty, which … is designed to ensure that there is no discrimination on the labour market' (Case C-281/98, *Angonese* [2000] ECR I-4139).

'proportionate' even if other towns in Germany and other EU member states did not adopt similar prohibitions due to different conceptions of 'human dignity'.[24]

WTO jurisprudence applies 'dynamic interpretations' and 'proportionality balancing' not only in 'horizontal' relations among WTO members, but also in protecting private economic actors against disproportionate governmental trade restrictions. For instance, in *Shrimp-Turtles II*, the Appellate Body concluded that the US administration of non-transparent and discriminatory certification procedures and import restrictions on shrimp had failed to protect the rights of exporting countries and of their individual exporters to 'basic fairness and due process'.[25] In the WTO jurisprudence on the protectionist 'zeroing practices' of EC and US antidumping authorities, the WTO Appellate Body rightly interpreted the WTO requirement of 'fair price comparisons' from the perspective of the reasonable interests of economic actors rather than – as advocated by some WTO panels – from the perspective of EC and US antidumping bureaucracies, which claimed that they had not intended to limit their 'sovereign right' to apply 'zeroing methodologies' by concluding the WTO Agreement on Antidumping.[26]

3.3 Protection of human rights in multilevel economic adjudication

The more the universal recognition of human rights and of 'constitutionalism' contributes to the globalization of principles of constitutional law, the more national and international courts resort to 'constitutional principles' for re-interpreting international law and justifying judicial decisions. Article 47 EUCFR protects the right to an effective remedy and to a fair trial as a cosmopolitan right of 'everyone', including alleged foreign terrorists. European courts (e.g. the CJEU, the EFTA Court and the ECtHR) cooperate very closely with national courts throughout Europe in protecting and 'balancing' civil, political, economic and fundamental rights at the request of European citizens. The four 'Kadi judgments' of the General Court and CJEU since 2005 relate to EU regulations that implement UN Security Council sanctions adopted under Article 41 UN Charter vis-à-vis Mr Kadi and other alleged terrorists in response to the terrorist attacks of 11 September 2001. The Security Council had identified Mr Kadi (a wealthy citizen of Saudi-Arabia) as a possible supporter of Al-Qaida and had ordered the freezing of his assets. In the first judgment of 2005 on Mr Kadi's legal challenge of the EU regulation that implements the Security Council sanctions, the General Court refused to fully review the EU regulation in view of the judicial immunity of the Security Council sanctions. The Court only reviewed whether the Security

24 Cf C-36/02 *Omega case* [2004] ECR I-9609.
25 WT/DS58/AB/R, adopted on 6 November 1998.
26 For an analysis of this jurisprudence see: S Cho, 'Global Constitutional Lawmaking' (2010) 31 *University of Pennsylvania Journal of International Law* 621–678.

Council had violated fundamental rights of Mr Kadi protected by *jus cogens*; it did not find such infringements. On appeal, the CJEU fully reviewed the lawfulness of the EU implementation regulation on the ground that all EU legal acts must remain consistent with the fundamental rights protected by EU law, even in case of implementation of UN Security Council sanctions. The Court found – without pronouncing on the legality of the UN Security Council measures – that the EU implementation of the Security Council sanctions had violated the claimant's fundamental right to be informed of the grounds for his subjection to sanctions, his right to be heard, his access to effective judicial review, and the right to protection of property.[27]

As the EU Commission and Council decided to maintain the sanctions, Mr Kadi appealed to the General Court once again. In its judgment of 2010, the General Court annulled the contested EU sanctions vis-à-vis Mr Kadi on the ground of infringements by the EU institutions of the rights of the defence, the right to respect for property and the principle of proportionality, and also of the right of Mr Kadi to effective judicial review. In its judgment of 18 July 2013, the CJEU rejected the appeal and concluded that effective 'judicial review is indispensable to ensure a fair balance between the maintenance of international peace and security and the protection of the fundamental rights and freedoms of the person concerned, those being shared values of the UN and the European Union'.[28]

The *Kadi*-judgment can be understood in conformity with the '*solange*-jurisprudence' of the German Constitutional Court and of the ECtHR to the effect that 'as long as' (which means *solange* in German language) the higher level of law (i.e. UN law in the *Kadi* cases, EU law in the *solange*-jurisprudence of the German Constitutional Court) does not guarantee equivalent protection of fundamental rights, the courts at lower levels of multilevel legal and judicial systems must guarantee such fundamental rights. Just as the German Constitutional Court and the ECtHR refrained from exercising their jurisdiction 'as long as' the CJEU protects fundamental rights in ways equivalent to the constitutional protection under German constitutional law and the ECHR respectively, the CJEU might limit its judicial review of EU measures implementing UN Security Council sanctions once UN law offers equivalent procedural and substantive legal protection of individual rights of the defence, property rights and effective judicial protection. Both the *Kadi*- and the '*solange*-jurisprudence' suggest that, as UN and regional human rights conventions leave states 'margins of appreciation' for implementing and protecting higher standards of human rights in their national legal systems, multilevel legal regulation and judicial protection of civil, political, economic, social

27 For comprehensive analyses of the *Kadi*-judgments see M Avbelj, F Fontanelli, G Martinico (eds), *Kadi on Trial* (Routledge 2014), see also Chapter 5 of this book.

28 Joined Cases C-584/10P, C-593/10P and C-595/10P, *Commission, Council, United Kingdom v Yassin Abdullah Kadi*, para. 131 (cf n 27).

and cultural rights must be based on mutually consistent interpretations and 'judicial comity' (e.g. regarding the local remedies rule in HRL), 'subsidiarity' and 'loyal cooperation' among the different levels of governance, with due respect for the sovereign rights of states to guarantee higher levels of constitutional protection at national levels than at international levels of governance.

4 Conclusions

UN law does not limit the 'sources' and 'rules of recognition' of international law to 'international conventions … recognized by states' (Article 38(a) of Statute of the ICJ). The additional sources – '(b) international custom, as evidence of a general practice accepted as law; (c) the general principles of law recognized by civilized nations; (d) …judicial decisions and the teachings of the most highly qualified publicists of the various nations, as subsidiary means for the determination of the rules of law' (Article 38 of ICJ Statute) – must be construed 'in conformity with principles of justice', including also 'human rights and fundamental freedoms for all', as explicitly recalled in the Preamble and Article 31:3(c) of the VCLT.[29] International and national HRL require subjecting state consent and multilevel governance to constitutional restraints as illustrated by the jurisprudence of European courts. In their judicial administration of justice, national and international courts of justice should use the customary rules of treaty interpretation for limiting intergovernmental power politics to the extent it ignores or violates 'human rights and fundamental freedoms for all' and other constitutional 'principles of justice' accepted by the parties to the dispute. If the international 'rules of recognition' are construed in conformity with the legal duties of all governance institutions to respect, protect and fulfil human rights and other constitutional rights 'retained by the people' (in the words of the Ninth Amendment to the US Constitution), the universal recognition of human rights and the corresponding duties of all UN member states to respect, protect and fulfil human rights remain the ultimate sources of multilevel regulation of PGs demanded by citizens. Citizens and democratic institutions may legitimately disagree on how to prioritize, balance and construe civil, political, economic, social and cultural rights in different legal, economic and political contexts. Hence, respect for democratic 'constitutional pluralism' and for the 'inalienable core' of human rights are more convincing justifications of modern IEL than mere state consent and economic utilitarianism. The three main claims of this contribution are:

- Cosmopolitan paradigms can regulate and justify multilevel governance of citizen-driven transnational PGs (like the world trading system) more coherently than the statist paradigms advocated by governments and

29 See also Chapter 13 of this book.

diplomats for justifying their power-oriented, 'disconnected' and fragmented UN/WTO governance.

- The historical lessons from 'republican constitutionalism' confirm that multilevel governance of transnational PGs must remain embedded into 'cosmopolitan constitutionalism' in order to protect rights of citizens effectively. As illustrated also by the temporary 'fragmentation' of European law (e.g. due to the creation of the European Coal and Steel Community, the EEC and EFTA) and by its subsequent re-integration (e.g. by the ECHR, EU-, EEA-law and related adjudication): 'consistent interpretations' and constitutionalism offer the most effective remedies to fragmentation processes; they enable 'de-fragmentation' of multilevel regulation of transnational PGs and better protection of the unity and overall coherence of multilevel HRL.
- Cosmopolitan and 'republican constitutionalism' also offer more coherent justifications for 'systemic coordination' of the 'multilevel dialogues among courts' with due respect for the reality of constitutional and legal pluralism.

11 A constitutionalised legal order

Exploring the role of the World Heritage Convention (1972)*

Andrzej Jakubowski

1 Introduction

Janet Blake has observed that '… it is not possible to state one single approach to the protection of cultural heritage under international law… cultural heritage means many things to many people (and groups of people) and the challenge facing international law in this field is to try to satisfy as many of the legitimate interests in heritage as possible, while at the same time operating within a system primarily established by and for sovereign and equal States'.[1] One can hardly agree more. Indeed, the complexity of the normative environment for the protection of cultural heritage poses a number of questions in terms of the fragmentation of the international legal order. The arguments on fragmentation particularly arise in the context of the different types of heritage protected under distinctive and multiple regimes (movable property, immovable property, tangible heritage and intangible heritage), marked by internal normative conflicts and tensions. These arguments also refer to technical or workflow issues related to both policy and management in dealing with cultural heritage questions. Another group of concerns addresses a primordial deficiency of international cultural heritage law, which lies in its opposing objectives, being the exclusive interest of states on one hand, and universal and community interests in the protection, enjoyment and management of cultural resources on the other. Concerns over fragmentation are also raised by the lack of established techniques to alleviate normative conflicts and tensions between international law norms on the protection of cultural heritage, and those belonging to other specialized regimes, such as human rights law and trade law. Finally, it is argued that international heritage law is greatly affected by the politics of expertise (so-called 'expertisation'), which

* The research on this chapter has been carried out and financed within the project 'HEURIGHT14-The Right to Cultural Heritage – Its Protection and Enforcement through Cooperation in the European Union, No. 30/DSAP-PF/HERITAGEPLUS/2015, ERA-NET Heritage Plus 'Cultural Heritage and Global Change', Horizon 2020.

1 J Blake, *International Cultural Heritage Law* (OUP 2015) 21–22.

leads to profound disagreements and fragmentation within this specific area of international law.[2]

On the other hand, a seemingly opposite doctrinal trend emphasizes that the current evolution of international cultural heritage law rises above its internal ruptures, due to the growing universal awareness that cultural heritage represents a holistic notion inherently linked to the identity of peoples and connected to both individual and collective human rights. In this regard, it is claimed that international law and its practice provide evidence that today certain general principles concerning the protection and enjoyment of cultural heritage have either already emerged at the level of customary international law or are in the process of emerging (*in statu nascendi*).[3] Accordingly, since the origin of such principles arises from the general interest of the international community, respect for cultural heritage constitutes the object of an obligation *erga omnes*.[4] Arguably, these voices may be encapsulated within theories on normative constitutionalisation, touching upon the foundations of the international legal order and the development of core values in international law.

This chapter brings together these two narratives and attempts to show how and to what extent they might be useful to explain and analyze the current challenges surrounding the international protection of cultural heritage. Taking the example of the 1972 World Heritage Convention (WHC)[5] and its current practical operationalistion, it seeks to identify which elements of its legal regime are the most plausible candidates to obtain the status of 'universal' or 'constitutional' principles of the international legal order. This analysis aims to demonstrate how different 'fragmented' practices of international law may contribute to the consolidation of a universal regime for the protection of cultural heritage globally.

2 Arguments on the fragmentation of cultural heritage law

Protection of cultural heritage constitutes a relatively new area of international law.[6] Its original fundamental rationale consisted in recognition of the right

2 In particular see L Lixinski, 'International Cultural Heritage Regimes, International Law, and the Politics of Expertise' (2013) 20 *IJCP* 407; L James and T Winter, 'Expertise and the Making of World Heritage Policy' (2015) *International Journal of Cultural Policy* (online edition of 07 May 2015).

3 F Francioni, 'Au-delà des Traités: l'Émergence d'un Nouveau Droit Coutimier pour la Protection du Patrimoine Culturel' (2007) 111 *RGDIP* 19.

4 Ibid., 41; AF Vrdoljak, 'Human Rights and Cultural Heritage in International Law' in F Lenzerini and AF Vrdoljak (eds), *International Law for Common Goods: Normative Perspectives on Human Rights, Culture and Nature* (Hart 2014) 139, 173.

5 Convention Concerning the Protection of World Natural and Cultural Heritage, adopted on 16 November 1972, entered into force on 17 December 1975, 1037 UNTS 151.

6 See Blake (n 1) 4–6; F Francioni, 'A Dynamic Evolution of Concept and Scope: From Cultural Property to Cultural Heritage' in AA Yusuf (ed), *Standard-Setting in UNESCO. Normative Action in Education, Science and Culture: Essays in Commemoration of the Sixtieth Anniversary of UNESCO*, vol. 1 (UNESCO 2007) 221; F Francioni, 'The Evolving International Legal Framework for the Protection of Cultural Heritage' in S Borelli, F Lenzerini (eds),

of every state to identify, physically control, and protect its tangible cultural heritage against irreparable loss in the event of armed conflict[7] and its unlawful removal from a state's territory during both war and peacetime.[8] This state-oriented perspective of international cultural heritage legislation, aimed at preserving national heritage against 'external' threats to its integrity, has been gradually broadened, and today encompasses a vast range of cultural manifestations and interests attached to them. The evolution of treaty law in this area, in particular the large UNESCO legal instrumentarium, reflects some current universal problems and concerns of the international community on the one hand, and the growing complexity and specialization of national cultural heritage legislation on the other. Consequently, cultural heritage law is now considered 'an established branch of international law'.[9] Yet most of the treaties in this area are still young, 'with all the uncertainties that this entails',[10] and thus it has been asserted that the effect of the expansion of distinct regimes 'concerning cultural heritage contributes to the fragmentation of international law'.[11] In fact, one of the basic arguments on the fragmentation of cultural heritage law – at both the national and international levels – refers to its compartmentalisation of the different types of heritage into tangible and intangible dimensions. It is often argued that 'the common feature of cultural heritage legislation is its fragmentation', since various aspects of cultural heritage are regulated under distinct instruments and fall under the competences of different authorities and monitoring bodies.[12] In addition, the protection of cultural heritage universally is challenged by the differences and inconsistency of national and/or regional regimes. This latter observation arguably touches upon the allegations of territorial and/or structural fragmentation. In this regard it is necessary to address the lack of well-developed mechanisms to deal with the variety of conflicts and tensions within international cultural heritage law, since 'the development of this autonomous regime has not been accompanied by the creation of a specific, comprehensive and efficient dispute settlement

Cultural Heritage, Cultural Rights, Cultural Diversity. New Developments in International Law (BRILL-Nijhoff 2012) 3.

7 UNESCO Convention for the Protection of Cultural Property in the Event of Armed Conflict, adopted on 14 May 1955, entered into force on 7 August 1956, 249 UNTS 240.

8 UNESCO Convention on the Means of Prohibiting and Preventing the Illicit Import, Export and Transfer of Ownership of Cultural Property, adopted on 14 November 1970, entered in force on 24 April 1972, 823 UNTS 231; Unidroit Convention on Stolen and Illegally Exported Cultural Objects, adopted on 24 June 1995, entered into force on 1 July 1998, (1995) 34 ILM 1322.

9 A Chechi, 'Evaluating the Establishment of an International Cultural Heritage Court' (2013) 18 *Art, Antiquity & Law* 31, 32.

10 Blake (n 1) 5.

11 Chechi (n 9) 32.

12 For instance see ETNOFOLK, 'Strategy for the Use of Cultural Heritage Resources' (2014) 6, available at <http://www.central2013.eu/fileadmin/user_upload/Downloads/outputlib/ETNOFOLK_Strategy_and_recommendations.pdf> accessed on 10 August 2015.

system',[13] nor by any established hierarchies or other techniques to manage normative conflicts. Hence it may be plausibly argued that the existing regimes do not offer any consistent and efficient international system for the protection of cultural heritage.

A second group of fragmentation arguments refers to the 'original sin' of the international legal system of cultural heritage law, i.e. its opposite objectives, which result in the dichotomy between state-oriented approaches and those designed to accommodate and enforce universal and community interests in the protection, enjoyment and management of cultural resources. Traditionally, these opposite 'ways of thinking' of cultural heritage have been framed in terms of John Henry Merryman's theories of 'cultural nationalism' and 'cultural internationalism'.[14] The former relates to the exclusivity and hegemony of the nation-state with respect to cultural material, 'to make the case for its retention within or return to the national territory',[15] as reflected in the regime of the 1970 UNESCO Convention. 'Cultural internationalism' sees the globalization of cultural exchange as a positive factor which contributes to international understanding, knowledge, research, and access to cultural material, rather than as a threat to its preservation and enjoyment.[16] Universal approaches emphasize the existence of commonly shared values and interests in cultural heritage, sometimes transcending narrowly defined states' interests.[17] In fact, 'the idea of basing protection on the notion of universal, global value, as a heritage of mankind, has been predominant throughout international law-making since the second half of the twentieth century and has formed the justification for international cooperation in this field'.[18] As a result of these two conflicting theories, very real interests driven by national or state-oriented objectives of cultural heritage protection 'are usually incompatible'[19] with those stemming from and/or reflecting universal values and concerns.[20]

13 Chechi (n 9) 32.

14 JM Merryman, 'Two Ways of Thinking of Cultural Property' (1986) 80 *AJIL* 831.

15 JM Merryman, 'The Nation and the Object' (1994) 3 *IJCP* 61, 64.

16 See J Cuno (ed), *Whose Culture?: The Promise of Museums and the Debate over Antiquities* (Princetown University Press 2009) 1–35.

17 Within the group of international treaties which embody such concerns are usually listed: the 1954 Hague Convention and two Protocols to it (1954, 1999); the 1972 World Heritage Convention; UNESCO Convention on the Protection of the Underwater Cultural Heritage, adopted on 2 November 2001, entered into force on 2 January 2009, UNESCO Doc.31C/RES.24, (2002) 41 ILM 37; UNESCO Convention for the Safeguarding of the Intangible Cultural Heritage, adopted on 17 October 2003, entered into force on 20 April 2006, 2368 UNTS 3; UNESCO Convention on the Protection and Promotion of the Diversity of Cultural Expressions, adopted on 20 October 2005, entered into force on 18 March 2007, 2440 UNTS 311.

18 Blake (n 1) 13.

19 D Lowenthal, *Heritage Crusades and the Spoils of History* (Viking 1997) 227.

20 Cf D Gillman, *The Idea of Cultural Heritage* (CUP 2010) 41 ff.; K Wangkeo, 'Monumental Challenges: The Lawfulness of Destroying Cultural Heritage During Peacetime' (2003) 28 *Yale Journal of International Law* 183, 186.

Fragmentation claims also relate to the expanding structure of global cultural heritage governance, which involves a growing multiplicity of authorities, actors and stakeholders and makes 'meaningful communication between them and solution-oriented thinking difficult'.[21] Indeed, there are a growing number of institutional actors – such as World Intellectual Property Organization – involved in cultural heritage issues, often applying contradictory or 'fragmented' *par excellence* solutions. In particular, the topics of culture and cultural heritage pose serious difficulties to international economic law, since cultural policies have been perceived as negative factors hampering international trade and investment.[22] Certain concessions have only been available under the 'cultural exception' clauses, giving effect to states' interests in limiting free trade in culture in order to protect and promote their artists and other elements of their culture.[23] Moreover, various aspects of cultural heritage are regulated under bilateral agreements on trade in cultural products, which are sometimes more restrictive in relation to the protection of cultural heritage than general multilateral regimes, resulting in a dichotomy known as 'strategic fragmentation'.[24] In addition, different tensions may be identified between cultural heritage law and other specialized regimes of international law. Importantly, a number of seemingly inextricable contradictions, both real and potential, can be observed between collective rights to cultural heritage and other (mainly) individual human rights. In particular these refer to inherent controversies between the objectives of protecting both cultural heritage and individual rights, especially with respect to the right to enjoy private property.

The last group of arguments on the fragmentation of cultural heritage law concerns its alleged expertisation. Laurajane Smith, in her influential book *Uses of Heritage*[25], has explored the growing importance of the role of professional experts – appointed as the rightful 'stewards' of heritage – in identifying and 'protecting' heritage *vis-à-vis* other multiple discourses and interests. In such a context, the role of experts in 'translating' the language of heritage into legal vocabulary in the 'Authorized Heritage Discourse' (AHD), can be seen as a tool both supporting and combating the fragmentation of international cultural heritage law.[26] On one hand, experts provide the 'impartial' knowledge necessary for the operationalisation of various cultural heritage

21 M Burri, 'The International Law of Culture: Prospects and Challenges' (2014) 19 *IJCP* 579, 579.

22 V Vadi, *Cultural Heritage in International Investment Law and Arbitration* (CUP 2014) 93 ff.

23 See generally J Shi, *Free Trade and Cultural Diversity in International Law* (Hart 2013) 139 ff. and 233 ff.; and L Richieri Hanania (ed), *Cultural Diversity in International Law: The Effectiveness of the UNESCO Convention on the Protection and Promotion of the Diversity of Cultural Expressions* (Routledge 2014).

24 L Lixinski, *Intangible Cultural Heritage in International Law* (OUP 2013) 58.

25 LJ Smith, *Uses of Heritage* (Routledge 2006).

26 Lixinski, 'International Cultural Heritage Regimes' (n 2) 423.

regimes, bridge 'the gap between the languages of law and of heritage',[27] and promote a consensus approach to history, smoothing over conflicts and social differences. On the other hand, the AHD dichotomizes heritage between intangible and tangible, as heritage professionals strive to expand their self-created professional legitimacy and importance.[28] This may lead to a lack of communication and harmony, even amongst the relatively few cultural heritage regimes under UNESCO. It may also contribute to unequal power/knowledge relations between the interests of experts and those of human communities,[29] thus undermining the effective enforcement of cultural heritage legislation and its objectives.

3 World heritage as a legal concept

Within the context of the proliferation of international regimes on the protection of cultural heritage, the WHC is undoubtedly the most recognizable instrument.[30] Being both a fruit of the post-World War Two trauma and the decolonisation which took place after the war (i.e. the loss of direct control by developed countries over cultural heritage sites located in developing countries), the WHC has gradually become a truly universal treaty (a 'jewel' of international cultural heritage law),[31] today binding 191 states.[32] 'The overarching benefit of ratifying the World Heritage Convention is that of belonging to an international community embracing appreciation and concern for universally significant properties that embody a world of outstanding examples of cultural diversity'.[33] Thus, state parties to this treaty, 'by joining hands to protect and cherish the world's ...... cultural heritage, express a shared commitment to preserving our legacy for future generations'.[34] Importantly, the system of the WHC bridges the two opposing perspectives: national and universal,[35] recognizing the principle that the international community as a whole has an interest and duty to cooperate in order to safeguard, valorise and guarantee the conservation of certain elements of cultural heritage of universal and outstanding value. In fact, 'the

27 Ibid., 407.
28 Smith (n 25) 29 ff.
29 Lixinski, 'International Cultural Heritage Regimes' (n 2) 412.
30 This chapter omits the issues related to the protection of the world's natural heritage under the WHC. On this environmental issue, see Chapter 15 in this book.
31 See S von Schorlemer, 'Compliance with the UNESCO World Heritage Convention: Reflections on the Elbe Valley and the Dresden Waldschlössen Bridge' (2009) 51 *GYIL* 321.
32 <http://portal.unesco.org/la/convention.asp?KO=13055&language=E&order=alpha>, accessed on 25 September 2015.
33 <http://whc.unesco.org/en/convention> accessed on 15 October 2015.
34 Ibid.
35 R Anglin, 'The World Heritage List: Bridging the Cultural Property Nationalism-Internationalism Divide' (2008) 20 *Yale Journal of Law & the Humanities* 241.

secret of its success lies in the careful combination of national legal orders, based on the principle of territorial sovereignty, with the international law concept of "world heritage" attached to properties of such exceptional value as to entail the general interest of the international community for their conservation and management'.[36]

The core of the 1972 UNESCO World Heritage regime consists of the World Heritage List (WHL). Under Article 11 of this treaty, the decision with respect to inscription rests with the World Heritage Committee (Committee), an organ elected by the states parties to the Convention. As provided in the Operational Guidelines,[37] the process of nominating properties for inclusion on the WHL begins with the states parties, which are exclusively empowered as sovereigns to identify and delineate the properties in their own territories which would form part of world heritage (Article 3). Thus, in contrast to other resources, defined by international law as the common heritage of mankind, World Heritage Sites remain subject to the jurisdiction of the territorial state.[38] Moreover, the inclusion of a property on the WHL requires the consent of the territorial state (Article 11(3)). On the other hand, the Committee has the power to consider and evaluate the proposed property, to approve or reject its inscription in the WHL, and to monitor its state of conservation, on which its world heritage status depends. Moreover, when such a property, forming part of the cultural and natural heritage, 'is threatened by serious and specific dangers', the Committee may, in case of 'urgent need', include this property, even without the consent of the state concerned, in the inventory of World Heritage Sites which require major operations for their conservation and for which 'assistance has been requested' – the List of World Heritage in Danger (Article 11(4)).[39] The WHC's provisions are also interpreted to mean that in particular cases, if and when an inscribed property loses its outstanding universal value, the Committee may decide to remove the property from the WHL.[40] Here too the consent of the state is not required.[41]

36 F Francioni, 'Public and Private in the International Protection of Global Cultural Goods' (2012) 23 *EJIL* 719, 725.

37 The Operational Guidelines for the Implementation of the WHC are periodically revised to reflect the decisions of the Committee. Latest version: UNESCO Doc. WHC. 13/01, July 2013, <http://whc.unesco.org/archive/opguide13-en.docx>, accessed on 15 October 2015.

38 See A Chechi, *The Settlement of International Cultural Heritage Disputes* (OUP 2014) 17–20; Wangkeo, 'Monumental Challenges' (n 20) 186; M Frigo, 'Cultural Property v Cultural Heritage: A "Battle of Concepts" in International Law?' (2004) 86 *International Review of the Red Cross* 367, 377; J Blake, 'On Defining the Cultural Heritage' (2000) 49 *ICLQ* 61, 69; K Baslar, *The Concept of the Common Heritage of Mankind in International Law* (Brill-Nijhoff 1998) 296.

39 GP Buzzini and L Condorelli, 'Article 11: List of World Heritage in Danger and Deletion of a Property from the World Heritage List' in F Francioni and F Lenzerini (eds), *The 1972 World Heritage Convention: A Commentary* (OUP 2007) 175, 177.

40 Ibid., 196–99.

41 Ibid., 199.

Thus, the legal regime of this UNESCO instrument provides for a particular reconciliation of national and universal visions and interests with respect to the protection of cultural heritage, vesting significant powers in an international organ. However, the dialectic between states' interests and that of the international community may produce grounds for continuous conflicts within the system of the WHC. In practice, conflicts between state sovereignty and the universal protection of world heritage have tended to be resolved 'in favour of a state-oriented approach'.[42] Moreover, the universal language of this convention may foster local or even political disputes stemming from conflicting claims to a given cultural heritage,[43] even though in an ideal world a universal vocabulary should transcend local or national conflicts. In addition, the system of nomination and evaluation of cultural properties to be inscribed on the WHL is profoundly affected by the AHD, as the Committee is formed by experts nominated by states and usually representing their interests as well as Western perceptions of cultural significance, and thus creating 'a cultural and discursive climate in which certain values and ideologies become dominant in defining cultural development and change'.[44] Within this conventional regime, the voices of communities raising various interests or concerns (economic, social or cultural) about a given heritage subject to internationalisation under the WHC have been scarcely considered, owing to the very weak mechanisms for fostering community involvement.[45] In such a guise, the expertisation of the World Heritage system may be seen as evidence of an unequal power/knowledge relationship between the interests of experts and those of human communities, contributing to the regime's internal deficiencies and shortcomings.

4 World heritage as a universal value

Irrespective of the above mentioned drawbacks of the WHC, its value-laded regime and vocabulary have recently induced some new developments in international practice and theory. Essentially, these confirm that the protection of world cultural heritage has reached the status of a nearly uncontested, universally recognized and accepted 'constitutional' value, and its protection constitutes both an international and national obligation and responsibility, stemming from the general interest of all humankind.

42 F Francioni and F Lenzerini, 'The Future of the World Heritage Convention: Problems and Prospects' in F Francioni and F Lenzerini (eds), *The 1972 World Heritage Convention: A Commentary* (OUP 2007) 401, 405.

43 Cf J Musitelli, 'World Heritage, between Universalism and Globalization' (2002) 11 *IJCP* 323, 330–332; A Jakubowski, *State Succession in Cultural Property* (OUP 2015) 304, 307–8; SA Bollens, *Cities, Nationalism and Democratization* (Routledge 2007) 188–89.

44 Smith (n 25) 100.

45 Lixinski, 'International Cultural Heritage Regimes' (n 2) 418–19; cfr James & Winter, 'Expertise and the Making' (n 2) 6–15.

4.1 Practices

When one 'persecutes people on the basis of their ethnicity or religion, destroys their monuments, their temples, deprives them of their intangible heritage, attacks their identities – they stop being humane'.[46] This statement by Irina Bokova, the Director-General of UNESCO, perfectly summarizes most recent international discourses relating to the protection of the cultural heritage under threat of destruction and pillage in Syria and Iraq. In fact, on 17 October 2015, fifty-three of UNESCO's Member States, including all the UN Security Council members, supported an appeal to add the protection of cultural property, in particular World Heritage Sites, to the list of tasks for UN peacekeeping forces.[47] Indeed, the images and clips of globally known sites being destroyed, broadcasted by Dáesh propaganda, have shocked the international community and generated appeals for more decisive measures to stop the destruction. Seen through this lens, the objective of protection of cultural heritage arguably seems parallel to that of providing for the protection and rescue of human communities. In particular the destruction of the archaeological site of Hatra in Iraq, inscribed on the WHL, moved UNESCO and the Islamic Educational, Scientific and Cultural Organization (ISESCO) to issue a joint statement[48] in which Abdulaziz Othman Altwaijri, Director-General of the latter organization, described the attacks against cultural heritage as acts against both local communities and all humankind, stating that 'with this latest act of barbarism against Hatra, Daesh shows the contempt in which it holds the history and heritage of Arab people, which had been rightly recognized as a World Heritage site'.[49]

As regards international law's normative framework, the protection of cultural sites inscribed on the WHL is clearly provided for under humanitarian treaty law and customary law.[50] More importantly, the Second Protocol to the 1954 Hague Convention[51] established a new category of enhanced

46 <https://www.rt.com/news/317632-unesco-isis-cultural-cleansing> accessed on 20 October 2015; see also 'Address by Irina Bokova, Director-General of UNESCO on the occasion of the Conference of the Secretaries-General of National Commissions to ISESCO', Baghdad, 28 March 2015, UNESCO Doc. DG/2015/057.

47 <https://news.artnet.com/art-world/un-blue-helmets-heritage-protection-342083> accessed on 20 October 2015.

48 <http://www.unesco.org/new/en/unesco/about-us/who-we-are/director-general/singleview-dg/news/destruction_of_hatra_marks_a_turning_point_in_the_cultural_cleansing_underway_in_iraq_say_heads_of_unesco_and_isesco/#.Vk24W784eY3> accessed on 15 September 2015.

49 Ibid.

50 See F Francioni and F Lenzerini, 'The Obligation to Prevent and Avoid Destruction of Cultural Heritage: From Bamiyam to Iraq' in BT Hoffman (ed), *Art and Cultural Heritage: Law Policy and Practice* (CUP 2006) 28.

51 Second Protocol to the Hague Convention of 1954 for the Protection of Cultural Property in the Event of Armed Conflict, signed on 26 March 1999, entered into force on 9 March 2004, 2253 UNTS 21.

protection relating to the safeguarding of and respect for cultural property that is of the greatest importance for humanity in the event of armed conflict (Article 10).[52] Accordingly, the parties to a conflict are obliged to 'ensure the immunity of cultural property under enhanced protection by refraining from making such property the object of attack or from any use of the property or its immediate surroundings in support of military action' (Article 12). Each party to this treaty presents a list of cultural properties for which it intends to request the granting of enhanced protection (Article 11.1). In practice, the current inventory of such cultural properties, managed by UNESCO, is comprised exclusively of World Heritage Sites.[53]

Violation of the prohibition against the intentional destruction of cultural heritage, in the event of both international and non-international armed conflict, gives rise to individual criminal responsibility. Accordingly, the 1954 Hague Convention obliges parties to undertake 'within the framework of their ordinary criminal jurisdiction, all necessary steps to prosecute and impose penal or disciplinary sanctions upon those persons, of whatever nationality, who commit or order to be committed a breach of the present Convention' (Article 28).[54] More recently, the Second Protocol to the 1954 Hague Convention provided the most advanced and detailed regime of individual criminal responsibility for offences against cultural heritage under enhanced protection, that is, being of the greatest importance to humanity. It also introduced the principle of universal jurisdiction over the most 'serious violations' of the norms on the protection of cultural heritage, and obliges the parties to prosecute or extradite the offender regardless of his or her nationality or the location of the violation committed.[55]

The principle of individual criminal responsibility for severe acts against cultural heritage in the event of armed conflict has also been introduced into the statutes of international criminal tribunals. Article 3(d) of the Statute of the International Criminal Tribunal for ex-Yugoslavia (ICTY)[56] defines the

52 See further N van Woundenberg, 'Enhanced Protection: A New Form of Protection under the 1999 Second Protocol' in N van Woudenberg and L Lijnzaad (eds), *Protecting Cultural Property in Armed Conflict* (Brill-Nijhoff 2010) 51.

53 <http://www.unesco.org/new/fileadmin/MULTIMEDIA/HQ/CLT/pdf/19542P-enhanced-protection-list-en_20140320.pdf> accessed on 15 April 2016.

54 These provisions are reinforced under Article 85(4)(d) of the 1977 Protocol I to the 1949 Geneva Conventions, which established the prosecution of offences against 'the clearly-recognized historic monuments, works of art or places of worship which constitute the cultural or spiritual heritage of peoples and to which special protection has been given by special arrangement, for example, within the framework of a competent international organization.' Protocol Additional to the Geneva Conventions of 12 August 1949, and relating to the Protection of Victims of International Armed Conflicts (Protocol I), signed on 8 June 1977, entered into force on 7 December 1978, 1125 UNTS 3.

55 M Hector, 'Enhancing Individual Criminal Responsibility for Offences Involving Cultural Property – the Road to the Rome Statute and the 1999 Second Protocol' in N van Woudenberg and L Lijnzaad (eds), *Protecting Cultural Property in Armed Conflict* (Brill-Nijhoff 2010) 69; R O'Keefe, *The Protection of Cultural Property in Armed Conflict* (CUP 2006) 236.

56 Statute of the International Tribunal for the Prosecution of Persons Responsible for Serious Violations of International Humanitarian Law Committed in the Territory of the Former Yugoslavia since 1991, adopted on 25 May 1993, UN Doc. S/RES/827 (1992).

'seizure of, destruction or wilful damage done to institutions dedicated to religion, charity and education, the arts and sciences, historic monuments and works of art and science' as violations of the laws or customs of war. The Rome Statute of the International Criminal Court (ICC)[57] includes similar provisions. Accordingly, it criminalizes, as serious violations of the laws and customs applicable in international armed conflict, intentional attacks directed 'against buildings dedicated to religion, education, art, science or charitable purposes, historic monuments, hospitals and places where the sick and wounded are collected, provided they are not military objectives' (Articles 8(2)(b)(ix) and 8(2)(e)(iv)). Although none of the statutes provides for a special category of crimes in relation to the acts against sites being of the greatest importance to humanity, World Heritage status has already been singled out and relied on in international criminal jurisprudence. The trials before the ICTY of military leaders involved in the shelling of the Old City of Dubrovnik, inscribed on the WHL in 1979, offer an instructive analysis in this regard. The Trial Chamber, in *Jokić*, held that 'this crime represents a violation of values especially protected by the international community'.[58] Moreover, it explained that while 'it is a serious violation of international humanitarian law to attack civilian buildings, it is a crime of even greater seriousness to direct an attack on an especially protected site'.[59] In turn, in *Strugar*[60] the ICTY found that a critical factor in imposing criminal liability on the military leaders who ordered bombardments of the historic city arose from the fact that its monumental and cultural substance enjoyed international protection.[61] In other words, acts against a cultural site of outstanding universal value constitute a violation of its protected status, which is derived from the interest of all mankind.

Attacks directed against a World Heritage Site are also the subject of the current proceedings before the ICC. On 26 September 2015, Mr Ahmad Al Mahdi Al Faqi (Abu Tourab), an alleged member of Ansar Dine, a Tuareg Islamic extremist militia in North Africa, was surrendered by the authorities of Niger to the ICC.[62] He is suspected of war crimes allegedly committed in 2012, in Timbuktu (Mali),[63] by intentionally directing attacks against buildings dedicated to religion and/or historical monuments (Art. 8 (2)(e)(iv) of

57 Statute of the International Criminal Court (Statute of Rome), adopted on 17 July 1998, entered into force on 1 July 2002, U.N. Doc. A/CONF.183/9, 2187 UNTS 90.

58 ICTY, *Prosecutor v Jokić*, No IT-01-42/1-S, Trial Chamber, Judgment of 18 March 2004, para, 46.

59 Ibid.

60 ICTY, *Prosecutor v Strugar*, No IT-01-42-T, Trial Chamber, Judgment of 31 January 2005.

61 Ibid., paras 327–329 and 461.

62 <https://www.icc-cpi.int/en_menus/icc/press%20and%20media/press%20releases/Pages/pr1157.aspx> accessed on 20 October 2015.

63 These buildings, mostly built in 15th and 16th centuries, comprise three large mosques, sixteen mausoleums and holy public places, and were inscribed on the WHL in 1988, due to their 'essential role in the spread of Islam in Africa' and function as 'outstanding witnesses to the urban establishment of Timbuktu, its important role of commercial, spiritual

the Rome Statute). The proceedings against Abu Tourab[64] constitute the first case concerning the destruction of cultural property to be brought before the ICC. Though its outcome is still unknown, one may expect that the great cultural value of properties in question, both for local populations of North Africa and the international community as a whole, may provide an important context in the ICC's reasoning.

The third area of international practice in which new 'uses' of the World Heritage regime are visible is that of state succession and cultural heritage obligations. In fact, the duty to protect World Heritage Sites, although arising from a multilateral treaty, can be arguably seen as continuously binding, irrespective of the replacement of one territorial state by another, since this obligation does not constitute a concern of merely domestic jurisdiction, but it lies in the general interest of the international community.[65] In fact, the application of this principle may refer, *inter alia*, to the joint concern and duty of successor states to cooperate to preserve and manage their common heritage within the framework of the WHC.[66] Perhaps this aspect of a state succession arrangement is the most meaningful and visible in light of the 2013 ICJ judgement in *Temple of Preah Vihear (Cambodia v Thailand)*.[67] This long-lasting territorial dispute, dating back to the colonial delimitation of borders between France, the colonial power, and the predecessor of the modern states of Cambodia and Siam (Thailand), substantially changed with the 2008 inscription of the ancient Hindu temple of Preah Vihear on the WHL. In this new light, the court held that 'the Temple of Preah Vihear is a site of religious and cultural significance for the peoples of the region and is now listed by UNESCO as a world heritage site'.[68] Accordingly, it recalled that 'under Article 6 of the WHC, to which both States are parties, Cambodia and Thailand must co-operate between themselves and with the international community in the protection of the site as a world heritage'.[69] The ICJ also pointed out that 'each State is under an obligation not to "take any deliberate measures which might damage, directly or indirectly" such heritage'. In other words, territorial disputes cannot undermine the implementation of binding obligations towards all humankind in relation to the protection of a cultural heritage site of outstanding universal value. This observation may also lead to a conclusion that the international regime under the WHC will play an important role in violent scenarios involving state succession, due to the general

and cultural centre on the southern trans-Saharan trading route, and its traditional characteristic construction techniques' <http://whc.unesco.org/en/list/119> accessed on 5 September 2015.

64 ICC, *Prosecutor v Ahmad Al Faqi Al Mahdi*, No ICC-01/12-01/15.

65 Read more Jakubowski, *State Succession* (n 43) 302 ff.

66 Ibid., 302.

67 *Request for Interpretation of the Judgment of 15 June 1962 in the Case concerning the Temple of Preah Vihear (Cambodia v Thailand),* Judgment of 11 November 2013, ICJ Reports 2013, 281.

68 Ibid., para. 106.

69 Ibid.

interest of all humankind in the cultural properties inscribed on the WHL. Thus the international obligations towards such heritage, undertaken prior to the date of state succession, will continue irrespective of any changes in state sovereignty over the territory where these sites are located.[70]

The role of the 1972 UNESCO legal regime has also been explored in relation to international investment law. The practice of managing conflicts between investor's rights and measures employed by host states in order to protect cultural heritage has, however, produced different outcomes. Some of them can be seen as shocking, or at the very least unexpected. Undoubtedly the deletion of the cultural landscape of Elbe Valley (near Dresden, Germany) from the WHL constitutes the most striking, well-known example. In fact, this is the only case in which cultural property was removed from the list. The Committee found that the site failed to keep its 'outstanding universal value as inscribed' in consequence of 'the building of a four-lane bridge in the heart of this unique cultural landscape'.[71] On the other hand, it is possible to observe a growing trend toward the recognition of cultural heritage considerations as a legitimate aim of host states allowing them to introduce certain measures that might have an impact on investors' rights, and thus on the execution of international investment treaties.[72] Accordingly, the International Centre for Settlement of Investment Disputes (ICSID)'s arbitral tribunals have found that the protection of World Cultural Heritage justifies certain interference in a host state's obligations under international investment law.[73] Yet, the far-reaching impact of the WHC's standards on international investment disputes is perhaps most visible in the reasoning of arbiters in the case of *Glamis Gold* (2009),[74] which concerned an investor's claims against the US under NAFTA Chapter 11 ('Settlement of Disputes between a Party and an Investor of

70 Jakubowski, *State Succession* (n 43) 264.

71 UNESCO Doc. 33 COM 7A.26; see von Schorlemer, 'Compliance with the UNESCO World Heritage Convention' (n 31).

72 A Peters, 'Constitutional Fragments: On the Interaction of Constitutionalization and Fragmentation in International Law' (2015) 2 *Working Paper* (Centre for Global Constitutionalism, University of St Andrews), 7, note 29. Undoubtedly, 'cultural policies are to be implemented at the complete discretion of the host state', but in order to be considered in investment disputes they 'need to be in conformity with relevant international law standards'; see Vadi, *Cultural Heritage in International Investment Law* (n 22) 115–116.

73 See *Southern Pacific Properties (Middle East) Limited v Arab Republic of Egypt*, ICSID Case No. Arb/84/3, Award of 20 May 1992; *Parkerings-Compagniet AS v Republic of Lithuania*, ICSID Case No. ARB/05/8, Award of 11 September 2007. The first case regarded a foreign tourist development project in one of the most important archaeological areas of the world: the Pyramid Fields from Giza to Dahshur (Memphis and its Necropolis), discontinued by Egypt in the context of the planned nomination of the site for inclusion in the WHL and its subsequent inscription. Yet, in given circumstances of the case, Egypt was liable to pay equitable compensation for the value of the expropriated investment. In the second case, the ICSID arbitral tribunal dealt with a dispute concerning a public tender launched by the city of Vilnius, Lithuania, for the construction of a modern car park in the historical city centre, inscribed on the WHL in 1994.

74 *Glamis Gold Ltd. v The United States of America*, UNCITRAL Arbitration (NAFTA), Award of 8 June 2009.

Another Party').[75] The dispute involved a mining project by a Canadian investor in an area of the Californian desert that the Quechan Indian tribe considered as a sacred place, partly because of certain cultural artefacts preserved therein, but more importantly in relation to the ceremonial use of this land and landscape. The investor claimed that the US, through various acts, wrongfully delayed approval of its open-pit gold-mining project and that, when federal approval appeared likely, the State of California rendered the project economically unfeasible by introducing a mandatory backfilling requirement in order to protect Native American sacred sites located in the area. The Arbitral Tribunal rejected the claim of the Canadian company and recognized the legitimacy of the regulatory measures imposed by the Californian authorities with a view to protect cultural heritage. In reaching its finding, it recalled the WHC, even though the site was not inscribed on the WHL,[76] treating this treaty as part of California's legislation to protect Native American culture. Interestingly, in its statement of relevant legal instruments, the tribunal recalled Article 12 of the WHC, stating that the fact that a property belonging to the World Cultural Heritage has not been inscribed on the WHL 'shall in no way be construed to mean that it does not have an outstanding universal value'.[77] Accordingly, one may argue that protective measures of a host state in relation to a cultural site may be deemed legitimate under an applicable investment treaty whenever the World Heritage status of the property in question is asserted, even if not confirmed by its inscription on the WHL.[78]

The above-described international practice in relation to the operationalization of the WHC system provides evidence of a certain quite consistent tendency in recognizing and enforcing universal cultural heritage values throughout distinct, seemingly fragmented, areas of international law. Another set of developments refer to the World Heritage regime itself. In fact, 'the appeal for a more decentralised regime supported by civil society… seems to have been heard'.[79] These voices have come from different directions. In 2002 Koïchiro Matsuura, UNESCO's Director-General, stated that: 'The identification, preservation and enhancement of sites reflecting our world's natural and cultural diversity can be assured only if governments, local authorities, business and, especially, local populations work at it together'.[80] Some voices have come also from NGOs and heritage experts, due to the increased understanding of

75 North American Free Trade Agreement, signed on 8, 11, 14 and 17 December 1992, entered into force on 1 January 1994, 32 ILM 605.

76 *Glamis Gold* (n 74) para. 84.

77 Ibid., para. 84, note 194.

78 Cf F Lenzerini, 'Article 12 Protection of Properties Not Inscribed on the World Heritage List' in F Francioni and F Lenzerini (eds), *The 1972 World Heritage Convention: A Commentary* (OUP 2008) 201, 204 ff.

79 JAR Nafziger, 'The World Heritage Convention and Non-State Actors' in LV Prott, R Redmond-Cooper and S Urice (eds), *Realising Cultural Heritage Law* (Institute of Art and Law 2013) 85.

80 Press Release, UNESCO, 'UNESCO Celebrates 30th Anniversary of World Heritage Convention in Venice', No. 2002–90 (2002) available at <http://www.unesco.org/bpi/eng/unescopress/2002/02-94e.shtml> accessed on 15 October 2015.

the various UNESCO cultural heritage regimes. Perhaps the strongest claim to alleviate the expertisation of the system of the WHC came from the African Commission on Human and Peoples' Rights (ACHPR), deeply concerned that the nomination and inscription mechanisms and practices sometimes overrode the rights and will of local communities and indigenous peoples, including their rights to development.[81] In 2011, this regional human rights monitoring body urged 'UNESCO and the World Heritage Committee to establish robust procedures and mechanisms to ensure that indigenous peoples are adequately consulted and involved in the management and protection of World Heritage sites and that their free, prior and informed consent is obtained when their territories are being nominated and inscribed as World Heritage sites'.[82] In fact, in the last decade the role of formal and informal commitments of non-state actors has visibly increased in relation to the nomination, management and protection of World Heritage Sites,[83] slowly contributing to overcoming its state-based exclusivity and the unequal power/knowledge relations between state-appointed experts and local or indigenous groups' interests and rights, at least on the level of a growing awareness within UNESCO.

4.2 *Doctrinal responses*

The developments in international practice, and in particular the consolidation of the international community and global public opinion against the destruction of cultural heritage committed by Daesh militants, seem to support the recurring doctrinal arguments on the universal, even constitutional, features of the WHC. In fact cultural heritage, particularly from the European perspective,[84] is often associated with 'global common goods' or 'global public goods'.[85] This concept has also been referred to by the UN Development Programme on various occasions,[86] and is reflected in

81 Further see S Disko, 'Indigenous Peoples' Rights and the World Heritage Convention' in W Logan, MN Craith, U Kockel (eds), *A Companion to Heritage Studies* (Willey Blackwell 2015) 355.

82 ACHPR, Resolution (197) on the Protection of Indigenous Peoples' Rights in the Context of the World Heritage Convention and the Designation of Lake Bogoria as a World Heritage site, done in Banjul, The Gambia, on 5 November 2011, available at <http://www.achpr.org/sessions/50th/resolutions/197> accessed on 25 October 2015.

83 Nafziger, 'The World Heritage Convention' (n 79) 79–85. Yet, it is also argued that actual UNESCO World Heritage decision-making (inscriptions on the WHL) becomes increasingly politicised and primarily reflects inter-state dynamics represented in the Committee. For intance, see L Meskell, C Liuzza, E Beracchini and D Saccone, 'Multilateralism and UNESCO World Heritage: Decision-Making, States Parties and Political Processes' (2015) 21 *International Journal of Heritage Studies* 423.

84 Blake, *International Cultural Heritage Law* (n 1) 327–28.

85 For instance, MT Albert and B Ringbeck, *40 Years World Heritage Convention: Popularizing the Protection of Cultural and Natural Heritage* (De Gruyter 2015) 7.

86 For instance, see I Kaul, I Grunberg, and M Stern (eds), *Global Public Goods: International Cooperation in the 21st Century* (OUP 1999).

the Convention's preamble: 'the deterioration or disappearance of any item of the cultural or natural heritage constitutes a harmful impoverishment of the heritage of all the nations of the world'. According to its guidelines, cultural heritage being of outstanding universal value shall be shared, enjoyed and protected by all the members of the international community. But while the concept of global common goods seems very appealing with respect to world cultural heritage, it is equally very problematic.[87]

Public goods, characterized by non-excludability and non-rivalry in their consumption, have long constituted an important concept in public economics.[88] In a global dimension, they are sometimes defined as those which 'tend towards universality in the sense that they benefit all countries, population groups, and generations',[89] making humanity as a whole both the beneficiary and custodian of global public goods.[90] Accordingly, such goods can comprise natural global commons (such as the ozone layer and climate stability), human-made global commons (such as scientific and practical knowledge, principles and norms, and *cultural heritage*), and global policy outcomes (such as peace, health and financial stability).[91] Sometimes, the concept of global common or public goods is also associated with that of common heritage of mankind.[92] In this regard cultural resources, in particular world heritage as defined under the WHC, would seem to be plausible candidates to be included in the category of global common goods. Yet cultural properties inscribed on the WHL cannot be considered as common property in the traditional sense.[93] World Cultural Heritage Sites are within the exclusive competences of territorial states and they do not always offer free, unhindered public access and use. In fact, the tangible dimension of a site and the cultural rights of a group which enjoys such heritage may give rise to claims to cultural exclusiveness, limiting their access to non-members or conditioning it on the religion practiced or gender. On the other hand, conceiving of world heritage as a common good may conceal 'external' state or international interventionism at the expense of human rights attached to a given cultural property.[94] Thus the conceptualisation of world heritage as global common goods would be better framed in relation to cultural diversity 'embodied in the

87 See V Vadi, 'Public Goods, Foreign Investments and the International Protection of Cultural Heritage' in F Lenzerini and AF Vrdoljak (eds), *International Law for Common Goods: Normative Perspectives on Human Rights, Culture and Nature* (Hart 2014) 231, 236–243.
88 P Samuelson, 'The Pure Theory of Public Expenditure' (1954) 43 *The Review of Economics and Statistics* 387; J Hudson and P Jones, '"Public Goods": An Exercise in Calibration' (2005) 124 *Public Choice* 167.
89 Kaul et al. (eds), *Global Public Goods* (n 86) 16.
90 For further analysis of the concept of 'global common goods' and its operation in international law, see Chapter 10 in this book.
91 Kaul et al. (eds), *Global Public Goods* (n 86) 453.
92 Cf FGI Inocencio, *Reconceptualizing Sovereignty in the Post-National State: Statehood Attributes in the International Order. The Federal Tradition* (AuthorHouse 2014) 72–73.
93 Wangkeo, 'Monumental Challenges' (n 20) 186.
94 Vadi, 'Public Goods' (n 87) 243.

uniqueness and plurality of the identities of the groups and societies making up humankind', leading to the conclusion that as 'a source of exchange, innovation and creativity, cultural diversity is as necessary for humankind as biodiversity is for nature'.[95] In international practice, cultural diversity has been recognized and promoted as a global common good for a variety of reasons and purposes, including its importance to peace and stability, progress and development, and the full realization of all human rights.[96] In such a guise, the protection of world cultural heritage, which demonstrates 'the importance, for all the peoples of the world, of safeguarding this unique and irreplaceable property, to whatever people it may belong'[97] can be seen as a universally recognized common good, whose value and significance arise from the protection of diversity of cultures, inherently linked to the identity of peoples and connected to both individual and collective human rights.

The universality of the 1972 UNESCO regime has also been analysed in terms of the normative foundations of protection of the World Cultural Heritage. Accordingly, it has been claimed that international obligations in this regard are part of general international law,[98] understood as rules rooted in both universal treaties and customary international law. In particular, the development of an international custom has been observed in the area of humanitarian law with respect to the obligation to protect cultural property from destruction and pillage in the event of armed conflicts. An extensive study of the International Committee of Red Cross (2005)[99] listed a vast catalogue of such norms which have emerged in recent decades.[100] Moreover, the 2003 UNESCO Declaration Concerning the Intentional Destruction of Cultural Heritage[101] explicitly stated that 'the development of rules of customary international law has also been affirmed by the relevant case-law, related to the protection of cultural heritage in peacetime as well as in the event of armed conflict'.[102] It also provided, under Article VI, that 'a state that intentionally destroys or intentionally fails to take appropriate measures to prohibit, prevent, stop, and punish any intentional destruction of cultural heritage of great importance for humanity, whether or not it is inscribed on a list maintained by UNESCO or another international organization, bears the responsibility for such destruction, to the extent provided for by international law'. This statement is clearly based on the well-rooted doctrinal argument that the WHC, as a particular multilateral treaty has given rise to

95 Article 1 of the UNESCO Universal Declaration on Cultural Diversity, adopted on 2 November 2001, UNESCO Doc. 31C/Res.
96 For further analysis see Vrdoljak, 'Human Rights and Cultural Heritage' (n 4) 168–172.
97 Fourth recital, Preamble, The 1972 World Heritage Convention.
98 See Francioni, 'Au-delà des Traités' (n 3).
99 JM Henckaerts, L Doswald-Beck, C Alvermann, *Customary International Humanitarian Law* (CUP 2005).
100 Ibid., vol. 1 127–138, 523–25; vol. 2, 723–813, 3452 *passim*.
101 Adopted on 17 October 2003, UNESCO Doc. 32 C/Res. 33 (2003).
102 Ibid., Preamble.

obligations *erga omnes contractantes*,[103] Indeed, the very nature and logic of the obligations under this treaty are of 'general or common interest'.[104] Thus a breach of the obligations towards cultural property protected under the 1972 UNESCO regime and situated in the territory of one state does not necessarily have to inflict a specific injury on another state, but amounts to an offence against all the State Parties to the Convention'.[105] Since the WHC has been ratified or acceded to by nearly all states of the world, the obligations that it creates may be deemed to be of an *erga omnes* nature on the level of general international law.[106] In relation to this, one may expect that such obligations not only bind states, but they would also apply to various non-state actors,[107] in particular armed groups controlling a given territory and who may be responsible for acts of destruction and plunder of the internationally protected cultural heritage sites, as it is now happing in Syria and Iraq.

But what are the consequences of violation of such an obligation(s)? Under the general regime of international responsibility a violation of an obligation owed to the international community as a whole would entitle any state, including those not directly injured, to invoke the responsibility of another state deemed to be in breach of such an obligation.[108] As the ICJ has recently confirmed, the 'common interest implies that the obligations in question are owed by any State party to all the other States parties' to a given multilateral treaty. 'These obligations may be defined as "obligations *erga omnes partes*" in the sense that each State party has an interest in compliance with them in any given case'.[109] Undoubtedly, a breach of the obligations created by the WHC would constitute an offence against the international community and the collective interest of all humankind. However, one needs to distinguish a situation of armed conflict, regulated under relevant provisions of international humanitarian law, and an occurrence during peacetime. As regards the former, a violation of the internationally protected status of cultural heritage gives rise both to state responsibility and criminal responsibility on the part of individual perpetrators, including members of non-state armed groups, since such groups *per se* can hardly be held accountable for the violations of international rules on the protection of cultural heritage in armed conflict.

103 C Forrest, *International Law and the Protection of Cultural Heritage* (Routledge 2010) 50, 277–78.
104 Buzzini and Condorelli, 'Article 11: List of World Heritage in Danger' (n 39) 178.
105 Ibid.
106 Francioni, 'Au-delà des Traités' (n 3) 41.
107 Cf Z. Howe, 'Can the 1954 Hague Convention Apply to Non-State Actors?: A Study of Iraq and Libya' (2012) 47 *Texas International Law Journal* 403.
108 Responsibility of States for Internationally Wrongful Acts, adopted by the International Law Commission at its Fifty-Third Session, November 2001, UN Doc. A/56/49(Vol I)/Coor.4.
109 *Questions relating to the Obligation to Prosecute or Extradite (Belgium v Senegal)*, Judgment of 20 July 2012, ICJ Reports 2012, 422, para. 68.

With respect to the consequences of a territorial state's own policies or actions – which often have caused serious damage to cultural properties inscribed on the WHL,[110] thus amounting to a violation of the obligations under the WHC – the responsibility of that state can be invoked but it would hardly be enforced. This is due to the structure of the Convention and its respect for state sovereignty, including the principle of non-intervention in domestic affairs. As Roger O'Keefe rightly noted: 'the law of State responsibility is, in practice, an unlikely and ill-adapted mechanism for compelling a State to preserve cultural heritage situated on its territory'.[111] Particularly difficult are questions regarding available and proportionate countermeasures.[112] Thus, in the great majority of cases diplomatic means and diplomatic pressure provide the only 'practicable option',[113] and the deletion of a property from the WHL might constitute the only frustrating consequence.

While the deficiencies of diplomatic intervention might be questionable, it needs to be stressed however that, though justified by the common interest of humanity, a more profound internationalization and scrutiny of cultural heritage policies adopted by territorial states may potentially produce serious negative effects. In particular, these may consist in imposing the hegemony of AHD at the expense of local cultural interests and trampling on the rights of communities which have created, enjoyed and used cultural heritage deemed to be of the greatest interest to all mankind. In other words, the strengthening of the universal or constitutional features of the 1972 UNESCO regime may serve as double-edged sword, capable of both enforcing or undermining the realization of cultural human rights attached to cultural heritage.

5 Conclusions

The analysis offered in this chapter has explored the use of arguments on the fragmentation of international law and/or global constitutionalisation in the context of international cultural heritage law, with particular focus on the regime of the WHC. The choice of this very specific context is not accidental. Indeed, the concept of world heritage and its practical operationalisation touches upon both arguments, since the very nature of international cultural heritage law lies in the dichotomies between particularism and universalism, regionalism and globalization, and between expert knowledge and community interests. Thus, the arguments over the fragmentation of this area of international law and those claiming its 'universal' and 'constitutional' features refer to its distinct, parallel dimensions. Clearly neither of them has been employed to impose particular legal concepts or interpretations in a

110 Wangkeo, 'Monumental Challenges' (n 20) 191–92.

111 R O'Keefe, 'World Cultural Heritage: Obligations to the International Community as a Whole?' (2004) 53 *ICLQ* 189, 207

112 Ibid., 207–08.

113 Ibid., 208.

hegemonic or exclusive fashion.[114] Instead, both arguments complement each other and lead to a more comprehensive vision of the relationship between the regime of the WHC and general international law in the area of cultural rights. They also provide valuable insights into how this regime operates *vis-à-vis* (and within) distinct specialized areas of international law. In fact, the arguments on fragmentation offer a rather descriptive analysis in relation to certain drawbacks of the system for the protection of world cultural heritage. In turn, the universality or constitutionalisation claim is more focused on the objectives and values of the WHC, primarily exploring the notion of the international community, wherein all share equally respect for cultural diversity and recognize that its deterioration and diminution may have adverse consequences on human dignity and human rights.

This chapter has also attempted to demonstrate how different 'fragmented' practices of international law contribute to a more consistent protection of the cultural heritage deemed to be of greatest importance and value to all mankind. It has examined to what extent the universal value of world heritage, stemming from the common concern and general interest of the international community, has been practically used or interpreted. In doing so, the major conclusion is that the obligations and standards created by the WHC have gradually transcended or overridden competing international regimes when it comes to a concrete dispute. In this regard, the protection of cultural heritage may be seen as a 'constitutional' principle of the international community.

114 Cf Peters, 'Constitutional Fragments' (n 72) 42.

12 Constitutionalisation through fragmented adjudication?

Mónika Ambrus

1 Introduction

Traditionally, (substantive) fragmentation (or diversification)[1] of international law has been described as the existence of various fields or islands of international law, such as international environmental law, international economic law, international human rights law and so on, among which there is no or hardly any relationship even though they are part of the same big family of international law (*sectoral fragmentation*). While diversification can be explained with several factors, proliferation of international courts and tribunals is generally seen as one of its main contributors. Importantly, proliferation has also led to what can be classified as *structural fragmentation*: (quasi-)judicial bodies working within the same field of law using different approaches to address a similar concept/problem. (For an overview of possible effects of proliferation of international quasi-judicial bodies (IQJBs), see Figure 12.1 below.) Proliferation of international (quasi-)judicial bodies and the ensuing fragmentation have been discussed quite extensively in the legal literature.[2] In the existing literature mainly the negative

1 Given that the term 'fragmentation' has a rather negative connotation, the term 'diversification' is often preferred when simply describing the existence of various fields of international law.

2 E.g. G Hafner, 'Pros and Cons Ensuing from Fragmentation of International Law' (2003–2004) 24 *Michigan Journal of International Law* 849; B Simma, 'Fragmentation in a Positive Light' (2003–2004) 25 *Michigan Journal of International Law* 845; M Koskenniemi and P Leino, 'Fragmentation of International Law? Postmodern Anxieties' (2003) 15 *LJIL* 553; A Martineau, 'The Rhetoric of Fragmentation: Fear and Faith in International Law' (2009) 22 *LJIL* 1; T Buergenthal, 'Proliferation of International Courts and Tribunals: Is It Good or Bad?' (2001) 14 *LJIL* 267; OK Fauchald and A Nollkaemper (eds), *The Practice of International and National Courts and the (De-)Fragmentation of International Law* (Hart 2012); J Pauwelyn, 'Bridging Fragmentation and Unity: International Law as a Universe of Inter-Connected Islands' (2003–2004) 25 *Michigan Journal of International Law* 903; CP Romano, 'The Proliferation of International Judicial Bodies: The Pieces of the Puzzle' (1999) 31 *NYU Journal of International Law and Policy* 709; Address by Judge Stephen M. Schwebel, President of the International Court of Justice, to the General Assembly of the United Nations, 26 October 1999; Address by H.E. Judge Gilbert Guillaume, President of the International Court of Justice, to the United Nations General Assembly, 26 October 2000; Speech by H.E. Judge Gilbert Guillaume, President of the International Court of Justice, to the General Assembly of the United Nations, 30 October 2001.

effects of proliferation have been emphasised,[3] and some attempts were also made to address these consequences.[4] It has been highlighted that the creation of various (quasi-)judicial bodies would lead to diverging approaches with regard to the application of similar concepts in public international law (*substantive fragmentation*) relating to the same (*structural fragmentation*) and different fields of law (*sectoral fragmentation*), resulting in inconsistency, legal uncertainty as well as negative effects on the effective implementation of law.[5] These conclusions are partly based on some outstanding case-law, such as the *Nicaragua*[6] and *Tadic*[7] cases and the *MOX Plant* saga,[8] or on hypothetical/potential collisions. These cases raise at least two types of problems: diverging approaches towards the substance of the law (e.g. *Nicaragua-Tadic* cases) and uncertainty as to the jurisdictional competences (e.g. *MOX Plant* saga). The *Nicaragua-Tadic* cases can be described as a problem of substantive fragmentation, and the *MOX Plant* cases can be referred to as jurisdictional collision. The former 'problem' was also addressed by the International Law Commission in an extensive report,[9] while it remained silent on the latter. Although it received particular attention and was the subject of several studies and discussions, the impact of proliferation on substantive fragmentation of international law still lacks a consistent and systemic analysis, which relies on a comparative assessment of different aspects of judicial decision-making. This contribution attempts to address, at least partly, this gap.

In order to gain insights into the actual effects of proliferation on substantive fragmentation of international law, this chapter will explore the extent of divergence/convergence in judicial practices in relation to procedural norms on the one hand and substantive norms on the other in terms of both structural and sectoral fragmentation. Procedural norms are rather interesting, as they are usually unwritten rules in international adjudication, so divergence in this regard might seem natural. To the contrary, substantive norms are mainly written rules, still they often leave ample space for interpretation and for judicial divergence.

Concerning procedural norms, the analysis will focus on the allocation of the burden of proof with regard to the right not to be discriminated against and the precautionary principle (section 2). As to the former, the chapter will compare the relevant mainstream cases in the practice of the European Court of Human Rights (ECtHR) with that of the Court of Justice of the

3 ILC, 'Risks Ensuing from the Fragmentation of International Law' (25 July 2000) (LII)/WG/LT/L.1/Add. 1.

4 ILC, 'Fragmentation of International Law: Difficulties Arising from the Diversification and Expansion of International Law' (1 May–9 June and 3 July–11 August 2006) UN Doc A/CN.4/L.682.

5 ILC (n 3) 35.

6 *Military and Paramilitary Activities in and against Nicaragua (Nicaragua v United States of America)* (Merits) [1986] ICJ Rep 1986.

7 *Prosecutor v Tadic* (Judgment) ICTY-94-1-A, A Ch (15 July 1999).

8 *The MOX Plant Case (Ireland v United Kingdom)* (Provisional Measures, Order of 3 December 2011) ITLOS Reports 2001; *The MOX Plant Case* (Order No. 6 – Termination of Proceedings, 6 June 2008) Arbitral Tribunal; Case C-459/03 *Commission of the European Communities v Ireland* [2006] ECR I-04635.

9 ILC (n 3).

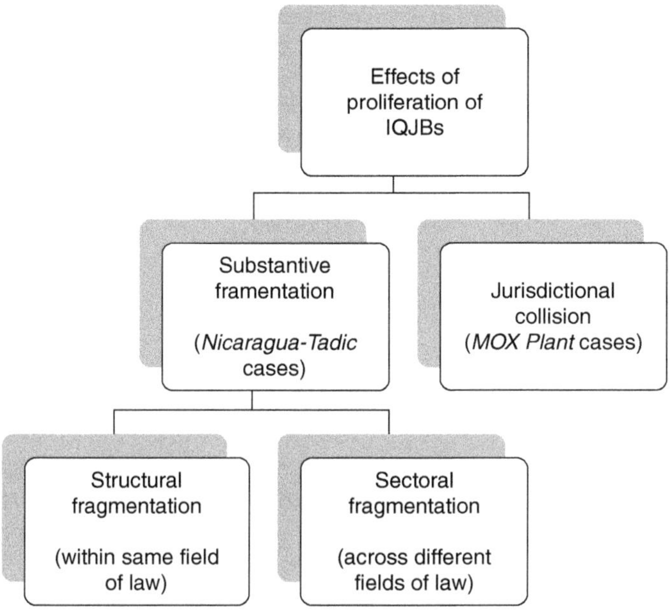

Figure 12.1 Overview of potential effects of proliferation

European Union (CJEU, earlier European Court of Justice, ECJ) (section 2.1). Given that these two judicial bodies operate within different fields of law, this can be described as sectoral fragmentation; however, due to certain overlaps between them (concerning human rights law) they also show signs of structural fragmentation. With regard to the latter, the comparison will focus on the allocation of the burden of proof when the precautionary principle was at stake in the case-law of the International Court of Justice (ICJ) and the World Trade Organisation's (WTO) panel and Appellate Body (section 2.2). Although the ICJ can also address trade-related matters, given that the relevant cases of the ICJ focused on environmental law, this comparison can be qualified as a form of sectoral fragmentation.

Two case studies will be selected for the comparative assessment of substantive norms, too (section 3). (For an overview of the case studies, see Table 12.1 below.) First, a comparison will be made between the manner in which water rights are devised by the Committee on Economic, Social and Cultural Rights in its General Comment No. 15 and how they are addressed by the European Court of Human Rights (section 3.1). Although the Committee is not a judicial body, nor are its General Comments (quasi-)judicial decisions in the strict sense, the comparison can still highlight whether or not judicial practice at a regional level diverges from international practice and guidelines. This comparison can mainly be qualified as an example of structural fragmentation (given their focus on human rights law), still these bodies also show signs of sectoral fragmentation due to their different focus within

Table 12.1 Overview of case studies in terms of the type of fragmentation at stake

	Structural fragmentation	*Sectoral fragmentation*
CJEU/ECtHR (burden of proof and discrimination law)	Signs	X
ICJ/WTO (burden of proof and the precautionary principle)	–	X
ESCRCee/ECtHR (water rights)	X	Signs
ICTY/ICTR (genocide)	X	–

human rights law (civil and political vs social, economic and cultural rights). Second, the concept of genocide as interpreted in the practice of the international criminal tribunals (International Criminal Tribunal for the former Yugoslavia (ICTY), International Criminal Tribunal for Rwanda (ICTR)) will be compared. Here, particular attention will be paid to the manner in which these judicial entities identify the members of the protected groups. This comparison is a clear case of structural fragmentation.

The main purpose of this comparative survey is to provide valuable insights into different aspects, areas and levels of adjudication enabling certain practical and theoretical conclusions as to the extent and/or nature of substantive fragmentation resulting from proliferation of international (quasi-) judicial bodies. Arguably, the opposite end of the fragmentation continuum is constitutionalisation. Accordingly, these insights will also reveal the status of constitutionalisation in international law, at least with regard to the case studies (section 4.1). Based on these comparisons and the extent of fragmentation/constitutionalisation certain conclusions can also be drawn as to the extent of convergence of a particular idea of justice driving these judicial bodies when interpreting the norm at stake (section 4.2). This last point raises interesting questions concerning the level of constitutionalisation: does it exist at the level of norm interpretation or at the level of sharing ideas of global justice?

2 Procedural norms and judicial practices

International courts and tribunals are established to assess the compliance with substantive rules – be they written or unwritten (in case of derived rules, customary international law or general principles of international law). However, in general their own procedural rules are not as extensive as the substantive rules or as domestic procedural rules. This indicates that oftentimes the rules based on which they proceed are unwritten rules. This section will take a closer look at one specific procedural rule, the allocation of the burden of proof, with regard to two different substantive rules, namely how it is applied in the case of prohibition of discrimination and with regard to the precautionary principle.

Burden of proof rules are closely related to the procedural positions of the parties. According to the general rule of the allocation of the burden of proof, the party alleging something is obliged to prove it (*onus probandi incumbit actori*).[10] Accordingly, the complainant/applicant has to bear the burden of proof with regard to the alleged interference with a particular rule, while the defendant/respondent has to bear the burden of proof with regard to the justification of his non-compliance with a certain rule, provided such justification is allowed.

In certain instances the burden of proof is (or argued to be) allocated in a somewhat different manner, which is often referred to as shifting the burden of proof. This 'shift' has been interpreted in various ways, but, arguably, conceptually this shift is limited to one specific interpretation. Namely, instead of the applicant, the respondent bears the initial burden of proof. Such a shift is often generated with the help of *presumption*, which should be established by the applicant. As soon as such a presumption is shown, the respondent has to prove that the claim does not stand, i.e. he bears the burden of persuasion in this regard. Should the respondent not be able to *negate* this presumption, the applicant's claim will be upheld. It has to be kept in mind that negating the presumption is not the same as *justifying* a particular conduct for which the respondent should in any event bear the responsibility. Negation means that the respondent bears the burden of proving that the presumption does not stand,[11] while in the justification phase it is accepted that the presumption is correct (the respondent could not negate it), but the respondent has good reasons for the interference.

Interestingly, the application of these special rules concerning the allocation of the burden of proof has been applied in discrimination cases[12] and has been argued to be applicable when the precautionary principle is at stake.[13] The main reason for arguing for a shift in the burden of proof in both cases is similar: given that the evidence with which the applicant could prove his case

10 F Palmer, 'Re-dressing the Balance of Power in Discrimination Cases: The Shift in the Burden of Proof' [2006] *European Anti-Discrimination Law Review* 23, 24; TR Hidma and GR Rutgers, *Bewijs* (Kluwer 2004) 46–49; U Erdal, 'Burden and Standard of Proof in Proceedings under the European Convention' (2001) 26 *European Law Review* 68, 81; J Kokott, *The Burden of Proof in Comparative and International Human Rights Law. Civil and Common Law Approaches with Special Reference to the American and German Legal Systems* (Kluwer 1998) 11.

11 See also M Ambrus, *Enforcement Mechanisms of the Racial Equality Directive and Minority Protection: Theory and Four Case Studies* (Eleven International Publishing 2011) chapter 2.

12 For an analysis of the allocation of the burden of proof in discrimination cases see Ibid.

13 See M Ambrus, 'The Precautionary Principle and a Fair Allocation of the Burden of Proof in International Environmental Law' (2012) 21 *Review of European Community and International Environmental Law* 259.

is oftentimes in the possession of the respondent, the applicant would be put in a rather difficult position should he have to make out his case.

2.1 Allocation of the burden of proof in discrimination cases

The prohibition of discrimination is a fundamental right and is laid down in several international legal documents, among which in Article 21 of the Charter of Fundamental Rights of the European Union, Article 6 of the Treaty of the European Union, and Article 14 of the European Convention on Human Rights (ECHR). The very first provision regulating the prohibition of discrimination between sexes in terms of payment was Article 119 of the EEC Treaty of 1957 (now Article 157 of the Treaty on the Functioning of the European Union (TFEU)). This was followed by the adoption of some directives,[14] and later on by Article 13 of the Treaty of Amsterdam (now Article 19 of the TFEU), which has authorised the Council to also adopt legislative measures outside the context of employment and industrial relations. This article paved the way for two important directives: the so-called Racial Equality Directive[15] and the Framework Equality Directive.[16] Both of these directives provide clear definitions of the different forms of discrimination, among which direct and indirect discrimination can be highlighted.[17] In addition, they also enshrine rules on the allocation of the burden of proof.[18] In the practice of the ECJ certain guidelines have been established as to when a differential treatment can be justified, which was later also confirmed in legislative documents.

Article 14 of the ECHR also enshrines the prohibition of discrimination on various grounds, however, it does not provide definitions of the different forms of discrimination. This article does not have an independent existence, the right to equal treatment needs to be invoked with regard to one of the other rights in the Convention.[19] Nevertheless, the Court emphasised that

14 Council Directive 75/117/EEC of 10 February 1975 on the approximation of the laws of the Member States relating to the application of the principle of equal pay for women and men [1975] OJ L045; Council Directive 76/207/EEC of 9 February 1976 on the implementation of the principle of equal treatment for women and men with respect to access to employment, vocational training and promotion, and working conditions (as amended by Council Directive 2002/73) [1976] OJ L204; Council Directive 97/80/EC of 15 December 1997 on the burden of proof in cases of sex discrimination [1997] OJ L014 (Burden of Proof Directive).

15 Council Directive of 2000/43/EC of 29 June 2000 implementing the principle of equal treatment between persons irrespective of racial or ethnic origin [2000] OJ L180 (Racial Equality Directive).

16 Council Directive 2000/78/EC of 27 November 2000 establishing a general framework for equal treatment in employment and occupation [2000] OJ L303/16 (Framework Equality Directive).

17 Racial Equality Directive, Article 2(2) a)-b); Framework Equality Directive, Article 2(2) a)-b).

18 Racial Equality Directive, Article 8; Framework Equality Directive, Article 10.

19 Article 1 of Protocol 12 of the ECHR has brought changes in this regard, in that it enshrines an independent right to equal treatment.

irrespective of its dependence on other articles, the right to equal treatment does have an autonomous meaning. Although this article does not provide for justification (unlike Articles 8–11 ECHR), the Court has very early explained that a justification clause is also embedded in this article.[20] So while the legislative environment is somewhat different, both courts have played an important role in the crystallisation of various rules relating to the concept of equal treatment.

The ECJ's approach towards the prohibition of discrimination on the grounds of gender was ground-breaking in many respects, but in particular with regard to the application of the special rules on the allocation of the burden of proof. The whole idea was developed starting from the *Danfoss* case in 1989.[21] Although the explanation of the ECJ was not always in line with what the special rules actually require or mean, the line of jurisprudence in this regard has led to the adoption of rules relating to the allocation of the burden of proof. First, the 1997 Burden of Proof Directive was adopted, and later its provision on the burden of proof has been repeated, as indicated above, in the Racial Equality Directive and the Framework Equality Directive, as well as in later directives on equal treatment. These two latter directives lay down that:

> when persons who consider themselves wronged because the principle of equal treatment has not been applied to them establish … facts from which it may be presumed that there has been direct or indirect discrimination, it shall be for the respondent to prove that there has been no breach of the principle of equal treatment.[22]

The earlier cases of the ECJ reveal two different approaches towards the allocation of the burden of proof. The first one can be observed in the *Danfoss* case, where the Court relied on the lack of transparency in the pay system as the main reason to 'shift' the burden of proof to the respondent.[23] This approach was also followed in the much debated *Brunnhofer* case, where the Court, exactly due to the fact that there was no lack of transparency, has rejected the application of the special rules.[24] The other approach neglects any transparency-related arguments, and as soon as the applicant managed to show a presumption of discrimination – usually with the help of statistical

20 *Case 'Relating to Certain Aspects of the Laws on the Use of Languages in Education in Belgium' v Belgium* App. nos 1474/62; 1677/62; 1691/62; 1769/63; 1994/63; 2126/64 (ECHR 23 July 1968).

21 Case C-109/88, *Handels- og Kontorfunktionærernes Forbund I Danmark v Dansk Arbejdsgiverforening, acting on behalf of Danfoss* [1989] ECR 3199 (*Danfoss*).

22 Racial Equality Directive, Article 8(1); Framework Equality Directive, Article 10(1).

23 '[W]here a system of pay which is totally lacking in transparency, it is for the employer to prove that his practice in the matter of wages is not discriminatory, if a female worker establishes, in relation to a relatively large number of employees, that the average pay for women is less than that for men.' *Danfoss* (n 21) para. 11.

24 Case C-381/99 *Susanna Brunnhofer v Bank der österreichischen Postsparkasse AG* [2001] ECR I-04961, para. 58.

data – the burden of proof is placed on the respondent.[25] This latter approach has prevailed both in the practice of the Court and in the legally binding documents, as indicated above. This does not mean, though, that the Court's approach has not been problematic. There is a steady and consistent line of jurisprudence with regard to indirect discrimination cases accepting the presumption of discrimination based on statistical data.[26] Indeed, the whole idea of 'shifting' the burden of proof was devised in indirect discrimination cases. However, in case of direct discrimination the Court was somewhat unclear about the meaning of the special allocation of the burden of proof. In the well-known *Feryn* case[27] the Court indicated that public statements revealing discriminatory practice establish a *prima facie* case of discrimination.[28] At the same time, it also concluded that such statements amount to discrimination. From the perspective of the allocation of the burden of proof this approach is somewhat problematic. Namely, the same fact is identified as a violation and as a presumption of the same violation. This double qualification actually shows that *de facto* the applicant has made out his case – due to the availability of the evidence. Put differently, in this case there was no real need for applying the special rules, given that the applicant had ample evidence to prove his case. Such an approach could also have a conceptually negative effect on whether the respondent can justify his treatment. All in all, even though there are binding legal provisions on the allocation of the burden of proof in cases of direct and indirect discrimination, their application still poses difficulties – at least in direct discrimination cases.

As far as the practice of the ECtHR is concerned, the picture is somewhat different. Importantly, the Court, based on the practice of the ECJ, has also tried to rely on the special rules for allocating the burden of proof, but it has encountered two main difficulties. First of all, the concept of indirect discrimination has not been embraced by the Court for a while, which was in the practice of the ECJ the door to the adoption of the special rules on the burden of proof.[29] Second, in direct discrimination cases it was rather reluctant to 'shift'

25 See, inter alia, Case C-127/92 *Dr. Pamela Mary Enderby v Frenchay Health Authority and Secretary of State for Health* [1993] ECR I-05535 (*Enderby*); Case C-237/94 *John O'Flynn v Adjudication Officer* [1996] ECR I-2617.

26 See, for instance, Case C-167/97 *Regina v Secretary of State for Employment, ex parte Nicole Seymour-Smith and Laura Perez* [1999] ECR I-623 paras 60–61; *Enderby* (n 25) para. 19; Case 170/84 *Bilka-Kaufhaus GmbH v Karin Weber von Hartz* [1986] ECR 1607 para. 29; *Danfoss* (n 21) para. 16; Case C-25/02 *Katharina Rinke v Ärztekammer Hamburg* [2003] ECR I-08349 [35].

27 Case C-54/07 *Centrum voor gelijkheid van kansen en voor racismebestrijding v Firma Feryn NV* [2008] ECR I-05187 (*Feryn*). On the *Feryn* case see also M Ambrus, M Busstra, K Henrard, 'The Racial Equality Directive and Effective Protection Against Discrimination: Mismatches between the Substantive Law and its Application' (2010) 3 *Erasmus Law Review* 165.

28 *Feryn* (n 27) para. 31.

29 See, for instance, *Timishev v Russia* App nos 55762/00 and 55974/00 (ECHR 13 December 2005); *D.H. and Others v The Czech Republic* App no 57325/00 (ECHR 13 November 2007); *Sampanis and Others v Greece* App no 32526/05 (ECHR 5 June 2008).

the burden of proof mainly due to the fact that it also expected evidence with regard to the intent to discriminate.[30] As far as the former is concerned, the *Hoogendijk* case was the first complaint before the Court in which it explicitly referred to the concept of indirect discrimination and accepted that a *prima facie* case of indirect discrimination can be established with the help of statistics.[31] Since then some other cases were also argued in terms of indirect discrimination, but it can be debated whether they were all concerned with this form of discrimination or rather (covert) direct discrimination.[32] The latest among them is the *Horváth and Kiss* case in which the applicants complained about 'the improper shunting of Roma children into special schools', which in their view 'constituted indirect discrimination'.[33] They argued that 'the tests used for placement had been culturally biased and knowledge-based, putting Roma children at a particular disadvantage'.[34] In the Court's view, the statistical data showing the overrepresentation of Roma children among pupils in special schools reveal 'a disproportionately prejudicial effect on the Roma',[35] which can be qualified as indirect discrimination.[36] Although the Court, at least 'verbally', accepted that the special rules should be applied, it mixed the presumption with the negation,[37] and thus gave the impression as if there is a presumption of discrimination only when the respondent cannot negate it. Nevertheless, this case comes the closest to the proper application of the special rules.

In direct discrimination cases, however, the Court has not been able to get even somewhat close to the application of the special rules on the allocation of the burden of proof, in particular in racial discrimination cases. The most outstanding examples in this regard are the *Nachova* and *Cobzaru* cases. In both cases the burden of proving (and not only the establishment of a presumption) that the disadvantageous treatment (ill-treatment) was based on racial or ethnic origin was placed on the applicants.[38]

Comparing the two jurisdictions both similarities and differences can be noticed. Both courts have had some conceptual difficulties as to what the special rules mean, i.e. that the original burden of persuasion is divided into two stages: presumption and negation, and that the respondent bears the burden

30 See, inter alia, *Nachova and Others v Bulgaria* App nos 43577/98 and 43579/98 (ECHR 6 July 2005) para. 157 (*Nachova*).

31 *Hoogendijk v the Netherlands* App no 58641/00 (ECHR 6 January 2005) para. 2.

32 See *D.H. and others v The Czech Republic* App no 57325/00 (ECHR 7 December 2006 (Chamber)) and (ECHR 13 November 2007 (Grand Chamber)).

33 *Horváth and Kiss v Hungary* App no 11146/11 (ECHR 29 January 2013) para. 90.

34 Ibid., para. 92.

35 Ibid., para. 110.

36 Ibid., para. 111.

37 For a brief analysis on the *Horváth and Kiss* case in relation to presumption and negation, see M Ambrus, 'The Burden of Proof in the *Horvath and Kiss v Hungary* case' (2013) <http://blog.eur.nl/esl/pil/2013/03/14/the-burden-of-proof-in-the-horvath-and-kiss-v-hungary-case> accessed 6 February 2014.

38 *Nachova* (n 30) para. 157; *Cobzaru v Romania* App no 48254/99 (ECHR 26 July 2007) paras 93–94 (*Cobzaru*).

of proving the latter one as well as the burden of proving the justification. However, while the ECJ was relatively able to apply the special rules in a conceptually correct manner in indirect discrimination cases, the ECtHR still struggles with the concept and its procedural consequences. Finally, the ECtHR was unable to apply the special rules in direct racial discrimination cases, while the ECJ seemed to be open to it – even though the language it used was rather unclear. Accordingly, in this context both divergence and convergence can be observed in terms of substantive fragmentation.

2.2 *Allocation of the burden of proof with regard to the precautionary principle*

Although the precautionary principle (PP) has been codified in several environmental treaties,[39] its precise meaning and scope have remained somewhat unclear.[40] The basic idea behind this principle is that scientific uncertainty should not be used to postpone action necessary for the protection of the environment.[41] In other words, 'decisions should err on the side of environmental preservation' (*in dubio pro natura*).[42] Importantly, the application of this principle has been extended to protect not only the environment, but also health more broadly.[43]

According to Wiener one of the archetypal versions of the precautionary principle means a shift in the allocation of the burden of proof.[44] As argued elsewhere,[45] however, rather than an alternative reading of the principle, the effect of the principle on the allocation of the burden of proof can be seen as a procedural approach towards the PP, which implies that it is complementary to the substantive archetypal versions. In simple terms, it could be argued that the principle inherently requires the application of the special rules on the allocation of the burden of proof.

The precautionary principle – either implicitly or explicitly – has been invoked both in the practice of the ICJ and the WTO. While in the former context it concerned the environment, in the practice of the latter it was

39 For an overview see inter alia D Freestone and E Hey, 'Origins and Development of the Precautionary Principle' in D Freestone and E Hey (eds), *The Precautionary Principle and International Law* (Kluwer Law International 1996) 3–15.

40 For an overview of the different interpretations of this principle see, inter alia, JB Wiener, 'Precaution' in D Bodansky, J Brunnée and E Hey (eds), *The Oxford Handbook of International Environmental Law* (Oxford University Press 2007) 597.

41 UNGA 'Report of the U.N. Conference on Environment and Development' (12 August 1992) UN Doc A/CONF.151/26/Rev. 1 (vol. I), Annex I Rio Declaration on Environment and Development, Principle 15.

42 A Arcuri, 'Reconstructing Precaution, Deconstructing Misconceptions' (2007) 21 *Ethics and International Affairs* 359, 362.

43 See, inter alia, Agreement on the Application of Sanitary and Phytosanitary Measures (adopted 15 April 1994, entered into force 1 January 1995) 1867 UNTS 493, Art. 5 (SPS Agreement).

44 Wiener (n 40) 597, 604–606.

45 Ambrus (n 13).

relied on in relation to health. Unlike the prohibition of discrimination, the PP was invoked both as an obligation with which one of the parties did not comply and as a justification for an alleged violation of an obligation under international law.

Two main relevant cases can be mentioned from the practice of the ICJ: the *Pulp Mills*[46] and the *Gabcikovo-Nagymaros* cases.[47] In the former case Argentina argued that Uruguay did not comply with its obligation to take precautionary measures, which the Court accepted and concluded that Uruguay was indeed 'obliged to use all means at its disposal in order to avoid activities … causing significant damage to the environment of another State'.[48] Although Argentina tried to make the argument that the burden of proof 'should not be placed on Argentina alone', the Court relied on the general rules for allocating the burden of proof. The Court explicitly pointed out that 'in accordance with the well-established principle of *onus probandi incumbit actori*, it is the duty of the party which asserts certain facts to establish the existence of such facts'.[49] In other words, the fact that a State did not take measures amounting to careful considerations had to be proven by the State challenging this. The application of the general rules required the applicant to carry out costly scientific assessments of the Uruguay River, which the respondent was initially obliged to do.

Somewhat differently, in the *Gabcikovo-Nagymaros* case Hungary tried to invoke the precautionary principle as justification for terminating the 1977 Treaty in which it undertook the obligation to build dam on the Danube.[50] In other words, the precautionary principle was not argued to have been violated (as was the claim in the *Pulp Mills* case or as happened in the above discussed discrimination cases), rather it was used to provide reason for violating the law of treaties. In this case the Court did not discuss the rules on the allocation of the burden of proof, from which it can be concluded that it was arranged in accordance with the general rules. Indeed, Hungary had to prove that the wrongfulness of the conduct could be justified by the fact that it was adopted as a precautionary measure; i.e. the party invoking the justificatory ground bears the burden of proving it. According to the Court, in order to justify its violation of treaty obligations, Hungary had to prove that the compliance with these obligations would have resulted in harm to the environment; i.e. that there was a (certain level of) risk. Had the special rules been applied, it would have sufficed if Hungary raised the presumption of a (certain level of) risk, which would have placed the burden of proof on Slovakia. All in all, the ICJ did not apply the special rules in these cases.

46 *Pulp Mills on the River Uruguay* (*Argentina v Uruguay*) [2010] ICJ Rep 14 (*Pulp Mills*).
47 *Gabcikovo-Nagymaros Project* (*Hungary v Slovakia*) [1997] ICJ Rep 7 (*Gabcikovo-Nagymaros*).
48 *Pulp Mills* (n 46) para. 101.
49 Ibid., para. 162.
50 *Gabcikovo-Nagymaros* (n 47) paras 49–58.

In the practice of the WTO, both explicit and implicit reference was made to the precautionary principle in the *EC-Hormones* case.[51] The US/Canada argued that the European Communities (EC) violated WTO law by restricting or prohibiting imports of meat and meat products from the US. One of the reasons the EC invoked was the precautionary principle to justify the adopted measure. While both the panel and the Appellate Body (AB) rejected the invocation of the precautionary principle under customary international law, as the AB itself also observed, this principle is also embedded in Article 3.3 of the WTO Agreement on Sanitary and Phytosanitary Measures (SPS Agreement).[52] There was some uncertainty as to whether in this case the precautionary principle constituted an obligation or justification – mainly because of the unclear relationship between Articles 3.1 and 3.3 of the SPS Agreement. According to the panel, an obligation-exception relationship existed between the mentioned two articles, which meant that it was for the EC to prove its justification. This approach implies the application of the general rules concerning the allocation of the burden of proof – who alleges something has to prove it. The AB departed from the panel's position concerning the explanation of this relationship as well as the allocation of the burden of proof stemming from this. In the AB's view each provision should be seen as separate obligations the violation of which was alleged by the applicants.[53] This position led the AB to essentially request the US/Canada to establish that there is a *prima facie* case of violation by the EC of its obligations. Although the AB spoke the language of the special rules on the allocation of the burden of proof, in fact they used the term '*prima facie*' to pinpoint who had to bear the burden of proof with regard to a specific issue, *in concreto* the US/Canada. Even though the special rules on the burden of proof were not applied, this approach of the AB (thus the position taken with regard to the relationship between the two rules) might be seen as advantageous for the EC since the US/Canada had to make out the case. However, the fact that the precautionary principle was seen as obligation also changed the emphasis of the examination of the case. When the precautionary principle is used as justification/exception, the party invoking it (thus the respondent) is required to prove the existence of a potential risk – in line with the general rules on the allocation of the burden of proof. However, when the precautionary principle is interpreted as an obligation, the party invoking its violation (thus the applicant) is required to prove the lack of risk.

51 WTO, *EC – Measures Concerning Meat and Meat Products – Report of the Panel* (18 August 1997) WT/DS26/R/USA (*EC-Hormones-Panel*); WTO, *EC – Measures Concerning Meat and Meat Products – Report of the Appellate Body* (16 January 1998) WT-DS26/AB/R (*EC-Hormones-AB*).

52 *EC-Hormones-AB* para. 124.

53 Ibid., para. 104.

All in all, both of the two international (quasi-)judicial bodies examined here are reluctant to apply the special rules on the allocation of the burden of proof when the precautionary principle is (either explicitly or implicitly) at stake – although for somewhat different reasons. Nevertheless, there also seems to be a revulsion against the different allocation of the burden of proof.

3 Substantive norms and judicial practices

One would presume that similar or same substantive norms would lead to less divergence than unwritten procedural rules. In a similar manner, there is also a presumption that derived rules, similarly to unwritten procedural rules, would also result in more divergence across judicial practices than the interpretation of explicitly enshrined rules. This section will provide examples for both aspects: first, the derived right to water will be the subject of assessment in the practice of the Committee on Economic, Social and Cultural Rights (ESCRCee, Committee) and the European Court of Human Rights, then the practice of the ICTR and ICTY towards a specific aspect of the crimes of genocide and persecution will be compared.

3.1 Water rights

The right to water as such is not enshrined in any international, legally binding documents. Nevertheless, it has been developed and elaborated on the basis of the International Covenant on Economic, Social and Cultural Rights (ICESCR),[54] in particular in the practice of the Committee on Economic, Social and Cultural Rights, and was explicitly defined in its famous General Comment 15 in 2002.[55] This comment is the first explicit acknowledgment of the existence of this right, which might be interpreted as the recognition that this right has an autonomous meaning, even though it is derived from the right to adequate standard of living (Article 11 ICESCR) and the right to the highest attainable standard of health (Article 12 ICESCR). Importantly, the General Assembly also confirmed this right in 2010.[56] Water-related aspects of human rights have also been addressed by the ECtHR interpreting the ECHR – even though it mainly focuses on civil and political rights. In the Court's case law reference to water-related rights can be discovered in the interpretation of right to life (Article 2 ECHR), right to fair trial (Article 6), right to private and family life, right to home and correspondence (Article 8

54 International Covenant on Economic, Social and Cultural Rights (adopted 16 December 1966, entered into force 3 January 1976) 993 UNTS 3 (ICESCR).

55 UN Committee on Economic, Social and Cultural Rights, 'General Comment No. 15 (2002). The Right to Water (arts 11 and 12 of the International Covenant on Economic, Social and Cultural Rights)' (20 January 2003) E/C.12/2002/11 (hereinafter General Comment 15).

56 UNGA Res 64/292 (28 July 2010) UN Doc A/RES/64/92.

ECHR), right to freedom of speech (Article 10 ECHR), and right to property (Article 1 of Protocol 1). Herewith, the main lines of the Committee's definition and elaboration of the right to water will be compared with the interpretation of the ECtHR of some of the above-mentioned rights.

Pursuant to General Comment 15, the main elements of the right to water are adequacy, availability, accessibility and quality.[57] The Comment lists certain core obligations, which, unlike other aspects of the rights under the Covenant, require progressive realisation, 'are of immediate effect'.[58] Among them the most important ones are the following: 'access to the minimum essential amount of water, that is sufficient and safe for personal and domestic uses to prevent disease', 'physical access to water and water facilities and services' and adopting 'measures to prevent, treat and control diseases linked to water'. The Comment also emphasises that states have both negative and positive obligations with regard to the realisation of the right to water, although in the Comment they are referred to as the obligations to respect, protect and fulfil – the last two being, strictly speaking, positive obligations. For instance, states must 'prevent third parties from interfering with the enjoyment of the right to water' (to protect), or states need to 'ensure that water is affordable' (to fulfil).

The relevant complaints in the practice of the Court are related to, among others, flood risk or effects of gold mining on the flora and fauna – and in particular on groundwater – and so on. The inclusion of water-related rights is not explicit in the practice of the Court, it can only be deduced from its reasoning. It has also been linked to both negative and positive obligations. For the sake of comparison, two main aspects of the right to water will be highlighted from the practice of the Court: the right to health and physical integrity (Article 8 ECHR) and the right to home and property (Article 8 ECHR and Article 1 of Protocol 1). As to the former the *Taskin* case[59] can be mentioned, which concerned the risk of contamination imposed by a gold mine. The case was decided on the basis of the procedural guarantees that were not present in this case. More concretely, the domestic administrative court had annulled the operation permit of the mine, which decision was not respected by the Council of Ministers having authorised the further operation of the mine. Importantly, in this context, the Court emphasised that this continuation imposed particular danger to the 'local ecosystem, and human health and safety' (para. 121) through the contamination of groundwater. Put differently, in terms of water-related rights the Court seems to interpret Article 8 ECHR as embedding the obligation to protect water from being polluted, which can be translated as the right to safe water or good water quality as well as adequate water. As far as the right to home and property is

57 The adequacy of water is defined by its availability, accessibility (physical, economic, information, non-discrimination) and quality. General Comment 15 para. 11.

58 General Comment 15 para. 37.

59 *Taskin and others v Turkey* App no 46117/99 (ECHR 10 November 2004).

concerned, the *Zander* case[60] deserves particular mentioning. This case was related to the right to property as a civil right under Article 6 ECHR.[61] The complaint in this case concerned the lack of judicial review with regard to a refusal of a request. The applicants requested the adoption of precautionary measures as a condition for authorising waste treatment activities by a certain company (VAFAB), which was located close to the applicants' land. Given that no damage had occurred yet, there was no possibility of appeal. In order to be able to address the complaint under Article 6 ECHR, the Court had to examine whether any 'civil right' was at stake. According to the Court 'the applicants' claim was directly concerned with their ability to use the water in their well for drinking purposes. This ability was one facet of their right as owners of the land on which it was situated'. In other words, the civil right of the applicants was related to the right to have clean drinking water, which was derived from the right to property.

In sum, the most important core obligations were also identified by the ECtHR, namely the right to safe and clean drinking water – in terms of the obligation to protect water from being contaminated and as an aspect of the right to property. Although the Court have not explicitly and directly analysed General Comment 15 (or the Committee's practice) or have taken it into account, there seems to be important convergence in the interpretation of the right to water between these two (quasi-)judicial bodies.

3.2 Genocide and persecution: identification of members of the protected group

Genocide is conceptually a rather complex crime – it includes different aspects that need to be proven, while they are also closely related to each other. Genocide is defined as the commitment of certain acts, such as killing members of a group, causing serious bodily or mental harm to members of a group and so on, with the intent to destroy, in whole or in part, this national, ethnical, racial or religious group.[62] As has been argued elsewhere, in addition to the discriminatory aspect of the special intent (intent to destroy the specific group as

60 *Zander v Sweden* App no 14282/88 (ECHR 25 November 1993).

61 One can invoke the right to fair trial only in relation to a *civil right* (or criminal charge against him/her). 'In the determination of his civil rights and obligations or of any criminal charge against him, everyone is entitled to a fair and public hearing within a reasonable time by an independent and impartial tribunal established by law.' Article 6(1) ECHR (emphasis added).

62 Convention on the Prevention and Punishment of Genocide (adopted 9 December 1948, entered into force 12 January 1951) 78 UNTS 277 (Genocide Convention), Article 2. The same definition was adopted in the Statute of the International Criminal Tribunal for the former Yugoslavia (adopted 25 May 1993 by UNSC Resolution 827, last amended 7 July 2009 by UNSC Resolution 1877), Article 4 (ICTY Statute); Statute of the International Criminal Tribunal for Rwanda (adopted 8 November 1994 by UNSC Resolution 955, last amended 16 December 2009 by UNSC Resolution 1901), Article 2 (ICTR Statute); and Rome Statute of the International Criminal Court (adopted 17 July 1998, entered into force 1 July 2002) 2187 UNTS 3, Article 6 (ICC Statute).

such), the conduct can also be interpreted (and arguably should be interpreted so in order to be conceptually consistent) as constituting discrimination against the individual members of the group. Persecution on political, racial, national, ethnic or religious grounds, a crime against humanity,[63] is often compared with genocide given the discriminatory component in both concepts. Namely, the intent to discriminate against a specific group in persecution cases is compared with the intent to destroy a protected group in genocide cases.[64] However, with regard to persecution one can also argue that the conduct itself needs to be discriminatory against the particular individuals, too. Given the limited number of genocide cases addressed by international criminal courts so far and the fact that different aspects of these cases were problematic in the practices of the tribunals,[65] the comparison will also include the identification of members of the protected group in persecution cases. The focus will be on the practice of the ICTY and the ICTR.

In light of the importance of the discriminatory aspect of genocide and persecution, it is not without further consequences what kind of approach international criminal courts apply for the identification of the members of these groups – if not carefully approached, the assessment of the potential victims might be under-exclusive (which is generally the case) or over-inclusive (even though courts have been rather careful not to include individuals who could not be linked to these groups in one way or another). Irrespective of the particular international criminal courts, in general two main approaches have been pinpointed in the case-law towards the identification of members of the protected group, that is the objective and subjective approaches. While the former argues to focus on so-called 'objective' features of the victims, the 'subjective' approach relies on the perception of the perpetrator.[66]

Interestingly, both approaches can be found in the practice of both the ICTY and ICTR. In other words, there is diversification even within their own practice in this regard. The example *par excellence* of the objective approach in genocide cases is the *Akayesu* case, where the question was raised whether serious bodily or mental harm inflicted on a Hutu woman can be regarded as forming part of the genocidal conduct against the Tutsi group.[67] The answer of the Chamber was in the negative. In the *Krnojelac* case concerning persecution a similar

63 ICTY Statute, Article 5; ICTR Statute, Article 3; ICC Statute, Article 7(h). Note that the prohibited grounds are not entirely the same under these statutes.

64 The special intent of the crime of genocide (i.e. the intent to destroy), however, constitutes a distinctive feature between these two crimes.

65 While in the practice of the ICTR the identification of members of the protected group proved to be the most important aspect of the case, in the case law of the ICTY the identification of the protected group itself (and thus not the members thereof) was seen as a complicated issue (including coverage of the protected group as well as the approach towards the identification of the protected group).

66 Sometimes the self-perception of the victim is also seen as a form of subjective approach, but this will not be addressed here.

67 *Prosecutor v Jean-Paul Akayesu* (Judgment) ICTR-96-4-T, T.Ch. I (2 September 1998) paras 521, 720–721.

approach was adopted both in theory and in practice by the ICTY, which was referred to as 'discrimination in fact'.[68] With regard to one of the detainees, who was tortured mistakenly for another detainee, the Trial Chamber did not accept that 'this act was in fact discriminatory' against him on political grounds.[69]

As far as the *subjective approach* is concerned, the ICTR did hint at the possibility that the perception of the perpetrator might also be used to identify a victim in the *Gacumbtsi* case. The Trial Chamber explained that '[e]vidence must also be tendered to show either that the victim belonged to the targeted ethnical, racial, national or religious group or that the perpetrator of the crime believed that the victim belonged to the said group'.[70] Likewise, in the *Kvocka* case concerning persecution, the ICTY accepted that 'persons suspected of being members of these groups are also covered as possible victims of discrimination'.[71]

This comparison allows for two conclusions. First, the divergence as to the identification of the members of the protected group is present within the practice of the same court as well as across the courts. Arguably, the divergence rather occurs across time than across courts – at least as far as genocide is concerned.[72] Second, divergence in this regard is also to be observed across different crimes including the same aspect. Both observations underlie the conceptual difficulty these tribunals had with this aspect of genocide and persecution, respectively. Importantly, the definitions of genocide and persecution are silent (or arguably are silent)[73] on this matter.

4 Institutional divergence and substantive convergence?

4.1 Relationship between proliferation and substantive fragmentation/constitutionalisation

As explained in the introduction, the four case studies represent different aspects of proliferation of (quasi-)judicial bodies. The comparison between the ECtHR and the CJEU is an example of an originally sectoral, and now increasingly more structural, fragmentation. The ICJ/WTO comparison represents a clear case of sectoral fragmentation. The ESCRCee vs ECtHR can mainly be seen as structural fragmentation, while showing signs of

68 *Prosecutor v Milorad Krnojelac* (Judgment) IT-97-25-T, T.Ch. (15 March 2002) para. 431.

69 Ibid., para. 456.

70 *Prosecutor v Sylvestre Gacumbtsi*, Judgment, ICTR-2001-64-T, T.Ch. III (17 June 2004) paras 254–255.

71 *Prosecutor v Miroslav Kvocka, Dragoljub Prcac, Milojica Kos, Mlado Radic, Zoran Zigic*, Judgment, IT-98-30/1-T, T.Ch. (2 November 2001) para. 195.

72 It seems that concerning genocide the prevailing view is that both approaches can be used (probably in a complementary manner), while with regard to persecution the objective approach seems more dominant both in the case law and in the legal literature.

73 The conduct elements of genocide (e.g. killing *members of the group*) are interpreted by some as requiring the reliance on the objective approach.

sectoral fragmentation as well (civil and political rights vs economic, social and cultural rights). Last but not least, the exploration of the case-law of the ICTY/ICTR is a good example of pure structural fragmentation. So what do the different comparisons teach us in terms of substantive fragmentation? Is there convergence or rather divergence in the manner in which the different (quasi-)judicial instances approach similar issues? Some surprising or unexpected conclusions can be drawn from the comparative analyses.

First, while one would have expected the highest convergence in case of structural fragmentation, the horizontal comparison could not give rise to such a straightforward conclusion. Obviously, given that the ICTY and ICTR operate in the same field of law, the influence on each other's approaches is much more extensive and intensive than in case of other forms of fragmentation. Second, also surprising is the finding based on the vertical-diagonal comparison between the ESCRCee and ECtHR. While the two entities compared 'adjudicate' with regard to somewhat different human rights as well as operate at different levels of governance, they devised (either explicitly or somewhat more implicitly) similar aspects of a non-explicitly stated right. Importantly, the ECtHR, although it often relies on the comparative law method, did not take into consideration General Comment 15 when addressing water-related complaints. Third, the comparison between the CJEU and the ECtHR can be identified as horizontal-diagonal. This analysis shows signs of both substantive fragmentation and constitutionalisation. If one looks at the temporal dimension of this divergence/convergence, it can be argued that from a clear case of divergence, we are heading towards increasingly more convergence – also in terms of the difficulties these judicial bodies are faced with. Finally, the horizontal-diagonal comparison between the ICJ and the WTO suggests the most convergence – even though the reasons provided by the two instances with regard to rejecting the application of the special rules on the allocation of the burden of proof are somewhat different. Put differently, while one would have expected more convergence (or more signs of constitutionalisation) when structural fragmentation is at stake and somewhat less in case of sectoral fragmentation, the opposite seems to be proven by the case studies. This last observation also indicates that in the original meaning of fragmentation the claim that there are no bridges in international law providing connections between the different islands might not be entirely correct. Undeniably, as the ICJ/WTO case study illustrated, there are elements of sector-specific approaches, still the 'final outcome' is rather similar. Although drawing the conclusion as to the existence of stable bridges between the islands might seem somewhat exaggerated, at least some temporary pontoon bridges can be discovered on the ocean of international law.

4.2 Convergence/divergence and global justice

Although differences do exist in the approaches in each case study, in general one could still see a line of convergence across judicial practices. This convergence could give rise to the presumption that, at least at the level of driving forces of the interpretation of the norms, there is an agreement between the judicial bodies.[74] The case studies on the allocation of the burden of proof in discrimination cases indicated that both courts acknowledge (although to a varying extent) the need to alleviate the burden of proof of the victim of discrimination – given the difficulty of getting access to evidence. Such an approach clearly encourages victims to submit their discrimination complaints, and would not impose too high a burden on the respondent. Interestingly, this driving force was not present in relation to the application of the precautionary principle even though similar considerations might also be applicable in these cases too – costs and difficulty of collecting evidence. It could be argued that such an approach would not support the protection of environment and health as well as the need to proceed with carefulness in adopting measures that might affect the environment or health. Rather it seems to be based more on a formal procedural justice approach, which does not take certain important differences as to the procedural position of the parties into account. From the water rights case study similar conclusions might be drawn: although implicit, both entities were willing to extend the scope of rights and adopt a broad interpretation. Such broad interpretations would, arguably, support a higher protection of the right to water, which is a basic need for each individual. Last but not least, the genocide and persecution cases also highlight a dilemma that played a role in the practice of both *ad hoc* tribunals, namely how to prove whether someone was mistreated due to his or her racial or ethnic origin etc. This approach can be compared with the formal procedural justice approach in relation to the precautionary principle. As argued elsewhere, the objective approach would not contribute to abolishing racial biases, which are the underlying causes of genocide and persecution. Admittedly, these differences in approaches might, to some extent, be explained by the institutional set-up of these (quasi-)judicial bodies, such as parties to the dispute, the nature of the judicial body, field of law in which they operate. Nevertheless, it is somewhat striking that concepts of formal justice seem to have so much influence on the interpretation of norms.

74 Cf Chapter 4 in this book.

13 From fragmentation to coherence

A constitutionalist take on the trade and public health debates

*Chien-Huei Wu**

1 Introduction

The Punta del Este Declaration launching the Uruguay Round in 1986 yielded fruit in the Final Act Embodying the Results of the Uruguay Round of Multilateral Trade Negotiations.[1] Of the contents of the Final Act, the Agreement on the Application of Sanitary and Phytosanitary Measures [hereinafter 'SPS Agreement'][2] and Agreement on Trade-Related Aspects of Intellectual Property Rights [hereinafter 'TRIPS Agreement'][3] are considered to have great repercussions on public health. Under the regulatory regime of the SPS Agreement, the joint WHO/FAO Codex Alimentarius Commission is explicitly recognized as a standard-setting organization for food safety; its role has been made well known through the *EC – Hormone* dispute.[4]

With regard to the TRIPS Agreement, the potentially adverse effects of the trade regime upon public health led to the adoption of the Doha Declaration on the TRIPS Agreement and Public Health,[5] and the Amendment of the TRIPS Agreement [hereinafter 'TRIPS Amendment'].[6] At that stage, access to medicine and compulsory licensing were central elements of the debates. In the Doha Declaration on the TRIPS Agreement and Public Health, Members

* The author gratefully acknowledges the grant of MOST research project 104-2410-H-001-087-MY2.

1 WTO Agreement: Marrakesh Agreement Establishing the World Trade Organization, 15 April 1994, 1867 UNTS 154, 33 I.L.M. 1144 (1994), first preambular.

2 Agreement on the Application of Sanitary and Phytosanitary Measures, 15 April 1994, 1867 UNTS 4.

3 Agreement on Trade-Related Aspects of Intellectual Property Rights, 15 April 1994, 1869 UNTS 299.

4 Appellate Body Report, *EC – Hormone*, adopted 13 February 1998. On this case, see e.g., B Hoekman, J Trachtman, 'Continued Suspense: EC–Hormones and WTO Disciplines on Discrimination and Domestic Regulation' (2010) 9 *World Trade Review* 151.

5 WTO, Doha Declaration on the TRIPS Agreement and Public Health, WT/MIN(01)/DEC/2 (14 November 2001).

6 WTO, Amendment of the TRIPS Agreement, Decision of 6 December 2005, WT/L/641 (8 December 2005).

agree 'that the TRIPS Agreement does not and should not prevent Members from taking measures to protect public health';[7] Members further affirm that 'the [TRIPS] Agreement can and should be interpreted and implemented in a manner supportive of WTO Members' right to protect public health and, in particular, to promote access to medicines for all'.[8] Members then point to the flexibilities provided in the TRIPS Agreement, including the interpretative approach which involves applying customary rules of interpretation of public international law; compulsory licensing; Members' right to determine national emergency and extreme urgency; and Members' freedom to establish regimes relevant for the exhaustion of intellectual property rights.[9] The TRIPS Amendment provides clearer rules regarding compulsory licensing for the production of pharmaceutical products and their export to an eligible importing Member.

Compared to the era when the WTO agreements were negotiated, the relationship between trade and public health is far more complicated. On the non-communicable diseases front, in 2010, at the same place where the Uruguay Round negotiations were launched, the Contracting Parties to the WHO Framework Convention on Tobacco Control (the WHO FCTC)[10] adopted the Punta del Este Decision on the Implementation of the WHO FCTC.[11] The pursuit of tobacco control has given rise to several trade-related issues, with plain packaging being one of the best known. In fact, in the WTO forum, Ukraine, Honduras, Dominican Republic, and Indonesia, have brought complaints against Australia concerning Australian trademark restrictions and other plain packaging requirements.

On the communicable disease front (and perhaps also the food safety concern front), the US in 2012 requested consultations with India on prohibitions of imports of US agricultural products over concerns related to avian influenza. In that dispute, the US argued that 'India's avian influenza measures, which are not based on the relevant international standards, are not based upon an assessment, as appropriate to the circumstances, of the risks to human, animal, or plant life or health, taking into account risk assessment techniques developed by the relevant international organizations'.[12] The Panel, supported by the Appellate Body, found unfavorably against India, on the ground that India's avian influenza measures were based neither on international standards, notably those adopted by

7 Doha Declaration on the TRIPS Agreement and Public Health, para. 4.

8 Ibid.

9 Ibid.

10 WHO Framework Convention on Tobacco Control, 21 May 2003, 2302 UNTS 166.

11 Conference of the Parties to the WHO Framework Convention on Tobacco Control, Punta del Este Decision on the Implementation of the WHO Framework Convention on Tobacco Control, para. 5, FCTC/COP4(5) (19 November 2010).

12 Request for the Establishment of a Panel by the United States, *India – Measures Concerning the Importation of Certain Agricultural Products*, p. 2, WT/DS430/3 (14 May 2012) [hereinafter '*India – Agricultural Products*'].

the World Organization for Animal Health (OIE), nor on scientific risk assessments.[13]

Acting on conventional food safety concerns, in 2012, Russia imposed an import ban on US beef and pork raised using the feed additive ractopamine.[14] Under the new regulatory regime, US beef and pork must be tested and certified free of ractopamine to be permitted entry into the Russian market. The US responded by threatening to lodge a complaint in the WTO forum. This dispute, like *EC – Hormones*, relates generally to the role of the WHO/FAO Codex Alimentarius Commission as an international organization capable of setting international standards, and specifically to the decision made by the WHO/FAO Codex Alimentarius Commission regarding the permissibility of ractopamine residue.

2 The tension between trade interests and public health objectives: regime collision

The tension between the WTO and the WHO stems from two driving forces. Firstly, the *raison d'etre* of these two organizations are marked by a stark contrast, with the former focusing on trade liberalization and the latter the promotion of public health. The intriguing point here is that trade governance and health governance are not separate but interrelated issues. This observation applies to the impact of trade liberalization upon public health as well as the impact of public health measures upon trade flows.

The impact of the WTO agreements on public health can be understood along three dimensions: harmful commodities and unhealthy products; liberalization of health services; and intellectual property rights. Harmful commodities and unhealthy products are regulated mainly under General Agreement on Tariffs and Trade 1994 [hereinafter 'GATT 1994'].[15] As a consequence of trade liberalization and opening markets, harmful commodities such as tobacco may enter domestic markets and thus undermine national public health policies. The popularity of unhealthy food is a result of the shift of dietary patterns, for which pervasive global trade in food is a driving force.[16] The liberalization of health services may lead to the erosion of equity and the emergence of inequitable two-tier health care systems; it may also result in an internal brain drain and decreased access and service quality

13 Panel Report, *India – Agricultural Products*, WT/DS430/R and Add.1, adopted 19 June 2015, as modified by Appellate Body Report WT/DS430/AB/R, para. 8.1.

14 It should be also noted that, with burst of Crimea crisis and in response to the sanctions imposed by European countries, Russia has also imposed a number of trade restrictive measures under the label of SPS measures. This evidences how trade politics can be transformed into high politics. The author owes this point to the editors.

15 General Agreement on Tariffs and Trade 1994, 15 April 1994, 1867 UNTS 187.

16 B McGrady, *Trade and Public Health: the WTO, Tobacco, Alcohol, and Diet* (CUP 2011) 5.

for vulnerable groups.[17] Intellectual property rights governing the availability and affordability of pharmaceutical products in developing countries, subsequently give rise to the issues of compulsory licensing, parallel imports, and exhaustion of intellectual property rights.[18]

Conversely, public health measures may also impact international trade flows, an illustrative example being the outbreak of Severe Acute Respiratory Syndrome (SARS) in 2002, which seriously interrupted international travel and commerce. This led eventually to the adoption of the 2005 International Health Regulations,[19] the purposes of which are to 'prevent, protect against, control and provide a public health response to the international spread of disease in ways that are commensurate with and restricted to public health risks, and [to] avoid unnecessary interference with international traffic and trade'.[20] Indeed, the predecessor of the International Health Regulations, the International Sanitary Regulations, adopted in the international sanitary conferences in the last half of the nineteenth century, were a compromise between developed and developing countries. The developed countries wished to control the international spread of disease, but feared that the flow of commerce might be unduly impeded by shipping and port authorities and thus undermine their export trade interests.[21]

In the contemporary era, global health governance is highly politicized, mainly because such policies, especially those relating to infectious diseases, do not operate in isolation. The high profile of global health politics in recent decades has been reflective of the emergence of new threats to health, which pose problems and challenges across to many policy areas.[22] The shaping and formulation of global health policies can greatly impact other governance spheres, such as trade and commerce.[23] This links to the second element of the tension: that between trade and public health.

The objective of the World Health Organization (WHO) – the attainment, by all peoples, of the highest possible level of health – is rooted in the

17 D W Bettcher, D Yach, G E Guindon, 'Global Trade and Health: Key Linkages and Future Challenges' (2000) 78 *Bullentin of the World Health Organization* 521, 523; on this topic, see contributions to Chantal Blouin, Nick Drager, Richard Smith (eds), *International Trade in Health Services and the GATS: Current Issues and Debates* (The World Bank 2006).

18 RD Smith, C Correa, C Oh, 'Trade, TRIPS and Pharmaceuticals' (2009) 37 *Lancet* 683, 685–687.

19 D P Fidler, 'Germs, Governance, and Global Public Health in the Wake of SARS' (2004) 113 *Journal of Clinical Investigation* 799, 801–802.

20 World Health Organization, International Health Regulation, Art. 2, adopted at 58th World Health Assembly on 23 May 2005 [hereinafter 'IHR 2005'].

21 M W Zacher, T J Keefe, *The Politics of Global Health Governance: United by Contagion* (Palgrave Macmillan 2008) 133–134; Bettcher, et al. (n 17) 522. See also D P Fidler, 'From International Sanitary Conventions to Global Health Security: The New International Health Regulations' (2005) 4 *Chinese Journal of International Law* 325.

22 D P Fidler, 'Architecture Amidst Anarchy: Global Health's Quest for Governance' (2007) 1 *Global Health Governance* 1, 5.

23 Zacher et al. (n 21) 133–134.

United Nations Conference on International Organization convened in San Francisco in 1945.[24] The subsequent International Health Conference, held in July 1946, adopted the WHO Constitution, which brought the organization into relations with the United Nations as one of the specialized agencies.[25] When the WTO came into being in 1995 it chose not to operate under the auspices of the United Nations, which prevents the Administrative Committee on Coordination from playing any meaningful role in bringing the fragmented institutional regimes into policy coherence – though the effectiveness of the Administrative Committee on Coordination is already highly questionable.[26]

Further, there is no institutional link between the WTO and WHO. The only embedded linkage between the WTO and WHO lies in the reference to the WHO/FAO Codex Alimentarius Commission as an international standard-setting organization in the SPS Agreement. Compared to the institutional linkage between the WTO and the Bretton Woods institutions, and the coherence mandate dictating that the WTO cooperate with the latter institutions in achieving greater coherence in global economic policymaking,[27] inter-agency cooperation and joint-initiatives between the WTO and the WHO remain remote. Thus, there exists a great danger of incoherence between the WTO and the WTO (and other public international organizations).[28] This necessitates greater coordination efforts. Currently, the WHO is granted observer status in the SPS Committee and TBT Committee, and may be granted *ad hoc* observer status in the TRIPS Council and GATS Council when public health issues are at stake.[29] Similarly, the WTO participates in some WHO activities, notably under the framework of the WHO FCTC. The mutual granting of observer status may contribute to mutual understanding, and trade and health communities may benefit from each other's perspective. However, access to each other's activities remains restricted and incongruence between these two organizations may arise from time to time.

24 G L Burci, C-H Vignes, *World Health Organization* (Kluwer Law International 2004) 15.

25 Constitution of the World Health Organization, 22 July 1946, Art. 69, 14 UNTS 185 [hereinafter 'WHO Constitution'].

26 On the potential role of the Administrative Coordination Committee on inter-agency cooperation in global governance, see Christian Tietje, 'Global Governance and Inter-Agency Co-operation in International Economic Law' (2002) 36 *Journal of World Trade* 501.

27 Declaration on the Contribution of the World Trade Organization to Achieving Greater Coherence in Global Economic Policymaking, adopted by the Trade Negotiations Committee on 15 December 1993, para. 5.

28 L A Winters, 'Coherence with No "Here": WTO Co-operation with the World Bank and the IMF' in D Nelson (ed), *The Political Economy of Policy Reform: Essays in Honor of J Michael Finger* (Elsevier 2004) 329.

29 K Lee, D Sridhar, M Patel, 'Bridging the Divide: Governance of Trade and Health' (2009) 373 *The Lancet* 416, 417.

The World Health Assembly [hereinafter 'WHA'], in recognition of the potential threats posed by international trade, adopted a resolution addressing the relationship between trade and health.[30] The WHA resolution underlined the importance of ensuring that 'the interests of trade and health are appropriately balanced and coordinated'[31] and requests that the Director General of the WHO *inter alia* 'continue collaborating with the competent international organizations in order to support policy coherence between trade and health sectors at regional and global levels'.[32]

At the policy level, while there is a joint-study on the *WTO Agreements and Public Health*,[33] this study is far from satisfactory. Robert Howse refers to this study as misleading and failing to taking into account the jurisprudence of the WTO Appellate Body, and as overstating the capacity of existent science in resolving trade disputes relating to health risks.[34] A recent product of the inter-agency collaboration is *Promoting Access to Medical Technologies and Innovation*.[35] Notwithstanding these joint efforts, progress in reconciling trade interests and public health concerns remains limited.

The potential conflicts between trade and health regimes evidences the threat of fragmentation of international law arising from differentiation of different types of international law[36] and the danger of regime collision. Regarding the fragmentation of international law as a consequence of differentiation, the International Law Commission [hereinafter 'ILC'] Study Group on the fragmentation of international law notes as follows:

> 'One aspect of globalization is the emergence of technically specialized cooperation networks with a global scope...spheres of life and expert cooperation that transgress national boundaries and are difficult to regulate through traditional international law. National laws seem insufficient owing to the transnational nature of the networks while international law only inadequately takes account of their specialized objectives and needs'.[37]

30 WHA, 59.26 International Trade and Health, 59/2006/REC/1, adopted at the Ninth plenary meeting (27 May 2006).
31 Ibid., preamble.
32 Ibid., para. 2(3).
33 WHO/WTO, 'WTO Agreements and Public Health: A Joint Study by the WHO and the WTO Secretariat' (WHO/WTO 2002).
34 R Howse, 'The WHO/WTO Study on Trade and Public Health: A Critical Assessment' (2003) 24 *Risk Analysis* 501, 501.
35 WTO/WIPO/WHO, 'Promoting Access to Medical Technologies and Innovation: Intersections between Public Health, Intellectual Property and Trade' (WTO/WIPO/WHO 2012).
36 'Fragmentation of International Law: Difficulties arising from the Diversification and Expansion of International Law', Report of the Study Group of the International Law Commission, A/CN.4/L.702, 18 July 2006, para. 55 [hereinafter 'ILC Report'].
37 ILC Report, para. 481.

The diversification and specialization of international law results in less attention being paid to general principles and practices of international law[38] and 'conflicts between rules or rule-systems, deviating institutional practices and, possibly, the loss of an overall perspective on the law'.[39]

With regard to the danger of regime collision, Günther Teubner and Peter Korth observe that, 'the appearance of global regimes does not entail the integration, harmonization or, at the very least, the convergence of legal orders; rather, it transforms the international differentiation of law thereby not producing unity but a new fragmentation of law'.[40] Teubner and Korth refer to this phenomenon as sectoral differentiation meaning 'the differentiation of global law into transnational legal regimes, which define their external reach of their jurisdiction along issue-specific rather than territorial lines, and which claim a global validity for themselves'.[41] In other words, there is a trend toward 'polycentric globalization', meaning 'an accelerated differentiation of society into autonomous social systems, each of which springs territorial confines and constitutes itself globally'.[42] This 'polycentric globalization' gives rise to 'clash of rationalities' as a consequence of 'polycentric globalization' seems inevitable given the attempt to maximize their rationality by different global functional systems in a process of functional differentiation. The root of such problems lies in the 'fragmented and operationally closed functional systems of a global society, which, in their expansionist fervor, create the real problems of the global society, and who at the same time make use of global law in order normatively to secure their own highly refined sphere logics'.[43]

In view of this threat of fragmentation and threat of regime collision, I will propose four different approaches to resolving potential conflicts between trade and public health, and reconciling the competing values. These approaches are interpretative, legislative, human rights and the global principle of subsidiarity. I will then link these four approaches via a constitutionalist approach toward international law with a view to bringing the fragmentation of international regimes into policy coherence.

38 ILC Report, paras 5–8.

39 Scholars nonetheless have divergent views as to the impact of fragmentation of international law. Some see it as the erosion of general international law, emergence of conflicting jurisprudence, forum shopping and loss of legal security while others view it as a natural consequence of the increase of international activities, which can be redressed by technical streamlining and coordination. ILC Report, para. 8.

40 G Teubner, P Korth, 'Two Kinds of Legal Pluralism: Collision of Transnational Regime in the Double Fragmentation of World Society' in M A Young (ed), *Regime Interaction in International Law: Facing Fragmentation* (CUP 2012) 39.

41 Ibid.

42 A Fischer-Lescano, G Teubner, 'Regime-Collisions: the Vain Search for Legal Unity in the Fragmentation of Global Law' (2004) 25 *Michigan Journal of International Law* 999, 1006–1007.

43 Ibid., 1007.

3 Reconciling trade interests and public health concerns

3.1 Interpretative approach

The first approach is the interpretative approach informed by the Vienna Convention on the Law of Treaties [hereinafter 'VCLT'].[44] This approach is strongly advocated by the ILC Study Group on the fragmentation of international law. The ILC Study Group relies heavily on Articles 31–32 of the VCLT, and refers to treaty interpretation as the integration of international legal systems. Systemic integration suggests that 'whatever their subject matter, treaties are a creation of the international legal system and their operation is predicated upon that fact'.[45] The ILC Study Group endorses giving particular weight to Article 31(3)(c) of the VCLT, which requires the interpreter of a treaty to take into account 'any relevant rules of international law applicable in relations between the parties'. This provision deals with cases in which material sources external to the treaty, including other treaties, customary rules or general principles of law, are relevant in its interpretation. When it comes to other treaties, 'such other [treaty] rules are of particular relevance where parties to the treaty under interpretation are also parties to the other treaty'.[46] They may constitute evidence of 'common understanding of the parties as to the object and purpose of the treaty under interpretation or as to the meaning of a particular term'.[47]

This interpretative approach is relied upon by many scholars interested in avoiding and resolving conflicts arising from conflicting regimes in the international legal system. In an attempt to achieve coherence between trade and public regimes, Chang-fa Lo also refers to the VCLT for proper interpretation of a WTO rule.[48] Joost Pauwelyn argues that in case of a conflict between a WTO treaty rule and a non-WTO rule, the WTO rule must be interpreted in the light of, and, to the extent possible, consistent with, the non-WTO rule whenever the non-WTO rule falls within the four categories set out for in Articles 31–32 of the VCLT; the same applies when the interpretation of a non-WTO rule is at stake.[49] In the context of the relationship between the WTO Agreement and multilateral environment agreements, Gabrielle Marceau argues that VCLT, in particular, Article 31(3)(c) 'aims at promoting some "coherence" in the interpretation of treaty obligations, so

44 Vienna Convention on the Law of Treaties, 23 May 1969, 1155 UNTS 331; 8 ILM 679 (1969); 63 *AJIL* 875 (1969), see also Chapter 10 in this book.

45 ILC Report, para. 17.

46 ILC Report, para. 21.

47 Ibid.

48 C-F Lo, 'External Regime Coherence: WTO/BIT and Public Health Tension as an Illustration' (2012) 7 *Asian Journal of WTO and International Health Law and Policy* 263, 276. Note that Lo sees the WTO system as a self-sufficient and closed regime, which is different from Pauwelyn's conceptualization of the WTO.

49 J Pauwelyn, *Conflicts of Norms in Public International Law: How WTO Relates to other Rules of International Law* (CUP 2003) 252.

that the treaty being interpreted and other relevant international law rules are read in a way that is mutually supportive and avoids conflict'.[50] Thus, VCLT may be used as an instrument for ascertaining the meaning of the provisions of WTO rules and for resolving the conflicts between WTO law and non-WTO law.

This interpretative approach has also been stressed in the Doha Declaration on the TRIPS Agreement and Public Health, declaring 'that the [TRIPS] Agreement can and should be interpreted and implemented in a manner supportive of WTO Members' right to protect public health and, in particular, to promote access to medicines for all'.[51] The Doha Declaration seems to give voice to confidence that trade and public health may be mutual supportive, and that potential conflicts may be resolved through this interpretative approach. Nonetheless, a closer look at the WTO jurisprudence reminds us of the high hurdles to be overcome.

Indeed, VCLT has long been a tool heavily relied upon by the Appellate Body, which in its first case held that the WTO Agreement is not to be read in clinical isolation from public international law.[52] As the Appellate Body explains, the general rule of interpretation as set out in the VCLT has attained the status of a rule of customary or general international law, and constitutes part of the 'customary rules of interpretation of public international law' which the Appellate Body has been directed to apply in clarifying the provisions of the covered agreements.[53]

In an attempt to ascertain the meaning of a generic term of 'exhaustible natural resources', as set out in Article XX(g) of the GATT 1994, the Appellate Body in *US – Shrimps* refers to other non-WTO treaties in ascertaining the meaning of 'exhaustible natural resources', as set out in Article XX(g) of the GATT 1994. The question before the Appellate Body is whether natural resources include living natural resources. By surveying relevant international treaties and declarations, such as the 1982 United Nations Convention on the Law of the Sea [hereafter 'UNCLOS'], the Convention on Biological Diversity [hereinafter 'CBD'], Agenda 21 and the Resolution on Assistance to Developing Countries, adopted in conjunction with the Convention on the Conservation of Migratory Species of Wild Animals [hereinafter 'CMS'], the Appellate Body held the term 'exhaustible natural resources' to cover living natural resources.[54] It should be noted that the CMS is not binding

50 G Marceau, 'Conflicts of Norms and Conflicts of Jurisdictions: The Relationship between the WTO Agreement and MEAs and other Treaties' (2001) 55 *Journal of World Trade* 1081, 1089.

51 Doha Declaration on the TRIPS Agreement and Public Health, para. 4.

52 Appellate Body Report, *US – Gasoline*, WT/DS2/AB/R, adopted 20 May 1996, p. 17.

53 Ibid.

54 Appellate Body Report, *US – Shrimps*, adopted 6 November 1998, WT/DS58/RW, adopted 21 November 2001, upheld by Appellate Body Report WT/DS58/AB/RW, paras 130–131. Relying on *US – Shrimps*, Lukasz Gruszczynski argues that by looking other non-WTO law with a view to ascertaining the ordinary meaning of a term in the provisions of the WTO law or to defining the WTO obligation, WTO judiciary may overcome its narrow approach

upon the disputing parties, the US and Malaysia, a fact of which the Panel on *US – Shrimp (Article 25 – Malaysia)* was fully aware.[55]

However, the scope of VCLT aid in resolving conflicts between trade and public health has its limit.[56] That limit is best illustrated in the restricted approach adopted by the Panel in *EC – Approval and Marketing of Biotech Products.* In that dispute, the Panel held that what is qualified as 'any relevant rules of international law applicable in the relations between the parties' as set out for in Article 31(3)(c) of the VCLT must be 'those rules of international law which are applicable in the relations between all parties to the treaty which is being interpreted'.[57] This restricted view makes it extremely difficult, if not impossible, for other international agreements, such as the WHO FCTC, to be taken into account in interpreting the WTO agreements.

In contrast to the restrictive approach adopted by the Panel in *EC – Approval and Marketing of Biotech Products*, the Appellate Body in *EC – Large Civil Aircraft* took a more balanced approach. The Appellate Body underlined two competing values in this interpretative exercise. On the one hand, 'the purpose of treaty interpretation is to establish the common intention of the parties to the treaty';[58] thus, the treaty interpreter has to be cautious in drawing from an international agreement to which not all the WTO Members are contracting parties. On the other hand, the Appellate Body, citing the ILC Report, held that Article 31(3)(c), principle of systemic integration, instructs the treaty interpreter to seek to ensure that 'international obligations are interpreted by reference to their normative environment' in a manner that gives 'coherence and meaningfulness' to the process of legal interpretation.[59] However, in conclusion, the Appellate Body did not rule on whether the bilateral agreement between the EU and US in question constitute 'any relevant rules of international law applicable in the relations between the parties' since the bilateral agreement was not relevant to the provision to be interpreted.

The Appellate Body is faced with a dilemma between internal coherence of WTO law and external coherence between WTO law and public international law. With the help of Article 31(3)(c), the principle of systemic

in restricting the parties as codified in Art. 31(3)(c) of the VCLT as 'all the parties'. L Gruszczynski, 'The New Tobacco Products Directive and WTO Law: Much Ado about Nothing' (2015) 10 *Asian Journal of WTO & International Health Law and Policy* 115, 130–131.

55 Panel Report, *US – Shrimp* (Art. 25 – Malaysia), para. 5.57.

56 Pauwelyn (n 49) 244–247; 272–274.

57 Panel Report, *EC – Approval and Marketing of Biotech Products*, WT/DS291/R / WT/DS292/R / WT/DS293/R / Add.1 to Add.9 and Corr.1, adopted 21 November 2006, para. 7.70. The ILC Report refers to this ruling by noting that 'the panel buys what it calls the "consistency" of its interpretation of the WTO Treaty at the cost of the consistency of the multilateral treaty system as a whole'. ILC Report, para. 450.

58 Appellate Body Report, *EC – Large Civil Aircraft*, para. 845.

59 Appellate Body Report, *EC – Large Civil Aircraft*, para. 845.

integration, and relaxing the scope of 'the parties' from 'all the parties' to the 'parties to the dispute', the Appellate Body will contribute to the coherence between WTO law and public international law by reading the WTO law in light of other public international law, including customary international law and international treaty law. Nonetheless, this move may undermine the coherence of the WTO since rights and obligations of the WTO agreements may differ from one Member to another.[60] Such pitfalls are in fact envisaged by the ILC Report. The antidote offered by the ILC Study Group to this relies on the distinction 'between "reciprocal" or "synallagmatic" treaties (in which case mere "divergence" in interpretation creates no problem) and "integral" or "interdependent" treaties (or treaties concluded erga omnes partes) where the use of that other treaty in interpretation should not be allowed to threaten the coherence of the treaty to be interpreted'.[61] With such distinction, it would release the concerns about consistency and coherence of WTO law as expressed in the Panel report on *EC – Approval and Marketing of Biotech Products.*

That said, given that there is currently no clear guidance from the WTO jurisprudence, some further aid must be sought for the exploration of the common understanding or common intention of WTO Members, which is then linked to the legislative approach.

3.2 Legislative approach

The second approach is the legislative, which can be employed in different stages of the formation of international legal regimes, and may take different forms. From the outset, when a set of international rules is formulated, there may be a built-in disposition of the relationship between such rules and other international laws. Such a practice can be seen in the IHR 2005, in which Article 57(1) regulates the relationship between the IHR and other international agreements. This provision puts forward two elements: first, the IHR 2005 and other relevant international agreements should be interpreted so as to be compatible; second, the IHR 2005 shall not affect the rights and obligations of any State Party deriving from other international agreements.[62]

After a set of international rules comes into being, the legislative approach may also be employed through authoritative interpretations, decisions or declarations adopted by competent treaty bodies or the decision-making bodies of international organizations. The legal force of authoritative interpretations is much stronger than those of decisions and declarations. In the WTO era, the WTO Members have rarely adopted authoritative interpretations. In contrast, both the WTO and the WHO FCTC frequently adopted decisions and declarations – the Doha Declaration on the TRIPS Agreement and Public

60 The author owes this point to the editors.
61 ILC Report, para. 472.
62 IHR 2005, Art. 57(1).

Health, and the Punta del Este Decision on the Implementation of the WHO FCTC being prime examples.

In *US – Clove Cigarettes*, the Appellate Body distinguished between authoritative interpretations and other sorts of Ministerial decisions or declarations. As the Appellate Body pointed out, Article IX:2 of the WTO Agreement sets out two specific requirements for the adoption of authoritative interpretations: '(i) a decision by the Ministerial Conference or the General Council to adopt such interpretations shall be taken by a three-fourths majority of Members; and (ii) such interpretations shall be taken on the basis of a recommendation by the Council overseeing the functioning of the relevant Agreement'.[63] As regards the second requirement, the Appellate Body held that 'the recommendation from the relevant Council is an essential element of Article IX:2, which constitutes the legal basis upon which the Ministerial Conference or the General Council exercise their authority to adopt interpretations of the WTO Agreement'.[64] Thus, in the view of the Appellate Body, the existence of a specific recommendation from the relevant Council is an essential element for a Ministerial decision or declaration to qualify as an authoritative interpretation.

The Appellate Body further clarified the nature of authoritative interpretations and other forms of Ministerial decisions and declarations, stating that, 'multilateral [authoritative] interpretations are meant to clarify the meaning of existing obligations'.[65] Besides, 'multilateral [authoritative] interpretations adopted pursuant to Article IX:2 of the WTO Agreement are most akin to subsequent agreements within the meaning of Article 31(3)(a) of the Vienna Convention'.[66] However, the Appellate Body cautioned that while authoritative interpretations, in view of their specific function under Article IX:2 of the WTO Agreement and their adoption by the Members sitting in the form of the highest organs of the WTO, are most akin to subsequent agreements on interpretation within the meaning of Article 31(3)(a) of the VCLT, they are not exhaustive or exclusive.[67] There are other forms of agreement, as will be shown below, and the Doha Declaration on the TRIPS Agreement and Public Health can be considered one of these subsequent agreements.

The Doha Declaration on the TRIPS Agreement and Public Health was adopted in response to demands for effective action to address public health problems facing developing countries and least developed countries.[68] After

63 Appellate Body Report, *US – Clove Cigarettes*, WT/DS406/AB/R, adopted 24 April 2012, para. 251.
64 Appellate Body Report, *US – Clove Cigarettes*, para. 254.
65 Appellate Body Report, *US – Clove Cigarettes*, para. 259.
66 Appellate Body Report, *US – Clove Cigarettes*, para. 259.
67 Appellate Body Report, *US – Clove Cigarettes*, para. 259.
68 For further exploration of the Doha Declaration on the TRIPS Agreement and Public Health, see F M Abbott 'The Doha Declaration on the TRIPS Agreement and Public Health: Lighting a Dark Corner at the WTO' (2002) 5 *Journal of International Economic Law* 469.

reinstating that the TRIPS 'Agreement can and should be interpreted and implemented in a manner supportive of WTO members' right to protect public health and, in particular, to promote access to medicines for all',[69] the Doha Declaration on the TRIPS Agreement and Public Health points to the flexibilities provided in the TRIPS Agreement to achieve this end. These flexibilities include the interpretative approach, which entails applying customary rules of interpretation of public international law; compulsory licensing; Members' right to determine what constitutes a national emergency or situation of extreme urgency; and Members' freedom to establish regimes relevant for the exhaustion of intellectual property rights.[70]

In the context of WTO law, the Doha Declaration on the TRIPS Agreement and Public Health constitutes a 'subsequent agreement between the parties' within the meaning of Article 31(3)(a) of the VCLT. In *US – Clove Cigarettes*, the Appellate Body was called upon to determine the legal nature of the Doha Ministerial Decision. The Appellate Body put forward two criteria for having a Ministerial Decision adopted by the WTO Members qualified as a 'subsequent agreement between parties': temporal and substantive. First, the decision must be adopted temporally later than the adoption of the relevant covered agreement. Second, 'the terms and content of the decision is expressive of an agreement between WTO Members on the interpretation and application of a WTO provision'.[71] In applying these two criteria to the Doha Declaration on the TRIPS Agreement and Public Health, the temporal element is easily satisfied. The remaining question relates to whether WTO Members agree on the interpretation and application of a WTO provision. The answer is also affirmative, which can find evidence from the declaration prescribing that the TRIPS Agreement can and should be interpreted and implemented in a manner supportive of the right of Members to protect public health and promote access to medicine. The emphasis on the flexibility provided in the TRIPS Agreement also reflects the WTO Members' consensus as to the application of the TRIPS Agreement. The Doha Declaration on the TRIPS Agreement and Public Health thus constitutes a 'subsequent agreement between the parties' within the meaning of Article 31(3)(a) of the VCLT. By referring to this legislative approach with an expression of their agreement as to the interpretation and application of the WTO laws, this 'subsequent agreement' can provide additional interpretative guidance to the treaty interpreter and, in this case, lend strength to a Member's argument on its right to protect public health.

The same technique is also employed by the Contracting Parties of the WHO FCTC. In response to the challenges posed by tobacco industries in various international fora, in particular Philip Morris International's investor claim against Uruguay in the International Center for the Settlement of Investment

69 Doha Declaration on the TRIPS Agreement and Public Health, para. 4.
70 Doha Declaration on the TRIPS Agreement and Public Health, para. 4.
71 Appellate Body Report, *US – Clove Cigarettes*, para. 262.

Disputes [hereinafter 'ICSID'][72] and potential complaints in the WTO, the WHO FCTC Contracting Parties adopted the Punta del Este Decision on the Implementation of the WHO FCTC with a view to shielding those countries adopting strict tobacco control measures. The WHO FCTC Contracting Parties firstly reinstated the right to health as enshrined in the WHO Constitution, reaffirmed the Contracting Parties' determination to prioritize the right to protect public health and referred to Article XX(b) of the GATT 1994, TRIPS Agreement and Doha Declaration on the TRIPS Agreement and Public Health. The Contracting Parties then declared that, *inter alia*, '[Contracting] Parties have the right to define and implement national public health policies pursuant to compliance with conventions and commitments under WHO, particularly with the WHO FCTC'[73] and that 'Parties may adopt measures to protect public health, including regulating the exercise of intellectual property rights in accordance with national public health policies, provided that such measures are consistent with the TRIPS Agreement'.[74]

The terms and language of this declaration cover similar materials to those of the Doha Declaration on the TRIPS Agreement and Public Health. But in the context of the WTO law, the Punta del Este Decision on the Implementation of the WHO FCTC is of a different legal nature. While this decision may be arguably deemed as a 'subsequent agreement between the parties' in the context of the WHO FCTC, the same does not hold true for WTO law. At best, this decision can only be considered to apply as 'any relevant rules of international law applicable in the relations between the parties', which are already questionable in the first place. The key point here is whether this declaration, a soft law instrument in nature, can be qualified as 'any relevant rules of international law applicable in the relations between the parties'.

The Appellate Body in *US – Anti-Dumping and Countervailing Duties (China)*, put forward three criteria for this: relevant; rules of international law; applicable in the relations between the parties. In addition to controversy of the scope of the parties, one has to further reflect whether the Punta del Este Decision on the Implementation of the WHO FCTC can be qualified as 'rules of international law'. The WTO judiciary refers to Article 38(1) of the Statute of the International Court of Justice[75] and opines that such rules cover international treaties and conventions, customary international law, and general principles of law.[76] In light of this formal and narrow reading of 'rules of international law', the Punta del Este Decision on the Implementation of

72 *Philip Morris Brands Sàrl, Philip Morris Products S.A. and Abal Hermanos S.A. v Oriental Republic of Uruguay*, ICSID Case No. ARB/10/, Decision on Jurisdiction (2 July 2013), Procedural Order No. 3 (15 February 2015), Procedural Order No. 4 (24 March 2015).

73 Punta del Este Decision on the Implementation of WHO FCTC, para. 5.

74 Punta del Este Decision on the Implementation of the WHO Framework Convention on Tobacco Control, para. 4.

75 Appellate Body Report, *US – Anti-Dumping and Countervailing Duties (China)*, para. 308.

76 Panel Report, *EC – Approval and Marketing of Biotech Products*, para. 7.67.

the WHO FCTC does not constitute a rule of international law and cannot be taken into account through the venue of Article 31(3)(c) of the VCLT.[77] A legislative approach with secondary rule-making or decision-making is of constraint in leaping from one regime to another.

Finally, members of an international organization, or Contracting Parties to an international agreement, may rely upon the legislative approach by amending treaty rules with a view to resolving or eliminating treaty conflicts. Such a practice can be seen in the TRIPS Amendment. With a view to resolving the difficulties facing those countries with insufficient, or entirely lacking, manufacturing capacities in the pharmaceutical sector in making effective use of compulsory licensing, the WTO Members adopted a TRIPS Amendment that inserts Article 31(b) after Article 31, and inserts the Annex to the TRIPS Agreement after Article 73. One of the major purposes of the TRIPS Amendment is to release a country resorting to compulsory licensing for a pharmaceutical product of its obligation to refrain from exporting the licensed product as dictated by Article 31(f) of the TRIPS Agreement. The rationale for this provision is that some developing and least developed countries in need of pharmaceutical supplies are not equipped with the capacity to produce such pharmaceutical products. Thus, a mechanism allowing for compulsory licensing in one country, from which the licensed pharmaceutical product is subsequently exported to an importing country in need, is thus required to address public health problems facing countries with limited manufacturing capacities.

Whereas this legislative approach may provide some help in resolving the conflicts between trade and public health, there are some pitfalls in this approach. To begin with, the amendment route is a lengthy one, as it takes quite a long time for all WTO Members to go through the processes of their domestic ratification procedures. The TRIPS Amendment, for example, has not yet entered into force. With regard to the Doha Declaration and the Punta del Este Decision, while they may provide some guidance in interpreting the WTO Agreement and the WHO FCTC, and offer some help in resolving the potential conflicting obligations, the legal force of such decisions and declarations are rather weak. In contrast, authoritative interpretations bear stronger legal force, but this very character may discourage Members from opting for this approach.

77 While the Punta del Este Decision on the Implementation of the WHO FCTC may not be taken into account through Art. 31(3)(c) of the VCLT, other soft law instruments adopted under the auspice of the WHO FCTC may constitute relevant international standards in terms of Art. 3.2 of the TBT Agreement and is thus of relevance to the WTO law. On this point, see e.g., L Gruszczynski, 'The World Health Organization Framework Convention on Tobacco Control as an International Standard under the Agreement on Technical Barriers to Trade' in A D Mitchell, T Voon (eds), *The Global Tobacco Epidemic and the Law* (Edward Elgar 2014) 105–125.

3.3 Human rights approach

The third route is the human rights approach, with the overarching right here being the right to health. Such a right to health can find its root not only in the WHO Constitution and relevant international health agreements, but also in WTO law. The WHO Constitution explicitly recognizes that the enjoyment of the highest attainable standard of health is one of the fundamental rights of every human being, and the WHO FCTC refers to various international legal instruments articulating the right to health, including the International Covenant on Economic, Social and Cultural Rights.[78] The relevance of the right to health is not limited to health regime, but also extends to trade regime. As the preamble of the WTO Agreement spells out clearly, trade liberalization in the context of the WTO is a means instead of an end. The end of trade liberalization is to raise standards of living.[79] The value of protection of human health is also recognized in various provisions in the WTO agreements, such as Article XX(b) of the GATT 1994 and Article 2.1 of the SPS Agreement. The right to health thus serves as an overarching right linking trade and health regimes.

The right to health is generally understood to be composed of three types of obligations: an obligation to respect; obligation to protect; and obligation to fulfil. As the United Nations Economic and Social Council explains in the General Comment 14:

> The right to health, like all human rights, imposes three types or levels of obligations on States parties: the obligations to respect, protect and fulfil. In turn, the obligation to fulfil contains obligations to facilitate, provide and promote. The obligation to respect requires States to refrain from interfering directly or indirectly with the enjoyment of the right to health. The obligation to protect requires States to take measures that prevent third parties from interfering with Article 12 guarantees. Finally, the obligation to fulfil requires States to adopt appropriate legislative, administrative, budgetary, judicial, promotional and other measures towards the full realization of the right to health.[80]

78 WHO FCTC, preamble. On the sources of international right to health, see OHCHR and WHO, *The Right to Health: Factsheet 31* (OHCHR/WHO 2008) 9–11; V A Leary, 'The Right to Health in International Human Rights Law' (1994) 1 *Health and Human Rights* 24, 28–35; A Ely Yamin, 'The Right to Health Under International Law and Its Relevance to the United States' (2005) 95 *American Journal of Public Health* 1156, 1156–1157; E D Kinney, 'The International Human Right to Health: What does This Mean to Our Nation and World?' (2001) 34 *Indiana Law Review* 1457, 1458–1467.

79 WTO Agreement, first preambular.

80 Committee on Economic, Social and Cultural Rights, General Comment 14, 'The right to the highest attainable standard of health' (Twenty-second Session, 2000), para. 33, U.N. Doc. E/C.12/2000/4 (2000), reprinted in Compilation of General Comments and General Recommendations Adopted by Human Rights Treaty Bodies, U.N. Doc. HRI/GEN/1/Rev. 6 at 85 (2003).

Moreover, whereas the right to health is subject to progressive realization, it nonetheless entails some core obligations, including to ensure the right of non-discriminatory access to, and equitable distribution of, health facilities, goods and services, and to provide essential drugs.[81]

The right to health approach has a number of virtues in trade and public health debates. First, the right helps to bridge the trade and health regimes, as public health is a value shared by both the WHO and the WTO. Secondly, a right to health approach contributes to the empowerment of individuals,[82] which subsequently demands public participation when public health is at stake. The right to health also entails entitlement, which can be best illustrated in the access to essential medicine aspect.[83] Thirdly, raising right to health concerns in the WTO context contributes to the prioritization of public health. As the Appellate Body held in *Brazil – Retreaded Tyres*, Article XX(b) 'illustrates the tensions that may exist between, on the one hand, international trade and, on the other hand, public health and environmental concerns'.[84] The WTO panel or Appellate Body, in assessing the least trade restrictiveness of a Member's measure relying on Article XX(b) of the GATT 1994 (or its necessity under Article 2.2 of the SPS Agreement), has to weigh and balance a series of factors, notably, the importance of the common interests or values protected, and the impact upon imports or exports.[85] Therefore, the recognition of the right to health and its fundamental value to human beings helps to endorse giving greater weight to public health in this weighing and balancing process. The right to health should, therefore, trump commercial interests[86] in case of a conflict between a country's obligation to protect human health and its obligation to honor trade liberalization commitments. To this end, the 'flexibilities' provided in the WTO agreements for a WTO Member to protect public health should be respected and utilized.

These flexibilities are reaffirmed in the Doha Declaration on the TRIPS Agreement and Public Health. A WTO Member has the right to grant compulsory licensing, the freedom to determine the conditions for doing so,

81 Ibid.; see further L Forman and others, 'What could a Strengthened Right to Health Bring to the post-2015 Health Development Agenda?: Interrogating the Role of the Minimum Core Concept in Advancing Essential Global Health Needs' (2013) 13 *BMC International Health and Human Rights* 1, 1–11.

82 On this point, see E U Petersmann, 'Time for United Nations "Global Compact" for Integrating Human Rights into the Law of Worldwide Organizations: Lessons from European Integration' (2002) 13 *EJIL* 621; cf P Alston, 'Resisting the Merger and Acquisition of Human Rights by Trade Law: A Reply to Petersmann' (2002) 13 *EJIL* 815.

83 Leary (n 78) 35–40.

84 Appellate Body Report, *Brazil – Retreaded Tyres*, WT/DS332/AB/R, adopted 17 December 2007, para. 210.

85 Appellate Body Report, *Korea – Various Measures on Beef*, WT/DS161/AB/R, WT/DS169/AB/R, adopted 10 January 2001, para. 164.

86 On rights as trumps, see, R Dworkin, *Taking Rights Seriously* (Harvard University Press 1977).

to decide what constitutes a national emergency or other circumstances of extreme urgency, and to define its national regulatory regime on the exhaustion of intellectual property rights. The aim of the Doha Declaration on the TRIPS Agreement and Public Health is to reinstate the flexibilities available to a WTO Member in putting forward public health measures without infringing WTO rules. These flexibilities then link to the fourth approach, the recognition of a principle of global subsidiarity, that opens up the possibility of there being a policy space for WTO Members in enhancing and safeguarding public health.

3.4 Principle of global subsidiarity

As defined by Andreas Føllesdal, the principle of subsidiarity 'regulates authority within a political order, directing that powers or tasks should rest with the lower-level sub-units of that order unless allocating them to a higher-level central unit would ensure higher comparative efficiency or effectiveness in achieving them'.[87] The principle of subsidiarity is a constitutional principle under EU law, but finds its roots in German law and a counterpart in United States federalism.[88] This principle has had an impact on international human rights law and WTO law.[89] In the context of the WTO, Robert Howse and Kalypso Nicolaidis argue that, in preserving and enhancing the legitimacy of the WTO, the intepretation of the WTO rules should engage competing and divergent human values. Howse and Nicolaidis underline the role of non-WTO institutions and norms representing values other than free or freer trade, and argue against the narrow definition of the WTO's constitutional *telos* as free trade, or isolated search within the WTO system for structural principles.[90] Thus, they call for a global principle of subsidiarity to be complemented by three basic principles: institutional sensitivity, political inclusiveness, and top-down empowerment. Institutional sensitivity means that the WTO should be sensitive, and deferent, to interests and values external to the trade regime, including those of nation states themselves. Political inclusiveness means international trade regimes should be more open to relevant stakeholders other than trade interests, both at the national and international levels. Top-down empowerment aims, with the

87 A Føllesdal, 'Survey Article: Subsidiarity' (1998) 6 *The Journal of Political Philosophy* 190, 190.

88 See G A Bermann, 'Taking Subsidiarity Seriously: Federalism in the European Community and the United States' (1994) 94 *Columbia Law Review* 331.

89 See e.g., P G Carozza, 'Subsidiarity as a Structural Principle of International Human Rights Law' (2003) 97 *AJIL* 38; R Howse, K Nicolaidis, 'Enhancing WTO Legitimacy: Constitutionalization or Global Subsidiarity?' (2004) 15 *Governance: An International Journal of Policy, Administration, and Institutions* 73; J P Trachtman, 'Trade and... Problems, Cost-Benefit Analysis and Subsidiarity' (1998) 9 *EJIL* 32.

90 Howse et al. (n 89) 75.

aid of global norms, to redressing the disadvantages facing local actors that are disempowered in their domestic context and subsequently biasing in the representation of their country at the global level.[91]

Such principle of global subsidiarity should then guide the WTO judiciary during its interpretative exercise when public health concerns are at stake. The value of human health is reinstated in a number of WTO provisions. For example, Article 20(b) of the GATT 1994 provides that 'nothing in this [GATT 1994] Agreement shall be construed to prevent the adoption or enforcement by any contracting party of measures necessary to protect human, animal or plant life or health'. A similar exception is provided in Article XIV(b) of the GATS. In addition, Article 2.1 of the SPS Agreement recognizes that 'Members have the right to take sanitary and phytosanitary measures necessary for the protection of human, animal or plant life or health'. These provisions nonetheless recognize that human health is a value which Members should be able to pursue with the maximum degree of freedom. Therefore, these provisions should not be reduced to mere exceptions to trade liberalization commitments, but should be read as an explicit recognition of the legitimacy of preserving national policy spaces to promote and protect public health. In this context, how to define the scope of Members' regulatory autonomy in pursuing public health objectives is the pivotal question. On the one hand, the Appellate Body views Members' right to regulate 'as an *inherent power* enjoyed by a Member's government, rather than a right bestowed by international treaties such as the WTO Agreement'.[92] On the other hand, such right to regulate is subject to the constraint of international obligations when a sovereign enters into international agreements based on its consent. The delimitation of Members' regulatory space is thus a delicate task. In this process, the global principle of subsidiarity would caution the treaty interpreter to be fully aware of values other than free or freer trade (in fact, public health is a value expressly recognized in the WTO agreements), or value external to the WTO regime. Moreover, it would guide the treaty interpreter to respect a Member's decision to protect national public health, and its efforts to realize the right to health with the boundary of its WTO obligations.

4 From fragmentation to coherence: the quest for global constitutional order

In recognition of the threat of fragmentation of international law and danger of regime collision between the WTO and WHO, four approaches are proposed with a view to reconciling the conflicts between trade and public health: the interpretative, legislative, and human rights approaches, and an

91 Ibid., 86–90.

92 Appellate Body, *China – Publications and Audiovisual Products*, paras 221–2 (emphasis added).

application of the global principle of subsidiarity. These four approaches address different dimensions of challenges facing international law arising from the proliferation of international legal regimes and the shift of regulatory authority from nation states to international organizations.

These four approaches address questions as to the' role of international organizations and treaty-bodies as lawmakers; how regimes interact with each other and general international law; the role of international adjudicators and their reliance on interpretation rule as codified in VCLT in resolving these conflicts, the role of individuals in international legal order and the protection of human rights; and whether and how an international regime should defer to values external to itself. Indeed, these questions are what constitutionalists of international law aim to answer.

For Jan Klabbers, the constitutionalization of international law does not merely suggest that the international legal order is 'governed by a clear fundamental, constitutive norm or set of norms',[93] which has been long the case since Westphalia, with the fundamental norm being sovereignty. The constitutionalization of international law entails deriving political legitimacy from the nature of its constitution.[94] Moreover, this global constitutional order has to be pluralist, composed of diverse actors and built upon multiply sources of global authority. It has to respect political pluralism as 'different people may have different interests and different perspectives on what they hold to be the good life'.[95] At the same time, it has to recognize normative pluralism as 'individuals, states and other actors act and behave in different webs of normative utterances'.[96]

However, the constitutionalization of international law may backfire on the vision of a global constitutional order: the major challenge comes from sectoral constitutionalization, meaning the emergence of constitutional elements of primary and secondary law of international organizations. Sectoral constitutionalization engenders the danger of fragmentation. The question here is: 'When different organizations have their own constitutions, how can they still be members of a global constitutional order?'[97] Ann Peters submits that the various processes of constitutionalization operative on different levels do not necessarily exclude each other. 'Global constitutional order is pluralist and it relates to multi-level governance. It implies nested constitutional orders'.[98] Therefore, members of a global constitutional order, notably, states and international organizations, may have their own sectoral constitutions, which will in the end result in multi-level constitutionalism.

93 J Klabbers, A Peters, G Ulfstein, *The Constitutionalization of International Law* (OUP 2009) 8.
94 Ibid.
95 Ibid., 43.
96 Ibid., 44.
97 Ibid., 202.
98 Ibid.

In this line, sectoral constitutionalization in the WHO and the WTO does not prevent the two organizations from being brought together under a global constitutional order. Nominally, the WHO has had a constitution since its inception, while the WTO Agreement has been widely referred to as the WTO Constitution.[99] That being said, the coexistence of these two organizations in the global constitutional order does not necessarily iron out the divergences between trade and health governance. Great efforts have to be made with a view to ensuring coherence between these two regimes and avoiding the threat of fragmentation. To this end, it is essential to recalibrate the understanding and expectation of the WTO interpretative community with regard to the interpretative value of human rights within a trade instrument. At the same time, public health advocates have to recognize that the use of right to health as an interpretative instrument does not unconditionally receive priority over trading rights and interests.[100]

Bearing this in mind, I propose four concrete approaches to resolve the potential conflicts between trade regime and health regime in this global constitutional order. These four approaches are embedded in a constitutionalist approach toward international law that is in search of a global constitutional order. The WTO Agreement should be transformed into a WTO Constitution focusing trade liberalization but open to, and respecting, non-economic values, which will then contribute to the integrity of the WHO Constitution. This constitutionalist approach will help to delineate the jurisdictional boundary of international organizations and clarify the allocation of competence between such international organizations and their member states. This constitutionalist approach will ensure that international adjudicators of a given regime respect values external to it. Finally, within such global constitutional order, individuals will be empowered with a right to health that the state will have an international obligation to respect, protect, and fulfill. Within this global constitutional order, a constitutionalist approach will thus help to link the four approaches presented above and thus reap the benefits arising from the synergy of these approaches.

6 Conclusion

When concluding the Uruguay Round Negotiations, the drafters of the WTO Agreement were aware of the potentially adverse effects of trade liberalization upon public health. At that time, the debates centered on harmful commodities and unhealthy products; the liberalization of health services; and intellectual

99 See e.g., J H Jackson, *The World Trading Organization: Constitution and Jurisprudence* (Royal Institute of International Affairs 1998) 102–103; E U Petersmann, 'From "Member-Driven Governance" to Constitutionally Limited "Multi-Level Trade Governance" in the WTO' in G Sacerdoti, A Yanovich, J Bohanes (eds), *The WTO at Ten: The Contribution of the Dispute Settlement System* (CUP 2006) 98.

100 J Tobin, *The Right to Health in International Law* (OUP 2012) 364.

property rights. During the past two decades, the debate between trade and public heath has intensified greatly, the best example being Australian tobacco control measures on plain packaging. The exacerbation of this debate is also reflective of the emergent phenomenon of regime collision, and engenders the threat of the fragmentation of international law.

With a view to resolving potential conflicts between trade liberalization measures and public health objectives, four approaches are proposed: interpretative, legislative, human rights approaches, and the application of the global principle of subsidiarity. The interpretative approach addresses the role of international adjudicators in relying on the interpretation rules as embodied in the VCLT to mitigate potential conflicts between international obligations. This approach takes its departure point from a presumption that the drafters of international treaties do not intend to set out conflicting international obligations, and international rules are thus to be interpreted as compatible. The legislative approach addresses the role of international organizations or treaty bodies as lawmakers. The drafters of a given international agreement may, from the outset, define its relationship with other international agreements. The treaty body or international organization may also subsequently decide or declare that an interpretative value will be applied to a potential conflict. Members of the international organization concerned may also refer to treaty amendment procedures to eliminate the conflict between different international obligations. The human rights approach aims to empower individuals with a right to health to wield against states in cases of competing values and interests arising from the debates over trade and public health, and endorse giving greater weight to public health in weighing and balancing processes. The global principle of subsidiarity instructs a given international regime to be sensitive to values external to itself. In an attempt to linking these four approaches, I argue that a constitutionalist approach toward international law in search of a global constitutional order is desirable and will help to reap benefits arising from synergies between these four approaches.

14 Access to environmental justice for NGOs

Interplay between the Aarhus Convention, the EU Lisbon Treaty and the European Convention on Human Rights

Marjolein Schaap - Rubio Imbers [1]

1 Introduction

The human right of access to justice[2] has been conceptualized by the UN/ECE Convention on Access to Information, Public Participation and Access to Justice ('Aarhus Convention')[3] as a right of access to environmental justice and recognizing an important role for non-governmental organizations (NGOs)[4] in the enforcement of this right.[5] The Aarhus Convention obliges its parties to guarantee procedural rights in decision-making in environmental matters; all EU member states and the EU itself are party to the Aarhus Convention and thus have committed themselves to ensure that these procedural guarantees are taken into account. Additionally, 43 out of 47 member states to the European Convention on Human Rights (ECHR) are party to the Aarhus Convention.[6]

1 An earlier version of this paper was presented at the COST Action IS1003 conference 'Constitutionalisation and Fragmentation of International Law Revisited' (18 November 2013), Warsaw, Poland. The author would like to thank the reviewers and Ellen Hey, Urszula Jaremba, Carina Olsthoorn and Federica Violi for their valuable comments on the chapter.

2 E.g. F Francioni, 'The Right of Access to Justice under Customary International Law' in F Francioni (ed.), *Access to Justice as a Human Right* (OUP 2007) 1; C Redgwell, 'Access to Environmental Justice' in *Access to Justice as a Human Right* 153.

3 UN ECE Aarhus Convention (adopted on 25 June 1998, entered into force on 30 October 2011) 2161 UNTS 447.

4 D Bodanksy, J Brunnée and E Hey, 'International Environmental Law: Mapping the Field' in Bodanksy, Brunnée and Hey (eds), *The Oxford Handbook on International Environmental Law* (OUP 2008) 6, 20–21; See further PJ Spiro, 'NGOs and Civil Society' in *The Oxford Handbook on International Environmental Law* 770–790.

5 MR Goldschmidt, 'The Role of Transparency and Public Participation in International Environmental Agreements' (2002) 29 *Environmental Affairs* 343, 347; M Macchia, 'Global Administrative Law Compliance: the Aarhus Convention Compliance Review System' (2008) 4 *ERPL/REDP* 1317, 1334.

6 All EU states are also party to the ECHR, see for status of ratifications http://conventions.coe.int/Treaty/Commun/ChercheSig.asp?NT=005&CM=&DF=&CL=ENG.

Each convention has its own compliance mechanism, thus resulting in overlapping mandates, interaction between the actors involved, and possibly, in diverging interpretation of overlapping rights. This interplay between the treaty regimes is highly fascinating, particularly in the context of the discourse on constitutionalisation and fragmentation of international law. As discussed by Peters, constitutionalisation within the field of international law refers to the '…gradual emergence of constitutionalist features in international law' which are expected to 'compensate for globalization-induced constitutionalist deficits on the national level.'[7] Constitutional features often mentioned include transparency, separation of powers, judicial review, limited exercise of public power and human rights protection. Access to justice as such has a strong foundation in international human rights law and is an essential right in enabling people to hold public actors to account for their exercise of public power.[8] Against this background, the right of access to environmental justice for NGOs will be examined in this chapter. This research will show whether and to what extent the right of NGOs to access to environmental justice is in the process of constitutionalisation[9] by mapping the overlapping, multilayered European treaty regimes on the basis of the legislation and case law stemming from each respective treaty regime.

The chapter takes as point of departure for the analysis the provisions on access to justice as defined by the Aarhus Convention which will be discussed in section 1; particular focus will be on the access to justice obligations following from Article 9(3) of this treaty. Section 2 analyses whether and to what extent the EU as party to the Aarhus Convention has interpreted and implemented the access to environmental justice obligations flowing from this convention in relation to the EU institutions. In particular, it emphasises that the criteria for legal standing at the level of EU Courts[10] should be interpreted in light of the Aarhus Convention. In turn, Section 3 examines whether and to what extent the (ECtHR) is already taking the access to justice obligations stemming from the Aarhus Convention into account in its

7 A Peters, 'The Merits of Global Constitutionalism' (2009) 16(2) *Indiana Journal of Global Legal Studies* 397–411, cited in A Wiener et al., 'Global Constitutionalism: Human Rights Democracy and the Rule of Law' (2010) 1 *Global Constitutionalism* 1, 4; D Bodanksy, 'Is there an International Environmental Constitution' (2008) 16 *Indiana Journal of Global Legal Studies* 565, 572.

8 D Shelton, *Remedies in International Human Rights Law* (OUP 1999) 358; Francioni 'The Right of Access to Justice' (n 2) 7–8.

9 See in this light the functional school of constitutionalism, JL Dunoff and JP Trachtman, 'A Functional Approach to International Constitutionalization' in JL Dunoff and JP Trachtman (eds), *Ruling the World: Constitutionalism, International Law and Global Governance* (CUP 2009) 1, 4.

10 Note that pre-Lisbon treaty terminology will be used when case law and treaty provisions are cited preceding the Lisbon treaty. In all other instances the post-Lisbon treaty terminology will be used.

case law. Section 4 explores the approach taken by the ECtHR in reviewing EU obligations until now and speculates whether access to environmental justice might be further protected and thus enhanced once the EU accedes to the ECtHR. Section 5 of this chapter concludes with answering the question whether and to what extent these converging layers might actually enhance access to environmental justice for NGOs within Europe leading to a constitutionalisation of this right.

2 The pillar of access to justice of the Aarhus Convention

There are currently 47 parties to the Aarhus Convention,[11] including the EU. The convention lays down minimum standards for access to information, public participation and access to justice in decision-making in environmental matters.[12] The compliance mechanism, the Aarhus Convention Compliance Committee (ACCC), allows members of the public[13] to communicate their concerns about a Party's compliance directly to a board of independent experts.[14] The mandate of the ACCC is quite different from the Court of Justice of the European Union (CJEU) and the ECtHR, as it takes a non-confrontational, non-judicial, and consultative approach when reviewing compliance and it can merely recommend (non-binding) solutions to ensure compliance.[15]

Access to justice is regulated by Article 9 of the Aarhus Convention. The public should have access to a court or another independent and impartial review body in order to be able to ask for review of environmental decision-making regarding alleged violations of the convention. The Aarhus Convention identifies three different strands of access to justice procedures, those relating to right to information procedures under Article 4, those that relate to Article 6 & 7 participation procedures and the remaining review procedures under Article 9(3) of the Convention, which will be the focus of the analysis. Article 9(3) ensures that members of the public, when they meet the national requirements (if any), must have access to administrative or judicial procedures to challenge acts and omissions concerned.[16] Public authorities have quite some flexibility in defining the criteria; however, it may

11 For current status of ratifications, http://www.unece.org/env/pp/ratification.html, accessed on 15 April 2016.

12 See also E Hey, 'The Interaction between Human Rights and the Environment in the European "Aarhus Space"' in A Grear & L J Kotzé (eds), *Research Handbook on Human Rights and the Environment* (Edward Elgar 2015) 353, 357–362.

13 Art. 2(4) Aarhus Convention:

> '"The public" means one or more natural or legal persons, and, in accordance with national legislation or practice, their associations, organizations or groups'.

14 Decision I/7 Review of Compliance, ECE/MP.PP/2/Add.8 (2 April 2004).

15 Art. 15 Aarhus Convention; see also Annex III to UN ECE *Guidance Document on the Aarhus Convention Compliance Mechanism* (2010), http://www.unece.org/fileadmin/DAM/env/pp/compliance/CC_GuidanceDocument.pdf at paras 41–43.

16 ACCC, *Communication ACCC/C/2008/23 concerning United Kingdom*, ECE/MP.PP/C.1/2010/6/Add.1 (October 2010) at para. 44.

not result in imposing such strict criteria effectively preventing NGOs from challenging acts or omissions that contravene national law relating to the environment.[17] Members of the public (including NGOs) should thus (in principle) have standing to directly or indirectly enforce the law:[18]

> ...[and have] access to adequate remedies against acts and omissions which contravene environmental laws, and with the means to have existing environmental laws enforced and made effective.[19]

The review procedures, as protected by Article 9 (paras 1–3) of the Aarhus Convention, should uphold certain minimum procedural guarantees. In general, they must be fair and equitable, timely, and not prohibitively expensive, and be carried out by independent and impartial bodies.[20]

3 Aarhus – EU: access to environmental justice for NGOs at EU courts

The Aarhus Convention was signed by the (then) European Community and approved via a Council Decision,[21] after which the EU institutions became bound by its legal regime. The provisions of the Aarhus Convention became an integral part of the EU legal order,[22] thus prevailing over secondary Community legislation.[23] The Aarhus Convention is a mixed agreement, concluded by

17 ACCC, *Communication ACCC/2005/11 concerning Belgium*, ECE/MP.PP/C1/2006/4/Add 2 (28 July 2006) paras 35–36; ACCC, *Communication concerning Denmark ACCC/C/2006/18*, ECE/MP.PP/2008/5/add.4 (29 April 2008) para. 29.

18 See Regional Environmental Center for Central and Eastern Europe (eds), *The Aarhus Convention: an Implementation Guide* (UN Publications 2000) 140; See also preamble, Aarhus Convention.

19 ACCC, *Denmark ACCC/C/2006/18* (n 17) para. 28.

20 Art. 9(4) Aarhus Convention; See e.g. ACCC, *Communication concerning Spain ACCC/2008/24*, ECE/MP.PP/C.1/2009/8/Add.1 (30 September 2010) paras 104–105, 112; see further J. Ebbesson and others, *The Aarhus Convention: an Implementation Guide* (UN Publications 2014) 190–204.

21 Council Decision 2005/370/EC, OJ 2005 L 124, at 1.

22 *Slovenian Wolf Forest Protection Movement* case against Slovenia (*Lesoochranárske Zoskupenie VLK v Ministerstvo Životného Prostredia Slovenskej Republiky* [2011] ECR C-240/09); in paras 30–33 the Court established that the Aarhus Convention provisions are considered to be an integral part of the EU legal order, and consequently the ECJ can interpret the Convention via preliminary ruling questions that are referred by national courts. For the role of the EU in enforcing Aarhus obligations within member states see e.g. S Kingston, 'Mind the Gap: Difficulties in Enforcement and the Continuing Unfulfilled Promise of EU Environmental Law' in Kingston (ed.), *European Perspectives on Environmental Law and Governance* (Routledge 2013) 147; JH Jans, 'Judicial Dialogue, Judicial Competition and Global Environmental Law' in JH Jans et al., (eds), *National Courts and EU Environmental Law* (Europa Law Publishing 2013) 145.

23 T- 338/08 *Stichting Natuur en Milieu and Pesticide Action Network Europe v European Commission* & T-396/09 *Vereniging Milieudefensie and Stichting Stop Luchtverontreiniging Utrecht v European Commission* (14 June 2012) para. 52.

both the EU and the member states on the basis of joint competence.[24] The EU has implemented the obligations flowing from this treaty at two different levels: firstly, compliance of EU member states[25] with the Aarhus obligations is regulated via the Aarhus Directives,[26] which will be left outside the scope of this case study; secondly, the EU has implemented the Article 9(3) obligations for the EU institutions via the Aarhus Regulation 1367/2006.[27] This section examines whether and to what extent this EU regulation sufficiently implemented the access to justice obligations. It explains that the standing requirements for the judicial review procedure via Article 263 TFEU (i.e. annulment procedure of EU acts) are quite impossible to be met for NGOs (sections 3.2 & 3.3) and explores whether the avenue providing for access to justice for NGOs via the Aarhus Regulation is sufficient in order to comply with Article 9(3) of the Aarhus Convention. Therefore, section 3.1 will discuss the Aarhus Regulation in light of compatibility with the Aarhus Convention, taking into account relevant CJEU case law. This section concludes with discussing the communication filed at ACCC in which communicants complained that the EU did not comply with its Aarhus obligations by providing only in restrictive situations access to environmental justice for NGOs.

3.1 The Aarhus Regulation: the possibility for NGOs to request for internal review

Article 1(d) of the Aarhus Regulation states that one of the purposes of the Regulation is to grant 'access to justice in environmental matters at Community level under the conditions laid down by this Regulation'. The Aarhus Regulation stipulates two criteria for access to justice. Firstly, it establishes which criteria NGOs need to fulfill in order to be able to request for internal review by one of the Community institutions (most often the Commission). Secondly, it sets out that internal review may only be asked of administrative acts under environmental law.[28]

The first set of criteria appears to be not too stringent. An NGO should be qualified as such according to a member state national law or practice, it should have as its primary objective to promote environmental protection, existed for more than two years, and lastly, the subject matter 'in respect

24 Art. 4(2)(e) TFEU; see e.g. para. 32 of *Slovenian Wolf Forest Protection Movement* case (C-240/09) (n 22).

25 All EU member states are also 'individually' party to the Aarhus Convention, thereby already obliged to comply with the Aarhus provisions. The EU Aarhus directives streamline and further enhance the protection necessitated by the Aarhus Convention for decision-making processes in environmental matters in light of EU obligations.

26 E.g. Directive 2003/4/EC and Directive 2003/35/EC, see further http://ec.europa.eu/environment/aarhus/legislation.htm; see Hey (n 12) 365–373.

27 Regulation No 1367/2006 (6 September 2006) OJ L 264/13 25.9.2006 (entry into force: 28 September 2006, became of application on 17 July 2007).

28 Arts 10–11 Aarhus Regulation.

of which the request for internal review is made [should be] covered by its objective and activities'.[29] This seems to be in accordance with the Aarhus Convention which stipulates that parties to the Convention may pose criteria, if any, in their national law in order for NGOs to have standing to request for review,[30] as long as the criteria do not effectively bar any NGO from accessing the review procedure.

The second criterion of the Aarhus Regulation is that NGOs fulfilling those criteria may only ask for internal review of administrative acts.[31] Administrative acts are defined in Article 2 of the Regulation as 'any measure of individual scope under environmental law, taken by a Community institution or body, and having legally binding and external effects'.[32] The definition of the concept of administrative act in the Aarhus Regulation was part of a dispute before the CJEU. In these cases – initiated by environmental NGOs – the applicants argued that the limitation in the Aarhus Regulation to be able to request internal review only for measures of individual scope was in contravention of Article 9(3) Aarhus Convention.[33] The General Court agreed with the applicants and concluded that the limitation of administrative acts to those of 'individual scope' in Article 10(1) Aarhus Regulation was incompatible with Article 9(3) Aarhus Convention.[34] In appeal, the CJEU concluded that Article 9(3) Aarhus Convention does not have a direct effect, as the provision is not unconditional and sufficiently precise and therefore cannot be relied upon for assessing the legality of Article 10(1) Aarhus Regulation.[35] The Court of Justice concluded that the General Court therefore erred in law by assessing its compatibility.[36] The criticism that administrative acts are interpreted too restrictively in the Aarhus Regulation is however wider voiced,[37] amongst others AG Jääskinen in his opinion to the CJEU appeal cases raised similar concerns.[38] This precise question on compatibility of the

29 Art. 11 sub (a)-(d) Aarhus Regulation.
30 Art. 9(3) Aarhus Convention.
31 Art. 10(1) Aarhus Regulation.
32 Art. 2(1)(g) Aarhus Regulation.
33 Case T-338/08; case T-396/09 (n 23).
34 Ibid., para. 83; also see paras 71–82.
35 Case C-404–12 P & C-405/12 P (13 January 2015) paras 52, 54, see also paras 46–51 in which the CJEU sets out how the doctrine of direct effect should be applied to the case at hand.
36 Ibid., para. 60; note that therefore the CJEU never examined the scope/definition of the concept of administrative act in the Aarhus Regulation.
37 See e.g. 'Submission on behalf of (observer) Friends of the Earth to the ACCC in relation to Communication ACCC/C/2008/32 (part II)' (23 February 2015) and the comments submitted by observers Dr. Eliantonio and Dr. Backes (26 June 2015), available via http://www.unece.org/env/pp/compliance/Compliancecommittee/32TableEC.html (last accessed 20 April 2016).
38 Opinion of AG Jääskinen to Joined Cases C-401/12 P, C-404/12 P and C-403/12 P (8 May 2014) paras 126–131, where he concludes that 'it must be held that Article 10 Aarhus Regulation does not fully implement the obligations arising under Article 9(3) Aarhus Convention'.

Aarhus Regulation also forms part of a communication pending with the ACCC initiated by an NGO against the EU.[39]

Those NGOs who have requested an internal review by the Commission in accordance with the Aarhus Regulation, may initiate proceedings at the level of EU Courts under Article 263(4) TFEU to request a review of the written response of the Commission to the request. NGOs then still need to fulfill the criteria for legal standing as stipulated in the EU treaties,[40] which should not be problematic as the NGO would request judicial review of the written response *addressed* to them and not of the act in question. However one may doubt whether and to what extent a review of the written response of the Commission by the EU Courts would ensure sufficiently access to justice in the context of the Aarhus Convention.[41] Additionally, does a review solely by the body who created the act itself suffice in terms of access to justice?

Besides the problems raised above, the majority of the NGOs will also have difficulty with meeting the legal standing criteria before the EU Courts. Those NGOs that choose not to request for internal review, NGOs that would like to request a review of an (administrative) act falling outside of the scope of the Aarhus Regulation,[42] NGOs that do not meet criteria imposed to them by the Aarhus Regulation, and NGOs that wish to have the substance of an administrative act reviewed by the EU Court,[43] need to go (immediately) via level of EU Courts and thereby need to meet the standing criteria of 263(4) TFEU in order to be able to ask for a review of the respective act. These procedures will be discussed below. Firstly, the individual and direct concern criteria (pre-Lisbon situation) will be discussed, and afterwards, the second possibility for review created by the third limb of Article 263(4) TFEU.

3.2 Legal standing of NGOs in judicial review procedure[44] at the level of EU courts: individually and directly concerned

Access to justice for members of the public – or in EU law jargon non-privileged applicants – was before the Lisbon Treaty regulated in Article 230(4) of the EC treaty. Non-privileged applicants had legal standing if the act they wanted to challenge was of *'direct and individual' concern* [emphasis added]

39 For further discussion see section 3.4 below.

40 Art. 12 Aarhus Regulation; see also case T-338/08 (n 23) para. 80–81, in which the General Court confirms that NGOs still need to fulfill the criteria of (then) 230(4) TEC, now 263(4) TFEU.

41 See also the critique voiced by AG Jääskinen (n 38) para. 130.

42 E.g. in T-338/08 ((n 23) para. 26 of General Court judgment) the Commission had determined that the request for internal review was inadmissible as it did not concern an act of individual scope nor a bundle of decisions qualifying as such.

43 These NGOs need to plead the illegality of the administrative act. See for instance, AG Jääskinen (n 38) para. 130.

44 Note that the chapter focuses on the annulment procedure of Art. 263(4) TFEU, former Art. 230(4) EC Treaty, explicitly not dealing with other EU judicial review procedures.

to them. The term 'individually concerned' was interpreted for the first time by the ECJ in the *Plaumann case*.[45] The *Plaumann* formula required that non-privileged applicants were to be affected by the act:

> ...by reason of certain attributes which are peculiar to them or by reason of circumstances in which they are differentiated from all other persons and by virtue of these factors distinguishes them individually just as in the case of the person addressed.[46]

Considering that environmental NGOs request review in order to defend common values, it resulted in a situation which made it practically impossible for NGOs to fulfill these criteria and hence acquire standing to challenge administrative acts.[47] This created an effective bar to (environmental) justice at the level of EU courts, something which seems to go against the spirit and obligations of the Aarhus Convention.

3.3 Legal standing post – Lisbon: the third limb of Article 263(4) TFEU

Access to justice for non-privileged applicants is now regulated in Article 263(4) TFEU, which has an extra paragraph added to the provision, the third limb, in comparison to old Article 230(4) TEC.[48] What is new is the possibility to request review as a non-privileged applicant when *directly concerned* by a 'regulatory act of general application which does not entail implementing measures'.[49] Regulatory acts should be

45 *Plaumann and Co v Commission Case 25/62* [1963] ECR 95. For further analysis of applicability 230(4) TEC in environmental cases, see e.g. Justice and Environment, 'Access to Justice in Environmental Matters' (2010), available at http://www.justiceandenvironment.org; T Crossen and V Niessen, 'NGO Standing in the European Court of Justice – Does the Aarhus Regulation Open the Door' (2007) 16(3) *Reciel* 33.

46 *Plaumann* (n 45) see also C-456/13 P, *T&L Sugars Ltd & Sidul Açúcares, Unipessoal Lda/ Commission* (28 April 2015) para. 63; Case T-18/10R, *Inuit Tapiriit Kanatami and Others v Parliament and Council* (6 September 2011) ECLI:EU:T:2011:419 para. 72. C-274/12 P *Telefonica v Commission* (19 December 2013) EU: C:2013:852 para. 46.

47 See e.g. AG Jacobs in the *UPA* case, who argued that the criteria are too strict (not particularly focusing on environmental law), failing to provide effective judicial protection and a potential breach of Art. 6 ECHR, Case C-50/00 P, *Union de Pequenos Agriculturos v Council* [2002] ECR-I 6677 para. 102; The applicability of the *Plaumann* formula to environmental law related cases was confirmed e.g. in *Greenpeace Stichting Council v Commission*, Case 231/95 ECJ [1998] ECR I-01651.

48 See also Case C-583/11P, GC *Inuit Tapiriit Kanatami and Others v Parliament and Council* (2 October 2013), EU:C:2013:625 para. 55.

49 In order to determine whether an act entails implementing measures should be assessed by reference to the position of the person pleading the right to bring proceedings, see *T&L Sugars Ltd* (n 46) paras 29-32; see also C Werkmeister, S Potters and J Traut, 'Regulatory Acts within Article 263(4) TFEU – A Dissonant Extension of *Locus Standi* for Private Applicants' (2010–2011) 13 *Cambridge Yearbook of European Legal Studies* 312; S Balthasar, 'Locus Standi Rules for Challenges to Regulatory Acts by Private Applicants: the New Article 263(4) TFEU' (2010) 35 *European Law Review* 542.

interpreted as all those acts of general application apart from legislative acts.[50] The term has further been interpreted by the General Court in the *Microban* case;[51] general application implies 'that it applies to objectively determined situations and it produces legal effects with respect to categories of persons envisaged in general and in the abstract'.[52] In view of the Court, the purpose of the third limb was to enable non-privileged applicants to bring under less stringent conditions actions for annulment of acts of general application.[53] Thus, NGOs do still have to meet the direct concern; at this moment it is not clear how easy or difficult it might be for NGOs to fulfill this criterion.[54] For the remaining NGOs, as reasoned by the CJEU:

> as regards persons who do not fulfil the requirements of the fourth paragraph of 263 TFEU (...), it is for the Member States to establish a system of legal remedies and procedures which ensure respect for the fundamental right to effective judicial protection.[55]

To sum up, environmental NGOs are permitted by 263(4) TFEU to institute proceedings at the level of EU Courts against:

- Acts, including regulations, addressed to the NGO (no requirement of direct/individual concern)[56]
- Acts of general application, including regulations, which are of individual and direct concern to the NGO[57]
- Regulatory acts of general application, meaning any acts of general application apart from legislative acts, which do not entail implementing measures and which are of direct concern to the NGO (third limb).[58]

50 See Case T-18/10 *Inuit Tapiriit Kanatami* (n 46) para. 56. Case T-262/10 *Microban International and Microban (Europe) v Commission* [2011] ECR II-0000 para. 21. Legislative acts are also excluded from review under Art. 2(2) Aarhus Convention. The ACCC states that label under domestic law should not be decisive; instead, what counts are the legal functions and effect of a decision, *Belgium* case (2005) (n 17) para. 29. The EU Courts determine this by the procedure followed to adopt the act, see e.g. *Microban*, para. 22, and Case T-338/08 (n 23) paras 62–65.

51 *Microban,* (n 50) para. 22.

52 Ibid., para. 23.

53 *Inuit* case (n 48) para. 60.

54 See *T&L Sugars Ltd* (n 46) para. 37.

55 Ibid., para. 49; also see GC *Inuit* case (n 48) para. 100.

56 This includes the response on a written request for internal review under the Aarhus Regulation.

57 The '*Plaumann* formula'; see *Inuit* case (n 48) para. 45, confirmed in *Microban* (n 50) and *Telefonica* (n 46).

58 See for further information on legal standing before EU Courts e.g. R Schütze, *European Union Law* (CUP 2015) 354–364.

3.4 Mapping the interaction between the ACCC and the CJEU on access to justice for NGOs at the level of the EU

The previous paragraphs discussed the Aarhus Regime and the EU access to justice regime for NGOs in environmental matters. This section assesses whether the EU has sufficiently implemented its obligations under the Aarhus Convention by ways of the Aarhus Regulation and 263(4) TFEU. This exact question was also posed by NGO ClientEarth, which filed in 2008 a communication concerning non-compliance of the EU with the Aarhus Convention at the ACCC.[59] This communication was split up into two parts, Part I focused on the *Plaumann* formula and the extent to which remedies available at the national level may compensate a certain lack of access to justice at the level of the EU (thereby on the pre-TFEU case law and regime). Part II of the communication was discussed on 1st of July 2015, after the final ruling of the CJEU in the *Stichting Milieudefensie* case.[60] It focused on the compatibility of the Aarhus Regulation with the Aarhus Convention and the extent to which 263(4) TFEU should be taken into account as a form of implementation measure for the Aarhus access to justice obligations.

The ACCC stated in Part I that it is up to parties to the Aarhus Convention to decide whether to apply criteria of legal interest as a threshold for standing; however, that the application of the criteria should not result in 'effectively barring all or almost all members of the public from challenging acts and omissions related to domestic environmental law.'[61] The ACCC examined the general jurisprudence and interpretation of standing criteria by the EU Courts, thereby looked whether (at least):

> ...some decisions, acts and omissions by the EU institutions are such as to be covered by article 9(3)[62] ... [ACCC] is convinced that for at least some acts and omissions by EU institutions, [the EU] must ensure that members of the public have access to administrative or judicial review procedures, as set out in article 9, paragraph 3.[63]

Therefore when assessing the *Plaumann* formula and how they were applied in cases in which environmental NGOs sought standing to challenge administrative acts of the EU relating to the environment, the ACCC reasoned that the:

> ...consequence of applying the Plaumann test to environmental and health issues is that in effect no member of the public is ever able to challenge a decision or a regulation in such case before the ECJ.[64]

59 ACCC, *Communication ACCC/C/2008/32 (part I) concerning compliance by the European Union, ('European Union 2008')* ECE/MP.PP/C.1/2011/4/add.1 (24 August 2011).

60 Case T-396/09 (n 23).

61 Ibid., para. 80.

62 Ibid., para. 72.

63 Ibid., para. 74; note though that Art. 263(4) TFEU only deals with acts and not omissions; omissions are dealt with by Art. 265 TFEU.

64 Ibid., para. 86.

Interestingly, the ACCC came to this 'finding' while they had stated that they were not in the position to come to findings as there were currently cases pending at the EU courts,[65] and that the case law cited by the communicants preceded the Lisbon Treaty and the Aarhus Regulation. However the ACCC did clearly state that a 'new direction of jurisprudence of EU courts should be established in order to ensure compliance with Convention',[66] giving a clear sign to the EU. Some argue therefore that the ACCC seemed to (try to) enter into a dialogue with the EU courts.[67] The ACCC further argued that it was disappointed that EU Courts had not taken Aarhus obligations into account in their reasoning after the Aarhus Convention entered into force.[68]

The EU reaction as expressed by the Commission was quite strong; the Commission was 'baffled' by the 'findings' of the Committee that the case law would be in contravention with the Aarhus Convention and stated that they did not have the authority to do so.[69] Furthermore, it reminded the ACCC that the EU Courts cannot be controlled by the EU; a change in the line of case law can only be achieved via Treaty amendments by the parties to the EU.[70] Moreover, although provisions of Union legislation must, as far as possible, be interpreted and applied in a manner that is consistent with international agreements:

> (…) an international agreement cannot affect the allocation of powers fixed by the Treaties or, consequently, the autonomy of the Community legal system. Thus, the powers conferred on the Court of Justice by the EC Treaty may be modified pursuant only to the procedure provided for to that effect by the Community legal order.[71]

The ACCC responded by referring to the general principles of international law on treaty interpretation;[72] according to Article 27 of the 1969 Vienna Convention on the Law of Treaties, a state may not invoke its internal (i.e. domestic) law as justification for failure to perform a treaty. As argued by the

65 Cases T-338/08 and T-369/09 (n 23).

66 ACCC, *European Union 2008* (n 59) para. 97.

67 Kingston (n 22) 167.

68 ACCC referred to Case C-435/97 *WWF and Others v Autonome Provinz Bozen and Others* [1999] ECR I-5613), in which the *Plaumann* formula were upheld; see also Kingston (n 22) at 165–167.

69 Submission of the European Commission on behalf of the European Community, (20 July 2011) at 1, accessible via http://www.unece.org/env/pp/compliance/Compliancecommittee/32TableEC.html.

70 Ibid.

71 Ibid.

72 ACCC, *European Union 2008* (n 59) para. 41; in the *Belgium* case (n 17) para. 43 the ACCC stated that altering established court practice is sometimes necessary in order to comply with Aarhus obligations.

ACCC, all the branches of government should make an effort to bring about compliance with an international agreement.[73]

The EU Commission further argued that, together with the system of preliminary ruling, a sufficient and effective judicial protection system existed with the EU,[74] which was recognized by the ECtHR via the 'presumption of equivalent protection doctrine'.[75] Therefore, there were no problems in regards of access to justice and procedural guarantees. The ACCC stated that the preliminary ruling system in itself – and as supplement – does not constitute an adequate and effective judicial remedy able to compensate for the lack of legal standing at the Courts of the EU, because it presupposes, amongst others, that NGOs have standing at the national level[76] and that national courts will decide to request a preliminary ruling under the conditions of 234 TEC (new 267 TFEU).[77]

After the ACCC report on communication Part I was published in 2011, the *Stichting Milieudefensie* case was decided in first instance by the General Court, and in appeal by the CJEU.[78] As discussed, the communicants had reasoned that the Aarhus Regulation is too restrictive and also that the *Plaumann* & *Microban* options via 263(4) TFEU were too restrictive and thereby could not supplement/remedy the lack of access to justice for NGOs at the EU Courts. The CJEU referred to the whole system of judicial protection including the preliminary ruling system and Article 263(4) TFEU. However, as argued, the CJEU did not provide an answer to the dispute regarding communication Part I.[79]

Now, at the ACCC, these precise EU judgments form part of ClientEarth's communication Part II. The communicant reasoned that the Aarhus Regulation is too restrictive by limiting internal review only to administrative acts of individual scope, that the general (restrictive) criteria of 263(4) TFEU still apply and that the CJEU continues to apply the exact same strict criteria which before were deemed to be in non-compliance by the ACCC.[80] The communicant requested the ACCC[81] to assess Articles 2 & 10 of the Aarhus Regulation in light of the Aarhus Convention and to 'recommend to the EU that the Courts change their interpretation of Article 263(4) TFEU,

73 ACCC, *European Union 2008*, (n 59) para. 42; note though that EU lawyers might question the applicability of the VCLT (1969) to the EU as it is an international organization and not a state. See also Art. 27 VCLT (1986).
74 See Submission of the European Commission (n 69).
75 See below section 3.8.
76 Not all member states grant (yet) NGOs access to environmental justice at the national level. Without the possibility to initiate a case at the national level, one cannot request a question to be referred to the ECJ on the interpretation or validity of EU/Aarhus obligations.
77 ACCC, *European Union 2008*, (n 59) para. 89.
78 Case T-396/09 (n 23).
79 See (n 35).
80 ClientEarth, *Communication ACCC/C/2008/32 (Part II)* (23 February 2015), available via http://www.unece.org/env/pp/compliance/Compliancecommittee/32TableEC.html.
81 Decision I/7 of the MoP (n 14) para. 18.

including the criterion of "direct concern" – last limb of the sentence – in a way to provide standing to NGOs'.[82] In short, the EU's position is that it had acted in accordance with the CJEU case law and that the EU fulfils its obligations under 9(3) Aarhus Convention.[83] The ACCC findings are expected end 2015 – beginning 2016.[84]

3.5 Reflecting on the Aarhus – EU interaction

In 2008, the ACCC had examined the general jurisprudence of the EU Courts on legal standing for NGOs, and was highly critical on its scope. Since then, there seems to be a huge improvement as now standing criteria for regulatory acts of general application not entailing implementing measures are more easily met when we look at the recent CJEU case law.[85] However, for the remaining part the CJEU relies for the implementation and enforcement of effective judicial protection on EU Member states in solving the problem,[86] which (according to the EU) is in line with the obligations under Article 19(1) TEU.[87] But when member states do not accord legal standing to NGOs and/or when national courts do not ask for a preliminary ruling, one may question whether there is indeed an effective system of judicial protection. Additionally the Aarhus Regulation seems to limit the access to justice for NGOs beyond what Article 9(3) Aarhus Convention permits. The positive note is however, as phrased by AG Jääskinen, the Aarhus Regulation at least facilitates *some* form of access to justice for NGOs:

> ...as such organisations do not have sufficient interest or maintain the impairment of a right in order to exercise [the right to judicial review] in accordance with article 263 TFEU.[88]

In regard to the interaction between the ACCC and the EU, one has to realize that this is not a standard interaction between two international regimes, or two international organizations as such, as can be found in the majority

82 Ibid., para. 90; note though that the recommendations by the ACCC are not legally binding upon the parties, the idea is to ensure compliance via dialogue and ultimately via the MoP.

83 Observations by the European Union to the Communicant's Commentary on the CJEU Judgments (11 June 2015) available at http://www.unece.org/env/pp/compliance/Compliancecommittee/32TableEC.html.

84 Findings will be published at http://www.unece.org/env/pp/compliance/Compliancecommittee/32TableEC.html.

85 Case T-18/10 *Inuit* (n 46).

86 GC *Inuit* case (n 48) paras 100–106; Case C-274/12 P, *Telefonica SA v* (n 46) paras 56–60.

87 Art. 19(1) TFEU: Member States shall provide remedies sufficient to ensure effective legal protection in the fields covered by EU law.

88 See conclusions AG Jääskinen to Cases-404/12 P & C-405/12 P (n 38) para. 124.

of scholarly work on interaction between courts focusing on overlapping mandates and converging/diverging interpretation of international law.[89] Instead, we have the EU – as a 'member state'[90] who is obliged to comply with the Aarhus Convention and provide for access to environmental justice. The situation in terms of interpretation and normative interaction is thereby, on paper fairly simple. The question of interpreting the treaty obligations of the Aarhus Convention for member states is dealt with by general treaty law and its rules for compliance (i.e. VCLT, as also referred to by ACCC in e.g. *Belgium* case and the AG opinion in the CJEU appeals cases). Therefore in terms of discourse, it is important to distinguish the two different roles/ relations with regard to EU, something that is not always that evident. For instance, the EU in responding to allegations of non-compliance with Aarhus relied several times upon the system of preliminary reference as complementing the judicial review system and relied on the recognition by ECtHR of the presumption of equivalent protection of fundamental rights within EU. However, the system of preliminary reference serves particularly to aid member states in interpreting the TFEU. Similarly EU member states who are also member states of the Council of Europe (CoE), and thus parties to the ECHR, may be confronted with double obligations which is 'solved' by the doctrine presumption of equivalence protection. This doctrine does not (yet?) relate to the conduct of EU institutions. In this regard case law of CJEU forms part of the conduct of EU and should be taken into account when assessing compliance of EU with Aarhus obligations and not as a form of authoritative interpretation of Aarhus obligations. Therefore, as also described by Kingston: In theory the relationship between the Compliance Committee and the EU Courts could be described as hierarchical, in the sense that the Committee is competent to assess the legality of the EU Courts' jurisprudence under the Convention.[91]

However, the problem is that the ACCC does not stipulate to be the ultimate authority to interpret the convention, additionally the ACCC is no Court and its findings are not formally binding on parties to the Convention.[92] Note also that the findings of the ACCC are always to be approved by the Meeting of Parties;[93] the question is when the ACCC would come to the conclusion that the EU is in non-compliance in Part II of the communication whether such

89 This fits in line with the general debate on fragmentation and constitutionalisation of international law, see e.g. for a critical reflection, Chapter 5 by Francois Finck and Chapter 10 by Ernst-Ulrich Petersmann in this book. Interestingly, Mónika Ambrus in Chapter 12 assessed how constitutionalisation might take place via fragmented adjudication.

90 This typification triggers a debate on how to qualify the relation between the EU – ACCC/ Aarhus, where public international law lawyers and EU Lawyers most likely have opposite positions.

91 Kingston (n 22) 166.

92 Idem.

93 Decision 1/7 ECE.MP.PP.2.add.8e, at 37; see also UN ECE, Guidance Document of the Aarhus Convention Compliance Mechanism, at 22.

agreement could be reached; and if not, what the possible normative implications of that decision could be for the relation between the ACCC and the EU and long-term what the implications might be for EU member states. Therefore the interaction between the ACCC and the EU seems to aim more for a 'dialogue… deliberately avoiding direct confrontation and, with that, a hierarchical solution'.[94] One may wonder, however, with the way the communication has been progressing since 2012 whether this still can be maintained or whether it should be maintained. In my perception the questions phrased by the ACCC to the EU in 2015 seem to hint in a more hierarchical direction, thereby aiming at a further constitutionalisation of the right to access to environmental justice for NGOs in Europe.

3.6 European Court of Human Rights' approach towards Aarhus

The third regional body that has dealt with environmental justice is the ECtHR. In terms of interaction between the ECtHR/ECHR and the ACCC/Aarhus Convention it is important to note that there are no formal institutional arrangements between the two bodies, the ECtHR does not have any obligation to incorporate the Aarhus Convention. The function of the ACCC and the ECtHR is similar, in that they both respond to individual complaints.[95] Of the 47 CoE member states, only 4 member states are not party to the Aarhus Convention. Even though the ECHR does not have a substantive provision on the right to a healthy environment, the ECtHR has recognized in various cases the undeniable link between international human rights law and environmental protection.[96] Extensive analysis exists on how the ECtHR incorporates procedural environmental obligations in its substantive ECtHR provisions and to what extent this is sufficient or not.[97] For instance, a crucial factor for observance by the ECHR in environmental cases is whether there was a fair transparent decision-making process, i.e. respect for public's right to information, participation and effective access to justice.[98] This section will,

94 Kingston (n 22) 167.
95 Hey (n 12) 354.
96 E.g. *Lopez Ostra v Spain* 16798/90 [1994] ECHR 46 (9 December 1994); Council of Europe, *Manual on the Protection of the Environment* (2nd edn, COE Publishing, 2012).
97 E.g. R Pavoni, 'Public Interest Litigation and the European Court of Human Rights: No Love at First Sight' in F Lenzerini and AF Vrdoljak (eds), *International Law for Common Goods: Normative Perspectives on Human Rights, Culture and Nature* (Hart 2014); L Loucaides, 'Environmental Protection Through the Jurisprudence of the European Convention on Human Rights' (2004) 75 *British Yearbook of International Law* 249; A Boyle, 'Human Rights or Environmental Rights? A Reassessment' (2006–2007) 18 *Fordham Environmental Law Review* 471; F Francioni, 'International Human Rights in an Environmental Horizon' (2010) 21 *EJIL* 41; see also Hey (n 12), on the contours of Aarhus Space: 'a space in which a right to the environment has emerged' amongst others due to the engagement of the ACCC, CJEU and ECtHR in shaping and protecting these rights.
98 *Hatton and Others v the United Kingdom* 36022/97 [2003] ECHR 338 (8 July 2003) paras 96–98, 104.

instead, only focus on access to environmental justice for NGOs in the context of Article 6 ECHR.

3.7 Access to environmental justice under Article 6 ECHR

NGOs participate in proceedings at the ECtHR mainly via the submission of *amicus curiae* briefs,[99] and not as applicants in a proceeding. This can be explained by the prohibition of *actio popularis* at the level of the ECtHR.[100] Further, certain rights as protected under the ECHR can only be enjoyed by natural persons and thereby NGOs cannot initiate a complaint.[101] Nevertheless, NGOs may initiate proceedings for an alleged violation of Article 6 (right to fair trial). However, there are still quite some hurdles for NGOs who wish to successfully submit a complaint to the ECtHR. In order for the 'civil limb' of Article 6(1) ECHR to be applicable there must be:

> ...a dispute over a "right" that can be said, at least on arguable grounds, to be recognized under domestic law. The dispute must be genuine and serious; it may relate not only to the actual existence of a right but also to its scope and the manner of its exercise. The outcome of the proceedings must be directly decisive for the right in question: mere tenuous connections or remote consequences are not sufficient to bring Article 6§1 into play.[102]

In other words, the ECtHR does not recognize a right to litigate *in abstracto* on behalf of the general interest. In *Gorraiz Lizarraga v Spain,* the ECtHR reasoned that Article 6(1) ECHR was applicable as, in addition to a defense of the public interest, the proceedings in question were intended 'to defend certain specific interests of the association's members'.[103] Interestingly, in *Collectif Stop Melox et Mox*[104] a complaint on an alleged violation of Article 6 ECHR was declared admissible of a NGO who had challenged national legislation that had authorized the enlargement of a nuclear plant. The ECtHR acknowledged that even though the NGO undoubtedly defended the general

99 Art. 36(2) ECHR; Pavoni (n 97) 22.

100 Art. 34 ECHR; note that the prohibition of *actio popularis* does not relate to access to justice standards at the national level, but that instead, it is a procedural rule at the international level to prevent overburdening the international human rights machinery.

101 E.g. required for Arts 2 & 8 ECHR. This analysis only concerns Art. 6 ECHR; see for the ECtHR approach to Arts 2, 8, 10 ECHR in light of environmental law e.g. Hey (n 12)

102 ECtHR, *Gorraiz Lizarraga and others v Spain* 62543/00 (27 April 2004) para. 43; ECtHR, (GC) *Bochan v Ukraine* App no 22251/08 (5 February 2015) para. 42.

103 *Gorraiz Lizarraga v Spain* (n 102) paras 45–48; this criterion was introduced for the first time in ECtHR (GC) *Balmer-Schafroth and others v Switzerland* case 22110/93 (28 August 1997).

104 *Collectif National d'Information et d'Opposition a l'Usine Melox – Collectif Stop Melox et Mox v France* 75218/01 (28 March 2006) para. 4.

interest, in this case it should not be interpreted as litigation *in abstracto* on behalf of the general interest.[105] The Court instead stated that Article 6(1) should not be interpreted restrictively, and the requirements of the civil right criterion should be applied with 'souplesse'[106] when complaints are lodged by NGOs. The Court thus recognized the important role NGOs play in defending the public interest and relied on the Aarhus Convention to show that public's right to information and participation require an important role for NGOs;[107] the participatory rights as accorded by the Aarhus Convention were considered civil rights which anyone having an interest should be able to enforce in courts.[108]

Once the complaint is admissible the question is whether in Article 6 ECHR, the ECtHR includes Aarhus related procedural guarantees in terms of access rights. The Court in the landmark case *Golder v UK*[109] interpreted access to justice as including a right to access courts. The ECtHR emphasized in a subsequent case that Article 6(1) does not create new substantive rights that can be enforced through the courts, but that its guarantees 'extend only to rights which can be said, at least on arguable grounds, to be recognized under domestic law'.[110] However, once domestic law recognizes a substantive right, domestic courts may not establish procedural bars that prevent individuals from accessing the courts to enforce that right.[111] Furthermore, the procedural guarantees as protected under Article 6(1) ECHR, of 'everyone is entitled to a fair and public hearing within a reasonable time by an independent and impartial tribunal established by law' seem to have at minimum – if not further – a same interpretation and scope as Article 9(4) Aarhus Convention.

Thus the problem regarding access to environmental justice for NGOs at the ECHR level lies at the threshold for applicability of ECHR and the limited standing at the ECtHR. In terms of fair trial, procedural guarantees seem to be similar or at least of equivalent protection with the Aarhus Convention.

Nevertheless, when looking at how the ECtHR includes procedural environmental obligations into its interpretation of substantive human rights obligations there is still a lot of progress to be made. It seems to result into a 'mismatch'[112] between at one side the increased role of NGOs at the national level as most prominently promoted by the Aarhus Convention and at the other side the restricted access of NGOs to the ECtHR.

105 If interpreted as such, the complaint should have been declared inadmissible as it would amount to an *actio popularis*. See also Pavoni (n 97).

106 *Collectif Stop Melox et Mox v France* (n 104) para. 4.

107 Ibid. the ECtHR referred to Art. 2(4) Aarhus Convention.

108 Ibid., para. 4; further see Pavoni (n 97) 25–26.

109 ECtHR, *Golder v United Kingdom,* 21 February 1975, Series A no 18, paras 34–35, 38.

110 ECtHR, *Roche v United Kingdom* [GC], Appl. no. 32555/96, para. 117, ECHR 2005-X, para. 117.

111 Ibid., para. 119.

112 Pavoni (n 97) 22.

There is a possibility for the ECtHR though to contribute to further constitutionalisation of procedural environmental rights in Europe via the living instrument line of reasoning, which implies that the ECtHR interprets the ECHR obligations 'in light of present-day conditions'.[113] The ECtHR has interpreted the Convention in a dynamic manner and taken environmental concerns into account and read them into the rights protected by the Convention.[114] One major step in this direction was taken in the *Taskin v Turkey* case in which the ECtHR reasoned that:

> … elements of international law other than the Convention, the interpretation of such elements by competent organs, and the practice of European States reflecting their common values. The consensus emerging from specialised international instruments and from the practice of Contracting States may constitute a relevant consideration for the Court when it interprets the provisions of the Convention in specific cases.[115]

The ECtHR took the procedural environmental guarantees as stipulated in the Aarhus Convention into account in relation to Turkey, while Turkey is a member of the CoE but not a party to the Aarhus Convention nor a member state of the EU.

When comparing the approach adopted by the ECtHR and the ACCC one can notice quite some differences. The ECtHR has always been typified as following a more classical (individualistic) approach to the human rights obligations of the Convention, whereas the ACCC adopts the common interest approach to the Aarhus obligations which fits in line with the environmental obligations which are by their nature general interest oriented. Francioni has criticized this classical human rights approach to environmental cases and called it counterproductive in that it tends to reduce environmental values to the limited sphere of individual interests thus altering their inherent nature as public good.[116] The problem of the ECtHR is that, as summarized by Hey:

> … the ECtHR recognizes that individual rights may be limited by the general interest in protecting the environment, but does not recognize that individuals may use their individual rights to protect the general interest in the protection of the environment.[117]

What seems to be leading for the ECtHR is the development of the inclusion of procedural environmental rights at the national level, in this context the

113 See e.g. ECtHR, *Tyrer v UK* app no 5856/72 (15 April 1978) para. 31.

114 See for further analysis of this approach by the ECtHR e.g. Hey (n 12) 362–365.

115 ECtHR, *Taskin and others v Turkey*, app no 46117/99 (10 November 2004) paras 99, 86: referring to Demir and Baykara: paras 85–86.

116 Francioni, 'International Human Rights' (n 97) 46, 55; see also Hey (n 12) 365.

117 Hey (n 12) 365, she also highlights that perhaps the new pilot judgments practice of the ECtHR might provide a solution in this regard.

EU as judicial oversight for EU member states and the ACCC for oversight on the Aarhus obligations at the national level play an important role. When these rights become increasingly part of domestic constitutions and access is increasingly recognized for NGOs, the ECtHR will most likely start taking it more into account as part of the common values across Europe.[118]

3.8 A third layer on the way: the limited review of the ECtHR of the EU

Even though the EU has not yet acceded to the ECHR,[119] the ECtHR has already dealt with EU obligations and case law of the EU Courts in various cases.[120] At this moment the ECtHR is already – to a marginal extent – conducting a review of judicial protection as offered by the system of the EU treaties. This can be witnessed particularly when looking at the development of the presumption of equivalent protection doctrine. The famous *Bosphorus* case[121] addressed the question to what extent a member state's action can be justified by its compliance with international obligations flowing from membership of an international organization to which it had transferred part of sovereignty.[122] The ECtHR examined the whole system of judicial protection within the EU as created by the treaty and interpreted by the case law of the Courts of the EU.[123] It recognized the limited standing for non-privileged applicants at the EU Courts and thereby the important role that national courts play in the protection and enforcement of EU law.[124] The equivalence of the protection should manifest itself both in substantive guarantees as in the mechanisms controlling their observance.[125] A presumption of equivalent protection[126] can only be rebutted when there is a manifest deficiency in the

118 See particularly *Taskin* case (n 115).

119 For current status, http://hub.coe.int/web/coe-portal/what-we-do/human-rights/eu-accession-to-the-convention; see also the draft agreement on Accession of the European Union to the European Convention on Human Rights; P Gragl, *The Accession of the European Union to the European Convention on Human Rights* (Hart 2013); P Graig, 'EU Accession to the ECHR: Competence, Procedure and Substance' (2013) 36 *Fordham International Law Journal* 1114.

120 See e.g. S Morano-Foadi & S Andreadakis, *A Report on the Protection of Fundamental Rights: A Reflection on the Relationship between the Court of Justice of the EU and the ECtHR Post Lisbon*' (Oxford Brookes University 2014), available at https://dm.coe.int/CED20140017597

121 ECtHR, *Bosphorus Hava Yollari Turizm Ve Ticarat Anonim Sirketi v Ireland* [GC] ECHR 2005-VI.

122 Ibid., para. 154; see also the preceding case law of the ECtHR dealing with EU and the concept of equivalent protection, *Melchers* (1990), *Cantoni* (1996), *Matthews* (1999).

123 *Bosphorus* (para. 120) paras 161–165.

124 The ECtHR referred to EU case law, showing its awareness of the *Plaumann* related problems with the issue of legal standing for NGOs, and the criteria for preliminary references, *Bosphorus* (n 121) paras 85–99.

125 Ibid., para. 155.

126 See also the *Al Dulimi* case in which the presumption of equivalent protection was used regarding states and their obligations following from UNSC resolutions; ECtHR,

judicial protection of the international organization.[127] Only in this case a full review of the compliance by the CoE/EU member state with the ECHR obligations will be conducted. The focus is thus on the procedural guarantees and the presumption is that they are of similar level, which could result into a gap in the judicial review system.

With the EU acceding to the ECHR one may doubt whether this approach adopted by the ECtHR, and the protected status of the EU may and should be upheld; for instance, Gragl argued that in light of the interest of other high contracting parties and the principle of equality the Union's privileged status should be given up after accession.[128] Time will tell which approach the ECtHR adopts towards the EU and how this might contribute to a further constitutionalisation or fragmentation of the right to (environmental) justice for NGOs.[129]

4 Concluding: situating the debate on the access to environmental justice for NGOs in terms of a process towards constitutionalisation

The chapter tried to map the complexity of the overlapping mandates created by the three European treaty regimes when dealing with access to environmental justice. Naturally, there is a chance that these converging layers and possible competing authorities might lead to conflicting interpretation of what is required for access to justice. For instance, the parallel systems may come up with incompatible conclusions, or instead the situation might result into 'synergies in compliance control, and further rather than impede the effectiveness of the access to justice in member states'.[130] Some argue that it might result in a positive judicial dialogue between the various courts and quasi-judicial bodies in Europe which 'would also be in the interest of the Community.'[131] Importantly, the system in itself has potential to contribute positively to the enforcement and further development of access to

Al-Dulimi and Montana Management Inc. v Switzerland 5809/08, ECHR 2013; in the *Klausecker v Germany* case the presumption of equivalent protection was upheld in relation to the EPO and their system of effective judicial remedies, ECtHR, *Klausecker v Germany* App no 415/07 (6 January 2015).

127 This was the case in the *Michaud v France* case, the ECtHR reasoned that because the French Conseil d'Etat did not ask for a preliminary ruling, i.e. the CJEU had no opportunity to examine the question, and because France had a margin interpreting the obligations following from the EU legislation (it was a directive) the presumption could not be upheld, *Michaud v France* App no 12323/11 ECtHR (6 March 2013) para.115.

128 Gragl (n 119) 264.

129 The approach to be adopted by ECtHR largely depends on the accession agreement to be concluded between the EU – Council of Europe in which the division of competences and scope of review mechanism are to be stipulated.

130 J Ebesson, 'Access to Justice at the National Level' in M Pallemaerts (ed.), *Aarhus Convention at Ten* (Europa Law Publishing 2011) 245, 252.

131 A Tanzi and C. Pitea, 'Interplay between EU law and International Law Procedures in Controlling Compliance' in *Aarhus Convention at Ten* (n 130) 367, 381.

(environmental) justice. Hey therefore argues that ACCC, the CJEU and the ECtHR all shape the European 'Aarhus Space', which is based on 'procedural environmental rights as opposed to a justiciable right to an adequate environment'.[132] Within this space, according to Hey, many of the barriers of international, regional and national law have been removed and members of the public 'can freely move between the various bodies of law in order to protect the environment' and which also shows the potential showing also the potential for cooperation between the various international institutions.[133]

Time will tell how the access to justice obligations in relation to acts by EU institutions will be interpreted by the ECtHR and how the Court will situate itself in the evolving dialogue taking place between the ACCC and the CJEU. The ECtHR and the CJEU place a strong emphasis on domestic implementation and protection of the procedural obligations and thereby do not address the gap at the level of the EU nor when it exists at the level of the domestic authorities. Therefore, the Aarhus Convention and the ACCC play an essential role in enabling NGOs to enforce access to environmental justice at the national level (and EU level). In the long term, once the obligations for access to environmental justice have been properly implemented and guaranteed at the domestic level, it could result into a strong 'constitutionalised' right to environmental justice for all members of the general public. However, at this moment, the implementation is not complete and even though the contours are visible of a constitutionalised right, one cannot yet argue that access to environmental justice for NGOs has a constitutional character in Europe.

132 Hey (n 12) 374.
133 Ibid., 376.

15 The reconciliatory approach

How multilateral environmental agreements can harmonise international legal obligations

Britta Sjöstedt

1 Introduction

International environmental law has developed to address complex and interrelated environmental problems that often have global effects. For instance, the destruction of the ozone layer, climate change, air pollution, biodiversity loss and water pollution affect large regions and have also adverse influences on each other.[1] Hence, environmental challenges require instruments that can counter multi-dimensional damage on an international scale.[2] Environmental treaties, also referred to as Multilateral Environmental Agreements (MEAs), are of essential importance in developing the field of international environmental law. There are over 500 MEAs,[3] each regulating a specific environmental issue, including the Biological Diversity Convention[4] (CBD), the Framework Convention on Climate Change (FCCC),[5] the Convention for the Protection of the Ozone Layer,[6] the Convention of International Trade in Endangered Species (CITES),[7] and the UNESCO[8]

1 S Maljean-Dubois, 'The Making of International Law Challenging Environmental Protection' in Y Kerbrat and S Maljean-Dubois (eds), *The Transformation of International Environmental Law* (Hart and Pedone 2011) 26.
2 N Matz, 'Approaches to Coordination of International Environmental Agreements' in R Wolfrum and N Matz, *Conflicts in International Environmental Law* (Springer 2003) 160.
3 P Roch and F Xaver Perrez, 'International Environmental Governance: the Strive Towards a Comprehensive, Coherent, Effective and Efficient International Environmental Regime' (2005) *Colorado Journal of International Environmental Law and Policy* 1.
4 Biological Diversity Convention (adopted 5 June 1992, entered into force 29 December 1993) 1760 UNTS 79 (CBD).
5 Framework Convention on Climate Change (adopted 9 May 1992, entered into force 21 March 1994) 1771 UNTS 107 (FCCC).
6 Convention for the Protection of the Ozone Layer (adopted 22 March 1985, entered into force 22 September 1988) 1513 UNTS 323.
7 Convention of International Trade in Endangered Species (adopted 3 March 1973, entered into force 1 July 1975) 993 UNTS 243 (CITES).
8 The WHC was adopted at the General Conference of UNESCO (short for United Nations Educational, Scientific and Cultural Organisation). Thus, UNESCO and the operation of the WHC are intertwined.

World Heritage Convention[9] (WHC). The MEAs often require collective and far-reaching measures to be undertaken, for example cutting down carbon emissions or preserving particular ecosystems and species. Such measures may interfere with other areas of international law creating tensions between MEAs and other bodies of international obligations, including international humanitarian law (IHL), human rights law, trade law, and investment law, as these areas may permit behaviour that is inconsistent with what the MEAs prescribe.[10]

Arising tensions between international legal areas with overlapping scope are often explained as a result of an increased diversification and fragmentation of international law.[11] Such diversification may be viewed as a development of the international legal system. However, as the system develops and becomes more complex, it needs responses to prevent inconsistency among its obligations. This chapter focuses on the tendencies as well as the opportunities of MEAs to respond to such development by reconciling with other international legal obligations.[12] As environmental protection is multifaceted, MEAs are inclined to intermingle with non-environmental areas of international law.[13] Most MEAs share certain elements in regard to their character, structure, and operation that facilitate such intermingling. I argue that MEAs – thanks to their particular design – could adopt an alternative 'reconciliatory approach.' This approach describes the MEA institutions' capability to go beyond treaty interpretations and adopt more practical and political oriented strategies to interact and harmonise with other areas of international law and at the same time to further their objectives. Such practices have the potential to endorse coherence within the international legal system.

This chapter examines the role of the institutions and the mechanisms established under MEAs in the processes of de-fragmentation and constitutionalisation of international law. It shows that specialised areas of international law, in this case international environmental law, can develop their own approaches to avoid tensions and conflicts among international legal norms.[14] I will demonstrate the implications of a reconciliatory approach by

9 Convention Concerning the Protection of the World Cultural and Natural Heritage (adopted 23 November 1972, entered into force 15 December 1979) 1037 UNTS 151 (World Heritage Convention).

10 For further reading, see e.g. M Tignino, 'The Legal Regime of Natural Resources in Times of Armed Conflict and its Weaknesses' in Kerbrat and Maljean-Dubois (eds) (n 1) 25.

11 See ILC, 'Fragmentation of International Law: Difficulties Arising from the Diversification and Expansion of International Law' (13 April 2006), ILC Report, UN Doc. A/CN.4/L.682.

12 Similar tendencies can also been seen in human rights law area, see L Lixinski, 'Treaty Interpretation by the Inter-American Court of Human Rights: Expansionism at the Service of the Unity of International Law' (2010) 21 *EJIL* 585.

13 L Boisson de Chazournes, 'Features and Trends in International Environmental Law' in Kerbrat and Maljean-Dubois (eds) (n 1) 14.

14 For additional angles on fragmentation in relation to international environmental law, see also H Van Asselt, F Sindaco and MA Mehling, 'Global Climate Change and the Fragmentation of International Law' (2008) 30(4) *Law & Policy* 423; A Wiersema, 'The

looking at the application of the WHC in relation to international humanitarian law and the UN Charter in the Democratic Republic of the Congo (DRC). The WHC is not a pure MEA as it also protects cultural heritage, but it has the same structure and it operates like an MEA. Also, it protects particular areas of great international environmental importance. Thus, it uses the concept of protected areas, which is a conservation tool used under MEAs to preserve certain ecosystems or species. In the DRC, maintaining the protection of the natural world heritage sites during armed conflict is conducted by adopting measures that are anticipated by a reconciliatory approach. Instead of determining which legal norm prevails, the WHC institutions have employed decisions and recommendations as well as cooperative measures extending over the borders of international legal areas.

The following section discusses the particular challenges connected with international environmental law and why traditional legal tools fail to adequately address them. The third section scrutinises the essential elements of the MEA structure, which are prerequisites for adopting a reconciliatory approach. Section 4 looks at the practice of reconciling norms illustrated in the case of applying the WHC to protect natural world heritage sites in relation to the wars in the DRC. The fifth section explores the utility of, and opportunities for, MEAs to adopt a reconciliatory approach. The sixth concluding section discusses how MEAs can reconcile their obligations with other bodies of international law, and thereby assisting in the de-fragmentation of the international legal system.

2 Multilateral Environmental Agreements and limits of the traditional approaches

MEAs have a tendency to affect other areas of international law when they address complex and global environmental problems.[15] The development of international environmental law has contributed to an increased fragmentation of international law. As more specialised areas of law develop, they do so without acknowledging and adapting to the content of the already existing law. Thus, in many cases such increased specialisation of international law can bring inconsistency among the legal obligations.[16] The UN International Law Commission has suggested a set of legal tools to respond to such situations.[17] These tools consist of: interpretation according to Articles 31–32

New International Law-Makers? Conferences of the Parties to Multilateral Environmental Agreements' (2009) 31 *Michigan Journal of International Law* 231.

15 Boisson de Chazournes (n 13) 14–16; Maljean-Dubois (n 1) 31.

16 See ILC (n 11).

17 According to the International Law Commission, the relationship between two or more legal norms is determined by either interpretation or conflict resolution. In the first case, a norm can assist in the interpretation of the other norm. In this case both norms can be applied in conjunction. In the latter, the norms are incompatible and a choice has to be made between them. See ILC, 'Conclusions of the Work of the Study Group on Fragmentation

in the Vienna Convention on the Law of Treaties[18] (VCLT), in particular Article 31(3)(c) which is referred to as the principle of systemic integration;[19] and classic conflict solution techniques, including the *lex specialis* and *lex posterior*.[20] In this section, I argue that these legal tools, which I refer to as the 'traditional approaches', have proven unable to respond satisfactorily when facing tensions between MEAs and other areas of international law. This is because of three specific challenges relating to the application of MEAs. Firstly, the MEAs consist of principles and flexibly worded provisions that their treaty institutions continue to develop. The treaty institutions largely rely on soft law, e.g. non-binding law, in the normative process as they frequently adopt non-binding recommendations and/or resolutions.[21] As the traditional approaches operate mainly among rules and principles without allocating soft law any particular significance, they thereby fail to fully address the normative processes taking place under the MEAs.[22]

The second challenge regards the employment of the conflict solution techniques, namely the *lex specialis* and *lex superior*. Most MEAs protect interests shared by all states parties and require compliance by all of them to achieve the common treaty objective.[23] Consequently, to employ conflict solutions techniques, which solve conflicts by allowing one rule to prevail at the expense of another, would undermine the operation of these types of treaties.[24] In case of normative tensions involving an MEA, a solution offered under the conflict solution techniques is not appropriate, as it has to take into account the need of compliance by all state parties to achieve a shared objective.[25] The substantive content of most MEAs pursues a common goal requiring cooperation among all the state parties, rather than exchanging performances.[26] It follows from the transboundary character of environmental degradation that instruments require collective responses. Environmental

of International Law: Difficulties Arising from the Diversification and Expansion of International Law' (2006) *Yearbook of the International Law Commission* para. 2.

18 Vienna Convention on the Law of Treaties (adopted 23 May 1969, entered into force 27 January 1980) 1155 UNTS 331(VCLT).

19 The principle of systemic integration requires the interpreter of a treaty to take into account 'any relevant rules of international law applicable between the parties' according to Art. 31(3)(c) VCLT. The Article allows for taking into account external material sources in the treaty interpretation, including other treaties, customary rules or general principles of law. For further reading, see ILC Conclusions (n 17) paras 17–23.

20 See ILC Conclusions (n 17).

21 M Kampto, 'Normative Uncertainties' in Kerbrat and Maljean-Dubois (eds) (n 1) 57. See also R Churchill and G Ulfstein, 'Autonomous Institutional Arrangements in Multilateral Environmental Agreements: A Little-Noticed Phenomenon in International Law' (2000) 94 *AJIL* 639; Wiersema (n 14).

22 C McLachlan, 'The Principle of Systemic Integration and Article 31(3)(c) of the Vienna Convention' (2005) 54 *ICLQ* 279, 290–291.

23 Boisson de Chazournes (n 13) 11.

24 Matz (n 2) 131–132.

25 Ibid., 131–132.

26 Ibid., 132.

challenges, such as climate change or protection of the ozone layer, cannot be remedied if only one state cuts its carbon emissions or usage of ozone depleting substances while the rest of the states maintain or increase theirs. To be effective, a larger group of states has to contribute together.[27] These shared obligations are binding for the group of states and are often concerned with extra-state interests of a non-reciprocal character. Because all states have a legal interest to address global environmental problems, these are concerns that have to be protected by all states parties at all times. States parties have to do what they can to prevent or at least minimise environmental harm. To allow states parties to derogate from these types of obligations would impede the effectiveness of MEAs. As a consequence, the conflict resolution techniques are limited methods when dealing with environmental treaties established to achieve a common objective shared by all states parties, or even shared by the whole international community.[28]

The third challenge is that the legal tools of interpretation and conflict solutions do not take into account the possibilities to solve tensions through cooperative arrangements between various stakeholders.[29] MEAs are frequently implemented through joint activities between different MEA institutions that could also extend to non-environmental bodies.[30] These arrangements are typical means to implement MEAs and form part of the broader international environmental governance system. International environmental governance comprises interaction between different actors striving to respond to global environmental issues through rules, practices, processes, soft law and institutions,[31] which may also have impacts on areas outside the environmental sphere. Soft law remains influential also in this aspect and is acknowledged in this system of environmental governance, which expands the opportunities for action to further international environmental protection. The traditional approaches fail to acknowledge and address the importance of cooperative activities in implementing MEAs.[32]

27 Ibid., 160.

28 Ibid., 131–133.

29 The ILC report excluded this aspect in its work, see ILC (n 11). See also, M Young, 'Introduction' in Young (ed), *Regime Interaction in International Law Facing Fragmentation* (CUP 2012) 4; N Matz-Lück in 'Norm Interpretation Across International Regimes in Young (ed), *Regime Interaction in International Law Facing Fragmentation* (CUP 2012) 201–205.

30 For instance, signs of cooperation between WTO law and FCCC focusing on how trade could bring about climate change benefits. See Van Asselt, Sindico and Mehling (n 14) 436–438. Similarly, CITES' secretariat and UN Food and Agriculture Organization (FAO) have established cooperative arrangements, see M Young, 'Creating, Implementing and Enforcing Law' in M Young (ed), *Regime Interaction in International Law* (n 29) 91.

31 See UNEP, 'Environmental Governance' (2009) <http://www.unep.org/pdf/brochures/EnvironmentalGovernance.pdf> accessed 4 May 2014.

32 Similar thoughts on defaults in traditional legal tools focusing on legal hierarchies and international judiciary have been expressed by J Dunhoff, 'New Approach to

Instead of relying on the traditional approaches of employing the legal tools of interpretation and conflict solution techniques to solve strained norm relations, MEAs are designed in a manner that enables the adoption of an alternative reconciliatory approach. This approach makes use of the MEA institutions' ability to interact and harmonise with other areas of international law and at the same time ensure continued operation of their instruments. This could be achieved through two methods. First, as MEA institutions are empowered to implement and develop the flexible provisions set out in the treaties, they can circumvent clashes with other legal areas by taking these into consideration in their decision-making.[33] This course of action is similar to what is prescribed by the principle of systemic integration pursuant to Article 31(3)(c) in the VCLT. Article 31(3)(c) permits that 'any relevant rules of international law applicable in the relation between the parties' may be considered while interpreting a treaty.[34] However, the MEA institutions are assigned with discretionary powers, which enable them to go beyond an interpretation process to achieve compromises between the MEA provisions and other legal obligations. Such compromises could also consider soft law, which has considerable normative influence within international environmental law, rather than merely 'rules of international law' as provided in Article 31(3)(c) VCLT.[35] Furthermore, Article 31(3)(c) is subject to another limitation. Being a rule of interpretation, it can only be used in a bigger context of interpretation to harmonise provisions in MEAs with other international rules.[36] Hence, it is only applicable if the provision requires interpretation. This may often be the case with the open-textured treaty rules in MEAs to provide meaning to unclear terms.[37] Nevertheless, means of interpretation cannot substitute, displace or modify provisions.[38] The treaty that is being interpreted maintains the principal position, while the other rules used for assisting in the interpretation process have a secondary role to interpret the provisions in the principal treaty.[39] Such interpretation is not able to reconcile tensions between norms of different instruments on an equal footing. Thus, Article 31(3)(c) in the VCLT cannot be taken out of the larger interpretation

Regime Interaction' in Young (ed), *Regime Interaction in International Law* (n 29) 137–139.

33 D Bodansky, *The Art and Craft of International Environmental Law* (Harvard University Press 2011) 155.

34 The principle of systemic integration and 'mutual supportive' is used by the ILC when referring to Art. 31(3)(c), see ILC Conclusions (n 17) paras 17–23.

35 See P Weil, 'Towards Relative Normativity in International Law' (1983) 77 *AJIL* 413 and J Klabbers, 'The Redundancy of Soft Law' (1996) 65 *Nordic Journal of International Law* 167.

36 McLachlan (n 22) 311–312.

37 ILC Conclusions (n 17) paras 20 (a) and 23.

38 N Matz-Lück, 'Harmonization, Systemic Integration, and "Mutual Supportiveness" as Conflict-Solution Techniques: Different Modes of Interpretation as Challenge to Negative Effects of Fragmentation?' (2006) *Finnish Yearbook of International Law* 50.

39 J Pauwelyn, *Conflict of Norms in Public International Law* (CUP 2003) 254.

context to deal with general application of treaties to resolve inconsistency between two overlapping legal instruments.[40] These limitations can, however, be overlooked by the MEA institutions, which confirms that they are concerned with tasks beyond treaty interpretation in their decision-making.

Second, MEA institutions are authorised under their treaties to cooperate with other actors to further the objectives of the treaties. Such cooperation could take place with actors outside the realm of international environmental law and may have a harmonizing effect on other areas of international law. Instead of determining which legal norm prevails, the MEA institutions can employ decisions and recommendations as well as cooperative measures extending over the borders of international legal areas. Obligations of different legal areas of law can be fulfilled by entering these collaborations and thereby have a reconciling effect.

To conclude, in many cases, tensions between obligations originating from different areas of international law need a political solution going beyond law. Hence, legal tools as the rules on interpretation as well as the classic conflict solution techniques may not always be suitable to resolve the tensions. A reconciliatory approach represents an opportunity to combine legal tools with political pragmatisms to achieve compromises between clashing international legal obligations. It allows MEA institutions to adopt measures that go beyond treaty interpretations and the legal techniques of conflict solutions. Such measures can be more practical and political oriented and involve institutionalised collaboration between MEA institutions and other actors, even with those outside the international environmental legal realm.

3 Elements of environmental treaties supporting reconciliatory tendencies

MEAs do not form a homogeneous group; nonetheless, most MEAs share four elements regarding their character, structure, and operation that enable the adoption of a reconciliatory approach.[41] The elements include: 1) open-ended treaty provisions; 2) establishment of treaty institutions; 3) compliance systems focused on supportive enforcement measures; and 4) the ability for the treaty institutions to cooperate among each other and with other actors including international organisations, non-governmental organisations and private actors. The elements are linked to the objectives of MEAs protecting the international environment as a shared concern of the states parties. The elements contribute to creating a system of global environmental governance of a multi-level collaboration with various actors involved – formally or

40 Nevertheless, if the state parties agree on using Art. 31(3)(c) beyond interpretation it is unlikely that such action would be questioned, see Matz-Lück (n 29) 223.

41 This would apply to the examples mentioned above including CBD, FCCC, Convention for the Protection of the Ozone Layer, CITES, and the WHC.

informally – in the production and implementation of rules, policies, and practices to respond to environment-related demands.[42]

In the following subsections, I use the WHC as an example to describe the four elements and how they facilitate the use of a reconciliatory approach for MEA institutions. The WHC, protecting natural and cultural world heritage sites of outstanding universal value for mankind, is regarded to have successful strategies to ensure its operation and its purpose.[43] According to Article 4 of the WHC, the states parties to the convention are under the obligation to identify, protect, preserve, present and transmit the cultural and natural heritage situated in their territory for future generations. Article 6(3) of the WHC requires states parties to refrain from deliberately causing damage, directly or indirectly, to the world heritage sites situated in the territory of other states parties. To enhance the protection, states parties can nominate sites in their territory to be inscribed on the World Heritage List in accordance with Article 11(2). For a site to be designated to that list, it has to fulfil the requirements set out in Articles 1 and 2 of the WHC.[44] Pursuant to Article 11(4), a separate 'List of World Heritage in Danger' (the 'Danger List') supports the World Heritage List. Sites on the Danger List are prioritised for international assistance under the WHC according to Article 21(2). Even though the WHC has a scope going beyond pure environmental protection as it also protects cultural heritage, it operates as an environmental treaty and it shares the four typical elements pointed out above. As it provides an area-based protection for the sites included on the World Heritage List, it applies a typical conservation tool often used under MEAs, including the Biological Diversity Convention and the Ramsar Convention. Furthermore, the WHC has proactively made use of the four elements to further its aims and it has demonstrated tendencies of adopting a reconciliatory approach as noted in the case of the DRC, which makes it an illuminating example. In this case, instead of determining which legal norm prevails, the WHC institutions have employed decisions and recommendations as well as cooperative measures extending over the borders of international legal areas.

3.1 First element: principles and open-ended provisions

Most, if not all, MEAs are framework conventions with open-ended provisions, providing general principles and adaptable obligations, which permit the states parties a flexible application.[45] This also applies to the

42 See UNEP, 'Environmental Governance' (n 31).

43 F Francioni and F Lenzerini, 'The Future of the World Heritage Convention: Problems and Prospects' in F Francioni and F Lenzerini (eds), *The 1972 World Heritage Convention: A Commentary* (OUP 2008) 402.

44 In accordance with Arts 1 and 2, these sites must all have elements that are of outstanding universal value.

45 P Birnie, A Boyle and C Redgwell, *International Law & the Environment* (OUP 2009) 17.

WHC. For instance, Article 4 of the WHC calls for states parties to do all they can to protect world heritage 'to the utmost of [their] own resources'. Likewise, Article 5(d) requires that each state party 'shall endeavour, in so far as possible, and as appropriate for each country to take the appropriate legal, scientific, technical, administrative and financial measures necessary for the identification, protection, conservation, presentation and rehabilitation' of its heritage sites. The wording used in both of these Articles allows states a degree of discretion to adapt the measures to the specific challenges within the national context taking into account geographical variations or the nature of the environmental problems.[46] Thus, the absence of distinct substantive obligations is an expression of the dynamic character of MEAs, in which the treaty text represents only the starting point of a normative process.[47]

There are two underlying reasons for the use of open-ended provisions. First, similarly to many human rights treaties, the provisions in the MEAs represent the result of compromises of negotiations.[48] Because of the difficulties to achieve political consensuses on global environmental issues, the treaties replicate half-steps agreed on by the negotiators.[49] Consequently, the MEAs provide platforms for continued dialogue on unsettled issues putting much emphasis on the future process of developing the rules. Second, because of the particularities of environmental problems, they need to be addressed using a less fixed application that can offer flexible and context-based responses.[50] The MEA provisions provide enough discretion so they can be modified to consider specific geographical, economic and social factors of the states parties or evolution of scientific knowledge.[51] In sum, MEAs are less concerned with how 'binding' a norm is, but rather on the normative processes more broadly, in which norms continuously develop. This partly explains the need for discretion to adopt pragmatic solutions and also why a traditional approach is insufficient to appreciate the particularities within international environmental law.

3.2 Second element: treaty institutions

Regarding the second element, MEAs establish institutions empowered to develop the open-ended provisions into substantive rules by adopting context-based secondary decisions, resolutions and/or recommendations.[52]

46 G Carducci, 'Articles 4–7, National and International Protection of Cultural and Natural Heritage' in Francioni and Lenzerini (eds) (n 43) 145.
47 Bodansky (n 33) 155.
48 Kampto (n 21) 57.
49 Churchill and Ulfstein (n 21) 628; Kampto (n 21) 57.
50 D Shelton, 'Comments on the Normative Challenge of Environmental "Soft Law"' in Kerbrat and Maljean-Dubois (eds) (n 1) 71.
51 Boisson de Chazournes (n 13) 10–11.
52 Wiersema (n 14) 53.

The MEA institutions provide for continued development.[53] Although the institutional architecture within the MEAs varies, there are some shared fundamental attributes. Typically, the main decision-making and executive treaty body consists of a 'Conference of the Parties' (COP). The WHC has a General Assembly with representation of all state parties, which is equivalent to a COP.[54] Some MEAs have separate executive bodies and compliance committees as well.[55] The WHC has established an executive World Heritage Committee (WH Committee) consisting of 21 state parties. The WH Committee has a broad mandate to ensure effective implementation of the convention, defining and developing the provisions of the WHC by adopting decisions, recommendations and guidelines.[56] In particular, the WH Committee has adopted a set of Operational Guidelines[57] that provide directions for the application of the WHC. In contrast to some other MEAs, the WHC has assigned all the decision-making competencies to the WH Committee as opposed to the COP, or the General Assembly in the case of the WHC.[58]

The wide-reaching mandate of the MEAs' bodies injects a political element into their application of the treaties. Much of the work of MEAs in developing and implementing the treaty provisions is expressed in non-binding documents such as declarations, activities, programmes etc. Furthermore, the institutions have political functions to some extent. As they are empowered to direct the general goals of the MEAs within the limits of the treaty provisions, they can adopt decisions guided by the context and pragmatic considerations that have more of a political than a legal character. While such decisions are more flexible and aim to achieve compromises between different interests, a legal decision would be more rigid and aimed at maintaining predictability, coherence and stability.[59] The content of a political decision can be more diverse and nuanced. Thus, the activities under the MEAs blur

53 Matz (n 2) 164.

54 The General Assembly corresponds to a conference of the parties, which is usually the supreme decision-making organ in MEAs. See D Zacharias, 'The UNESCO Regime for the Protection of World Heritage as Prototype of an Autonomy-Gaining International Institution' (2008) 9 *German Law Journal* 1842.

55 This is the case in Convention on Long-Range Transboundary Air Pollution (adopted 13 November 1979, entered into force 16 March 1983) 1302 UNTS 217 (LTRAP); Convention on the Protection of the Marine Environment of the Baltic Sea Area (adopted 9 April 1992, entered into force 17 January 2000) 1507 UNTS 167 (Helsinki Convention); and the Convention for the Protection of the Marine Environment of the North-East Atlantic (adopted 22 September 1992, entered into force 25 March 1998) 2354 UNTS 67 (the OSPAR Convention).

56 The WH Committee meets at least once a year. See *The Operational Guidelines for Implementation of the WHC* (hereinafter the Operational Guidelines) (November 2011) available at <whc.unesco.org/archive/opguide11-en.pdf>, accessed 4 May 2014.

57 Ibid.

58 Matz (n 2) 166.

59 M Cerar, 'The Relationship Between Law and Politics' (2010) 15 *Annual Survey of International and Comparative Law* 19, 33–34.

the line between political decision-making and treaty interpretation as well as law-making. Hence, the establishment of MEA institutions with degrees of context-based decision-making authority enable compromises that characterise a reconciliatory approach to solve tensions. These can go beyond pure legal treaty interpretation and conflict solution techniques to seek more political oriented solutions.[60]

3.3 *Third element: non-confrontational compliance mechanisms*

The majority of the MEAs share the third element of having supportive compliance mechanisms. These mechanisms are designed to facilitate state parties' fulfilment of their obligations, rather than punishing failures.[61] The non-confrontational mechanisms build from the idea that state parties are unable but not unwilling to comply.[62] The MEA institutions collect and share information on the implementation procedure, analyse causes of non-compliance and provide recommendations and assistance for the state parties rather than engage in robust enforcement measures.[63] The purpose is to change behaviour among the states parties rather than achieve a specified result.

Almost all MEAs, including the WHC, use a self-reporting system that requires states parties to submit national reports to the MEA bodies to be evaluated on how they fulfil their commitments.[64] The reports are also the basis for the MEA institutions to provide guidance for decisions, recommendations and/or initiate activities for enhanced implementation. This could be achieved through establishing action plans, providing financial and technical support, implementing capacity building measures including workshops, consultations, and training etc.[65] Under the WHC, states parties can request international assistance from the WH Committee for the purposes of securing the protection, conservation, presentation or rehabilitation of the world heritage sites.[66] International assistance can be offered in terms of studies, the provision of experts, skilled labour, training of staff and specialists,

60 On the need for political process to respond to fragmentation, see N Matz-Lück, 'Harmonization, Systemic Integration, and "Mutual Supportiveness" as Conflict-Solution Techniques: Different Modes of Interpretation as Challenge to Negative Effects of Fragmentation?' (2006) 17 *Finnish Yearbook of International Law* 50.

61 Churchill and Ulfstein (n 21) 629; N Goeteyn and F Maes, 'Compliance Mechanisms in Multilateral Environmental Agreements: An Effective Way to Improve Compliance?' (2011) 10 *Chinese Journal of International Law* 791, 797–799.

62 Goeteyn and Maes (n 61) 799.

63 See Bodansky (n 33) 226–227, and in particular on the WHC compliance mechanism, see EJ Goodwin, 'World Heritage Convention, the Environment, and Compliance' (2009) 20 *Colorado Journal of International Environmental Law and Policy* 157.

64 Goeteyn and Maes (n 61) 791, 797, 811.

65 Ibid., 814.

66 The Committee grants the requests in accordance with Art. 13(1) of the WHC.

supply of equipment, low-interest or interest-free loans or the granting of non-repayable subsidies under the WHC.[67] According to Article 22(4) of the WHC, assistance in the form of equipment supply should be of such nature that the state party does not possess or is not in a position to acquire it. The WHC has also established a World Heritage Fund to provide financial support.[68] Other MEAs also have established funds[69] or receive funding from the Global Environment Facility (GEF) to finance implementing activities.[70] Another measure undertaken in the WHC for effective implementation is through the Danger List for sites that are under threat for various reasons so these can receive strengthened protection.[71] The Danger List demonstrates how the WHC proactively tries to ensure protection for the sites, rather than punishing the states parties for not adequately protecting them. In rare cases, a world heritage site could be deleted from the list. This would happen if the site has lost its outstanding value due to wilful mistreatment, neglect or accident and does no longer constitute a world heritage.[72] Deletion from the World Heritage List is an unwanted measure to adopt under the WHC, as its main objective is to make sure that the world heritage is preserved.

However, there are MEAs that have punitive components in their compliance mechanisms, such as naming and shaming, warnings, sanctions and financial penalties.[73] Some MEAs also provide for traditional dispute settlements together with the supportive compliance mechanisms.[74] Nevertheless, classical judicial dispute settlements may not be suitable means to advance the shared aims of most MEAs. By the same token, using means provided under the VCLT such as withdrawal, suspension, and termination would not be helpful to address non-compliance.[75] The primary aim of the compliance mechanisms installed under MEAs is to assist and motivate state parties to

67 WHC, Art. 22.
68 WHC, Art. 15.
69 For instance, the COP of FCCC recently created a new fund, the Green Climate Fund for financing the implementation of the convention. See <http://www.dlapiper.com/~/media/Files/Insights/Publications/2012/12/Green%20Climate%20Fund%20GCF/Files/Climate_Change_Alert_Renewables_Dec_2012/FileAttachment/Climate_Change_Alert_Renewables_Dec_2012.pdf> accessed 4 April 2016.
70 The GEF, the world's largest public financer of global environment issues, will operate a new landmark fund to help developing countries to ratify and implement a key international agreement to conserve and sustainably use biodiversity. For further information see <http://www.thegef.org/gef/Press_release/GEF_establishes_NPIF 195> accessed 4 April 2016.
71 See Art. 11(4) of the WHC.
72 This happened in case of Oryx Sanctuary in Oman as well as with Dresden Waldschlosschen Bridge and Elbe Valley Cultural Landscape in Germany.
73 CITES provides for economic inducements such as trade sanctions for the non-compliant party. See also Goeteyn and Maes (n 61) 800.
74 Such mechanism is provided in Art. 18 in the Convention on the Conservation of European Wildlife and Natural Habitats (adopted 19 September 1979, entered into force 1 June 1982) 1284 UNTS 209 (Bern Convention).
75 Churchill and Ulfstein (n 21) 646.

be in full compliance and to secure the MEA objective, and not that parties withdraw from the treaty.[76] The opportunities to adopt measures to help state parties to be in compliance provides further degrees of flexibility, moving the MEAs away from being pure legal instruments but providing them with tools for pragmatic solutions, which could involve reconciliation across legal fields if needed to ensure compliance. Such tools advance further a political dimension into the MEAs.

3.4 *Fourth element: institutional cooperation*

The fourth element relates to how the MEA institutions comprising COPs, executive bodies, secretariats and subsidiary bodies are often encouraged in the treaties to cooperate with other stakeholders. This element is closely related to the character of environmental problems, which requires a collective response to achieve a higher level of efficacy for the MEAs.[77] The MEAs can either explicitly or implicitly empower institutions to instigate cooperation with other actors.[78] Regarding the WHC, pursuant to Article 13(7), the WH Committee is authorised to cooperate with other organisations, bodies and individuals to implement projects and programmes.[79] The WHC, as with most MEAs, does not further specify the forms of collaboration. Generally, the provisions set out in the MEAs provide for great flexibility as to how to conduct the collaboration. The cooperation seems to be performed on a voluntary basis as encouraged in the treaty text.[80] As the cooperation is not restricted to certain forms or actors, it could be undertaken with actors engaged in other areas of international law. The involvement of MEA institutions in such collaborations could contribute to reconciling tensions with the other legal obligations.[81] However, the lack of concrete guidance on how to formulate these collaboration efforts can be rectified by decisions of the COPs or other bodies under the MEAs.[82]

In sum, most MEAs have a similar structure enabling them to develop and respond to global environmental challenges in a flexible manner. The four elements allow MEAs to reconcile and interact with other areas of law by adopting strategies that combine political decision-making with legal interpretation and law-making. Bringing a political component into the

76 Goeteyn and Maes (n 61) 815.
77 Matz (n 2) 119 and 170.
78 Young 'Creating, Implementing' (n 30) 99; Matz (n 2) 167.
79 On the WHC website, there is a list of different actors which are WHC partners, including Earth Watch Institute, Panasonic, International New York Times, Norwegian Foreign Ministry of Affairs, GTZ, Belgian Federal Science Policy, see <http://whc.unesco.org/en/partners/> accessed 10 April 2016.
80 Matz (n 2) 161.
81 In relation to cooperation between WTO and FCCC institutions, there are no legal obstacles, only if anything political. See Van Asselt, Sindico and Mehling (n 14) 437 and 440.
82 Matz (n 2) 164–165.

legal domain of applying and interpreting MEAs facilitates a reconciliatory approach, as it builds on pragmatics and compromises to solve tensions between legal norms.[83]

4 Opportunities in the application of environmental treaties: the example of the World Heritage Convention

As mentioned earlier, MEAs often interfere with other bodies of international obligations. Such interference has been witnessed in regard to the application of the WHC in relation to the armed conflicts taking place in the DRC. In this case the WHC has affected obligations of IHL as well as the UN Charter creating normative tensions between different legal obligations. To overcome these tensions, the UNESCO and the WH Committee have employed a reconciliatory approach by adopting decisions adjusted to a conflict context and initiated collaboration with other actors. Similar practices involving the WHC can also be noted in other cases, for instance during the hostilities taking place in Kosovo, Bosnia, Jerusalem, Cambodia-Thailand. The UNESCO is involved in the protection work on many cultural heritage sites in conflict contexts collaborating with other actors. Notably, the UNESCO and the UN peacekeeping mission deployed in Mali collaborate under a specified Security Council mandate to support the Malian authorities in protecting Mali's cultural and historic sites from hostile attacks.[84] However, these cases concern cultural heritage, which is protected besides under the WHC, also under specific instruments applicable during armed conflicts and thereby forming part of the IHL framework.[85] As cultural protection is already an issue under IHL, there is less risk of normative tensions.

In this section, I examine the application of the WHC during the armed conflicts taking place in the DRC between 2000 and 2011.[86] The purpose is to show its potential to reconcile with other legal obligations and still remain in operation in different types of situations, such as during armed conflicts.

4.1 Background to the Congolese armed conflicts

Several armed conflicts have taken place in the DRC since 1996.[87] The warfare has severely impacted five protected natural world heritage sites

83 For the discussion on law and politics, see Cerar (n 59) 32.

84 See UN Security Council Resolution adopted on 25 April 2013 (UN Doc. S/RES/2100) para. 16 (f).

85 In particular, the 1954 Hague Convention and its two Protocols.

86 The DRC ratified the WHC on 23 September 1974; see <www.whc.unesco.org/en/states-parties> accessed 10 April 2016.

87 The First Congo War occurred between 1996–1998, during which Rwanda, Uganda and Angola were involved. The Second Congo War occurred between 1998–2000. The DRC, Rwanda, Uganda, Zimbabwe, Burundi, Angola, Namibia, Chad, Eritrea and Sudan to varying degrees were involved. A peace agreement was concluded between warring parties

located in the DRC.[88] As they are rich in natural resources, controlling these sites has become a goal in the armed conflict for both strategic and economic reasons.[89] The armed groups have used the isolated environment of the sites as part of their military operations, both as hiding places and to set up base camps.[90] Economic motives have been prominent for armed groups to settle inside the sites to poach wildlife and exploit natural resources. The revenues are used for financing warfare but also for personal profit.[91]

The armed groups' usage of the world heritage sites has turned parts of them into military objectives.[92] In such cases, a substantial amount of damage can be done lawfully to these areas under IHL.[93] To prevent the armed groups to use the sites in their warfare, the Congolese army has entered the world heritage sites. It has carried out operations that have adversely impacted the sites by, for example, cutting down trees and placing army camps inside the sites.[94] It may take decades for the sites' sensitive ecosystems to recover from the damage resulting from a single attack. Nevertheless, such operations are permitted measures according to IHL. In addition, the Security Council has determined that the situation in the DRC constitutes a threat to international peace and security. Therefore, it has deployed a UN peacekeeping mission

in April 2002. The hostilities have remained with such intensity and organisation among the concerned armed groups, including the Congolese army, that it may be classified as a non-international armed conflict with international elements. The lines are however blurring. Cf. with OCHA, *Democratic Republic of the Congo Mapping Exercise* (2010) 8–10, documenting the most serious violations of human rights and international humanitarian law 1993–2003 <www.ohchr.org/Documents/Countries/ZR/DRC_MAPPING_REPORT_FINAL_EN.pdf> accessed 15 April 2016.

88 The DRC has five natural world heritage sites protected under the WHC.

89 A Crawford and J Bernstein, *MEAs, Conservation and Conflict – A Case Study of Virunga National Park, DRC* (International Institute for Sustainable Development 2008) 17–18.

90 See UNESCO Docs: WHC-01/CONF.208/24, 17–19; WHC-07/31.COM/7A, 7–20; WHC-08/32.COM/7A, 7–31. See also Crawford and Bernstein (n 89) 17–18. For example, between 2008 and 2009, armed rebel groups occupied the gorilla sector of the world heritage site of Virunga. See UNESCO Doc. WHC-09/33.COM/7A, 12.

91 UNESCO Docs: WHC-06/30.COM/7A, 12–34; WHC-08/32.COM/7A, 7–31; see also Crawford and Bernstein (n 89) 17–18.

92 B Sjöstedt, 'The Role of Multilateral Environmental Agreements in Armed Conflict: "Green-Keeping" in Virunga Park. Applying the UNESCO World Heritage Convention in the Armed Conflict of the Democratic Republic of the Congo' (2013) 82 *NJIL* 129, 135–136.

93 A military objective is e.g. all objects that are not 'military objectives'. These principles are codified in the Rules 7–10 in the Customary Law Study by ICRC expand the application to also include non-international armed conflict, in J-M Henckaerts and L Doswald-Beck (eds), *Customary International Humanitarian Law Study* vol. 1 (CUP 2005) 25–35.

94 In 2006 it was reported that four brigades totalling 12,000 soldiers, were deployed inside or close to the world heritage site of Virunga Park, some of them with their families. See UNESCO Docs: WHC-06/30.COM/7A, 19, 22, 27; WHC-08/32.COM/7A, 7–31; see also J Kalpers, 'Overview of the Armed Conflict and Biodiversity in Sub-Saharan Africa: Impact, Mechanisms and Responses' (2001) Biodiversity Support Program, Washington DC, 13.

in accordance with Chapter VII of the UN Charter.[95] The UNESCO and the WHC Committee has criticised the peacekeeping mission for harmfully affecting the sites.[96] At the same time, the DRC is under the obligation to protect and preserve the natural heritage situated in its territory pursuant to Article 4 of the WHC. All five of the Congolese natural world heritage sites have been put on the Danger List partly because of the threat posed by the armed conflicts taking place in and around the sites.[97]

4.2 Applying the World Heritage Convention and international humanitarian law

In the event of an armed conflict, IHL applies as the legal framework particularly designed for such events. Thus, the application of the WHC during armed conflict has to be simultaneous with IHL. In fact, there already exists a linkage between IHL and world heritage law regarding cultural property. As the 1954 Convention on the Protection of Cultural Property in the Event of Armed Conflict (1954 Hague Convention) and its two Protocols were adopted under the auspices of UNESCO,[98] the UNESCO has already been involved in protection work in relation to armed conflicts.[99] The UNESCO has an established mandate to review the compliance with the cultural protection rules, which also involves collaboration with other UN agencies, the International Criminal Tribunal for Former Yugoslavia (ICTY) and other institutions.[100]

However, there is no explicit legal protection under IHL in relation to natural heritage. The UN International Law Commission concluded in the course of its work on the 'Effects of Armed Conflict on Treaties', that there is a general presumption that environmental treaties continue to operate during

95 UNSC Resolution, adopted on 28 July 2003 (UN Doc. S/RES/1493) in preamble para. 12.

96 UNESCO Doc. WHC-11/35.COM/20, 12; UNESCO Doc. WHC-11/35.COM/7A. Add, 27 May 2011, 13.

97 See UNESCO Docs: WHC-94/CONF.003/16; WHC-96/CONF.201/21; WHC-97/CONF.208/17; WHC-99/CONF.209/22.

98 S Freeland, *Addressing the Intentional Destruction of the Environment during Warfare under the Rome Statue of the International Criminal Court* (Intersentia 2015) 73; see also Chapter 11 in this book.

99 It was suggested to include protection for the natural heritage under the cultural property regime during the negotiations of the Second Protocol to the 1954 Hague Convention. This suggestion was rejected because the protection of the natural heritage appeared to not be compatible with that of cultural property. Such inclusion would have required a new instrument and not only an update of the existing regime, which was the purpose of the 1999 Second Protocol. L Lixinski, 'Environment and War: Lessons from International Cultural Heritage Law' in R Rayfuse (ed), *War and the Environment. New Approaches to Protecting the Environment in Relation to Armed Conflict* (Brill 2014) 163.

100 See for instance the UNESCO Report on the implementation of the 1954 Hague Convention and its two (1954 and 1999) Protocols, available at <http://www.unesco.org/new/fileadmin/MULTIMEDIA/HQ/CLT/pdf/periodic_report_2011_en.pdf>.

armed conflict.[101] Thus, this would also apply for the WHC. In Article 11(4) in the WHC, the "outbreak of an armed conflict" is expressly identified as a threat that can put a world heritage site on the Danger List for strengthened protection. For instance, all of the Congolese world heritage sites have been put on the Danger List partly because of the armed conflicts.[102] Several scholars share the view that the WHC applies during armed conflict.[103] However, in the case of a normative conflict, IHL generally prevails over peacetime law – such as the WHC – as being the *lex specialis* during armed conflict.[104] The definition and determination of the existence of a normative conflict is a thorny issue, which makes the application of *lex specialis* difficult. For instance, IHL does not obligate states to destroy the world heritage sites, but it permits such acts if they contribute to successful military operations. Simultaneously, the same lawful acts under IHL are prohibited under the WHC, which bans any harmful acts to the sites. There is not necessarily a clash between the two legal frameworks, as the DRC could avoid harming the sites in its warfare and successfully comply with both legal frameworks. Nonetheless, this causes tensions between them, as WHC would restrict the permitted military action under IHL.

To ensure that the Congolese world heritage sites receive continued protection throughout the hostilities, the WH Committee launched a project in 2000.[105] In its decisions regarding the project's implementation, the WH Committee criticised the Congolese army for conducting operations that

101 In the course of its work on the 'Effects of Armed Conflict on Treaties', the UN International Law Commission (ILC) concluded, in its Draft Article 3, that 'the existence of an armed conflict does not *ipso facto* terminate or suspend the operation of treaties'. Annexed to Draft Article 7, the ILC incorporated an indicative list of treaties whose subject matter implies continued application during armed conflict. This list includes environmental treaties Draft Articles on the Effects of Armed Conflicts on Treaties, with Commentaries, adopted at the 63rd session of the ILC (2011), Draft Articles 3 and 7 and annexed indicative list of treaties. <untreaty.un.org/ilc/texts/instruments/english/commentaries/1_10_2011.pdf>.

102 See (n 97).

103 S Vöneky, 'Peacetime Environmental Law as a Basis of State Responsibility for Environmental Damage Caused by War' in J Austin and C Bruch (eds), *The Environmental Consequences of War* (CUP 2000) 224–225; J Austin and C Bruch, 'Legal Mechanisms for Addressing Wartime Damage to Tropical Forests' (2003) 16 *Journal of Sustainable Forestry* 161, 171–172.

104 This has been confirmed by the International Court of Justice in *Legality of the Threat or Use of Nuclear Weapons, Advisory Opinion*, ICJ Reports 1996, p. 226, para. 25.

105 The partnership consists of the UNESCO's World Heritage Centre and Division of Ecological Sciences in cooperation with Institut Congolais pour la Conservation de la Nature (ICCN), the International Union for Conservation of Nature (IUCN), German Technical Cooperation (GTZ), and a task force of conservation non-governmental organisations including International Rhino Foundation, International Gorilla Conservation Programme, Wildlife Conservation Society, the World Wide Fund for Nature, and the Gilman International Conservation. In addition, the European Union and states (i.e. Belgium, Italy and Germany) as well as UN agencies or programmes (i.e. UN Development Programme, UN Environmental Programme) and the UN Mission to DRC (MONUC) collaborate with the Committee and the World Heritage Centre to address issues relating to the safeguarding of World Heritage properties in the DRC. See L Patchett, 'Articles

adversely affected the world heritage sites, regardless whether they were lawful under IHL. At the same time, the WH Committee acknowledged the need for the army to ensure security inside the sites. Given the particular national circumstances in the DRC with ongoing hostilities within the sites, the call for the army to protect the sites by the WH Committee can be regarded as a 'measure' in accordance with Article 5 of the WHC. Through military operations, the Congolese army has succeeded, as required by the WH Committee, to drive rebel groups out from several of their positions in and around the world heritage sites. In one of the world heritage sites, the army even appointed a brigade with the specific mandate to protect the site.[106] By involving the Congolese army in its decisions, the WH Committee has made the army aware of the need to protect the world heritage sites and thereby, hopefully prevent military operations damaging the sites. The support provided under the WHC has been important for the Park rangers, which are employed to protect the world heritage sites. In addition, the WHC project has provided funding for salaries, equipment, and training activities for the Park rangers.[107] Facilities at the Park stations and patrol posts have been rehabilitated and reconstructed,[108] and the Park rangers have been able to continue their work to protect the Park because of the international assistance provided under the WHC. Management by the Park rangers has been strengthened by the acquisition of equipment including trucks, speedboats, an airplane, communication systems, and computer systems.[109] In 2011, it was reported that all Park stations in the world heritage site of Virunga Park have mobile phone coverage, which enables coordination of the Park activities.[110] The activities undertaken by the WH Committee have enabled the Park rangers to perform their conservation work. Furthermore, these activities, undertaken as part of implementing the WHC, are adapted to the particular situation of the DRC with the aim of sustaining protection of the world heritage sites during the particular situation of armed conflict without necessarily interfering, but rather reconciling with the IHL obligations.

4.3 Applying the World Heritage Convention and the UN Charter obligations

As the Security Council has concluded that the situation in the DRC is a threat to international peace and security, a UN peacekeeping mission has

17–18, Activities to Support the World Heritage Fund' in Francioni and Lenzerini (eds) (n 43) 298; and the World Heritage website <whc.unesco.org/en/congobiodiversity> accessed 4 May 2014.

106 UNESCO Doc. WHC-11/35.COM/7A.Add, 13.

107 During the first phase of the pilot project (2001 to 2005) approximately USD 900 000 was spent on salaries, equipment etc. See UNESCO Doc. WHC-06/30.COM/7A, 26.

108 UNESCO Doc. WHC-11/35.COM/7A.Add, 4.

109 This equipment was financed by the European Union, one of the partners within the WHC project, UNESCO Doc. WHC-11/35.COM/7A.Add, 4.

110 UNESCO Doc. WHC-10/34.COM/7A, 12.

been installed in accordance with Chapter VII of the UN Charter.[111] The Security Council has authorised the peacekeepers to use all necessary means, including military, to support the DRC to improve the security situation.[112] In its work to stabilise the region, the peacekeeping mission has contributed to harm the world heritage sites, for instance by establishing base camps without a proper waste management system inside the sites.[113] The UNESCO and the WHC Committee have criticised this behaviour as being inconstant with the WHC. Pursuant to Article 103 of the UN Charter, obligations stemming from the Charter prevail over other treaty obligations, such as those in the WHC. Consequently, the decisions of the Security Council taken in accordance with the UN Charter would have precedence over the parallel WHC obligations in case they are incompatible with each other. Thus, the Committee cannot modify the decisions of the Security Council because they may hamper the protection of world heritage. It does not have the authority to direct the peacekeeping mission, as the UN is not a party to the WHC. By the same token, it cannot expect the DRC to adopt measures contrary to its obligations under the UN Charter in order to comply with the WHC.

Still, as the WHC protects a common concern of its states parties, possibly also of the international community, the protection of the world heritage sites represents a universal interest that all states parties to the WHC have a legal obligation to uphold. At the same time, the peacekeepers have a lawful right to stay in these areas and perform the tasks necessary for their mission. The DRC has consented to the deployment of the mission and it is under an obligation to respect the Security Council's decisions pursuant to the UN Charter. This may imply that the protection of the world heritage sites face colliding obligations when the peacekeepers monitor the areas encompassing the sites, which aims at maintaining international peace and security – also a universal interest. However, instead of accepting the precedence of the obligations according to Article 103 in the UN Charter, the WHC Committee has invited the peacekeeping mission to assist the Park rangers to evacuate armed rebel groups from the world heritage sites.[114] Since October 2003, the Committee has collaborated with the peacekeeping forces.[115] The peacekeepers have helped the Park rangers to monitor the world heritage sites and they have also conducted disarmament operations of rebel groups in

111 UNSC Resolution, adopted on 28 July 2003 (UN Doc. S/RES/1493) in preamble para. 12.

112 See the following UNSC Resolutions adopted in 2003–2011: UN Doc. S/RES/1493 (2003) paras 17–20 and 25–26; UN Doc. S/RES/1565 (2004) paras 4–6; UN Doc. S/RES/1592 (2005) para. 7; UN Doc. S/RES/1756 (2007), paras 2–4; UN Doc. S/RES/1856 (2008) paras 3–5; UN Doc S/RES/1906 (2009) paras 5–6; UN Doc S/RES/1925 (2010) paras 11–12; UN Doc. S/RES/1991 (2011) para. 1.

113 The peacekeeping mission has been requested by WH Committee to establish a waste management system for their camp in Rwindi within one of the world heritage sites. See UNESCO Docs: WHC-11/35.COM/20, 12; WHC-11/35.COM/7A.Add), 13.

114 UNESCO Doc. WHC-03/27.COM/24, 10.

115 UNESCO Doc. WHC-04/28/COM/26, 52.

cooperation with the Park rangers.[116] Such cooperation has not, however, been formalised between the peacekeeping mission or the Security Council and the Committee.[117] However, in March 2015 an attempt to include an expressed mandate for the UN peacekeeping mission to protect the world heritage sites was initiated by the peacekeeping mission together with the UN Environmental Programme (UNEP). Although such a protection was included in the draft decision, it did not end up in the Security Council's final decision.[118] Thus, the protection of the world heritage site per se remains outside the scope of the peacekeepers' mandate, at least formally.[119]

The collaboration (even in its limited form) has enabled the WH Committee to acquire assistance from an exterior actor to safeguard the world heritage sites. The Security Council has acknowledged that there is a link between illegal exploitation of natural resources and the outbreak or continuation of armed conflict, which threatens international peace and security.[120] As the WH Committee and the peacekeeping mission have common goals, they can benefit from each other's expertise and competence to advance these. The peacekeeping forces having the ability to use military means provides safety within the sites to enable the Park rangers to monitor the sites. At the same time, the Park rangers can assist the peacekeepers to control the exploitation of natural resources inside the parks and also to provide intelligence information. Of course, ideally to fully comply with the WHC, all military activities should be banned inside the world heritage sites. However, as long as hostilities are ongoing in the DRC, the cooperation with the peacekeepers represents a pragmatic approach to deal with the situation that at the same time reconciles conflicting obligations within the international legal system.[121]

116 UNESCO Doc. WHC-04/28.COM/15A Rev, 7–10.

117 UNESCO Doc. WHC-09/33.COM/7A, 14; UNESCO Doc. WHC-11/35.COM/7A. Add, 5.

118 At the experts meeting, the following statement was proposed for consideration by the UNSC during the review of the mandate of the peacekeeping mission installed in the DRC: 'Authorizes MONUSCO [the peacekeeping mission] to support national and regional efforts to investigate, prosecute and sanction members of armed groups and criminal networks engaged in national and transnational organized crime including, but not limited to, the illicit exploitation and trade in natural resources, such as gold and other minerals, wildlife, charcoal and timber, with special emphasis on addressing sources of conflict and safeguarding protected areas from armed groups, particularly, but not limited to, UNESCO World Heritage Sites.' UNEP MONUSCO Draft report from expert meeting, 'Background paper on illegal exploitation and trade in natural resources benefitting organized criminal groups and its implications on MONUSCO's role in fostering stability and peace in eastern DR Congo', Goma, DRC, 21 March 2015. Report is not yet published, but on file with the author.

119 In 2011, it was noted that contact was maintained but that little support was provided by the peacekeepers to the Park rangers, see UNESCO Doc. WHC-11/35.COM/7A.Add, 5, 9, 14.

120 UNSC Resolution, adopted 14 September 2005, UN Doc. S/RES/1625, para. 6.

121 For further reading on this collaboration, see Sjöstedt (n 92) 129–153.

5 The significance of a reconciliatory approach

MEAs are designed to deal with various situations to address global environmental problems. The advantage of having the first element of open-ended provisions combined with the second element of institutional decision-making is that the obligations can be developed on the basis of the contextual challenges for a particular state party. The third and fourth elements of supportive compliance mechanisms and cooperative initiatives, respectively, can together form a useful vehicle to mobilise international support from different stakeholders at the time when a state party may struggle to protect its environment. The interesting part with MEAs is that they can be implemented with limited state involvement by relying on cooperation with other treaty bodies, other states, international organisations, non-governmental organisations or private actors etc. For instance, the compliance measures can be provided through funds supporting a non-governmental organisation's project to further the aims of an MEA.

In the case of the DRC, the WH Committee's way of dealing with the situation has elements of a reconciliatory approach. The WH Committee has resumed its implementation of the WHC by avoiding accepting the existence of potential normative conflicts. The WH Committee did not address the possibility of the IHL to prevail as *lex specialis* during armed conflict or the primacy of UN Charter obligations in accordance with Article 103 in the Charter. Instead, the WH Committee adopted measures adjusted to the current circumstances that reconcile the obligations in the WHC with those in IHL and the UN Charter. For instance, the WH Committee has adopted decisions aimed at changing the Congolese army's behaviour inside the sites; provided international assistance including equipment and training that are suitable during armed conflict; and initiated institutional cooperation directly with the UN peacekeepers. As the WH Committee, as with many other institutions of the MEAs, has both expressed and implied powers to act in a manner to advance the object and purpose as set out in the treaty, they may use the powers to little by little extend the normative scope to act. The state parties can of course prevent such expansion, but in case there is no reaction from states, the MEAs can continue to develop in a dynamic normative manner. To operate during armed conflicts, the WH Committee adjusted to the context of the hostilities and considered other needs than those set out in the Convention. The adjustment probably contributes to ensure that the state parties accept the recommendations, decisions and other measures adopted under the WHC.

The usefulness of the strategies that reflect the reconciliatory approach is two-fold. First, it implies that state parties should try to achieve the MEAs' aims as far possible and not allow derogation from them in cases of normative conflict. MEA institutions can make sure that the treaty is in operation by adapting to the situation and thereby minimizing the risk of disrespecting the MEA obligations in difficult situations, including during armed conflict.

Moreover, the justification of the Committee's activities in relation to the DRC may be grounded in the objectives set out in the WHC to protect a universal interest.[122] Thus, the approach permits considerations of the need to ensure protection for a shared interest requiring collective responses of the state parties, such as those objectives of most MEAs.

Second, the approach functions using the discretionary powers of the MEA institutions to compromise and cooperate with other actors involved in implementing activities in other legal areas. The institutional arrangements established under the MEAs constitute a mix between treaty implementation and environmental governance. As state parties have transferred discretionary decision-making powers to institutions of the MEAs, they are able to compromise for the ends of ensuring effective treaty implementation based on the particular context the treaty is operating within.[123] The decisions and activities may be more political than legal measures by including features of pragmatism at the expense of predictability.

6 Conclusions

Global environmental problems pose a specific challenge to the international legal system as they request extensive and collective measures of the international community. As a consequence, the obligations in international environmental treaties often permeate into other areas of law and create normative tensions. Legal tools cannot respond satisfactorily to solve the tensions in many cases. This is because of the influence of soft law and the practice of institutional arrangements within the international environmental law-making and implementation process as well as the need to solve such tensions politically rather than legally. However, the MEAs have enabled its institutions to overcome the tensions by adopting a reconciliatory approach. The approach describes how normative and institutional interactions take place under MEAs for the purpose of avoiding conflicts and tensions with other international legal obligations but at the same time it furthers a common concern to mitigate global environmental problems. Thus, a reconciliatory approach can contribute to the constitutionalistion of international law, by facilitating the enforcement of certain obligations vested to the international community to address a general concern.

The significance of a reconciliatory approach lies in its ability to combine legal tools with political pragmatisms to achieve compromises and ad hoc solutions between clashing international legal obligations. MEAs are injected with such political pragmatism to overcome normative tensions with other

122 Art. 6(1) of the WHC establishes a duty on the international community to cooperate to protect world heritage. Art. 7 establishes a system for international cooperation under the WHC to achieve this end.

123 Matz (n 2) 175.

legal areas. They have the capability to go beyond treaty interpretations and adopt more practical and political oriented strategies to further their objectives. The decision-making bodies of MEAs can take into account other legal obligations and contextual concerns for its state parties. International cooperation can be instigated in various types of constellations and feed from the competence and resources of other stakeholders to implement the MEAs. The WH Committee adopted a reconciliatory approach when applying the WHC to protect the world heritage sites during the armed conflicts in the DRC. Other MEAs sharing the four structural elements of open-ended provisions, treaty institutions, supportive compliance mechanisms and ability to enter into institutional cooperation arrangements, can initiate similar activities to harmonise with other legal fields and at the same time advancing environmental protection.

Index

Aarhus convention 11, 244–64
access to justice 172, 244–46, 248, 250–51, 253, 255–56, 258–60, 263–64
accountability 9, 26, 96–97, 118–19, 122–23, 129, 151, 169–73, 178
ad hoc tribunals 140, 154–56, 221–22
aggression 139, 148; *see also* international crimes
Agreement on the Application of Sanitary and Phytosanitary Measure (SPS Agreement) 212, 214, 222, 226, 237, 238, 240
Arbitration 165, 170–71, 173, 176–77, 187
armed conflict 73, 126, 132–45, 185, 191–93, 199–200, 266, 278–85, 287
Article 103 of the UN Charter 72, 74–75, 80–82, 85, 93, 97, 151, 283–85; *see also* Charter of the United Nations
attribution 95–97, 140
Authorized Heritage Discourse (AHD) 187–88, 190, 201

burden of proof 175, 204–21

centralised authority 17, 48, 51
Charter of Fundamental Rights of the European Union (EUCFR) 76, 169, 177, 208
Charter of the United Nations (UN Charter) 97–98, 99–101, 124, 125, 144, 145, 148–51, 166–67, 170, 174, 179, 267, 278, 280, 282–83, 285; *see also* Article 103 of the UN Charter
coexistence 24, 70, 75, 92, 94, 159, 242
coherence 2, 3, 7, 8, 10, 58, 65–66, 68–69, 75, 85, 89, 90, 110, 132, 141, 145, 156, 182, 226, 228–32, 242, 266, 274
colonialism 164, 167–68, 194
commercial law 172–73
compartmentalisation 2, 185
complementarity 8–9, 119–23, 126, 127, 150, 156–57, 159
consistent interpretation 7, 44, 69, 71, 79–85, 181–82
constitutional rights 45, 109, 163–65, 167, 174, 181
constitutionalisation 1–12, 15, 32, 33–42, 47, 52, 53–55, 58–61, 63–68, 89–95, 105, 109, 110, 146, 149, 163–64, 167–69, 184, 202, 205–6, 219, 220, 263, 266
constitutionalism 2–6, 10, 15–17, 19–21, 23–30, 34–38, 40–44, 53–54, 56–57, 58–59, 60–61, 64, 65–68, 69, 76, 90, 91–94, 110, 118, 147, 149, 151, 163, 165–66, 172, 174, 177, 179, 182, 195, 241
convergence 11, 146, 204, 206, 212, 217, 219–21, 228
cosmopolitan constitutionalism 10, 41, 44, 57, 163, 172, 182
Council of Europe (CoE) 76, 110, 257–58, 261–63
Court of Justice of the European Union (CJEU) 11, 102, 104, 105, 106, 111–17, 166, 169, 178, 179, 180, 205, 206, 219, 220, 246, 248–49, 249, 251–53, 255, 256–57, 264; *see also* European Court of Justice (ECJ)
crimes against humanity (CAH) 119, 126, 127, 144, 148, 150, 155; *see also* international crimes

cultural diversity 154, 187–88, 196, 198–99, 202
cultural heritage law 10, 183–88, 191, 196–97, 201, 280

decentralisation 5–6, 9, 33, 35–36, 46, 48–49, 51–52, 105, 146, 163, 165, 173, 196
decolonisation 188
de-constitutionalisation 3, 19, 92
de-fragmentation 3, 10, 182, 266–67
democracy 26, 105, 151, 153, 164, 167
divergence 11, 19, 38, 90, 95, 146, 160, 204, 212, 215, 219–20, 232, 242
diversification 56, 85, 146–47, 149, 153, 156–57, 159–60, 203, 218, 228, 266
Doha Declaration on the TRIPS Agreement and Public Health 222, 233, 234
Drittwirkung 50
droit de regard 46
due diligence 6, 35, 46, 49–51

economic adjudication 179
environmental justice 11, 244–48, 251, 255, 257–60, 263–64
environmental law 11, 175, 203, 205, 247–49, 251, 253, 259, 265–67, 270–71, 273, 275, 286
environmental rights 261, 264
erga omnes 4, 24, 30, 46–48, 51, 66, 90, 175, 184, 200, 232
EU law 97, 105, 110, 115, 169, 173, 180, 239, 250, 262
Eurocentrism 20
European Convention on Human Rights = Convention for the Protection of Human Rights and Fundamental Freedoms (ECHR) 8, 11, 76, 77, 78, 82, 83–85, 96, 98, 100, 101, 114, 116, 135, 139, 164, 166, 169, 173, 180, 208–9, 215–17, 244, 258–61
European Court of Human Rights (ECtHR) 11, 47, 76–78, 79, 82–4, 90, 94–9, 100–4, 139, 142, 166, 179, 180, 204–6, 210, 215–16, 219, 220, 245–46, 257–58, 259–64
European Court of Justice (ECJ) 76, 90, 94, 99, 103, 104, 205, 208–12, 251, 253; *see also* Court of Justice of the European Union
European Economic Area (EEA) law 169, 173, 182
European Union 8, 18, 43, 76, 89, 92, 104, 106–7, 109–11, 113–14, 117, 180, 205, 208, 246, 282
expertisation 44, 183, 187, 190, 197

fair trial 102, 105, 127, 179, 215, 217, 259–60
foreign investment 108, 164–65, 170, 172–73, 176–77, 187, 195–96, 198
fragmentation 1–3, 5–12, 15, 16, 29, 39, 40–44, 48, 65, 66, 69, 70, 75, 77–79, 85–87, 89–90, 93, 95, 108, 110, 118, 128, 132, 133, 142, 144, 145, 146–8, 156–57, 159, 163–66, 182–84, 185–87, 195, 201, 202–6, 212, 219, 220, 227–29, 240, 241–44, 245, 263, 266–67
fundamental rights 26, 77, 83, 93–94, 99, 104, 111, 150, 152, 169, 170, 171, 173, 176, 178–80, 208, 237, 257

General Agreement on Tariffs and Trade (GATT) 164, 166, 167, 168, 169, 171, 172, 224, 230, 235, 237–38, 240
genocide 50, 119, 125–27, 144, 148–49, 158, 206, 215, 217–19, 221; *see also* international crimes
global constitutionalism 15, 16, 23, 26–8, 57, 61, 64
global governance 4, 8–9, 20, 57, 64, 95, 105, 127–28, 226
global justice 119, 127, 149, 206, 220
globalisation 1–3, 17–21, 23, 36, 38–39, 118, 120, 128, 130–31, 147, 163, 165, 179, 186, 201, 227–88, 245
Grundnorm 41, 43, 55, 147

harmonisation of norms 11, 78–79, 95, 97–98, 100–1, 105, 143–44, 228, 265–66, 270–71, 275, 287
hierarchy of norms 1–3, 11, 21, 24, 27, 30, 37–38, 42–43, 48, 56, 66, 71–74, 77, 79, 81, 85, 91–92, 100–1, 105, 132, 140, 145, 150–52, 159–60, 186, 258, 269
hostilities 9, 133, 135–38, 141–42, 158, 278, 281–82, 284–85
human rights 2, 6–12, 16, 26, 28, 32–35, 37, 39, 40–44, 46, 48–52, 57,

64, 70, 74, 76–7, 79, 82–84, 89–90, 92, 96–98, 100, 102, 104–5, 108, 119, 120–21, 125, 127, 129–30, 132, 135, 140, 143, 146, 163–67, 169, 170, 173–81, 184, 187, 197–99, 201–3, 215, 220, 228, 237, 240, 242–43, 244–45, 258–61, 273
human rights law (HRL) 12, 34, 39–42, 44–45, 47, 49–51, 83, 98, 132, 140, 143, 164, 183, 203, 205, 239, 245, 258, 266
humanisation 6, 24, 32, 35, 47, 51
humanitarianism 2, 39
humanity/humankind 1, 8, 23, 57, 62, 64, 71, 118–21, 125–29, 131, 139, 144, 148, 170, 190–95, 198–201; *see also* mankind
humanity law 144

imperialism 20, 164
individual criminal responsibility 52, 132, 140, 160, 192
institutionalisation 27, 41, 123, 172, 271
Inter-American Commission and Court 42, 44, 46, 266
International Centre for Settlement of Investment Disputes (ICSID) 173, 177, 195, 235
international community 4, 6, 18, 20, 23–24, 26, 28, 36–37, 40, 50, 56, 63, 70–72, 74–75, 93–94, 109, 118–19, 123–26, 128–29, 144, 147–49, 151, 163, 184–85, 188–91, 193–94, 197–98, 200–2, 269, 283, 286; *see also* international (global) society
International Court of Justice (ICJ) 47, 58, 72–73, 135–36, 149, 173, 175–77, 181, 194, 200, 203–6, 213, 219–20, 235, 281
International Covenant on Civil and Political Rights (ICCPR) 100, 108, 134
International Covenant on Economic, Social and Cultural Rights (ICESCR) 215, 237
international crimes 9, 119, 127–28, 152–53, 156–57, 160; *see also* war crimes, aggression, crimes against humanity, genocide
International Criminal Court (ICC) 122–23, 126–27, 129, 139, 146–47, 148–60, 193–94; *see also* Rome Statute
international criminal law (ICL) 8, 9, 121, 128–29, 132, 139, 140, 142–45, 146–47, 149, 152–57, 159, 160, 173
International Criminal Tribunal for Rwanda (ICTR) 140, 153–55, 158, 206, 218–20; *see also ad hoc* tribunals
International Criminal Tribunal for the former Yugoslavia (ICTY, ICTFY) 73, 140, 153–55, 158, 192–93, 205–6, 215, 217–20, 280; *see also ad hoc* tribunals
international economic law (IEL) 10, 108, 163–67, 169, 172, 176, 178, 181, 187, 203
international humanitarian law (IHL) 9, 12, 132–45, 193, 200, 266–67, 278–82, 285
International Law Commission (ILC) 2, 47, 65–66, 78, 80–82, 90, 133, 137, 143, 145, 203–4, 217, 227, 229, 231–32, 267, 280
international (global) society 24, 27, 30, 33, 36, 45, 52–60, 62, 66, 107, 163, 168, 196, 228; *see also* international community
internationalisation 6, 19, 33–35, 44–45, 49, 51–52, 57, 59, 91, 123, 130, 186, 190, 201
Internet 8, 106–11, 113, 115–17
investment law 172–3, 177, 195, 266
ius ad bellum 138

judicial review 93, 99–102, 104–5, 167, 180, 217, 245, 248, 250, 253, 256–57, 263
jus cogens 4, 24, 27, 30, 47, 51, 62, 90, 97, 119, 144, 151, 175, 180
jus inter gentes 47
justice 118, 120, 122–23, 127–28, 130–1, 146–47, 149, 153, 156, 158, 159, 160–78, 181, 206, 220–1, 244–48, 250–58, 260, 263–64

legal language 6, 17, 26–27, 36, 38, 53–55, 57–61, 63, 65, 67, 83–84, 89, 91–93, 99–100, 127, 156, 188, 190, 212, 214, 235
lex specialis 135–37, 139, 268, 281, 285

mankind 64, 186, 189, 193, 198, 201–2, 272; *see also* humanity/humankind
multilateral environmental agreement (MEA) 12, 265, 267

New Haven school 21, 64, 168
non-governmental organisations (NGOs) 177, 197, 244–46, 248–53, 255–56, 259–60, 262–64
North American Free Trade Agreement (NAFTA) 170, 195

Permanent Court of International Justice 54
Persecution 215, 217–19, 221
pluralisation 2, 9, 146, 156–57
pluralism 2, 7, 25, 29, 39, 40, 43–4, 63, 69, 70, 86, 92, 130, 148, 157, 160, 169, 175, 181–82, 241
politicisation xvii, 2
polity 36, 45, 91–2
precautionary principle 204–7, 212–15, 221
procedural rights 244
proliferation 4, 10, 11, 65, 71, 75, 89, 140, 145, 153–54, 188, 203–6, 219, 241
proportionality 140, 144, 164, 177, 180
proportionality balancing 176–77, 178–79
public goods (PGs) 10, 163, 165–69, 171, 173, 181–82, 197–98
Punta del Este Declaration 222

Reciprocity 3, 49, 175
reconciliatory approach 12, 266–67, 270–72, 275, 278, 285–87
regime collision 224, 227, 228, 240, 243
regional constitutionalisation 8, 89, 105
regionalisation 2, 201
responsibility 6, 9, 35, 47, 49–52, 64, 80–82, 96, 119–21, 125, 127, 140, 143, 145, 177, 190, 200–1, 281
Responsibility to Protect (R2P; RtP) 28, 35, 50, 51, 118–20, 121, 124–27, 129–30
right to be forgotten 8, 107, 109, 113–14, 116–17
right to health 216, 235, 237–38, 240, 242–43
right to life 132, 139, 215
right to possession 132
right to privacy 8, 109–10
Rome Statute of the ICC (RS) 9, 119, 121–22, 140, 146–51, 155–57, 193–94
rule of law 25–6, 54, 59, 62, 91–4, 105, 119, 121, 153, 164, 167, 170, 172–73, 177

scientist community 58
Second World War (WWII) 45
Security Council (or UN Security Council; SC) 3, 4, 24, 72–73, 81, 83–84, 90, 94–99, 101–5, 122–27, 148, 157, 179, 180, 191, 278–79, 282–84
Security Council Sanctions Committee 101
Shoah 45
soft law 52, 235, 268–70, 286
sovereignty 1, 3–4, 8, 9, 17–18, 22, 28, 33, 39, 45–47, 51–52, 118–21, 124, 127–28, 130–31, 147, 150, 164, 189–90, 195, 201, 241, 262
state 3, 4, 6, 9, 10–11, 17–18, 21-23, 27, 30–37, 46–52, 58–69, 80–84, 91–92, 95, 97–101, 104–5, 114, 118–20, 123–28, 130–31, 135–36, 138, 140, 143–45, 148–53, 156–57, 159, 163–67, 173–81, 183, 185–86, 188–90, 194, 196, 200–1, 210, 213, 216, 220, 232, 235, 237, 239, 240–44, 248, 252–58, 260–69, 272–78, 285; *see also* sovereignty
succession 194–5
specialisation 2, 185, 228, 267
subsidiarity 11, 164, 181, 228, 239–41, 243

targeting 9, 132–34, 136–37, 139–45
torture 132, 135, 219
TRIPS Agreement 222–23, 230, 233–36, 238–39
TRIPS Amendment 222–23, 236

UN Human Rights Committee 46
United Nations (UN) 8, 23, 27, 70, 72–73, 80, 82, 95, 97–99, 102, 104, 106, 110, 149, 164, 226, 230; *see also* Charter of the United Nations; Security Council
United Nations Educational, Scientific and Cultural Organization (UNESCO) 170–71, 185, 188–89, 191–92, 194–95, 197, 199–201, 265, 278, 280, 283
unity of international law 1–3, 7–8, 36, 42, 56–57, 59, 65–66, 68, 89, 124, 153–54, 182, 228

universalism 65–66, 190, 201

verticalisation 21–22, 38
Vienna Convention on the law of treaties (VCLT) 70, 77, 79, 85, 90, 145, 163, 165, 167, 174, 177–78, 181, 229–34, 236, 241, 243, 254–55, 257, 268, 270, 276

war crimes 119, 126–27, 132, 142, 144–45, 148, 155, 193; *see also* international crimes
water rights 205–6, 215, 221
Westphalian model/system/regime 33, 52, 122, 164, 173
WHO FCTC 223, 226, 232–37
World Health Organization (WHO) 11, 73, 170, 171, 224–27, 231–33, 235, 240, 242
world heritage: cultural 10, 47, 183–202, 280; natural 12, 266–67, 271–87
World Heritage Convention (WHC) 10, 183–202, 266–67, 271–87
World Intellectual Property Organization (WIPO) 187, 227
World Organisation for Animal Health (OIE) 224
World Trade Organization (WTO) 11, 19, 76, 205–6, 212, 214, 219–20, 223–24, 226–27, 229, 230, 232–39, 240, 242
WTO Agreement 168, 172–73, 179, 214, 223–24, 227–33, 236–38, 240, 242
WTO law 171–72, 214, 230–35, 237, 239

For Product Safety Concerns and Information please contact our EU
representative GPSR@taylorandfrancis.com
Taylor & Francis Verlag GmbH, Kaufingerstraße 24, 80331 München, Germany

www.ingramcontent.com/pod-product-compliance
Ingram Content Group UK Ltd.
Pitfield, Milton Keynes, MK11 3LW, UK
UKHW020018200926
475702UK00014B/1943

* 9 7 8 0 8 1 5 3 5 5 2 9 8 *